THE
ESSENTIALS
OF
CONDITIONING
AND
LEARNING

FOURTH EDITION

MICHAEL DOMJAN

AMERICAN PSYCHOLOGICAL ASSOCIATION

Washington, DC

Published by
American Psychological Association
750 First Street, NE
Washington, DC 20002
www.apa.org

APA Order Department
P.O. Box 92984
Washington, DC 20090-2984
Phone: (800) 374-2721; Direct: (202) 336-5510
Fax: (202) 336-5502; TDD/TTY: (202) 336-6123
Online: www.apa.org/pubs/books
E-mail: order@apa.org

In the U.K., Europe, Africa, and the Middle East, copies may be ordered from
Eurospan Group
c/o Pegasus Drive
Stratton Business Park
Biggleswade Bedfordshire
SG18 8TQ United Kingdom
Phone: +44 (0) 1767 604972
Fax: +44 (0) 1767 601640
Online: https://www.eurospanbookstore.com/apa
E-mail: eurospan@turpin-distribution.com

Typeset in Meridien by Circle Graphics, Inc., Columbia, MD

Printer: Sheridan Books, Chelsea, MI
Cover Designer: Naylor Design, Washington, DC

Library of Congress Cataloging-in-Publication Data

Names: Domjan, Michael, 1947- author.
Title: The essentials of conditioning and learning / Michael Domjan.
Description: Fourth Edition. | Washington, DC : American Psychological
  Association, [2018] | Revised edition of the author's The essentials of
  conditioning and learning, c2005. | Includes bibliographical references
  and index.
Identifiers: LCCN 2017015947 | ISBN 9781433827785 | ISBN 1433827786
Subjects: LCSH: Conditioned response. | Reinforcement (Psychology) |
  Learning, Psychology of.
Classification: LCC BF319 .D653 2018 | DDC 153.1/526—dc23 LC record available at
https://lccn.loc.gov/2017015947

British Library Cataloguing-in-Publication Data
A CIP record is available from the British Library.

Printed in the United States of America
Fourth Edition

http://dx.doi.org/10.1037/0000057-000

10 9 8 7 6 5 4 3 2 1

To Deborah

Contents

PREFACE   *xv*

1. Basic Concepts and Definitions   *3*

Fundamental Features of Learning   *4*

    Learning and Other Forms of Behavior Change   *4*

    Learning, Performance, and Levels of Analysis   *6*

    A Definition of Learning   *8*

Naturalistic Versus Experimental Observations   *8*

The Fundamental Learning Experiment   *9*

    The Control Problem in Studies of Learning   *10*

    The General-Process Approach to the Study of Learning   *12*

    The Use of Nonhuman Participants in Research on Learning   *13*

Summary   *14*

Technical Terms   *14*

2. The Structure of Unconditioned Behavior   *15*

Shaping and Homogeneous Versus Heterogeneous Substrates of Behavior   *16*

The Concept of the Reflex   *17*

Complex Forms of Elicited Behavior   *18*

    Modal Action Patterns   *19*

    Sign Stimuli   *20*

The Organization of Elicited Behavior   *23*

    Motivational Factors   *23*

    Appetitive and Consummatory Behavior   *23*

    Behavior Systems   *24*

Summary   *26*

Suggested Readings   *26*

Technical Terms   *26*

3. Habituation and Sensitization   27

Effects of the Repeated Presentation of an Eliciting Stimulus   29

Characteristics of Habituation Effects   *31*

Characteristics of Sensitization Effects   *36*

The Dual-Process Theory of Habituation and Sensitization   37

The S–R System and the State System   *37*

Implications of the Dual-Process Theory   *38*

Summary   *40*

Suggested Readings   *41*

Technical Terms   *41*

4. Pavlovian Conditioning: Basic Concepts   43

Pavlov's Proverbial Bell   *44*

Contemporary Conditioning Situations   *45*

Appetitive Conditioning   *45*

Aversive or Fear Conditioning   *46*

The Nature of the Conditioned Response   *48*

Conditioned Modifications of the Unconditioned Response   *49*

Stimulus Factors in Classical Conditioning   *50*

CS Novelty and the Latent Inhibition Effect   *51*

CS–US Relevance and Selective Associations   *51*

The Control Problem in Pavlovian Conditioning   *53*

Prevalence of Pavlovian Conditioning   *55*

Summary   *56*

Suggested Readings   *57*

Technical Terms   *57*

5. Stimulus Relations in Pavlovian Conditioning   59

Temporal Relation Between CS and US   *60*

Common Conditioning Procedures   *60*

Effects of the CS–US Interval   *62*

Temporal Encoding of When the US Occurs   *63*

Signal Relation Between CS and US   *64*

The Blocking Effect   *64*

CS–US Contingency   *65*

Higher Order Relations in Pavlovian Conditioning: Conditioned Inhibition   *67*

Inhibitory Conditioning Procedures   *67*

Behavioral Measurement of Conditioned Inhibition   *70*

Higher Order Relations in Pavlovian Conditioning: Conditioned Facilitation   *72*

Associations Learned in a Conditioned Facilitation Procedure   *73*

Summary   *75*

Suggested Readings   *75*

Technical Terms   *76*

6. Pavlovian Conditioning Mechanisms and Theories   77

What Is Learned in Pavlovian Conditioning?   *78*

How Are Pavlovian Associations Learned?   *81*

The Rescorla–Wagner Model   *81*

Attentional Models of Conditioning   *87*

Temporal Factors and Conditioned Responding   *88*

The Comparator Hypothesis   *89*

Summary   *92*

Suggested Readings   *93*

Technical Terms   *93*

7. Instrumental or Operant Conditioning   95

The Traditions of Thorndike and Skinner   *97*

Methodological Considerations   *97*

The Initial Learning of an Instrumental or Operant Response   *101*

Learning Where and What to Run For   *101*

Constructing New Responses From Familiar Components   *102*

Shaping New Responses   *102*

The Importance of Immediate Reinforcement   *104*

Associative Mechanisms in Instrumental Conditioning   *105*

The R–O Association   *106*

The S–R Association and Thorndike's Law of Effect   *106*

The S–O Association   *107*

The S(R–O) Association   *108*

Implications for Biological Constraints on Instrumental Conditioning   *109*

Implications for Neural Mechanisms of Instrumental Conditioning   *110*

Summary   *111*

Suggested Readings   *111*

Technical Terms   *112*

8. Schedules of Reinforcement   113

The Cumulative Record   *114*

Simple Schedules of Reinforcement   *115*

Ratio Schedules   *115*

Interval Schedules   *117*

Mechanisms of Schedule Performance *119*

Feedback Functions for Ratio Schedules *119*

Feedback Functions for Interval Schedules *120*

Feedback Functions and Schedule Performance *121*

Concurrent Schedules *122*

Concurrent-Chain Schedules and Self Control *124*

Summary *126*

Suggested Readings *127*

Technical Terms *127*

9. Theories of Reinforcement *129*

Thorndike and the Law of Effect *130*

Hull and Drive Reduction Theory *131*

Primary Reinforcers *132*

Secondary Reinforcers and Acquired Drives *132*

Sensory Reinforcement *133*

The Premack Principle *133*

The Premack Revolution *134*

Applications of the Premack Principle *134*

Theoretical Problems *135*

The Response Deprivation Hypothesis *136*

Response Deprivation and the Law of Effect *136*

Response Deprivation and Response Probability *136*

Response Deprivation and the Locus of Reinforcement Effects *137*

Response Allocation and Behavioral Economics *137*

Imposing an Instrumental Contingency *138*

Responding to Schedule Constraints *139*

Contributions of Response Allocation and Behavioral Economics *141*

Summary *141*

Suggested Readings *142*

Technical Terms *142*

10. Extinction of Conditioned Behavior *143*

Effects of Extinction Procedures *144*

Extinction and Original Learning *145*

Spontaneous Recovery *145*

The Renewal Effect *146*

Reinstatement of Conditioned Excitation *148*

Enhancing Extinction Performance *149*

"Paradoxical" Reward Effects in Extinction   *151*

    Overtraining Extinction Effect   *152*

    Magnitude of Reinforcement Extinction Effect   *153*

    Partial Reinforcement Extinction Effect   *154*

    Mechanisms of the Partial Reinforcement Extinction Effect   *155*

Summary   *158*

Suggested Readings   *159*

Technical Terms   *159*

11. Punishment   *161*

Effective and Ineffective Punishment   *162*

    When Punishment Fails   *163*

    When Punishment Succeeds   *164*

Research Evidence on Punishment   *164*

    Response–Reinforcer Contingency   *165*

    Response–Reinforcer Contiguity   *165*

    Intensity of the Aversive Stimulus   *165*

    Signaled Punishment   *167*

    Punishment and the Mechanisms Maintaining
       the Punished Response   *168*

    Punishment and the Reinforcement of Alternative Behavior   *168*

    Paradoxical Effects of Punishment   *169*

Can and Should We Create a Society Free of Punishment?   *170*

Alternatives to Abusive Punishment   *172*

    Time-Out   *172*

    Differential Reinforcement of Other Behavior   *172*

Summary   *173*

Suggested Readings   *174*

Technical Terms   *174*

12. Avoidance Learning   *175*

Dominant Questions in the Analysis of Avoidance Learning   *176*

Origins of the Study of Avoidance Learning   *177*

Contemporary Avoidance Conditioning Procedures   *177*

    Discriminated Avoidance   *177*

    Nondiscriminated or Free-Operant Avoidance   *179*

Two-Factor Theory of Avoidance   *181*

    Evidence Consistent With the Two-Factor Theory   *182*

    Evidence Contrary to the Two-Factor Theory   *183*

Conditioned Temporal Cues in Avoidance Learning   *184*

Safety Signals and Avoidance Learning   *184*

Extinction of Avoidance Behavior   *186*

Avoidance Learning and Unconditioned Defensive Behavior   *187*

    Species-Specific Defense Reactions   *187*

    The Predatory Imminence Continuum   *188*

Summary   *189*

Suggested Readings   *190*

Technical Terms   *190*

13. Stimulus Control of Behavior   *191*

Measurement of Stimulus Control   *192*

    Stimulus Generalization Gradients   *194*

    Stimulus Generalization and Stimulus Discrimination   *195*

    Contrasting Conceptions of Stimulus Generalization   *196*

Determinants of Stimulus Control: Sensory and Motivational Variables   *196*

    Sensory Capacity   *196*

    Sensory Orientation   *197*

    Stimulus Intensity or Salience   *197*

    Motivational Factors   *197*

Determinants of Stimulus Control: Learning Factors   *198*

    Pavlovian and Instrumental Conditioning   *198*

    Stimulus Discrimination Training   *199*

    Multiple Schedules of Reinforcement   *201*

Determinants of the Precision of Stimulus Control   *201*

    Interdimensional Versus Intradimensional Discriminations   *203*

Stimulus Equivalence Training   *205*

Summary   *206*

Suggested Readings   *206*

Technical Terms   *207*

14. Memory Mechanisms   *209*

Stages of Information Processing   *210*

The Matching-to-Sample Procedure   *210*

    Simultaneous Versus Delayed Matching to Sample   *212*

    Procedural Controls for Memory   *212*

Types of Memory   *213*

    Reference and Working Memory   *214*

    Trace Decay Versus Active Memory Processes   *214*

    Retrospective Versus Prospective Memory   *216*

Sources of Memory Failure   *218*

    Interference Effects   *219*

    Retrieval Failure   *220*

Consolidation, Reconsolidation, and Memory Updating   *222*

Summary   *224*

Suggested Readings   *225*

Technical Terms   *225*

GLOSSARY   *227*

REFERENCES   *241*

INDEX   *267*

ABOUT THE AUTHOR   *277*

Preface

Conditioning and learning are core topics that have shaped how we think about and investigate problems in many areas of psychology and allied disciplines. The purpose of this book is to provide a concise, current, and sophisticated summary of the essentials of conditioning and learning for students and professionals in those areas.

Although this field of conditioning and learning is more than 100 years old, new discoveries continue to be made, and new applications of the basic research continue to be explored to solve major clinical problems, such as the treatment of fears and phobias, the development of training procedures for autism spectrum disorder and developmental disabilities, and the treatment of drug addiction and other forms of compulsive behavior. Recent research has led to a more comprehensive account of the effects of instrumental conditioning, including economic analysis of instrumental conditioning effects. Considerable new progress has been also made in basic research on Pavlovian conditioning, extinction, memory consolidation, and memory reconsolidation. This book provides a concise and highly accessible summary of these new perspectives.

Concepts from conditioning and learning are frequently used in the neurosciences, developmental psychology, psychopharmacology, and comparative psychology. Researchers in these areas are interested in how nonverbal organisms learn, process, and remember information. Investigations of learning and cognition in nonverbal subjects invariably require using conditioning procedures in some way. Developmental psychologists, for example, frequently use habituation and instrumental conditioning procedures to study infant cognition. Neuroscience programs often include a "behavioral core" that is devoted to collecting behavioral data on learning and memory to complement data from more molecular levels of analysis. A major goal of this book is to provide easy access to the "essentials" of conditioning and learning for students and scientists who use these procedures and concepts in their own areas of specialization.

The basic procedures of habituation, classical conditioning, and instrumental conditioning are familiar to many students and professionals. However, our understanding of these procedures has changed dramatically in recent decades, and as a result, many common presumptions about learning are no longer valid. Did you know, for example, that

- contiguity between a conditioned and an unconditioned stimulus is neither necessary nor sufficient for Pavlovian conditioning?
- in many cases the most important result of Pavlovian conditioning is how it changes the organism's responses to the unconditioned stimulus rather than the development of a new response to a conditioned stimulus?
- instrumental conditioning does not "strengthen" the instrumental response?
- extinction procedures leave much of the associative structure of instrumental behavior intact?
- failure to remember something is rarely due to forgetting?
- consolidated memories are not permanent but can be changed when they are reactivated or retrieved?

Studies of basic conditioning mechanisms have moved heavily into the neurosciences, with numerous investigators studying the neural bases of conditioning and learning. However, one cannot examine the neural mechanisms of learning without being well informed about conditioning and learning procedures and phenomena at the level of behavior. Some graduate students and scientists in the neurosciences have had little or no training in behavioral techniques. Others are only familiar with the small number of behavioral techniques that are pertinent to the experiments they are working on. Such limited knowledge handicaps them from achieving a more comprehensive view of how behavior is related to neural mechanisms. It also limits their investigation to a remarkably small number of learning procedures. This book is intended to address this problem by exposing these scientists to at least the "essentials" of conditioning and learning.

Students (and professionals) in developmental and clinical psychology face similar challenges. These investigators also rely on conditioning and learning procedures, but their knowledge is often limited to specific procedures, without understanding the broader intellectual context for those procedures or contemporary theoretical analyses of those phenomena. Such a limited exposure to the field of conditioning and learning as a whole prevents these investigators from fully exploiting conditioning procedures to advance their areas of inquiry. For example, the "standard" therapy for overcoming pathological fears and phobias involves some form of extinction. Extinction is one of the most exciting areas of contemporary research in conditioning and learning, with numerous new techniques and perspectives discovered in recent years. Yet few of these have made their way into the clinical psychology curriculum.

Another area that is closely related to studies of conditioning and learning is applied behavior analysis, which originated in studies of operant conditioning carried out by B. F. Skinner and his intellectual descendants. Unfortunately, since its emergence as a separate field, applied behavior analysis has not maintained strong ties to the basic science on which it was founded. For example, many characterizations of Pavlovian conditioning in texts on applied behavior are seriously out of date. By making contemporary perspectives readily available in a brief and accessible format, this book may encourage updating the scientific roots of applied behavior analysis.

This book can serve as the primary text for an introductory course on conditioning and learning. It can also serve as a supplemental text for courses in neuroscience, clinical psychology, applied behavior analysis, developmental psychology, and psychopharmacology. Finally, the book can be used to provide the foundations for an advanced course, supplemented with journal articles and other assigned readings. To facilitate that, each chapter ends with a list of suggested readings.

As an additional resource for professors, I have also put together a companion website with sample PowerPoint slides, quiz questions, and more (see http://pubs.apa.org/books/supp/domjan).

In preparing this book, I was guided by my students, who have encouraged me over the past 45 years to keep searching for ways to explain concepts more simply and directly. This fourth edition includes updates and clarifications of the text that are too numerous to list. It also includes numerous new references and suggested readings.

I would like to thank Chris Kelaher, Beth Hatch, and everyone else at the American Psychological Association who worked on the book with great professionalism and enthusiasm. I would also like to thank my wife, Deborah Stote, for her steadfast support.

THE
ESSENTIALS
OF
CONDITIONING
AND
LEARNING

Basic Concepts and Definitions 1

Did you know that

- learning can result in either an increase or a decrease in responding?
- learning may not be readily apparent in the actions of an organism? Special test procedures may be required to see evidence of learning.
- learning may be investigated at the level of behavior, neural circuits and neurotransmitter systems, or individual neurons and their synapses?
- learning is a cause of behavior change? Therefore, learning can only be investigated with experimental methods that identify causal variables.
- control procedures are as important in studies of learning as training or experimental procedures?

Learning is of great interest because it is the primary means by which organisms make long-term adjustments in their behavior so as to become better attuned to the world in which they live. Learning requires flexibility in how one responds to the environment and therefore was considered evidence of intelligence by Darwin and other early comparative psychologists (Darwin, 1897; Romanes, 1882). Contemporary scientists study learning to gain insights into how the mechanisms of behavior are altered by experience.

http://dx.doi.org/10.1037/0000057-001
The Essentials of Conditioning and Learning, Fourth Edition, by M. Domjan

Learning procedures are often used in studies of clinical, developmental, and cognitive psychology, as well as behavioral neuroscience and psychopharmacology.

Learning is a pervasive feature of human behavior and is evident in many other animal species as well. It has been found in creatures as diverse as fruit flies, sea slugs, honeybees, rodents, birds, and monkeys. Thus, *learning* is one of the fundamental characteristics of behavior.

Fundamental Features of Learning

People learn to recognize friends as different from strangers. They learn how to hold a telephone and how to answer it when it rings or vibrates. They also learn to swim, to ride a bicycle, and to avoid stepping in potholes. In all of these cases, learning is identified by a change in behavior. An experienced swimmer or cyclist behaves very differently from someone who has not learned to swim or ride a bike.

Learning to swim or ride a bicycle involves learning new hand, leg, and body movements and coordinating these movements to achieve balance and forward locomotion. Many, but not all, instances of learning involve the acquisition of new responses. We also learn to *not* do certain things. Children learn to keep quiet in church, to hold still when being examined by a doctor, and to not run into the street without first looking to see if it is safe. Learning to inhibit or suppress behavior is often as important as learning new responses. Riding a bicycle, for example, requires learning to pedal as well as learning not to lean too much to one side or the other. Thus, the change in behavior that is used to identify learning can be either an increase or a decrease in a particular response.

LEARNING AND OTHER FORMS OF BEHAVIOR CHANGE

Although all learning is identified by some kind of change in behavior, not all instances in which behavior is altered are instances of learning (see Figure 1.1). Therefore, it is important to distinguish learning from other sources of behavior change.

A major feature of learning that makes it different from other forms of behavior change is that learning is relatively long lasting. This serves to distinguish learning from various short-term or temporary changes in behavior. *Fatigue* and drowsiness can cause widespread and large changes in behavior (many of your actions become slower and less vigorous). However, such changes are temporary and can be reversed by a good rest. Major short-term changes in behavior can also be caused by changes in *motivation*. For example, people are much more reactive to stimuli related to food when they are hungry than after a hearty meal. Changes in stimulus conditions can also cause widespread but short-term changes in behavior. If you get a stone in your shoe, the discomfort is likely to change the way you walk and may encourage you to stop and empty your shoe. But the disruption is likely to be short lasting; you will resume your usual gait once the stone is removed. Learning, by contrast, involves longer term changes. The assumption is that once something is learned, it will be

FIGURE 1.1

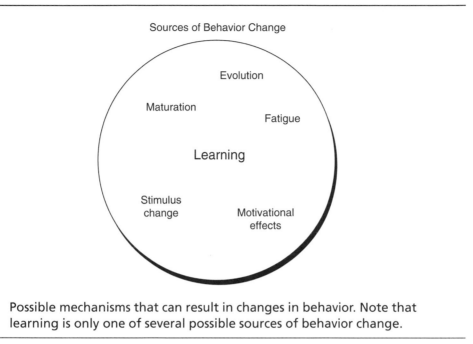

Sources of Behavior Change

Evolution

Maturation

Fatigue

Learning

Stimulus
change

Motivational
effects

Possible mechanisms that can result in changes in behavior. Note that
learning is only one of several possible sources of behavior change.

remembered for a substantial period of time. For example, you are not considered to have learned a new concept discussed in class if you cannot remember it the next day.

Although learning involves enduring changes in behavior, not all long-term changes are due to learning. Long-term changes in behavior can also be produced by physical growth or *maturation*. Children become more skillful in lifting heavy objects and reaching a cookie jar on a high shelf as they get older. These changes result from physical growth and maturation rather than learning.

Behavioral changes due to learning and changes due to maturation can be interrelated and difficult to distinguish. As a child becomes stronger and taller with age, these maturational changes facilitate the learning of new skills. However, one important difference between learning and maturation is that maturation does not require practice with things specifically related to the skill that is being acquired. A child will become better able to reach high shelves as she gets older whether or not she ever practices reaching for cookies. *Practice* is not needed for maturation, but it is required for learning.

Practice is obviously necessary to learn a skill such as swimming or riding a bicycle. One cannot become an expert bicycle rider without extensive practice with pedaling, steering, and balancing. Other things can be learned very quickly. A child will learn not to touch a burning log in a fireplace after just one painful encounter. Regardless of the amount of practice involved, however, all learning requires some practice or experience specifically related to the acquired behavior.

Another difference between maturation and learning is that the same maturational process can produce behavioral changes in a variety of situations. As a child grows taller, she will be able to reach taller shelves, climb taller trees, and catch butterflies that are flying higher off the ground. In contrast, behavior changes due to learning are more limited to the practiced response. Learning to operate a kitchen stove will help you cook indoors but will not improve your skill in building a fire for cooking on a camping trip. This is not to say that learning about one thing cannot help you do something else. Some generalization of learning can occur. However, generalization of learning tends to be limited. What you learn in one situation only generalizes to other similar situations. For example, learning to operate a particular gas stove will improve your ability to work other similar stoves but may not help if you are trying to cook with a microwave oven.

Another type of long-term change that has to be distinguished from learning is change due to *evolution*. Evolution can change not only the physical attributes of organisms but also their behavior. Furthermore, evolutionary changes, like learning, are a result of interactions with the environment. However, evolutionary changes occur across generations. In contrast, learning creates changes in behavior much more quickly within the lifetime of an individual organism.

Although learning is clearly distinguishable from evolution, learning is no doubt the product of evolutionary processes. Considering how pervasive learning is in the animal kingdom, it is safe to assume that it has evolved in particular environmental niches because organisms with the ability to learn are more successful in producing offspring in those environments (Domjan, Mahometa, & Matthews, 2012). The greater reproductive fitness of individuals with the ability to learn increases the likelihood that their genes (and the genetic bases of learning) will be passed on to future generations. This evolutionary process produces changes in the mechanisms of behavior from one generation to the next. Learning, in contrast, involves changes in behavior during an individual's own lifetime.

LEARNING, PERFORMANCE, AND LEVELS OF ANALYSIS

That learning has occurred can only be determined by observing a change in behavior; the change, however, may only be evident under special circumstances. A physics student, for example, may not be able to provide an adequate definition of a quark, suggesting that he has not learned the concept. However, the same student may be able to pick out the correct definition from a list of alternative possibilities. Children can learn many things about driving a car by watching adults drive. They can learn what the steering wheel does and what are the functions of the gas and the brake pedals. However, they may show no evidence of this knowledge until they are old enough to take driving lessons. These examples illustrate that learning can be behaviorally silent—having no visible behavioral manifestation. In such cases, special procedures must be used to determine what the individual has learned.

Learning may not be evident in the actions of an organism for a variety of reasons. One possibility is that what is learned is a relationship between stimuli or events in the environment rather than a particular response. For example, we may learn to associate the color red with ripe strawberries. The learning of an association between two stimuli is called *stimulus–stimulus learning*, or S-S learning. A learned association between red and ripeness will not be reflected in what we do unless we are given a special task, such as judging the ripeness of strawberries based on their color. S-S learning is usually not evident in the actions of an organism unless special test procedures are used.

The things an individual does, a person's observable actions, are collectively referred to as *performance*. Performance depends on many things, including motivation and the stimulus conditions or behavioral opportunities provided by the environment. Learning is just one of the many factors that determine performance. You may be an excellent flute player, but if you do not have the opportunity or the inclination to play the flute, no one will be able to tell what an accomplished musician you are.

I describe a number of behaviorally silent forms of conditioning and learning in the following chapters. Examples of behaviorally silent learning suggest that learning cannot be equated with a change in behavior. Rather, learning involves a change in the potential for doing something.

Where does the change in the potential for action reside? Behavior is the product of the nervous system. Therefore, learning involves long-lasting changes in the neural mechanisms of behavior. In fact, early neuroscientists, such as Ivan Pavlov, considered behavioral studies of learning to be studies of how the nervous system works. Pavlov regarded learning procedures as techniques for the investigation of neural function.

Because learning involves changes in the nervous system, it may be investigated at a variety of levels of analysis (see Figure 1.2). We may study learning at the level of molecular changes in nerve cells (or neurons), and their connections (or synapses).

FIGURE 1.2

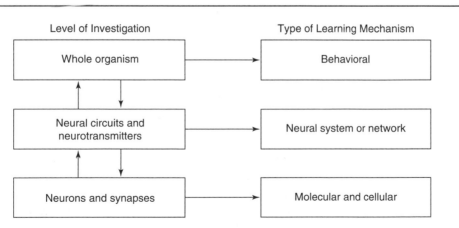

Levels of analysis of learning. Learning mechanisms may be investigated at the organismic level, at the level of neural circuits and transmitter systems, and at the level of nerve cells (neurons) and their synapses.

We may also study learning at the level of neural systems, such as neurotransmitter systems and neural circuits. Finally, we may study learning at the level of changes in the behavior of intact organisms.

Historically, studies of learning began at the level of the intact organism, and learning has been investigated most extensively at the behavioral level. However, with recent advances in the neurosciences, concepts and terms that have been developed for the behavioral analysis of learning have also been applied to investigations at the level of neural circuits and neurotransmitter systems, as well as at the cellular and molecular level. In fact, studies of the neural mechanisms of learning represent one of the largest areas of contemporary research in learning. A major challenge in the coming years will be to integrate knowledge from studies of learning that concentrate on different levels of analysis. Understanding how learning occurs at the behavioral level is critical for this integration (Delamater & Lattal, 2014). This book describes the behavioral analysis of learning.

A DEFINITION OF LEARNING

I identified a number of characteristics of learning in the preceding discussion. Learning involves a change in the potential or neural mechanisms of behavior. This change is relatively long lasting and is the result of experience with environmental events specifically related to the behavior in question. These characteristics are combined in the following definition:

> Learning is a relatively enduring change in the potential to engage in a particular behavior resulting from experience with environmental events specifically related to that behavior.

Naturalistic Versus Experimental Observations

Behavior occurs in many ways and in many situations. Basically, however, just two approaches to the study of behavior are available, naturalistic observations and experimental observations. *Naturalistic observations* involve observing and measuring behavior as it occurs under natural conditions, in the absence of interventions or manipulations introduced by the investigator. In contrast, *experimental observations* involve measuring behavior under conditions specifically designed by the investigator to test particular factors or variables that might influence the learning or performance of the behavior.

Consider, for example, activities involved in foraging for food by tree squirrels. Foraging can be investigated using naturalistic observations. One could watch squirrels in a park, for example, and count how often they picked up a seed, how often they ate the seed right away, and how often they buried the seed for later retrieval. Making such observations throughout the day and across seasons would provide detailed information about the foraging behavior of the squirrels in that park. However, such observations would not reveal why the squirrels did what they did. Observing squirrels undisturbed cannot tell us why they select one type of seed instead of another, why they devote more effort to foraging during one part of the day than another, or why they eat some seeds right away and bury others to eat later. Naturalistic observations cannot provide answers to questions that probe the *causes* of behavior. They may help us formulate questions or hypotheses about why animals do certain things, but naturalistic observations cannot identify causal variables.

The causes of behavior can only be discovered using experimental methods. Experimental observations require the investigator to manipulate the environment in special ways that facilitate reaching a causal conclusion. Using naturalistic observations, you may find that squirrels bury more seeds in the fall than in the winter. What might cause this outcome? One possibility is that more seeds are available in the fall than in the winter. We could test this possibility by comparing squirrels under two different conditions. Under one condition, the squirrels would be provided with excess food by spreading lots of peanuts in the observation area. Under the second condition, the squirrels would not be provided with extra peanuts. In all other relevant respects, the test conditions would be the same. Temperature, changes in daylight from day to day, and the extent of foliage in the trees would be identical. Given these identical conditions, if the squirrels buried more seeds when food was plentiful than when food was scarce, we could conclude that excess food encourages or causes the burying of seeds.

Although experimental observations permit us to draw conclusions about the causes of behavior, it is important to realize that they cannot be observed directly. Rather, causes must be inferred from differences in behavior observed under different experimental conditions. When we conclude that excess food causes seed burying, we are not describing something we have actually observed. What we saw in our hypothetical experiment is that squirrels bury more seeds when food is plentiful than when food is scarce. The conclusion that excess food causes seed burying is an inference arrived at by comparing the two experimental conditions. Causal conclusions are inferences based on a comparison of two (or more) experimental conditions.

Uncontrolled naturalistic observations can provide a wealth of descriptive information about behavior. We have learned a great deal from naturalistic observations about foraging for food, courtship and sexual behavior, maternal behavior, parental behavior, and defensive and territorial behavior. Considering that learning is ultimately also evident in the behavior of human and other animals, one might suppose that observational techniques can also be useful in the study of learning. In fact, some have advocated that detailed investigations of learning should begin with naturalistic observations of learning phenomena (Miller, 1985). However, naturalistic observations are inherently unsuitable for studies of learning because they cannot identify causal variables.

The Fundamental Learning Experiment

A critical aspect of the definition developed in this chapter is that learning is a result of past experiences. As such, learning is a causal variable, one that involves past experience with relevant environmental events. To conclude that learning has occurred, we have to be sure that the change in behavior we are seeing is *caused* by past experience.

As I noted earlier, causes cannot be observed directly. Instead, they have to be inferred from experimental observations. This idea has profound implications for the study of learning. Because learning is a causal variable, it cannot be observed directly. Rather, learning can only be investigated by means of experimental manipulations that serve to isolate a specific past experience as the cause of a change in behavior.

To conclude that a change in behavior is due to a specific past experience, or learning, one has to compare individuals with and without that experience under otherwise identical circumstances. The specific past experience is the independent variable (IV), and the resultant change in behavior is the dependent variable (DV). Consider, for example, the fact that most 8-year-old children can ride a bicycle proficiently, whereas 3-year-olds cannot. A reasonable interpretation is that the older children are expert riders because they have had more time to practice riding. That is, the change in behavior from 3 to 8 years of age may be caused by experience with bicycles. To support this conclusion, it is not enough to point to the fact that 8-year-olds are better riders than 3-year-olds. Such a difference could be due to physical growth and maturation. It is also not compelling to point out that 8-year-olds spend more time riding bicycles than 3-year-olds because this may be an effect rather than a cause of the greater skill of 8-year-olds. Some kind of experiment has to be conducted to prove that proficient riding is a result of past experience or learning.

One way to prove that bicycle riding is a learned skill would be to conduct an experiment with 3-year-old children who have never ridden a bicycle. We could assign the children randomly to one of two treatment groups: an *experimental group* and a *control group*. The experimental group would receive three 1-hour lessons in riding a bicycle. This would be the IV. The control group would also receive three 1-hour lessons through which they would become familiar with bicycles. However, the children in the control group would not be taught to ride. Rather, they would be told about the various parts of a bicycle and how the parts fit together. At the end of the lessons, both groups of children would be tested for their skill in riding. Proficiency in bicycle riding would be the DV. If proficient riding is learned through relevant practice, then the children in the experimental group should be more proficient than the children in the control group.

The preceding example illustrates the *fundamental learning experiment* (see Figure 1.3, left panel). To conclude that a behavior change is a result of learning, we have to compare the behavior of individuals under two conditions. In the *experimental condition*, participants are provided with the relevant environmental experience or training. In the *control condition*, participants do not receive the relevant training but are treated identically in all other respects. The occurrence of learning is inferred from a comparison between the two conditions. One cannot conclude that learning has occurred by observing only individuals who have acquired the skill of interest. Rather, conclusions about learning require a comparison between the experimental and control conditions.

THE CONTROL PROBLEM IN STUDIES OF LEARNING

Are there any special consequences because learning can only be inferred from a comparison between individuals with a particular training history and others who

FIGURE 1.3

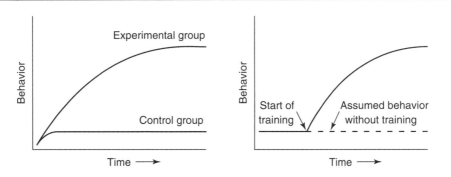

Two versions of the fundamental learning experiment. In the left panel, two groups of individuals are compared. The training procedure is provided for participants in the experimental group but not for participants in the control group. In the right panel, a single individual is observed before and during training. The individual's behavior during training is compared with what we assume its behavior would have been without training.

lack that history? Yes, indeed. One important consequence is that learning cannot be investigated using naturalistic observations. Under natural circumstances, individuals with a particular training history often differ in a number of respects from individuals who do not have the same history. Therefore, the requirements of the fundamental learning experiment are not satisfied under entirely natural circumstances.

A second important consequence of the fact that learning requires comparing an experimental condition with a control condition is that the control procedure must be designed with as much care as the experimental procedure. In fact, some landmark contributions to the study of learning have come not from analyses of experimental procedures for producing learning but from analyses of control procedures (e.g., Church, 1964; Rescorla, 1967; see also Papini & Bitterman, 1990). Different training procedures require different control procedures. I discuss this issue in greater detail as I examine various types of learning in the following chapters. For now, suffice it to say that the design of a control procedure is dictated by the particular aspect of past experience one wishes to isolate as being responsible for the behavioral change of interest.

In the example of children learning to ride a bicycle, we were interested in whether practice riding is critical for becoming a skillful rider. Children who practice riding also learn a lot about how a bicycle works (e.g., how the pedals make the wheels turn). This is why we designed the procedure for the control group so that the children in that group got to learn about the parts of a bicycle and how those parts go together. However, the children in the control group were not provided with practice in sitting on a bicycle and pedaling it. Thus, the design of the control procedure allowed us to isolate practice in riding as the critical factor involved in learning to ride a bicycle.

A third important consequence of the fact that learning can only be inferred from a comparison between experimental and control conditions is that learning is usually investigated with at least two independent groups of participants, an experimental group and a control group. An experimental design that involves comparing two separate groups of participants is called a *between-subjects experimental design*.

An important exception to the traditional between-subjects experimental design was developed in the Skinnerian tradition of learning research. Skinner advocated the extensive investigation of individual subjects rather than groups of participants. This led to the development of *single-subject experimental designs* (Sidman, 1960). However, even single-subject experiments involve comparisons between experimental and control conditions (see Figure 1.3, right panel). Basically, single-subject experiments require that the individual's behavior be understood well enough to permit accurate assumptions about how the individual would have behaved if it had not received a training procedure or intervention.

Consider, for example, a 4-year-old child who is unable to catch a ball tossed to him. If we spend several hours a day teaching the child how to catch a ball, he will become proficient within a few days. From this we may conclude that the child has learned to catch a ball. Notice, however, that this conclusion is based on our assumption that the child would not have acquired the skill so rapidly if he had not received instruction. Only if we have sufficient knowledge to make this assumption can we infer that the child learned to catch the ball. Thus, the study of learning in individual subjects also involves a comparison between an experimental and a control condition. The only difference is that the control condition is not provided by an explicit control group but by evidence obtained from other sources that gives us confidence that the behavior would not have changed without the training procedure.

THE GENERAL-PROCESS APPROACH TO THE STUDY OF LEARNING

In addition to relying on experimental techniques, investigators of learning typically use a general-process approach. Such an approach assumes that learning phenomena are the products of fundamental or basic processes that operate in much the same way in different learning situations.

The general-process approach is common in science and engineering. For example, in designing cars, engineers assume that the basic principles of how an internal combustion engine operates are pretty much the same whether the engine is used to propel a small four-door sedan or a large sport utility vehicle. In an analogous fashion, the basic principles involved in learning are assumed to be the same whether the learning involves children learning to operate a computer tablet or rats navigating a maze to obtain food. The general-process approach focuses on underlying commonalities across learning situations, with the goal of identifying universal learning principles.

The assumption that universal, basic laws of association are responsible for learning phenomena does not deny the diversity of stimuli different animals may learn about, the diversity of responses they may learn to perform, and species differences in rates of learning. The generality is assumed to exist in the rules or processes of learning, not in the contents or speed of learning.

If we assume that universal rules of learning exist, then we should be able to discover those rules in any situation in which learning occurs. Thus, an important methodological implication of the general-process approach is that general rules of learning may be discovered by studying any species or response system that exhibits learning. The general process approach to learning has been challenged by discoveries of various "biological constraints" that have encouraged a more ecological approach to the analysis of animal learning. However, even contemporary studies that incorporate an ecological perspective have sought to identify general principles that are applicable to all species and learning situations (Krause & Domjan, 2017).

THE USE OF NONHUMAN PARTICIPANTS IN RESEARCH ON LEARNING

Many of the basic principles of learning that I describe in the course of this book were first established in research with nonhuman animal participants and were only later extended to humans. There are many advantages to studying learning in nonhuman laboratory subjects. These include (a) better knowledge and control of the prior learning experiences of the research participants, (b) greater precision and control over the learning environment and administration of the learning procedures, (c) the ability to observe the same individuals under precisely the same conditions over repeated training and test trials, (d) knowledge of and ability to control the genetics of the participants, (e) greater control over motivational variables that might affect learning, (f) better chance to minimize the role of language, and (g) better chance to minimize efforts by the participants to please or displease the experimenter. Without the use of laboratory animals such as rats and mice, scientists would also be unable to develop behavioral tasks and tests that are critical to the study of the neurobiology and neuropharmacology of learning and memory. Such studies are beginning to provide treatments for serious maladies such as Alzheimer's disease.

Although nonhuman laboratory animals provide numerous advantages for the study of learning, some have argued in favor of alternatives. Four common alternatives have been proposed: (a) observational research, (b) studying plants, (c) studying tissue cultures, and (d) and studying computer simulations. As I pointed out previously, observational techniques do not involve the kind of precise experimental manipulations that are critical for studies of learning. Studying plants is not a viable alternative because plants do not have a nervous system, which is critical for learning. Tissue cultures can be useful in isolating the operation of specific cellular processes. However, without behavioral research involving intact organisms, one cannot determine the importance of a particular cellular process for the behavioral changes that characterize learning at the organismic level. Finally, computer simulations cannot replace experimental research because we first have to figure out how learning occurs in live organisms before we can build a computer simulation of learning.

Summary

Although learning is a common human experience, what it is and how it must be investigated are not obvious. Learning is evident in a change in behavior—either the acquisition of a new response or the suppression of an existing response. However, not all instances of altered behavior involve learning, and not all instances of learning produce immediately observable changes in behavior. The term *learning* is restricted to cases in which there is an enduring change in the potential to engage in a particular behavior that results from prior experience with environmental events specifically related to that behavior.

Learning mechanisms may be examined at the level of intact organisms, the level of neural circuits or systems, or the level of neurons and their synapses. However, because learning is a causal variable, it can be investigated only with experimental methods. Naturalistic observations may provide suggestions about learning but cannot provide definitive evidence. The basic learning experiment involves comparing an experimental and a control condition. The experimental condition includes the training procedure or experience whose effects are being tested. The control condition is similar but omits the relevant training experience. Learning is inferred from a difference in outcomes between the experimental and control conditions. For this reason, control procedures are as important for studies of learning as are experimental procedures.

Studies of learning have been based on a general-process approach, which assumes that diverse learning phenomena reflect the operation of universal elemental processes. This general-process approach and other conceptual and methodological considerations have encouraged the use of nonhuman animal subjects in learning experiments. Given the nature of learning phenomena, alternatives to the study of intact organisms are not viable.

Technical Terms

Between-subjects experiment
Control condition
Evolution
Experimental condition
Experimental observation
Fatigue
Learning

Maturation
Motivation
Naturalistic observation
Performance
Practice
Single-subject experiment
Stimulus–stimulus learning

The Structure of Unconditioned Behavior

2

Did you know that

- learning is constrained by the organism's unconditioned or unlearned behavior?
- unconditioned behavior is organized in complex and systematic ways?
- organized elicited behavior can result in well-coordinated social interactions?
- behavior in a complex environment can be governed by small, isolated stimulus features?
- sometimes the most effective stimulus for eliciting a response is not a naturally occurring stimulus but an artificial "supernormal" stimulus?
- species-typical or instinctive behavior is not invariant but modulated by the animal's motivational state?

Learning enables organisms to benefit from experience. Through learning, behavior can be altered in ways that make individuals more effective in interacting with their environment. Animals can forage more effectively by learning where and when food is likely to be available (Stephens, Brown, & Ydenberg, 2007). They can defend themselves more successfully by learning when and where they are likely to encounter a predator (e.g., Hollis, 1999).

http://dx.doi.org/10.1037/0000057-002
The Essentials of Conditioning and Learning, Fourth Edition, by M. Domjan

And they can be more effective in their sexual responses and produce more offspring by learning when and where they are likely to encounter a potential sexual partner (Domjan & Akins, 2011).

Shaping and Homogeneous Versus Heterogeneous Substrates of Behavior

In all instances of learning, the behavior of an organism is modified or shaped by its previous experience. B. F. Skinner introduced the term *shaping* in reference to a particular type of conditioning procedure that I describe in greater detail in Chapter 6. For our present purposes, it is sufficient to point out that through shaping, an organism's behavior can be gradually changed to enable it to perform new responses. A child's uncoordinated arm and leg movements, for example, can be gradually shaped to enable him to swim rapidly across a pool.

Skinner chose the term *shaping* by analogy with the way in which a sculptor gradually changes and molds a lump of clay into a recognizable object (Skinner, 1953). A sculptor interested in making a statue of a swan, for example, starts with an unformed lump of clay. She then cuts away excess clay here and there and molds what remains in special ways. As this process continues, a recognizable swan gradually emerges. In an analogous fashion, learning can change or shape an organism's behavior, with the result that the individual comes to respond in new ways.

The analogy with molding a block of clay into a swan captures some of the aspects of how behavior is changed through learning. However, the analogy has a serious shortcoming. Clay is a homogeneous substance that can be molded in any direction with equal ease. Behavior is not like that. Behavior cannot be changed in any direction with equal ease. Changes in behavior occur in the context of genetically programmed predispositions that make certain changes easier to produce than others. For example, it is much easier to train animals to approach and manipulate food-related stimuli (Hearst & Jenkins, 1974) than it is to train them to release or withdraw from stimuli related to food (Breland & Breland, 1961; Timberlake, Wahl, & King, 1982).

Learning procedures do not shape new behavior in the way that a sculptor shapes clay into a new object. A more apt analogy for the behavioral substrate of learning is provided by wood rather than clay (Rachlin, 1976). Unlike clay, wood has a heterogeneous or uneven consistency. It is grainy and has knots. Cutting with the grain is easier and results in a smoother line than cutting against the grain, and cutting around knots is easier than cutting through them. Because of this heterogeneity, if you are carving a statue out of wood, you have to pay close attention to how the statue is oriented in relation to the grain and the knots in the wood. Analogously, learning psychologists must pay close attention to how the new skills they are trying to teach fit with the organism's preexisting behavioral tendencies. This chapter is devoted to a description of these preexisting behavioral tendencies.

All instances of learning reflect an interaction between the training procedures used and the individual's preexisting behavior. Changes brought about by learning are not applied to a homogeneously modifiable substrate. Rather, learning is super-imposed on a heterogeneous preexisting behavioral structure. Therefore, understanding how learning occurs requires an appreciation of the heterogeneous behavioral substrate that organisms bring to a learning situation.

The dependence of learning on unlearned aspects of behavior has been emphasized in some areas of learning more than others. The interaction between conditioned and unconditioned aspects of behavior has been the focus of attention in studies of Pavlovian conditioning and avoidance learning (see Chapters 4 and 12). However, as we will see, unlearned behavioral tendencies are important in many other forms of learning as well.

The Concept of the Reflex

The smallest unit of unconditioned behavior is the reflex. The concept of a reflex was formulated by the French philosopher René Descartes (1596–1650). Descartes made numerous contributions to Western philosophy, including ideas about behavior that are familiar to most of us today but were innovative in the 17th century. Like other philosophers of his time, Descartes believed that important aspects of human behavior were voluntary. However, he was also impressed with the seemingly automatic and involuntary nature of some actions and proposed the concept of the reflex to characterize involuntary behavior.

Descartes based his concept of the reflex on animated statues that he saw in public parks in France. Sophisticated animated characters, such as those created by Disney Studios, were not available in Descartes's time. But some of the parks Descartes frequented had statues whose limbs would move when someone walked by. Through a series of levers and linkages, the limbs and joints of the statue were connected to stepping-stones along the walkway near the statue. Whenever someone stepped on one of these stones, the pressure on the stepping-stone was transferred to the statue, causing its arm or leg to move.

The moving statues appeared lifelike, and it seemed to Descartes that some aspects of human and animal behavior were similar to the behavior of the statues. Descartes pointed out that animals and people also perform certain actions in response to particular environmental stimuli. For example, we quickly withdraw our finger when we touch a hot stove, we "instinctively" flinch when we hear a sudden noise, and we extend our arm when we lose our footing. Such responses to particular stimuli are examples of *elicited behavior*.

The movements of the statues Descartes saw were elicited by the stimulus or force applied to the associated stepping-stones. Thus, the movements were reflections of the eliciting stimulus. Descartes coined the term *reflex* to capture this idea of behavior being a reflection of an eliciting stimulus. The entire unit from stimulus input to response output was termed the *reflex arc* (see Figure 2.1).

Reflexes are involved in many aspects of behavior important for sustaining critical life functions. Respiratory reflexes provide us with sufficient air intake. The

FIGURE 2.1

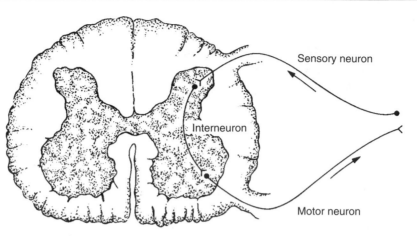

Cross-section of spinal cord

Neural organization of simple reflexes. The environmental stimulus for the reflex response activates a sensory neuron, which transmits the sensory message to the spinal cord. Here the neural impulses are relayed to an interneuron, which in turn passes the impulses to the motor neuron. The motor neuron activates muscles involved in the reflex response.

suckling reflex provides a newborn's first contact with milk. Chewing, swallowing, and digestive reflexes are important in obtaining nutrients throughout life. Postural reflexes enable us to maintain stable body positions, and withdrawal reflexes protect us from focal sources of injury.

For about 250 years after Descartes, investigators of reflexes were primarily concerned with physiological questions. Scientists studied the neural circuitry of the reflex arc, the mechanisms of neural conduction, and the role of reflexes in various physiological systems. These investigations continued at an accelerated pace in the 20th century. In addition, the idea of elicited behavior was extended to more complex forms of behavior. Much of this work was done in the newly emerging field of ethology, which is a specialty in biology concerned with the evolution and development of functional units of behavior (Baerends, 1988).

Complex Forms of Elicited Behavior

Ethologists discovered that complex social behavior in various species is made up of response components that are elicited by social stimuli. A male stickleback fish, for example, establishes a small territory and builds a nest tunnel during the mating season. After the territory has been set up, the approach of a male intruder elicits an aggressive defensive response from the resident male. In contrast, if a female enters the territory, the resident male engages in courtship zigzag swimming movements. The courtship zigzag movements stimulate the female to follow the resident male to the nest tunnel. Once the female is in the tunnel, with her head at one end and her tail at the other, the male prods the base of the female's tail. This causes the female to release her eggs. The female then leaves the nest and the male enters and fertilizes the eggs. After that, he chases the female away and fans the eggs to provide oxygen until the eggs hatch (see Tinbergen, 1952).

In this complex behavioral duet, the male and female each has its own special role. Stimuli provided by the female trigger certain actions on the part of the resident male (zigzag swimming); the male's behavior in turn provides stimuli that trigger other responses on the part of the female (following the resident male to the nest); the female's behavior then leads to further responses from the male; and so on. The outcome is a sequence of nicely coordinated social responses. The behavior sequence progresses only if the male's behavior provides the necessary stimulation to elicit the next response from the female, and vice versa. If the response of one participant fails to produce the next response in its partner, the sequence of actions is interrupted, and the social interaction may come to an end.

MODAL ACTION PATTERNS

Careful observations by ethologists have revealed numerous examples of complex social and nonsocial behaviors that are made up of sequences of elicited responses of the sort illustrated by the sexual behavior of sticklebacks. Elicited responses have been shown to be involved in, among other things, nest building, incubation, parental feeding of the young, grooming, foraging, and defensive behavior (Alcock, 2013). Each unit of elicited behavior is made up of a characteristic response and its corresponding eliciting stimulus.

The units of elicited behavior I have been discussing are commonly called *modal action patterns*, or MAPs. The phrase *action pattern* is used instead of *response* because the activities involved are not restricted to a single muscle movement, such as the blink of an eye or the flexion of a leg muscle. Elicited responses involved in grooming, foraging, courtship, and parental behavior require a coordinated set of various different muscles. The word *modal* is used to signify that most members of the species perform the action pattern in question and do so in a highly similar fashion. An action pattern is a characteristic of the species. For example, infant mammals typically feed by suckling, infant gulls typically feed by gaping and receiving food from a parent, and infant chickens typically feed by pecking small spots on the ground. Because modal action patterns are characteristic of a species, they are examples of *species-typical behavior.*

Originally, modal action patterns were called *fixed action patterns*, to emphasize that they are a stable feature of a species. However, the responses are not "fixed" in the sense that they occur exactly the same way each time. Because there is some variability in the elicited responses from one occasion to another, the phrase "modal action pattern" is now used in preference to "fixed action pattern."

Modal action patterns are evident in the behavior of all animals, including human beings. Our facial expressions (how we smile or express anger) are species-typical responses elicited by social and other stimuli. Suckling in infants is a modal action pattern, as is chewing in older individuals. How we comfort one another also reflects species typical modal action patterns.

SIGN STIMULI

Modal action patterns occur in the context of rich and complex arrays of stimulation. Consider, for example, a male quail that becomes sexually attracted to a female who comes into view. The female is a source of a variety of visual cues provided by what her head, neck, torso, and legs look like and by her movements. She may also provide auditory and olfactory stimulation, and if she comes close enough to the male, she provides tactile stimulation. Interestingly, most of these cues are not critical for eliciting sexual behavior in male quail.

To determine which of the various stimuli provided by a female quail are sufficient to attract a sexually motivated male, experimenters tested males with both live females and taxidermic models of females (see Figure 2.2). In one study (Domjan & Nash, 1988), for example, some of the models consisted of the head and entire body of a female. Other models consisted of just the head and neck of the female or just

FIGURE 2.2

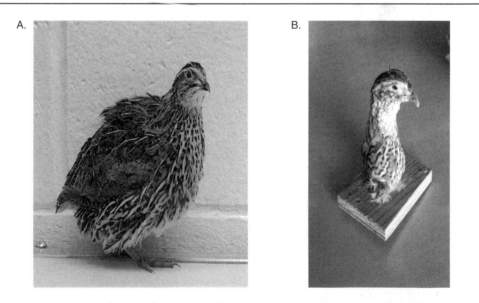

Photograph of a live female quail (A) and of a taxidermic model of a female's head and neck (B).

the body without the head. Figure 2.3 shows the tendency of male quail to approach and remain near these various types of female stimuli.

The male quail responded as vigorously to a complete taxidermic model of a female as they responded to a live female. This result shows that movement cues and auditory and olfactory stimuli provided by a live female are not necessary to elicit the approach response. The males also responded vigorously to just the visual cues of a female's head and neck. In fact, they approached the head-and-neck model almost as much as they responded to a complete female model. This is a remarkable outcome. Evidently male quail can identify a female by means of the visual cues of the female's head and neck alone. The rest of her body, her calls, her smell, her movements—all of these are unnecessary.

The restricted set of stimuli that are required to elicit a modal action pattern is called a *sign stimulus*. As far as male quail are concerned, the female's head and neck are the "sign" that she is a female. Similar results have been obtained with turkeys (Schein & Hale, 1965).

A sign stimulus is often a remarkably small part of the cues that ordinarily precede a modal action pattern. The pecking response of gull chicks, for example, is elicited by a prominent red spot on their mother's or father's bill (see Figure 2.4).

FIGURE 2.3

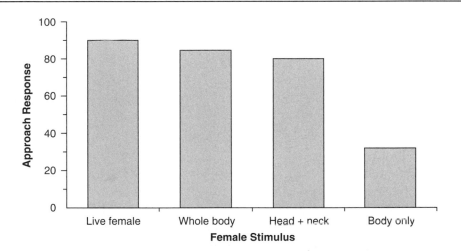

Approach response of sexually experienced male quail to a live female and to taxidermic models consisting of the whole body of a female, a female's head and neck only, and a female's body without the head and neck. From "Stimulus Control of Social Behaviour in Male Japanese Quail, *Coturnix coturnix Japonica*," by M. Domjan and S. Nash, 1988, *Animal Behaviour, 36*, p. 1013. Copyright 1988 by Elsevier. Adapted with permission.

FIGURE 2.4

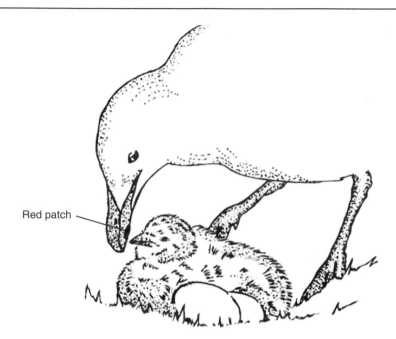

Red patch

The sign stimulus for the pecking response of gull chicks is a red spot near the tip of the parent's bill.

The pointed shape of the parent's bill, together with this prominent spot, stimulates the chicks to peck the parent's bill, which then causes the parent to feed the chick by regurgitating food. Other aspects of the parent (the shape of her head, her eyes, how she lands on the edge of the nest, the noises she makes) are not important (Tinbergen & Perdeck, 1950).

Artificial models are typically used to isolate the sign stimulus that is critical for eliciting a behavioral response. Once a sign stimulus has been identified, it can be increased in size and intensity to produce an even larger response. Such exaggerated forms of natural eliciting stimuli are called *supernormal stimuli.*

Sign stimuli are also prominent in the control of various aspects of human behavior, and businesses have become highly adept at enhancing the effectiveness of these cues by creating supernormal stimuli (Barrett, 2010). The taste of sugar and fat, for example, are sign stimuli for human food selection and ingestion. The food industry has taken advantage of this fact to increase sales by increasing the sugar and fat content of various food products. The creation of supernormal stimuli is also the goal of the cosmetic industry, to increase sexual attractiveness. In a similar fashion, the excessive violence in computer games involves the use of supernormal stimuli that elicit aggressive behavior.

The Organization of Elicited Behavior

If each reflex or modal action pattern occurred automatically whenever its eliciting stimulus was encountered, behavior would be somewhat disorganized. Elicited responses do not occur independently of each other. Rather, they are organized in special ways. As we will see in the following chapters, some of this organization is a result of learning and experience. Here I describe aspects of behavioral organization that are not obviously a product of learning.

MOTIVATIONAL FACTORS

One prominent factor that serves to coordinate modal action patterns is the motivational state of the organism. In numerous species, for example, courtship and sexual responses occur only during the breeding season, or only in the presence of sufficiently high levels of sex hormones. In fact, the necessary conditions can be even more restrictive. Male sticklebacks court females only if they are in the breeding season and they previously established a territory and built a nest. These preconditions serve to prime or create the motivation for courtship behavior.

Motivational factors have been identified for a variety of modal action patterns, including aggression, feeding, and various aspects of parental and sexual behavior. The motivational state sets the stage for a modal action pattern, the actual occurrence of which is then triggered by a sign stimulus. In a sense, the sign stimulus releases the modal action pattern when the animal is in a particular motivational state. For this reason, a sign stimulus is also sometimes referred to as a *releasing stimulus*.

Ethologists considered the motivational state of the organism to be one of the key factors involved in the organization of behavior (e.g., Lorenz, 1981). Using motivational concepts, they formulated an influential model of how modal action patterns are organized, referred to as the *hydraulic model* of behavior. The hydraulic model assumes that certain factors lead to the buildup of a particular type of motivation or drive. The term *hydraulic* was used by analogy with a hydraulic engine, in which the buildup of pressure causes pistons to move until the pressure is released or dissipated. The hunger drive, for example, is created by the expenditure of energy and the utilization of nutrients. This drive in turn induces selective attention to food-related stimuli and lowers the threshold for activating food-related modal action patterns. Once food is found and eaten, the motivational state of hunger is discharged. Thus, the motivational state facilitates modal action patterns related to eating, and the opportunity to perform those responses in turn reduces the motivational state.

APPETITIVE AND CONSUMMATORY BEHAVIOR

Elicited behavior is also organized sequentially. Certain responses tend to occur before others. Ethologists characterized the response sequence involved in the discharge of a drive state as consisting of two major components. The first of these is *appetitive behavior*. In the case of the feeding system, appetitive behavior consists of responses involved in searching for a patch of food. Appetitive behavior is quite variable and occurs in response to general spatial cues. For example, in searching for a patch of food, a squirrel will focus on spatial cues that help identify trees and bushes that may contain nuts and fruit. Appetitive behavior tends to occur over a wide area and involves a range of possible activities. During the course of its foraging, the squirrel may run across open grass, scramble over rocks, climb trees, jump from one tree limb to another, and so on.

Once the squirrel encounters an edible nut, its behavior becomes much more stereotyped and restricted. Now the squirrel remains in one place, sits back on its hind legs and tail, takes the nut in its front paws, cracks it open, and chews and swallows the food. These more stereotyped species-typical activities are examples of *consummatory behavior* because they complete or consummate the response sequence. Consummatory modal action patterns end the response sequence because these responses discharge the motivation or drive state.

In the feeding system, consummatory behavior involves the consumption of food, but the apparent similarity in wording in this case is merely a coincidence. In the sexual behavior system, consummatory behavior consists of the copulatory or coital responses that serve to complete a sexual interaction. In the defensive behavior system, consummatory behavior consists of the circa strike responses an animal makes when it is not just threatened but physically attacked by a predator (see Chapter 12).

Another way to think about appetitive and consummatory behavior is that appetitive behavior consists of activities that enable an organism to come into contact with the sign stimuli that will elicit the modal action patterns that permit completing the response sequence. For example, the appetitive sexual behavior of the male involves searching for a female. Once the female is encountered, the stimuli provided by her elicit a more restricted range of courtship and copulatory responses. These copulatory or coital responses then discharge the motivation to engage in sexual behavior, thereby consummating or ending the sexual behavior sequence.

BEHAVIOR SYSTEMS

Recent research on the structure of unconditioned behavior has suggested that elicited behavior sequences should be subdivided into more than just the two response categories (appetitive and consummatory responses) provided by classical ethology. Timberlake (2001), for example, characterized the feeding system as consisting of at least three components (see Figure 2.5). According to this more detailed view, the feeding behavior sequence starts with the *general search mode* in which the animal reacts to general features of the environment with responses that enable it to come in contact with a variety of potential sources of food. A honeybee, for example, may fly all around looking for bushes or other plants with flowers.

Once an animal has identified a potential source of food, it switches to a more restricted response mode, the *focal search mode*. In the focal search mode, the bee will concentrate on one bush, going from flower to flower. Upon encountering a specific flower, the bee will switch to the food-handling and ingestion mode. This last response mode is similar to what ethologists referred to as consummatory behavior and consists of responses required to extract nectar from the flower and ingest the nectar.

FIGURE 2.5

Components of the feeding behavior system. The feeding behavior sequence begins with a general search for potential food sites. Once a potential food site has been identified, the animal engages in a focal search of that site. Upon finding the food, the animal engages in food-handling and ingestion responses.

Behavior systems have been described for a variety of functions that organisms have to accomplish in their lives: caring for young, grooming, defense, and reproduction. As we will see, behavior systems are highly relevant to predicting the behavioral manifestations of learning. Several features of behavior systems are important in contemporary studies of learning:

1. Behavior systems usually consist of a sequence of three or more modes of behavior, rather than just appetitive and consummatory behavior. The organism moves from one mode of responding to another (general search to focal search) depending on the environmental events that it encounters.
2. The sequence of response modes is linear. An animal typically moves from one response mode to the next without skipping any steps in the sequence. A squirrel cannot handle food, for example, without first having encountered the food in its focal search mode.
3. Although the response sequence is linear, it is not unidirectional. An animal may go either forward or backward in the sequence depending on the circumstances. If the focal search behavior of a squirrel is not successful in locating nuts, the squirrel will move back to its general search mode.
4. Because response sequences are ordered in a linear fashion, they are also organized in time. General foraging responses tend to occur farther in time from the end of the feeding behavior sequence than ingestive responses. Because of this, temporal variables in learning are related to temporal factors in preexisting behavior systems.
5. Finally, each response mode involves not only characteristic responses but also increased sensitivity or attention to particular kinds of stimuli. In the general search mode, a foraging bee is likely to be looking for flowering bushes as opposed to bushes that don't have flowers. In the focal search mode, it is apt to focus on where the flowers are in the bush it has chosen to search and which flower is ready to harvest for nectar. Finally, in the food-handling mode, it will focus on the part of the flower that contains the nectar. Thus, various modes of behavior differ not only in terms of the types of response that are involved but also in the types of stimuli that guide the behavior.

Summary

All instances of learning reflect an interaction between the training procedures that are used and the individual's preexisting behavioral structures. Therefore, understanding how learning occurs requires an appreciation of unconditioned behavioral mechanisms. Unconditioned behavior is not homogeneous and modifiable in any direction but has its own determinate structure. The simplest unit of unconditioned behavior is the reflex, which consists of a specific eliciting stimulus and a corresponding elicited response. More complex forms of elicited behavior, studied by ethologists, involve modal action patterns that are elicited by sign stimuli or releasing stimuli. Ethologists identified motivational factors involved in the control of modal action patterns and pointed out that elicited behavior consists of a predictable sequence of activities that begins with appetitive responses and ends with consummatory behavior. These ideas have been extended in contemporary conceptualizations of behavior systems. A behavior system is a set of response modes that is activated in a coordinated fashion to achieve an important behavioral outcome such as nutrition, defense, or reproduction. The response modes are organized sequentially, and each response mode is characterized by particular responses and increased sensitivity to particular types of stimuli.

Suggested Readings

Baerends, G. P. (1988). Ethology. In R. C. Atkinson, R. J. Herrnstein, G. Lindzey, & R. D. Luce (Eds.), *Stevens' handbook of experimental psychology* (Vol. 1, pp. 765–830). New York, NY: Wiley.

Barrett, D. (2010). *Supernormal stimuli: How primal urges overran their evolutionary purpose*. New York, NY: Norton.

Timberlake, W. (2001). Motivational modes in behavior systems. In R. R. Mowrer & S. B. Klein (Eds.), *Handbook of contemporary learning theories* (pp. 155–209). Mahwah, NJ: Erlbaum.

Tinbergen, N. (1951). *The study of instinct*. Oxford, England: Clarendon Press.

Technical Terms

Appetitive behavior
Behavior system
Consummatory behavior
Elicited behavior
Ethology
Focal search mode
General search mode

Hydraulic model
Modal action pattern
Reflex
Reflex arc
Releasing stimulus
Sign stimulus
Species-typical behavior

Habituation and Sensitization 3

Did you know that

- reflexive behavior is not automatic and invariant but can increase or decrease as a result of experience?
- the vigor of elicited behavior is modified by opposing processes of habituation and sensitization?
- elicited behavior is determined not only by the eliciting stimulus but also by other recently encountered events?
- habituation effects are evident in decreased responding; sensitization effects are evident in increased responding?
- habituation and sensitization effects are both determined by the intensity and frequency of the eliciting stimulus?
- habituation is more specific to the eliciting stimulus than is sensitization?
- habituation is an inherent property of all elicited behavior?
- sensitization reflects a modulatory influence on the mechanisms of elicited behavior?

Having considered the structure of unconditioned behavior in Chapter 2, we are now ready to examine some of the ways in which behavior can be changed or modified by experience. We begin with the phenomena of habituation and sensitization because these phenomena are two of the simplest and most common forms of behavior change. It also is important to consider habituation and sensitization early in an account of learning because

http://dx.doi.org/10.1037/0000057-003
The Essentials of Conditioning and Learning, Fourth Edition, by M. Domjan

habituation and sensitization may occur in any of the more complex learning proce-dures that are described in subsequent chapters.

Habituation and sensitization have been investigated most extensively in reflex systems. A reflex is a fairly simple response that occurs in reaction to a specific elicit-ing stimulus. Suckling, for example, is readily elicited in a newborn infant by placing a nipple-shaped object in the infant's mouth. As I noted in Chapter 2, the concept of the reflex was originally formulated by Descartes, who assumed that reflexes have two major features. First, Descartes believed that the vigor of the elicited response is directly related to the intensity of the eliciting stimulus. In fact, he thought that the energy required for the reflex response was provided by the eliciting stimulus. Second, he believed that a reflex response will always occur when its eliciting stimu-lus is presented. For Descartes, reflexes were "automatic" or inevitable reactions to eliciting stimuli.

Descartes was correct in pointing out that certain actions are triggered by eliciting stimuli. But he was wrong in characterizing reflexes as invariant and energized by their eliciting stimuli. Nevertheless, his views continue to dominate how laypersons think about reflexes. People commonly consider reflexes to be automatic and fixed. In fact, the term *reflexive* is sometimes used as a synonym for *automatic.* However, scien-tists have shown that this view of reflexes is incorrect. As we will see in this chapter, elicited and reflexive behavior can be remarkably flexible. Responses to an eliciting stimulus may increase (showing sensitization) or decrease (showing habituation), depending on the circumstances.

Why should reflexive behavior be modifiable? Why do we need habituation and sensitization? Basically, these processes help us avoid responding to stimuli that are irrelevant and allow us to focus our actions on things that are important. Habituation and sensitization modulate our reflex responses and increase the efficiency of our interactions with the environment. Human and nonhuman animals live in complex environments that provide many forms of stimulation all the time. Even during an activity as seemingly uneventful as sitting quietly in a chair, a person is bombarded by visual, auditory, olfactory, tactile, and internal physiological stimuli. All of these are capable of eliciting responses, but if they all did (as Descartes originally thought), we would be reacting to lots of things that are unimportant. Without habituation and sen-sitization, behavior would be totally enslaved to the vicissitudes of the environment.

Consider, for example, the *orienting response.* We look and turn toward novel visual and auditory stimuli (e.g., someone entering the room). However, if all of the stimuli in our environment were to elicit an orienting response, we would be wasting much of our effort looking here, there, and everywhere. Many stimuli are not important enough to warrant our attention. While talking to someone in the living room, we need not orient to the sounds of a refrigerator humming in the background or a car going by in the street. Habituation and sensitization serve to modulate our respon-sivity. They ensure that we respond vigorously to some stimuli while ignoring others.

In Chapter 2, I noted that the vigor of elicited behavior is determined by motiva-tional factors and that the sequence of elicited responses is determined by the inher-ent structure of the behavior system that is activated. I also noted in passing that response systems are sometimes organized by learning and experience. Habituation and sensitization are the first behavioral principles that we will consider that serve to organize behavior based on experience.

Effects of the Repeated Presentation of an Eliciting Stimulus

The relationships that I describe here for habituation and sensitization are general characteristics that may be observed for just about any form of elicited behavior. Habituation procedures are widely used in studies of infant visual attention (Colombo & Mitchell, 2009). The basic experimental method is illustrated in Figure 3.1. The infant is seated comfortably in front of a screen that is used to present visual stimuli. When a stimulus appears on the screen, the infant looks at the display. The infant's visual attention is measured by timing how long his eyes remain fixated on the stimulus before he shifts his gaze elsewhere. How long the infant looks at the stimulus depends on what the stimulus is and how often it has been presented.

Figure 3.2 shows the results of a simple experiment that was conducted with two groups of 4-month-old babies (Bashinski, Werner, & Rudy, 1985). For each group,

FIGURE 3.1

Experimental setup for the study of visual attention in infants. The infant is seated in front of a screen that is used to present various visual stimuli. How long the infant looks at the display before diverting his or her gaze elsewhere is measured on each trial.

FIGURE 3.2

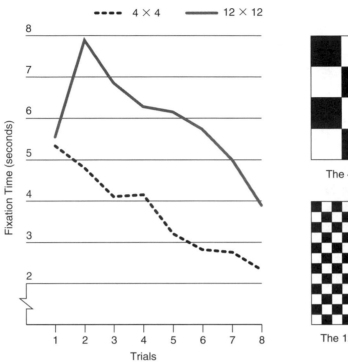

The 4 × 4 stimulus

The 12 × 12 stimulus

Visual fixation time for two groups of infants presented with a visual stimulus on eight successive trials. The stimulus was a 12 × 12 checkerboard pattern for one group and a 4 × 4 checkerboard pattern for the other group. From "Determinants of Infant Visual Fixation: Evidence for a Two-Process Theory," by H. S. Bashinski, J. S. Werner, and J. W. Rudy, 1985, *Journal of Experimental Child Psychology*, *39*, p. 588. Copyright 1985 by Elsevier. Reprinted with permission.

a 10-second visual stimulus was presented eight times, with a 10-second interval between trials. The complexity of the visual stimulus differed for the two groups. A 4 × 4 checkerboard pattern was presented to one group and a more complex 12 × 12 checkerboard pattern was presented to the other group. Notice that the duration of the visual fixation elicited by each stimulus was not invariant or "automatic." Rather, fixation time changed in different ways depending on the stimulus. With the complex 12 × 12 pattern, fixation increased from Trial 1 to Trial 2, then declined thereafter. With the simpler 4 × 4 pattern, visual fixation declined from each trial to the next.

A decrease in the vigor of elicited behavior is called a *habituation effect*. In contrast, an increase in responsivity is called a *sensitization effect*. Habituation was evident throughout the experiment with the 4 × 4 checkerboard pattern. Habituation was also evident with the 12 × 12 pattern from Trial 2 to Trial 8, but sensitization occurred from Trial 1 to Trial 2.

Another common experimental preparation for the study of habituation and sensitization involves the *startle response*. The startle response is a sudden movement or flinch caused by a novel stimulus. If someone broke a balloon behind you (making a loud popping sound), you would suddenly hunch your shoulders and pull in your neck. Startle is a common human reaction in a variety of cultures (Simons, 1996). The sudden movement that characterizes the startle reflex can easily be measured, which has encouraged numerous studies of habituation and sensitization of the startle reflex in a variety of species (e.g., Davis, Antoniadis, Amaral, & Winslow, 2008; Halberstadt & Geyer, 2009).

A sudden but soft sound may cause you to startle the first few times it occurs, but you will quickly stop responding to the sound. Similar results are obtained with mild tactile stimuli. When you first put on a comfortable pair of shoes, you feel the gentle pressure of the shoes against your feet. However, even though the tactile pressure remains, your reaction quickly habituates; soon you will be entirely unaware that you are wearing the shoes.

If the tactile stimulus is more intense (because the shoe does not fit as well), it will be more difficult to get used to it, and the pattern of responding may be similar to what we saw in Figure 3.2, with the visual attention of infants to a 12 × 12 checker board pattern. In such cases, responding increases at first and then declines. Similar results are obtained with the startle reflex if the eliciting stimulus is an intense tone.

If the eliciting stimulus is very intense, repetitions of the stimulus may result in a sustained increase in responding. If a pebble in your shoe is creating intense pressure, your irritation will increase with continued exposure to that stimulus, and this will last as long as the pebble remains in your shoe. Similarly, a sustained increase in the startle response may occur if the eliciting stimulus is an intense noise. Soldiers and civilians in a war zone may never get used to the sound of nearby gunfire.

As these examples illustrate, elicited behavior can change in a variety of ways with repetitions of the eliciting stimulus. Sometimes the response shows a steady decline or habituation effect. In other cases, a sensitization effect occurs at first, followed by a decline in responding. Elicited behavior can also show evidence of sustained sensitization.

CHARACTERISTICS OF HABITUATION EFFECTS

Numerous factors have been found to influence the course of habituation and sensitization effects. Here I consider some of the major variables.

Effects of Stimulus Change

Perhaps the most important feature of habituation is that it is specific to the particular stimulus that has been repeatedly presented. If a new stimulus is presented, the habituated response will recover, with the degree of recovery determined by how similar the new stimulus is to the habituated one. Stimulus specificity is a defining feature of habituation (Rankin et al., 2009).

The stimulus specificity of habituation turns out to be a very useful property to help rule out fatigue as a possible cause of the response decrement. Response fatigue is an obvious culprit when responding declines with repeated stimulations. However, if habituation were due to fatigue, the participant would not respond even when the eliciting stimulus was changed. The recovery of responding that occurs with a change in the eliciting stimulus rules out response fatigue and is one of the pieces of evidence indicating that habituation reflects a central neural process rather than changes in peripheral motor mechanisms.

Tests with novel stimuli are routinely carried out in studies of habituation with infants. Infants can stop looking at a visual stimulus for a variety of reasons. They may become tired or fussy or may fall asleep. To be sure that they are still paying attention and actively participating in the experiment, novel stimuli are introduced. The results of the experiment are considered valid only if the novel stimuli produce recovery of the habituated response.

Investigators have taken advantage of the stimulus specificity of habituation to study a wide range of issues in infant perception and cognition (Colombo & Mitchell, 2009). Before they are able to talk, infants cannot tell us in words which stimuli they consider to be similar and which they consider to be different. However, they can provide answers to such questions in their responses to test stimuli following habituation.

The infant habituation task has been used, for example, to determine whether 5-month-old infants perceive body postures based on a holistic representation of the body or representations of individual body parts. In one experiment (Hock, White, Jubran, & Bhatt, 2016), the infants were first habituated to the image of a person in a particular posture (Figure 3.3A) or to a disconnected arm and a leg presented in similar positions (Figure 3.3B). After habituation, one arm of the person was presented in a novel position, with a similar change in the disconnected arm. The infants showed recovery of the visual attention response only with the image of the person in a new posture (Figure 3.3A). They did not recognize the disconnected arm presented in a new position as a new stimulus (Figure 3.3B). This result suggests that the infants were processing body postures based on a holistic representation of the body rather than its parts.

Effects of Time Without Stimulation

Habituation effects are often temporary. They dissipate or are lost as time passes without presentation of the eliciting stimulus. A loss of the habituation effect is evident in a recovery of responding. This is illustrated in Figure 3.4. Because the response recovery is produced by a period without stimulation (a period of rest), the phenomenon is called *spontaneous recovery*.

Spontaneous recovery is a common feature of habituation (Rankin et al., 2009). If your roommate turns on the radio while you are studying, you may notice it at first, but then you will come to ignore the sound if it is not too loud. However, if the radio is turned off for an hour or two and then comes back on again, you will notice it again. The degree of spontaneous recovery is related to the duration of the period

FIGURE 3.3

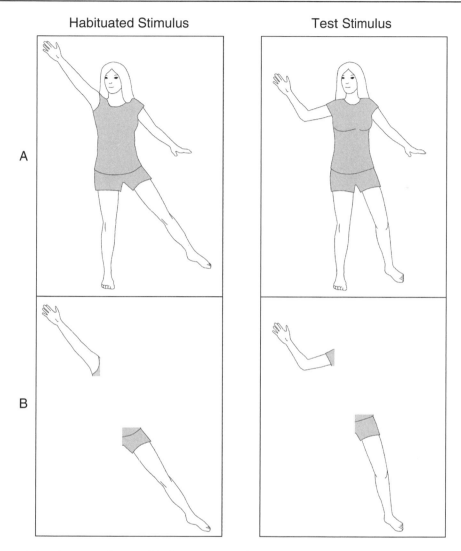

Stimulus specificity of habituation. Infants were first habituated to the image of a person in a particular posture (Panel A) or to a disconnected arm and a leg presented in similar positions (Panel B). After habituation, the infants were tested with a change in the position of the arm. The infants showed recovery of the visual attention response only when the arm was a part of a person. From "The Whole Picture: Holistic Body Posture Recognition in Infancy," by A. Hock, H. White, R. Jubran, and R. S. Bhatt, 2016, *Psychonomic Bulletin & Review, 23*, p. 428. Copyright 2016 by Springer. Adapted with permission.

FIGURE 3.4

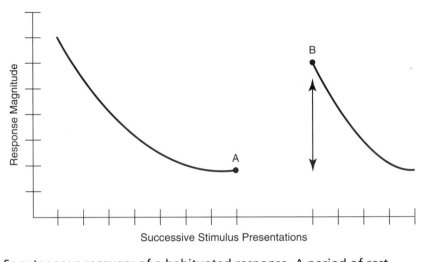

Spontaneous recovery of a habituated response. A period of rest without stimulus presentations occurred between points A and B, which caused a recovery of the habituated response. Data are hypothetical.

of without the radio playing. Longer periods without presentation of the eliciting stimulus result in greater recovery of the response. Less and less spontaneous recovery occurs with repetitions of the spontaneous recovery procedure. How much of a rest period is required to observe spontaneous recovery of habituation varies across different situations. For example, habituation of the novelty response to taste shows little spontaneous recovery even after a week or two.

Animals, including people, are cautious about ingesting a food or drink that has an unfamiliar flavor. This phenomenon is known as *flavor neophobia*. Flavor neophobia probably evolved because things that taste new or unfamiliar may well be poisonous. With repeated exposure to a new taste, the neophobic response becomes attenuated. Coffee, for example, often elicits an aversion response in a child who tastes it for the first time. However, after drinking coffee without ill effect, the child's neophobic response will become diminished or habituated. Once this has occurred, the habituation is likely to be long lasting. Having become accustomed to the flavor of coffee, a person is not likely to experience a neophobic response even if he goes a couple of weeks without having any coffee. Studies with laboratory rats have shown no spontaneous recovery of flavor neophobia over periods as long as 17 and 24 days (Domjan, 1976).

Habituation effects have been classified according to whether they exhibit spontaneous recovery. Cases in which substantial spontaneous recovery occurs are called *short-term habituation*, whereas cases in which significant spontaneous recovery does not occur are called *long-term habituation*. Short-term and long-term habituation are not mutually exclusive. Sometimes both effects are observed. Long-term habituation effects are genuine learning effects because they satisfy the criterion of being long lasting. In contrast, short-term habituation effects provide less convincing evidence of learning because they are less enduring.

Effects of Stimulus Frequency

The frequency of a stimulus refers to how often the stimulus is repeated in a given period of time—how often the stimulus occurs per minute, for example. The higher the stimulus frequency, the shorter the period of rest between repetitions of the stimulus. As we saw in the phenomenon of spontaneous recovery, the duration of rest between stimulations can significantly influence responding. Because higher stimulus frequencies permit less spontaneous recovery between trials, responding generally declines more rapidly with more frequent presentations of the stimulus (Davis, 1970). One way to reduce habituation is to substantially increase how much time occurs between repetitions of an eliciting stimulus.

Effects of Stimulus Intensity

Habituation is also determined by the intensity of the eliciting stimulus. In general, responding declines more slowly if the eliciting stimulus is more intense (Rankin et al., 2009). For example, laboratory rats are slower to lose their neophobic response to a strong flavor than to a weak flavor (Domjan & Gillan, 1976).

Effects of Exposure to a Second Stimulus

One of the remarkable features of a habituated response is that it is not determined only by the eliciting stimulus. The level of responding is also influenced by other stimuli the organism encounters at the time. In particular, exposure to a novel stimulus can result in recovery of responding when the previously habituated stimulus is reintroduced. This phenomenon is called *dishabituation* (Rankin et al., 2009).

The results of an experiment on dishabituation are summarized in Figure 3.5. The visual fixation of human infants was measured in response to a 4 × 4 checkerboard pattern (Kaplan, Werner, & Rudy, 1990). As expected, repetition of the visual stimulus resulted in a decline or habituation of the looking response of the infants. After Trial 8, a tone (1,000 Hz, 75 dB) was presented as a dishabituating stimulus along with the checkerboard pattern. Figure 3.5 shows that presentation of the tone caused significant recovery of visual fixation to the 4 × 4 pattern. The response to the original habituated visual stimulus was thus enhanced by presentation of the dishabituating tone.

The phenomena of dishabituation is useful in ruling out *sensory adaptation* as a cause of habituation. Sensory adaptation is a reduction in the efficacy of a sensory receptor to respond to stimulation. If the decrease in responding to the visual stimulus in Figure 3.5 had been due to sensory adaptation of the visual system, the presentation of a dishabituating tone would not have produced recovery of the visual attention response. Dishabituation, along with the stimulus specificity of habituation, indicates that habituation reflects a central neural process rather than changes in peripheral sensory or motor mechanisms.

FIGURE 3.5

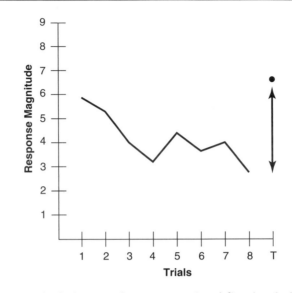

Dishabituation of a habituated response. Visual fixation in infants became habituated to a checkerboard stimulus presented in Trials 1 through 8. Presentation of a tone with the visual stimulus caused dishabituation of the attentional response during a subsequent test trial (T). From *Advances in Infancy Research* (Vol. 6, p. 98), by C. Rovee-Collier and L. P. Lipsitt (Eds.), 1990, Norwood, NJ: Ablex. Copyright 1990 by Elsevier. Adapted with permission.

Unfortunately, the term *dishabituation* is used inconsistently in the research literature. In studies with human infants, the term *dishabituation* is used to refer to recovery of a habituated response that occurs when the habituated stimulus is changed and a novel stimulus is tested (e.g., Kavšek, 2013). In contrast, in research with other species and response systems, *dishabituation* is reserved for cases in which the introduction of a second stimulus produces recovery in responding to the original habituated stimulus. This latter usage was advocated by Thompson and Spencer (1966) in their seminal work that provided the foundations of contemporary research on habituation. The distinction between the stimulus specificity of habituation and dishabituation remains important in contemporary neuroscience (Rankin et al., 2009).

CHARACTERISTICS OF SENSITIZATION EFFECTS

Sensitization effects are influenced by the same stimulus intensity and time factors that govern habituation phenomena. In general, greater sensitization effects (greater increases in responding) occur with more intense eliciting stimuli (Groves, Lee, & Thompson, 1969).

Like habituation, sensitization effects can be short-term or long-term (e.g., Davis, 1974). *Short-term sensitization* decays as a function of time without presentations of the stimulus. Unlike the decay of short-term habituation, which is called *spontaneous recovery*, the decay of short-term sensitization has no special name. It is not called spontaneous recovery because responding declines (rather than recovers) as sensitization dissipates. In contrast to short-term sensitization, *long-term sensitization* is evident even after appreciable periods without stimulation. As was the case with long-term habituation, long-term sensitization effects satisfy the durability criterion of learning, whereas short-term sensitization effects do not.

One important respect in which sensitization is different from habituation is that sensitization is not as specific to a particular stimulus. As I noted earlier, habituation produced by repeated exposure to one stimulus will not be evident if the stimulus is altered substantially. In contrast, sensitization is not so stimulus-specific. For example, the startle response to a brief loud auditory stimulus can be sensitized by exposure to a fear-eliciting stimulus. Fear-potentiated startle has been well documented in studies with both laboratory animals (Davis et al., 2008) and human participants (Bradley, Moulder, & Lang, 2005). In a similar fashion, the experience of illness increases or sensitizes the flavor neophobia response, and once flavor neophobia has been sensitized, the participants show heightened finickiness to a variety of different taste stimuli (Domjan, 1977).

The Dual-Process Theory of Habituation and Sensitization

So far, I have described the behavioral phenomena of habituation and sensitization. I have not discussed what underlying processes or machinery might produce these behavioral effects. Here we consider a prominent theory of habituation and sensitization, the dual-process theory of Groves and Thompson (1970). Although the theory was proposed some time ago, it remains relevant (Thompson, 2009). The theory was based on neurophysiological studies of habituation and sensitization, but it can be described as close to the level of a behavioral theory.

The dual-process theory is based on two underlying processes, a habituation process and a sensitization process. Unfortunately, the processes have the same names as the behavioral phenomena I described earlier. However, habituation and sensitization *processes* are distinct from habituation and sensitization *phenomena* or *effects*. Habituation and sensitization *phenomena* are performance effects; they are observable changes in behavior. In contrast, habituation and sensitization *processes* refer to the underlying neural events that are responsible for the observed behavioral changes.

THE S–R SYSTEM AND THE STATE SYSTEM

According to the dual-process theory, habituation and sensitization processes operate in different parts of the nervous system. One of these is called the *S–R system*; the other is called the *state system*. The S–R system is the shortest path in the nervous system between an eliciting stimulus and the resulting elicited response. The S–R system corresponds to Descartes's reflex arc. It is the minimal physiological machinery involved in a reflex. Minimally, the S–R system consists of three neurons: the *sensory* (or *afferent*) *neuron*, an *interneuron*, and an *efferent* (or *motor*) *neuron*. The eliciting stimulus activates the afferent neuron. The afferent neuron in turn activates the interneuron, which then activates the efferent neuron. The efferent neuron forms a synapse with the muscles involved in making the elicited response and triggers the behavioral response.

The *state system* consists of all neural processes that are not an integral part of the S–R system but influence the responsivity of the S–R system. Spinal reflexes, for example, consist of an afferent neuron that synapses with an interneuron in the spinal cord and an efferent neuron that extends from the spinal cord to the relevant muscle (see Figure 2.1). This is the S–R system of a spinal reflex. However, the spinal cord also contains neural pathways that ascend to the brain and ones that descend from the brain. These ascending and descending fibers serve to modulate spinal reflexes and make up the state system for spinal reflexes.

After one understands the distinction between the S–R system and the state system, the rest of the dual-process theory is fairly simple. As I noted earlier, the dual-process theory presumes the existence of separate habituation and sensitization processes. A critical aspect of the theory concerns where these processes are located. The habituation process is assumed to take place in the S–R system, whereas the sensitization process is assumed to take place in the state system.

Habituation and sensitization processes are not directly evident in the behavior of the organism. Rather, observable behavior reflects the net effect of these processes. Habituation and sensitization processes serve as opponent mechanisms that modulate reflex responsivity. Whenever the habituation process is stronger than the sensitization process, the net effect is a decline in behavioral output. This is illustrated in the left panel of Figure 3.6. The opposite occurs if the sensitization process is stronger than the habituation process. In that event, the net effect of the two processes is an increase in behavioral output. This is illustrated in the right panel of Figure 3.6.

After being activated, both the habituation process and the sensitization process are assumed to decay with time. This temporal decay assumption is needed in order to explain short-term habituation and short-term sensitization effects.

IMPLICATIONS OF THE DUAL-PROCESS THEORY

Like Descartes's reflex arc, the S–R system is the minimal or most primitive mechanism of elicited behavior. Therefore, the S–R system is activated every time an eliciting stimulus is presented. Because the habituation process operates in the S–R system, each activation of the S–R system results in some buildup of the habituation process. This makes habituation a universal feature of elicited behavior. Whenever an eliciting stimulus is presented, the habituation process is activated to some extent.

The universality of the habituation process does not mean that a decrement in responding will be always observed. Whether a habituation effect is evident will depend

FIGURE 3.6

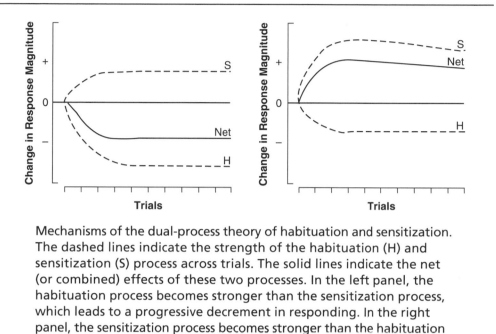

Mechanisms of the dual-process theory of habituation and sensitization. The dashed lines indicate the strength of the habituation (H) and sensitization (S) process across trials. The solid lines indicate the net (or combined) effects of these two processes. In the left panel, the habituation process becomes stronger than the sensitization process, which leads to a progressive decrement in responding. In the right panel, the sensitization process becomes stronger than the habituation process, which leads to a progressive increment in responding.

on whether the habituation process is counteracted by activation of the sensitization process. Another important factor is the interval between successive presentations of the eliciting stimulus. If this interval is long enough, habituation created by the previous stimulus presentation will have a chance to decay before the stimulus is repeated, and a decrement in responding will not be observed. On the other hand, if the interval between stimulus presentations is too short to permit decay of the habituation process, a decrement in responding will occur.

In contrast to the habituation process, the sensitization process is not always involved when an eliciting stimulus is presented. Sensitization occurs in the state system. The state system modulates responsivity of the S–R system, but it is not essential for the occurrence of elicited behavior. Elicited behavior can occur through the S–R system alone. Therefore, sensitization is not a universal property of elicited behavior.

When is the sensitization process activated? An informal way to think about this is that sensitization represents arousal. Sensitization or arousal occurs if the organism encounters a stimulus that is particularly intense or significant. You can become aroused by a loud, unexpected noise or by someone telling you in a soft voice that a close friend was seriously hurt in an accident. The state system and the sensitization process are activated by intense or significant stimuli.

The sensitization process can be activated by the same stimulus that elicits the reflex response of interest. This is the case if an intense or significant stimulus is used as the eliciting stimulus. The right panel of Figure 3.6 illustrates such a situation. In that example, the eliciting stimulus produced a substantial degree of sensitization, with the result that the net behavioral effect was an increase in responding.

The sensitization process can also be activated by some event other than the eliciting stimulus. Because the state system is separate from the S–R system, the state system can be activated by stimuli that are not registered in the S–R system of the response that is being measured. This is a critical feature of the dual-process theory and another respect in which sensitization is different from habituation. In contrast to habituation, sensitization is not necessarily produced by the eliciting stimulus of interest.

The fact that the sensitization and habituation processes can be activated by different stimuli permits the dual-process theory to explain a number of key phenomena, including dishabituation. As I noted earlier (see Figure 3.5), the presentation of a dishabituating stimulus can result in recovery of a habituated response. In the example summarized in Figure 3.5, the presentation of a tone caused recovery of the habituated visual fixation response to a checkerboard pattern. According to the dual-process theory, this occurred because the tone activated the state system and produced enough sensitization to overcome the previous buildup of habituation to the visual stimulus. In other words, dishabituation is produced by the addition of the sensitization process to a behavioral situation rather than the reversal or weakening of the habituation process. (For other evidence that supports this interpretation, see Groves & Thompson [1970] and Thompson [2009].)

The dual-process theory is remarkably successful in characterizing short-term habituation and short-term sensitization effects. However, the theory was not designed to explain long-term habituation and long-term sensitization. Explanations of long-term habituation and sensitization typically include mechanisms of associative learning, which I discuss in Chapters 4 through 6.

Summary

Reflexive or elicited behavior is commonly considered to be an automatic and invariant consequence of the eliciting stimulus. Contrary to this notion, repeated presentations of an eliciting stimulus may result in a monotonic decline in responding (a habituation effect), an increase in responding (a sensitization effect) followed by a decline, or a sustained increase in responding. Thus, far from being invariant, elicited behavior is remarkably sensitive to different forms of prior experience. The magnitude of habituation and sensitization effects depends on the intensity and frequency of the eliciting stimulus. Responding elicited by one stimulus can also be altered by the prior presentation of a different event (as in the phenomenon of dishabituation).

Many of the findings concerning habituation and sensitization may be explained by the dual-process theory, which holds that the processes that produce decreased responding occur in the S–R system, whereas the processes that produce sensitization occur in the state system. The S–R system is activated every time an eliciting stimulus is presented, making habituation a universal property of elicited behavior. Sensitization, by contrast, occurs only when the organism encounters a stimulus that is sufficiently intense or significant to activate the state system. Through their additive effects, the processes of habituation and sensitization serve to modulate the vigor of elicited behavior.

Suggested Readings

Colombo, J., & Mitchell, D. W. (2009). Infant visual habituation. *Neurobiology of Learning and Memory, 92*, 225–234. http://dx.doi.org/10.1016/j.nlm.2008.06.002

Epstein, L. H., Temple, J. L., Roemmich, J. N., & Bouton, M. E. (2009). Habituation as a determinant of food intake. *Psychological Review, 116*, 384–407. http://dx.doi.org/10.1037/a0015074

Kavšek, M. (2013). The comparator model of infant visual habituation and dishabituation: Recent insights. *Developmental Psychobiology, 55*, 793–808. http://dx.doi.org/10.1002/dev.21081

Rankin, C. H., Abrams, T., Barry, R. J., Bhatnagar, S., Clayton, D. F., Colombo, J., . . . Thompson, R. F. (2009). Habituation revisited: An updated and revised description of the behavioral characteristics of habituation. *Neurobiology of Learning and Memory, 92*, 135–138. http://dx.doi.org/10.1016/j.nlm.2008.09.012

Technical Terms

Afferent neuron
Dishabituation
Efferent neuron
Flavor neophobia
Habituation effect
Interneuron
Long-term habituation
Long-term sensitization
Motor neuron

Orienting response
S–R system
Sensitization effect
Sensory neuron
Short-term habituation
Short-term sensitization
Spontaneous recovery
Startle response
State system

Pavlovian Conditioning
Basic Concepts

4

Did you know that

- Pavlov viewed classical conditioning as a technique for studying the brain?
- classical conditioning is not limited to glandular and visceral responses?
- the conditioned response is not always like the unconditioned response?
- conditioned stimuli become part of the behavior system activated by the unconditioned stimulus?
- conditioning not only results in new responses to the conditioned stimulus, but it also changes how organisms interact with the unconditioned stimulus?
- which stimulus can serve as a conditioned stimulus in classical conditioning depends on the unconditioned stimulus that is used?
- associative learning is possible in the random control procedure?
- Pavlovian conditioning is involved in a wide range of behaviors, including preferences and aversions, fears and phobias, drug tolerance and addiction, and maternal and sexual behavior?

http://dx.doi.org/10.1037/0000057-004
The Essentials of Conditioning and Learning, Fourth Edition, by M. Domjan

n Chapter 3, I described ways in which behavior is changed by experience with individual stimuli. Habituation requires presenting the same stimulus over and over again and is sometimes referred to as *single-stimulus learning*. We are now ready to consider how organisms learn to put things together—how they learn to associate one event with another. *Associative learning* is different from single-stimulus learning in that the change in behavior that develops to one stimulus depends on when that stimulus previously occurred in relation to a second stimulus. Associative learning involves learning about combinations of stimuli. The first form of associative learning that we will consider is Pavlovian or classical conditioning.

Pavlov's Proverbial Bell

The basic elements of Pavlovian or classical conditioning are familiar to most of students. Accounts usually describe an apocryphal experiment in which Professor Pavlov rang a bell just before giving a bit of food powder to the dogs that he was testing. The dogs were loosely harnessed and hooked up to an apparatus that enabled Pavlov to measure how much they salivated. At first the dogs salivated only when they were given the food powder. However, after several trials with the bell being paired with the food, the dogs also came to salivate when the bell sounded.

The story of Professor Pavlov training his dogs to salivate to a bell is useful for introducing some important technical vocabulary. A stimulus such as food powder that elicits the response of interest without prior training is called an *unconditioned stimulus*, or *US*. Salivation elicited by the food powder is an example of an *unconditioned response*, or *UR*. The bell is an example of a *conditioned stimulus*, or *CS*, and the salivation that develops to the bell is called the *conditioned response*, or *CR*.

Pavlov's proverbial bell illustrates associative learning because salivation to the bell depends on presenting the bell in combination with food powder. Ringing the bell each time the dog is about to receive a bit of food presumably results in an association of the bell with the food. Once the bell has become associated with the food, the dog starts to respond to the bell as if it were food; it salivates when it hears the bell.

Although Pavlov's bell is familiar and helpful in introducing the technical terms used to describe Pavlovian or classical conditioning, the story is misleading in several ways. First, Pavlov rarely, if ever, used a bell in his experiments. Initial demonstrations of classical conditioning were conducted with visual CSs (the sight of the food that was to be placed in the dog's mouth) rather than auditory cues. Second, the story suggests that classical conditioning primarily involves the modification of visceral and glandular responses. B. F. Skinner elevated this implication to an axiom, postulating that classical conditioning can only modify glandular and visceral responses (e.g., Skinner, 1953). However, subsequent research has shown this assumption to be unwarranted (Domjan, 2016). Pavlovian conditioning can produce many types of CRs, including approaching a signal for food or approaching the food cup, both of which are skeletal rather than glandular or visceral responses.

Contemporary Conditioning Situations

Although classical conditioning was discovered in studies of salivary conditioning with dogs, dogs are not used in such experiments any longer, and salivation is rarely the response that is conditioned. Instead, pigeons, rats, rabbits, and college students commonly serve in the experiments, and various skeletal and physiological responses are conditioned. In some contemporary Pavlovian conditioning situations, the US is a desirable or appetitive stimulus, like food. These preparations are used to study *appetitive conditioning*. In other situations, an unpleasant or aversive event is used as the US. Such preparations are used to study *aversive* or *fear conditioning*.

APPETITIVE CONDITIONING

Appetitive conditioning is frequently investigated with pigeons and laboratory rats. Pigeons that serve in appetitive conditioning experiments are mildly hungry and are tested in a small experimental chamber called a *Skinner box* (see Figure 4.1). The CS is a circular spot of light projected onto a small plastic disk or touch screen above a food cup. Pecks at the light are automatically detected. The conditioning procedure consists of turning on the key light for a few seconds and then presenting a small amount of food.

FIGURE 4.1

Typical trial for conditioning sign tracking or autoshaping in pigeons. The conditioned stimulus (CS) is illumination of a small circular disk or pecking key for 6 seconds. The unconditioned stimulus (US) is access to food for 4 seconds. CS–US trials are repeated, with an intertrial interval of about 1 minute.

After a number of pairings of the key light with food, the pigeons come to approach and peck the key when it is lit (Hearst & Jenkins, 1974; Tomie, Brooks, & Zito, 1989). The conditioned approach and pecking behavior develop even if the key light is located some distance from the food cup (Boakes, 1979). The light becomes a signal for food, and the pigeons go where the light is located. Hence, this type of conditioned responding is called *sign tracking*. Because the procedure results in the pigeons pecking the response key without elaborate training or shaping by the experimenter, the procedure is also called *autoshaping*.

Laboratory rats are also used in studies of Pavlovian conditioning with food as the US. If an auditory cue is used as the CS that is presented before each food delivery, the rats approach and search the food cup as the CR to the auditory cue (Meyer, Cogan, & Robinson, 2014). This type of behavior is referred to as *goal tracking* because the CR tracks the location of the goal object or food. Sign tracking and goal tracking have been also found in sexual conditioning with domesticated quail, where the CS comes to signal access to a potential sexual partner (Burns & Domjan, 2001).

Whether sign tracking or goal tracking develops as the CR depends on the CS that is employed and other details of the conditioning procedure. In addition, there are significant individual differences that determine which type of conditioned behavior occurs. These individual differences have been discovered in studies with rats using a retractable lever apparatus (Flagel, Akil, & Robinson, 2009). In these experiments, the extension of a response lever into the experimental chamber was used as the CS. Each conditioning trial started with extension of the response lever, followed by the delivery of food into a food cup (see Figure 4.2 for an example of a rat in lever-press apparatus). With this procedure, about one third of the rats developed sign tracking and approached and made contact with the lever. Another third of the rats showed goal tracking and approached and searched the food cup. The remaining subjects showed a combination of these responses.

Individual differences in sign tracking versus goal tracking have attracted a great deal of interest because they are reflections of individual differences in the propensity to acquire incentive motivation. Incentive motivation plays a major role in addictions where exposure to signals for the drug of choice makes the procurement of an appetitive reinforcer irresistible. Individuals addicted to alcohol, for example, find the urge to drink irresistible when they see or smell an alcoholic drink. For them, the sight and smell of alcohol has become a strong incentive stimulus. Responses to the sight and smell of alcohol are sign tracking CRs (Zito & Tomie, 2014). Fascinating research has shown that individual differences in sign tracking and goal tracking are genetically based and related to neurobiological differences associated with impulsivity and drug abuse (Flagel et al., 2011).

AVERSIVE OR FEAR CONDITIONING

Aversive conditioning has been extensively investigated using the eye-blink response. The eye-blink is an early component of the startle reflex. Eye-blink conditioning was first developed with human participants (see Kimble, 1961, pp. 55–59). A mild puff

FIGURE 4.2

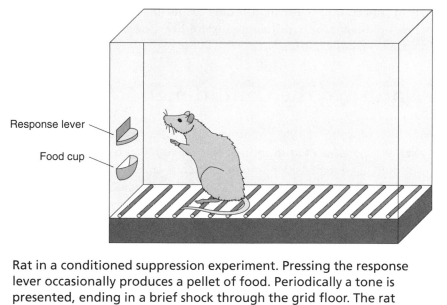

Response lever

Food cup

Rat in a conditioned suppression experiment. Pressing the response lever occasionally produces a pellet of food. Periodically a tone is presented, ending in a brief shock through the grid floor. The rat comes to suppress lever pressing during the tone.

of air to one eye served as the US, and a light served as the CS. After a number of pairings of the light with the air puff, the light came to elicit a conditioned eye-blink response. Subsequently, techniques for studying eye-blink conditioning were also developed for use with albino rabbits and rats to facilitate investigations of the neurophysiology of learning. With these species, irritation of the skin near one eye serves as the US, and a brief visual or auditory cue serves as the CS. Pairings of the CS and US result in a conditioned eye-blink response when the CS is presented (Gormezano, Kehoe, & Marshall, 1983).

Another common laboratory technique for studies of aversive conditioning is fear conditioning. This procedure, typically carried out with rats or mice, takes advantage of the fact that animals (including people) tend to become motionless, or freeze, when they are afraid. A tone or light serves as the CS, and a brief shock applied through a grid floor serves as the US. After a few pairings of the tone or light with the shock, the CS comes to elicit a freezing response. In the freezing posture, the rat exhibits total lack of movement except for breathing (N. S. Jacobs, Cushman, & Fanselow, 2010).

In a variant of fear conditioning known as the *conditioned suppression* procedure, rats are placed in an experimental chamber that has a response lever that is continually present (rather than being inserted into the chamber as a signal for food). The rats are trained to press the lever to obtain a pellet of food. Food is then provided only intermittently for lever presses, which keeps the rats pressing the lever at a steady rate. After the lever pressing is well established, aversive conditioning trials are introduced. On each of these trials, a tone or light CS is presented for a minute, followed by a brief foot shock. Within a few conditioning trials, presentation of the CS results in suppression of the food-reinforced lever-press response. The degree of lever-press suppression provides a measure of how much fear has become conditioned to the CS (Ayres, 2012).

The Nature of the Conditioned Response

In Pavlov's salivary conditioning experiments, the CR (salivation to a CS) was a glandular visceral response similar in form to the UR (salivation to food powder). These features of the CR were considered to be universal characteristics of classical conditioning during much of the 20th century. Pavlovian conditioning was considered to be primarily a mechanism for adjusting physiological and glandular responses to the environment through experience (Skinner, 1938), and the CR was assumed to always be similar to the UR (e.g., Mackintosh, 1974). However, neither of these assumptions is valid for the laboratory situations that are commonly used in contemporary research on Pavlovian conditioning.

Sign tracking, goal tracking, and conditioned eye-blink responses are skeletal rather than glandular responses. In eye-blink conditioning, the CR is similar to the UR. But this is not the case in fear conditioning. Here the foot shock that serves as the US elicits a vigorous startle and jump response, but the CS comes to elicit a contrasting freezing response. In many Pavlovian situations, the CR is not similar to the responses that are elicited by the US.

If we cannot assume that the CR will always be similar to the UR, how can we predict what kind of behavior will develop with Pavlovian conditioning? This remains a challenging question. A promising approach to answering the question is based on the identification of preexisting behavior systems that may be activated by a Pavlovian conditioning procedure.

I introduced the concept of behavior systems in Chapter 2. The concept is relevant to the present discussion because the US in a Pavlovian conditioning procedure activates the behavior system relevant to that US. Presentations of food to a hungry animal activate the feeding system, presentations of shock activate the defensive behavior system, and presentations of a sexual US activate the reproductive behavior system. The CR that develops depends on how the CS becomes incorporated into the behavior system activated by the US (Domjan & Krause, in press).

The feeding system, for example, involves a sequence of response modes starting with general search and then moving on to focal search and ingestive or consummatory behavior (see Figure 4.3). If a CS is presented before the animal receives each portion of food, the CS will become incorporated into one of the response modes of the feeding behavior system, which will in turn determine what type of CR the organism will perform (Timberlake, 2001). If the CS becomes incorporated into the focal search mode, the CR will consist of focal search responses such as sign tracking or goal tracking (Wasserman, Franklin, & Hearst, 1974). In contrast, if the CS becomes

FIGURE 4.3

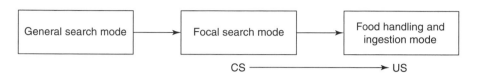

Behavior systems and Pavlovian conditioning. Conditioning procedures with food as the unconditioned stimulus (US) involve the feeding system. As a result of pairings of the conditioned stimulus (CS) with food, the CS becomes incorporated into the feeding system and comes to elicit food-related responses.

incorporated into the ingestive, consummatory response mode, the CR will involve handling and chewing the CS (Boakes, Poli, Lockwood, & Goodall, 1978).

In aversive conditioning, the nature of the CR is determined by the defensive behavior system (Rau & Fanselow, 2007). Foot shock used in studies of conditioned fear is an external source of pain, much like being bitten by a predator, and the response to shock is similar to the response to being bitten. When a rat is bitten by a snake, it leaps into the air. Similarly, rats jump when they receive a brief shock to the foot. The rat's defensive response to an impending or possible attack is different from its response to the attack itself. If a rat sees or smells a snake that is about to strike, the rat freezes. In the fear conditioning procedure, the CS signals an impending attack. Therefore, the CS comes to elicit the freezing defensive behavior.

Because the CS usually precedes the presentation of a US in a Pavlovian conditioning procedure, responses to the CS are anticipatory responses. What kind of anticipation is appropriate depends on how long you have to wait during the CS before the US is presented. Therefore, the interval between the onset of the CS and the onset of the US is critical in determining the nature of the CR. In aversive conditioning, for example, a long CS–US interval results in conditioned anxiety, whereas a short CS–US interval results in conditioned fear or panic (Waddell, Morris, & Bouton, 2006). In sexual conditioning, a long CS–US interval activates the general search mode, whereas a short CS–US interval activates the focal search mode (Akins, 2000).

Conditioned Modifications of the Unconditioned Response

In the preceding discussion, I followed the common practice of talking about Pavlovian conditioning as learning to anticipate a biologically significant event, the US. Why should organisms respond in anticipation of something? What is the advantage of anticipation? The value of anticipating a significant event is that you can deal with that event more effectively when it occurs. This suggests that Pavlovian conditioning should alter how organisms interact with the US. That is in fact the case. There is a growing body of evidence confirming that presentation of a CS alters how organisms interact with the US.

One of the first areas of research in which Pavlovian conditioning was found to change how organisms interact with the US is drug conditioning. When we take a drug for either recreational or therapeutic reasons, we focus on its pharmacological or unconditioned effects. However, there is also a strong conditioning component because drugs are typically administered using a ritual of some sort. The pharmacological effects of caffeine or a glass of wine, for example, are preceded by the smell and taste of the drinks and the particular place or time of day when the drugs are ingested. Smell, taste, and other cues related to drug administration function as CSs that become associated with the unconditioned pharmacological effects of caffeine and alcohol.

Drugs are disruptive to normal physiological functioning or physiological homeostasis. With repeated administrations of a drug, the body comes to anticipate these disruptive effects and learns to make compensatory adjustments in anticipation of the drug. The anticipatory adjustments are elicited by drug-conditioned cues and serve to attenuate the impact of the drug once it is ingested. Through this process, the impact of the drug is gradually reduced, an outcome known as *drug tolerance*.

An important implication of these learning mechanisms is that tolerance to a drug can be reversed if the drug is taken in a new place or in the absence of the usual drug-administration cues. Extensive research has confirmed this prediction, as well as numerous other implications of the conditioning model of drug tolerance (Siegel, 2008). One unfortunate consequence of the reversal of drug tolerance is that familiar doses of a drug that previously were not lethal become life threatening if the drug is taken in the absence of the usual drug-administration cues (Siegel, 2016).

The conditioning model of drug tolerance is not only of clinical significance. It also supports the idea that Pavlovian conditioning serves to modify how organisms respond to the US. This new perspective has been documented in a variety of Pavlovian conditioning situations, including fear conditioning, defensive conditioning, and sexual conditioning (Domjan, 2005). In the sexual conditioning of male quail, for example, a CS is paired with access to a sexually receptive female and ensuing copulation or coitus. With repeated pairings, the CS will acquire incentive motivational properties and elicit sign tracking. However, a more important result is that exposure to a sexual CS significantly changes how the male copulates with the female. The sexual CS reduces the male's latency to initiate copulation, it increases courtship responses, it increases the efficiency of copulatory behavior, and it enhances the release of sperm and the fertilization of eggs (Domjan & Akins, 2011). All of these changes in behavior represent changes in how the male interacts with the US, which in this case is a female sexual partner.

Stimulus Factors in Classical Conditioning

Early investigators of Pavlovian conditioning assumed that just about any stimulus the organism could detect could be effectively used as a CS. This assumption has turned out to be incorrect. In this section, I describe two factors that determine the effectiveness of a CS: the novelty of the CS and the nature of the US.

CS NOVELTY AND THE LATENT INHIBITION EFFECT

Novelty of a stimulus is a powerful factor determining its behavioral impact. As we saw in Chapter 3, repeated exposures to a stimulus may result in a habituation effect, making highly familiar stimuli less effective in eliciting vigorous behavioral reactions than novel stimuli. Habituation can also reduce the effectiveness of a stimulus that is later used as a CS in a Pavlovian conditioning procedure. This phenomenon is called the *latent inhibition effect* (Lubow & Weiner, 2010).

Studies of the latent inhibition effect are usually conducted in two phases, the preexposure phase and the conditioning phase. In the preexposure phase, participants are given repeated presentations of the stimulus that will be used later as the CS. For example, a tone that subsequently will be paired with food may be presented a number of times during the preexposure phase. During this phase, the tone is presented by itself, without the US. After the preexposure phase, the tone is paired with the food US, using conventional classical conditioning procedures. The typical outcome is that CS preexposure retards the subsequent development of conditioned responding to the tone.

The CS preexposure effect has been interpreted as reflecting attentional processes. Repeated presentations of a tone (for example) during the preexposure phase are assumed to reduce the participant's attention to the tone, and this in turn is assumed to disrupt subsequent Pavlovian conditioning of the tone (e.g., Schmajuk, 2010). Because of the involvement of attentional processes, the latent inhibition effect has become popular as a technique for studying brain mechanisms and disorders such as schizophrenia that involve deficits in attention (Lubow, 2011).

CS–US RELEVANCE AND SELECTIVE ASSOCIATIONS

The effectiveness of a stimulus as a CS in Pavlovian conditioning also depends on the US that is used. As I noted earlier, presentations of a US (e.g., food) serve to activate the behavior system relevant to that US. Thus, the feeding behavior system is activated when food is repeatedly presented to a hungry pigeon. As I previously emphasized, each behavior system is associated with its own distinctive set of responses. Behavior systems are also characterized by enhanced reactivity to a distinctive set of stimuli. Pigeons, for example, tend to locate food by sight and become highly attuned to visual cues when their feeding system is activated. This makes visual cues especially effective in Pavlovian conditioning with food for pigeons.

The first clear evidence that the effectiveness of a CS depends on the US that is used was obtained in studies of aversion conditioning in laboratory rats. The conditioned suppression phenomenon illustrates one type of aversion conditioning. Here a tone or light is paired with shock, with the result that the CS acquires aversive properties. Another type of aversion conditioning is *taste-aversion learning*. Here a novel taste is followed by postingestional illness (e.g., a mild case of food poisoning), and the organism learns an aversion to the novel taste as a result.

The conditioned suppression and taste-aversion learning phenomena demonstrate that both auditory and visual cues and taste cues are highly effective as CSs. Interestingly, however, they are effective only in combination with their own particular US (see Figure 4.4). Rats do not easily learn an aversion to an auditory or visual cue paired with illness, nor do they easily learn an aversion to a taste cue paired with shock (Garcia & Koelling, 1966). Such results illustrate the phenomenon of *CS–US relevance*, or *selective association*. The Garcia–Koelling selective association effect met with great skepticism when it was first reported, but much of that skepticism has been laid to rest by subsequent research that has confirmed the phenomenon in a variety of contexts and under circumstances that have ruled out various alternative interpretations (Domjan, 2015).

Like laboratory rats, people also learn aversions to stimuli selectively. People who experience some form of gastrointestinal illness are more likely to learn an aversion to a novel food they ate just before becoming sick than they are to learn an aversion to other types of stimuli they may have encountered. Consistent with the selective association effect, people do not report acquiring a food aversion if they hurt themselves in a physical accident or if they develop an irritating skin rash (Logue, Ophir, & Strauss, 1981; Pelchat & Rozin, 1982). Only illness experiences are effective in inducing a food aversion.

Since the initial demonstration of the selective association effect in aversion learning, such effects have been found in other forms of learning as well. For example, Shapiro, Jacobs, and LoLordo (1980) found that pigeons are more likely to associate a visual stimulus than an auditory stimulus with food. However, when the birds are conditioned with shock, the auditory cue is more likely to become conditioned than the visual cue. Selective associations also occur in primate fear conditioning (Mineka & Öhman, 2002). Monkeys and people learn to be fearful of the sight of snakes more easily than the sight of flowers. This seems to be the result of an evolutionary predisposition. Enhanced sensitivity to the sight of snakes has been observed in human infants as young as 8 to 14 months of age (LoBue & DeLoache, 2010).

FIGURE 4.4

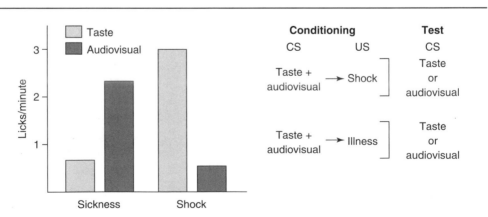

Procedure and results of the experiment by Garcia and Koelling (1966) demonstrating selective associations in aversion learning.

The Control Problem in Pavlovian Conditioning

The critical feature of Pavlovian conditioning is that it involves the formation of an association between a CS and a US. Therefore, before any change in behavior can be attributed to Pavlovian conditioning, one must demonstrate that the effect is not produced by other factors that do not involve an association.

To promote the development of an association, the conditioned and US have to be presented in combination with one another. It is particularly effective, for example, to present the CS just before the presentation of the US on each conditioning trial. (I have more to say about this in Chapter 5.) In addition, a number of conditioning trials are usually needed to get a learning effect. Thus, a Pavlovian conditioning procedure involves repeated presentations of the CSs and USs. However, as we saw in Chapter 3, repeated presentations of stimuli can also result in habituation and sensitization effects. This implies that habituation and sensitization effects can occur during the course of Pavlovian conditioning.

Habituation and sensitization effects due to repeated CS and US presentations do not depend on the formation of an association between the CS and US and therefore do not constitute Pavlovian conditioning. Habituation effects are typically of little concern because habituation results in decreased responding, whereas Pavlovian conditioning involves increased responding to the CS. Increased responding to the CS can be due either to sensitization resulting from CS exposures or to dishabituation or sensitization resulting from US presentations. Control procedures have to be used to rule out such sensitization effects in studies of Pavlovian conditioning.

A universally applicable and acceptable solution to the control problem in Pavlovian conditioning has not been found. Instead, a variety of control procedures have been used, each with its own advantages and disadvantages. In one procedure, CS sensitization effects are evaluated by repeatedly presenting the CS by itself. Such a procedure, called the *CS-alone control*, is inadequate because it does not take into account the possibility of increased responding to the CS due to dishabituation or sensitization effects of the US. Another control procedure involves repeatedly presenting the US by itself (the *US-alone control*) to measure US-induced sensitization. This procedure, however, does not consider possible sensitization effects due to repeated CS presentations.

In 1967, Rescorla proposed an ingenious solution, known as the *random control* procedure, that appeared to overcome the shortcomings of the CS-alone and US-alone controls. In the random control procedure, the CS and US are both presented repeatedly, but at random times in relation to each other. The random timing of the CS and US presentations is intended to prevent the formation of an association between them without interfering with sensitization processes.

The random control procedure became popular soon after its introduction, but as investigators began to examine it in detail, they discovered some serious difficulties (Papini & Bitterman, 1990). Studies demonstrated that this procedure is not entirely without effect, or neutral, in producing learning. Associative learning can develop in a random control procedure (e.g., Kirkpatrick & Church, 2004). One source of such learning is that random CS and US presentations permit occasional instances in which the CS is presented in conjunction with the US. If such occasional CS–US pairings occur early in a sequence of random CS and US presentations, conditioned responding may develop (Benedict & Ayres, 1972).

Associative learning can also result when the US is presented without the CS in a random control procedure. In such instances the US is being presented with the background contextual cues of the experimental chamber. These background cues were ignored throughout much of the early development of Pavlovian conditioning theory. However, more recent research has shown that the repeated presentation of a US in the absence of an explicit CS can result in substantial conditioning of background cues (Balsam & Tomie, 1985).

Although no entirely satisfactory control procedure for Pavlovian conditioning is available, the *discriminative control* procedure is a reasonable strategy. This procedure is summarized in Figure 4.5. The discriminative control involves two CSs, a CS^+ and a CS^-. The two CSs may be, for example, a brief tone and a brief light. On half the trials, the CS^+ is presented and paired with the US. (The + sign indicates that the US is presented with the CS.) On the remaining trials, the CS^- is presented, and the US does not occur. (The − sign indicates that the US is omitted.) CS^+ and CS^- trials are alternated randomly. For half the participants, the tone serves as the CS^+, and the light serves as the CS^-; for the remaining participants, these stimulus assignments are reversed.

What would happen if presentations of the US only sensitized responding to the light and tone CSs? Sensitization is not based on an association and thus does not depend on the pairing of a stimulus with the US. Therefore, sensitization is expected to elevate responding to both the CS^+ and the CS^-. If only sensitization occurred in the discriminative control procedure, the participants would respond to the CS^+ and CS^- in a similar fashion.

FIGURE 4.5

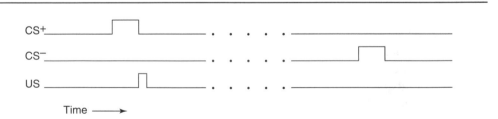

Time ⟶

Diagram of the discriminative control procedure for Pavlovian conditioning. Two types of trials occur in random alternation. On some trials, one conditioned stimulus, the CS^+, is paired with the unconditioned stimulus (US). On the remaining trials, another conditioned stimulus, the CS^-, is presented alone. Stronger conditioned responding to CS^+ than to CS^- is evidence of associative learning rather than some form of sensitization.

How about associative learning? In contrast to sensitization, associative learning should be specific to the stimulus that is paired with the US. Therefore, associative learning should elevate responding to the CS⁺ more than the CS⁻. Greater responding to the CS⁺ than to the CS⁻ in the discriminative control provides strong evidence of associative learning.

The discriminative control procedure permits the evaluation of associative effects within a single group of subjects (based on how those subjects respond differently to the CS⁺ and the CS⁻). Another approach that is frequently used is the *unpaired control procedure*. In this procedure, the CS and US are presented repeatedly, but the stimulus presentations are deliberately scheduled so that the CS and US never occur together or on the same trial. This procedure is administered to a control group, which is compared with an experimental group that receives the CS paired with the US. Greater responding in the paired group compared with the unpaired group is considered evidence of associative Pavlovian conditioning.

Prevalence of Pavlovian Conditioning

Classical conditioning is typically investigated in laboratory situations. However, we do not have to know a lot about classical conditioning to realize that it is common outside the laboratory as well. Classical conditioning is most likely to develop when one event (the CS) reliably occurs shortly before another (the US). This happens in many areas of life. Most of the stimuli we encounter occur in an orderly temporal sequence because of the physical constraints of causation. Some things simply cannot happen before other things have occurred. Social institutions and customs also ensure that events occur in a reliable sequence. Whenever one stimulus reliably precedes another, classical conditioning may take place, enabling you to predict what will happen next on the basis of antecedent events that serve as CSs.

One area of research that has been of particular interest is how people come to judge one event as the cause of another. In studies of human causal judgment, participants are exposed to repeated occurrences of two events (e.g., pictures of a blooming flower and a watering can briefly presented on a computer screen) in various temporal arrangements. In one arrangement, for example, the watering can always occurs before the flower; in another, it occurs at random times relative to the flower. After observing numerous presentations of both objects, the research participants are asked to indicate their judgment as to the strength of the causal relation between them.

Studies of human causal judgment are analogous to studies of Pavlovian conditioning in that both involve repeated experiences with two events and responses based on the extent to which those two events are related to one another. In view of these similarities, one might expect that there is considerable commonality between the results of causal judgment and Pavlovian conditioning experiments. That expectation has been borne out in numerous studies (Allan, 2005), suggesting that Pavlovian associative mechanisms may play a role in the numerous informal judgments of causality we all make in the course of our daily lives.

I described earlier in this chapter how Pavlovian conditioning can result in the acquisition of fear. The mechanisms of fear conditioning are of considerable interest because of the role of fear conditioning in anxiety disorders, phobias, and panic disorder (Craske, Hermans, & Vansteenwegen, 2006; Oehlberg & Mineka, 2011). As I already discussed, Pavlovian conditioning is also involved in drug tolerance and addiction (Siegel, 2008). Cues that reliably accompany drug administration can come to elicit drug-related responses through conditioning. In discussing this type of learning on the part of crack addicts, Dr. Scott Lukas of McLean Hospital in Massachusetts described the effects of drug-conditioned stimuli by saying that "these cues turn on crack-related memories, and addicts respond like Pavlov's dogs" (Newsweek Staff, 2001, p. 40).

Pavlovian conditioning is also involved in infant and maternal responses during nursing. Suckling involves mutual stimulation for the infant and mother. To successfully nurse, the mother has to hold the baby in a special position, which provides special tactile stimuli for both the infant and the mother. The tactile stimuli experienced by the infant may become conditioned to elicit orientation and suckling responses on the part of the baby (Blass, Ganchrow, & Steiner, 1984). Olfactory cues experienced by the infant also become conditioned during suckling episodes. Infants come to prefer suckling-associated cues, with the preference evident as long as a year after the conditioning episode (Delaunay-El Allam et al., 2010).

Pavlovian conditioning is also important in learning about sexual situations. Clinical observations indicate that human sexual behavior can be shaped by learning experiences, but the most extensive experimental evidence for sexual conditioning has been obtained in studies with laboratory animals (Domjan & Akins, 2011). In these studies, males typically serve as participants, and the US is provided either by the sight of a sexually receptive female or by physical access to a female. Subjects come to approach stimuli that signal the availability of a sexual partner. The presentation of a sexually CS also facilitates various aspects of reproductive behavior. After exposure to a sexual CS, males are quicker to perform copulatory responses, compete more successfully with other males for access to a female, show more courtship behavior, release greater quantities of sperm, show increased levels of testosterone and luteinizing hormone, and produce more offspring.

Summary

Although studies of Pavlovian conditioning began with the conditioning of salivation and other glandular responses in dogs, contemporary investigations focus on conditioning skeletal responses in sign tracking, fear conditioning, and eye-blink conditioning. These investigations have shown that different types of CRs can develop, depending on the nature of the CS and the behavior system activated by the US.

Because Pavlovian conditioning involves the learning of an association between a CS and a US, behavioral changes due to mere repetition of the CS and US have to be excluded. The random control procedure is not effective in this regard because it can result in associative learning. Although an entirely satisfactory control procedure is not available, the discriminative control and unpaired control procedures are reasonably effective. In the discriminative control procedure, one CS is paired with the US and another CS is presented without the US. Differential responding to the two CSs provides evidence of associative learning. In the unpaired control procedure, the CS is presented at times when the US is certain to not occur.

Pavlovian conditioning may occur wherever one event reliably precedes another. Examples include causality judgments, drug tolerance and addiction, suckling and nursing, and learning to predict potential sexual encounters.

Suggested Readings

Bouton, M. E., Mineka, S., & Barlow, D. H. (2001). A modern learning theory perspective on the etiology of panic disorder. *Psychological Review, 108*, 4–32. http://dx.doi.org/10.1037/0033-295X.108.1.4

Domjan, M. (2005). Pavlovian conditioning: A functional perspective. *Annual Review of Psychology, 56*, 179–206. http://dx.doi.org/10.1146/annurev.psych.55.090902.141409

Flagel, S. B., Akil, H., & Robinson, T. E. (2009). Individual differences in the attribution of incentive salience to reward-related cues: Implications for addiction. *Neuropharmacology, 56*(Suppl. 1), 139–148.

Papini, M. R., & Bitterman, M. E. (1990). The role of contingency in classical conditioning. *Psychological Review, 97*, 396–403.

Siegel, S. (2008). Learning and the wisdom of the body. *Learning & Behavior, 36*, 242–252. http://dx.doi.org/10.3758/LB.36.3.242

Technical Terms

Appetitive conditioning
Associative learning
Autoshaping
Aversive conditioning
CS–US relevance
Conditioned response (CR)
Conditioned stimulus (CS)
Conditioned suppression
Discriminative control
Latent inhibition
Random control
Selective association
Sign tracking
Skinner box
Taste-aversion learning
Unconditioned response (UR)
Unconditioned stimulus (US)
Unpaired control procedure

Stimulus Relations in Pavlovian Conditioning

5

Did you know that

- delaying the unconditioned stimulus (US) a bit after the onset of the conditioned stimulus (CS) produces stronger evidence of conditioning than presenting the CS and US simultaneously?
- a gap of just half a second between the CS and US can seriously disrupt excitatory fear conditioning?
- taste aversions can be learned with a delay of several hours between the CSs and CSs?
- CS–US contiguity is neither necessary nor sufficient for Pavlovian conditioning?
- different CS–US contingencies produce different levels of conditioned responding because of differences in the conditioning of contextual cues?
- in addition to CS–US associations, organisms can learn higher order relations in which one CS signals how a second CS will be paired with the US?

In Chapter 4, I introduced Pavlovian conditioning as a type of learning that involves establishing an association between two stimuli, the conditioned stimulus (CS) and the unconditioned stimulus (US). For two stimuli or events to become associated with one another, they have to be related to each other in some way. In the present chapter, I describe various relations that can exist

http://dx.doi.org/10.1037/0000057-005
The Essentials of Conditioning and Learning, Fourth Edition, by M. Domjan

between a CS and US. I also describe how different stimulus relations determine what is learned in Pavlovian conditioning.

Temporal Relation Between CS and US

Historically, the most prominent relation in Pavlovian conditioning is the temporal relation between the CS and US—when in time the stimuli occur relative to each other. In thinking about various temporal arrangements that are possible between a CS and a US, consider a railroad crossing on a roadway. Railroad crossings have flashing lights that indicate a train is about to arrive. In this example, the flashing lights are the CS, and the train crossing the road is the US.

COMMON CONDITIONING PROCEDURES

Simultaneous Conditioning

Perhaps the simplest temporal arrangement is the presentation of a CS and a US at the same time. Such a procedure is called *simultaneous conditioning* and involves perfect *temporal contiguity*, or coincidence, between CS and US (see Figure 5.1). Because simultaneous conditioning brings the CS as close as possible to the US, one might presume that it would be the most effective temporal relation to produce associative learning. Surprisingly, simultaneous conditioning rarely produces strong evidence of learning.

FIGURE 5.1

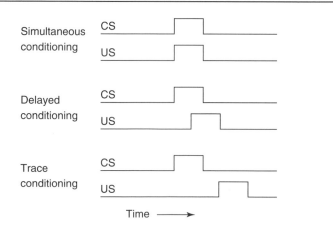

Procedures for simultaneous, delayed, and trace conditioning. One conditioning trial (involving a presentation of the conditioned stimulus [CS] and unconditioned stimulus [US]) is shown for each procedure. In a typical experiment, the conditioning trial is repeated until evidence of learning develops.

For example, simultaneous conditioning does not produce an eye-blink response to the CS (M. C. Smith, Coleman, & Gormezano, 1969).

Using the railroad crossing analogy, if simultaneous conditioning were used, the flashing lights would start when the train was already at the crossing. In this case, the flashing light would not provide any new or predictive information about the arrival of the train. You could not avoid getting hit by the train by responding to the flashing lights. Thus, simultaneous conditioning does not lead to an anticipatory conditioned response. However, a CS presented simultaneously with shock does acquire aversive properties, which are evident if one measures withdrawal or escape from the CS (Esmorís-Arranz, Pardo-Vázquez, & Vásquez-García, 2003).

Delayed Conditioning

Most of the evidence for associative learning comes from a type of procedure in which the CS starts shortly before the US on each trial (Schneiderman & Gormezano, 1964). Such a procedure is called *delayed conditioning* because the US is delayed after the start of the CS (see the middle panel of Figure 5.1). Notice that in the delayed conditioning procedure, the CS remains present until the US occurs, without a gap between the stimuli. Common measures of conditioning (conditioned eye-blink, sign tracking and goal tracking, and conditioned freezing) reflect the anticipation of the US and are readily observed with a delayed conditioning procedure.

Warning signals at railroad crossings typically use a delayed conditioning procedure. The flashing lights begin before the train arrives at the crossing, enabling you to anticipate that the train will be there soon. The most effective delayed conditioning procedure is one in which the CS begins shortly before the US. Unfortunately, that is often not the case with railroad crossings. The lights begin to flash some time before the arrival of the train, not immediately before the train arrives. This encourages people to cross the tracks quickly before the train shows up. The use of a shorter interval between the signal and the arrival of the train would discourage such risky behavior.

Trace Conditioning

Introducing a gap between the CS and the US changes a delayed conditioning procedure into *trace conditioning*. A trace conditioning trial is presented in the bottom panel of Figure 5.1 for contrast with the delayed conditioning trial shown in the middle panel. The gap between the CS and the US is called the *trace interval*.

Using our railroad crossing example, a trace conditioning procedure would be one in which the flashing lights ended 5 or 10 seconds before the train arrived. If you knew that the flashing lights would end before the train arrived, you would be less likely to stay off the tracks when the lights started flashing. Rather, you would avoid the tracks when the flashing lights ended.

Introducing a gap or trace interval between the CS and the US can drastically reduce the degree of conditioned responding that develops. In an early experiment on fear conditioning, Kamin (1965) found that introducing a trace interval of as little as a half a second significantly reduced the level of conditioned responding that occurred.

Since the work of Kamin (1965), investigators have found stronger evidence of trace conditioning in a number of different learning situations. Trace conditioning is of considerable interest because it requires a process that bridges the gap in time between the CS and the US. Such a time-bridging process is not required for delayed conditioning. Investigations of the neural bases of trace conditioning have identified various ways in which the neural circuits required for trace conditioning are different from those that are involved in delayed conditioning (Kalmbach, Ohyama, Kreider, Riusech, & Mauk, 2009; Raybuck & Lattal, 2014).

EFFECTS OF THE CS–US INTERVAL

Another temporal relation that is critical for associative learning is how much time passes between the start of the CS and the presentation of the US on each conditioning trial. The interval between when the CS begins and when the US is presented is called the *CS–US interval* or the *interstimulus interval*.

As I noted earlier, in many conditioning situations, there is little evidence of learning with simultaneous conditioning, where the CS–US interval is zero. Conditioned responding is more likely with delayed conditioning procedures, where the CS–US interval is greater than zero. However, the benefits of delaying the US after the start of the CS are limited. As the CS–US interval becomes longer and longer, evidence of learning declines. How rapidly responding declines as the CS–US interval is increased depends on the response system that is being conditioned.

Figure 5.2 illustrates the effects of the CS–US interval in three conditioning preparations. The left panel represents data from conditioning of the nictitating membrane response of rabbits. The nictitating membrane is a secondary eyelid present in many species. Like closure of the primary eyelid, closure of the nictitating membrane can be elicited unconditionally by a puff of air to the eye. The best results in conditioning the nictitating membrane response are obtained with CS–US intervals of 0.2 to 0.5 second. If the CS–US interval is shorter, less conditioned responding develops. Moreover, conditioned responding drops off quickly as the CS–US interval is extended past half a second. Little if any learning is evident if the CS–US interval is more than 2 seconds.

Fear conditioning or conditioned suppression represents an intermediate case. The strongest fear is learned with a CS–US interval that is less than a minute, but learning can also occur with CS–US intervals in the range of 2 to 3 minutes.

Learning over the longest CS–US intervals is seen in taste-aversion learning. In the conditioned taste aversion procedure, the ingestion of a novel flavored food (or drink) results in some form of illness or interoceptive distress (Lin, Arthurs, & Reilly, 2017; Reilly & Schachtman, 2009). The novel flavor is the CS, and the illness experience serves as the US.

A taste aversion can be learned even if the illness experience is delayed several hours after ingestion of the novel flavor. This phenomenon was first documented by John Garcia and his associates (e.g., Garcia, Ervin, & Koelling, 1966) and is called *long-delay learning* because it represents learning with CS–US intervals that are a great deal longer than the intervals that will support eye-blink conditioning or conditioned

FIGURE 5.2

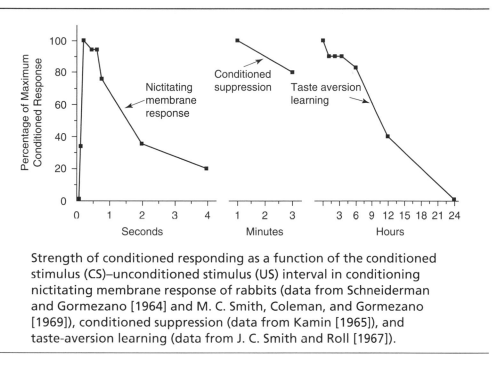

Strength of conditioned responding as a function of the conditioned stimulus (CS)–unconditioned stimulus (US) interval in conditioning nictitating membrane response of rabbits (data from Schneiderman and Gormezano [1964] and M. C. Smith, Coleman, and Gormezano [1969]), conditioned suppression (data from Kamin [1965]), and taste-aversion learning (data from J. C. Smith and Roll [1967]).

suppression. However, as Figure 5.2 illustrates, even with flavor-aversion learning, less conditioned responding is observed with longer CS–US intervals.

TEMPORAL ENCODING OF WHEN THE US OCCURS

The differences in learning that occur among simultaneous, delayed, and trace conditioning and the CS–US interval effects I have just described illustrate that Pavlovian conditioning is highly sensitive to time factors. A growing and impressive line of evidence indicates that participants learn a great deal about the precise time when the US is presented in relation to the CS. This type of learning is called *temporal coding* (Molet & Miller, 2014). Evidence of temporal coding indicates that Pavlovian conditioning involves more than just an "association" between the CS and US. Rather, Pavlovian conditioning involves learning precise information about when USs occur relative to other events in the environment. In fact, some have suggested that this type of temporal learning is more central to what occurs in Pavlovian conditioning than the familiar concept of a CS–US association (Balsam, Drew, & Gallistel, 2010).

Drivers who cross a railroad track when the lights at the crossing begin to flash are demonstrating temporal coding. They have learned not only that the flashing lights are associated with the train's arrival but also how long the lights are on before the train actually arrives. Knowledge of the timing of the train's arrival encourages drivers to cross the tracks before the lights have been on very long. Unfortunately, the learning of precise temporal information takes a bit of practice. At a railroad crossing inadequate temporal learning can have fatal consequences.

Signal Relation Between CS and US

In the previous section, I described some of the ways in which the temporal relation between the CS and US is important in Pavlovian conditioning. Another important factor is the signal relation, or informational relation, between the CS and US. In general, conditioned responding develops most rapidly with procedures in which the CS provides reliable information about the occurrence of the US. In these cases the CS serves as a reliable signal for the US.

In the typical delayed conditioning procedure, each conditioning trial consists of the presentation of the CS, followed shortly by the presentation of the US. Furthermore, the US does not occur unless it is preceded by the CS. Thus, occurrences of the US can be predicted perfectly from occurrences of the CS. The CS signals occurrences of the US perfectly, resulting in rapid acquisition of a conditioned response to the CS.

THE BLOCKING EFFECT

How might the signal relation between the CS and US be disrupted? One way is to present the target CS with another cue that already predicts the US. If there is another cue that already predicts the US, the target CS will be redundant, and you may not learn much about it. If one of your passengers has already pointed out to you that your car is about to run out of gas, a similar warning from a second passenger is redundant and less likely to command much of your attention. This idea, first developed experimentally by Kamin, has come to be known as the *blocking effect* (Kamin, 1969).

Kamin studied the blocking effect using the conditioned suppression procedure with laboratory rats, but the phenomenon may be illustrated more effectively with a hypothetical example of human taste-aversion learning. Let us assume that you are allergic to shrimp and get slightly ill every time you eat shrimp. Because of these experiences, you acquire an aversion to the flavor of shrimp. On a special occasion, you are invited to a private dinner by your pastor, and the main course is shrimp served with a steamed vegetable you don't remember eating before. Because you don't want to offend your host, you eat some of both the vegetable and the shrimp. The vegetable tastes pretty good, but you end up getting a bit sick after the meal.

Will you attribute your illness to the shrimp or to the new vegetable you ate? Given your history of bad reactions to shrimp, you are likely to attribute your illness to the shrimp and may not acquire an aversion to the vegetable. In this situation, the presence of the previously conditioned shrimp blocks the conditioning of the novel vegetable even though the novel vegetable was just as closely paired with the illness US.

The blocking effect shows that what individuals learn about one CS is influenced by the presence of other cues that were previously conditioned with the same US. The CSs Kamin used in his seminal experiments were a light and a broadband noise (see Figure 5.3). For the blocking group, the noise CS was first conditioned by pair-

FIGURE 5.3

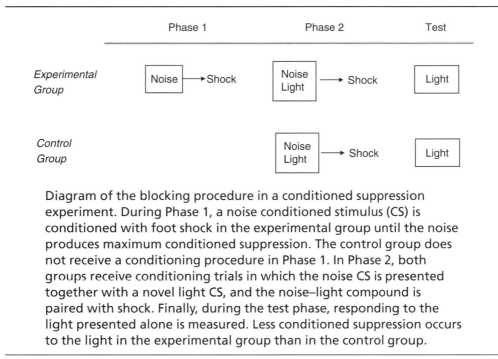

Diagram of the blocking procedure in a conditioned suppression experiment. During Phase 1, a noise conditioned stimulus (CS) is conditioned with foot shock in the experimental group until the noise produces maximum conditioned suppression. The control group does not receive a conditioning procedure in Phase 1. In Phase 2, both groups receive conditioning trials in which the noise CS is presented together with a novel light CS, and the noise–light compound is paired with shock. Finally, during the test phase, responding to the light presented alone is measured. Less conditioned suppression occurs to the light in the experimental group than in the control group.

ing it with foot shock a sufficient number of times to produce strong conditioned suppression to this auditory cue. In the next phase of the experiment, the noise and light CSs were presented simultaneously, ending in the shock US. A control group also received the noise–light compound paired with shock, but for this group, the noise had not been previously conditioned. For the control group, the noise and light were both novel stimuli. The focus of the experiment was on how much fear became conditioned to the novel light CS. Because of the prior conditioning of the noise in the blocking group, less conditioned suppression developed to the light in the blocking group than in the control group.

The blocking phenomenon is important because it illustrates that temporal contiguity between a CS and a US is not sufficient for successful Pavlovian conditioning. A strong signal relation is also important. The temporal relation between the novel light CS and the shock US was identical for the blocking and the control groups. Nevertheless, strong conditioned suppression developed only if the light was not presented with the previously conditioned noise. The prior conditioning of the noise reduced the signal relation between the light and shock and disrupted fear conditioning to the light.

CS–US CONTINGENCY

Historically, an important approach to characterizing the signal relation between a CS and US has been in terms of the *contingency* between the two stimuli (Rescorla, 1967).

The "contingency" between two events is a formal characterization of the extent to which the presence of one stimulus can serve as a basis for predicting the other. The CS–US contingency is defined in terms of two probabilities (see Figure 5.4). One of these is the probability that the US will occur given that the CS has been presented [p(US/CS)]; the other is the probability that the US will occur given that the CS has not happened [p(US/noCS)].

A situation in which the US always occurs with the CS and never by itself illustrates a perfect positive contingency between the CS and US. Smoke, for example, always indicates that something is burning. Therefore, the presence of the US (fire) can be predicted perfectly from the presence of the CS (smoke). In contrast, a situation in which the US occurs when the CS is absent but never occurs on trials with the CS illustrates a perfect negative contingency. In this case, the CS signals the absence of the US. If you use sunblock when you are at the beach, you are likely to avoid the sunburn that you would otherwise get from spending a day at the beach. The sunblock signals the absence of an aversive sunburn. Finally, if the US occurs equally often with and without the CS, the CS–US contingency is said to be zero. When the contingency between the CS and US is zero, the CS provides no useful information about whether the US will occur or not. This is the case if a dog barks indiscriminately whether or not there is an intruder present. A zero CS–US contingency is also characteristic of the random control procedure I described in Chapter 4.

FIGURE 5.4

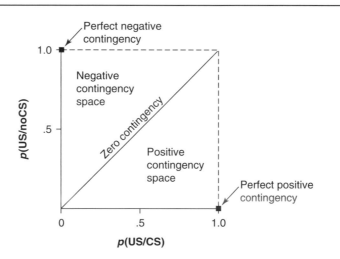

Contingency between a conditioned stimulus (CS) and an unconditioned stimulus (US). Contingency between a CS and US is determined by the probability of the US occurring given that the CS has occurred (represented on the horizontal axis) and the probability of the US occurring given that the CS has not occurred (represented on the vertical axis). When the two probabilities are equal (the 45° line), the CS–US contingency is zero.

Originally, the contingency between a CS and US was thought to determine the formation of CS–US associations directly. Since then, it has become more common to consider CS/US contingency as a procedural variable that predicts how much conditioned responding will develop. Contemporary analyses of contingency effects have focused on conditioning of the background cues that are present in any situation in which an organism encounters repeated presentations of discrete conditioned and unconditioned stimuli. Procedures involving different CS–US contingencies result in different degrees of context conditioning.

Consider, for example, a procedure involving a zero CS–US contingency. Such a procedure will involve presentations of the US by itself, presentations of the CS by itself, and occasional presentations of the CS together with the US. The US-alone trials can result in conditioning of the background or contextual cues in which the experiment is conducted. The presence of these conditioned background contextual cues may then block future conditioning of the explicit CS on those few occasions when the CS is paired with the US (Tomie, Murphy, Fath, & Jackson, 1980) or disrupt performance of conditioned responding through a comparator process, which I discuss in Chapter 6.

Higher Order Relations in Pavlovian Conditioning: Conditioned Inhibition

In the examples of Pavlovian conditioning I have discussed thus far, the focus of interest was on how a CS is directly related to a US. Now let us turn to more complex stimulus relations in Pavlovian conditioning. In higher order stimulus relations, the focus of interest is not on how a CS signals a US but on how one CS provides information about the relation between a second CS and the US. Thus, the term *higher order stimulus relation* refers to the signaling or modulation of a simple CS–US pairing by another CS. The adjectival phrase *higher order* is used because one of the elements of this relation is a CS–US associative unit. In considering higher order stimulus relations, I first discuss conditioned inhibition or negative occasion setting. Then I move on to the phenomenon of facilitation or positive occasion setting.

INHIBITORY CONDITIONING PROCEDURES

Conditioned inhibition was the first higher order signal relation to be extensively investigated. Concepts of inhibition are prominent in various areas of physiology. Being a physiologist, Pavlov was interested not only in processes that activate behavior but also in those that are responsible for the inhibition of responding. This led him to investigate conditioned inhibition. He considered the conditioning of inhibition to be just as important as the conditioning of excitation (Pavlov, 1927).

In excitatory conditioning procedures, the CS becomes a signal for the impending presentation of the US. In inhibitory conditioning, by contrast, the CS of interest becomes a signal for the absence of the US. However, this only occurs under special circumstances because ordinarily the absence of something has no particular psychological significance. If I tell you out of the clear blue that I have decided not to give you a thousand dollars, you are not likely to be upset, because you had no reason to expect that I would ever give you that much money. If the absence of something is not psychologically meaningful, a CS cannot become a signal for that nonevent. For successful inhibitory conditioning, the absence of the US has to be made salient or important.

I can make you disappointed in not getting a thousand dollars by telling you that you had been entered into a sweepstakes contest and had been selected as the winner of a thousand dollar prize. The absence of something is psychologically powerful if you have reason to believe that the event will take place. In inhibitory conditioning procedures, the absence of the US is made salient by excitatory conditioning that creates a positive expectation that the US will occur.

The Standard Conditioned Inhibition Procedure

The standard conditioned inhibition procedure is analogous to a situation in which something is introduced that prevents an outcome that would otherwise occur. A red traffic light at a busy intersection is a signal of potential danger (the US). However, if a police officer indicates that you should cross the intersection despite the red light (perhaps because the traffic lights are malfunctioning), you will probably not have an accident. The red light and the gestures of the officer together are not likely to be followed by danger. The gestures inhibit or block your hesitation to cross the intersection because of the red light.

The standard conditioned inhibition procedure involves two different CSs (A and B) and a US (see Figure 5.5). In the example of a malfunctioning traffic light, stimulus A was the red traffic light, and stimulus B was the police officer's gesture for you to cross the intersection. In laboratory experiments, stimulus A might be a light, stimulus B a tone, and the US a brief shock. On some trials, stimulus A is paired with the US. These

FIGURE 5.5

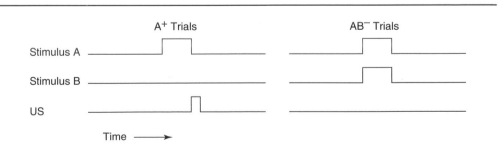

The standard procedure for conditioned inhibition. On A⁺ trials, stimulus A is paired with the unconditioned stimulus (US). On AB⁻ trials, stimulus B is presented with stimulus A, and the US is omitted. The procedure is effective in conditioning inhibition to stimulus B.

trials are represented as A+ (A plus), with the "+" sign indicating pairings with US. As a result of the A+ trials, the participant comes to expect the US when encountering stimulus A. This sets the stage for inhibitory conditioning.

On inhibitory conditioning trials, stimulus B is presented with stimulus A (forming the compound stimulus AB), but the US does not occur. These trials are represented as AB⁻ (AB minus), with the "−" sign indicating the absence of the US. The presence of stimulus A on the AB⁻ trials creates the expectation that the US will occur. This makes the absence of the US psychologically meaningful and serves to condition inhibitory properties to stimulus B.

Typically, A+ and AB⁻ trials are presented in an intermixed order in the standard inhibitory conditioning procedure. As training progresses, stimulus A gradually acquires conditioned excitatory properties and stimulus B becomes a conditioned inhibitor (Campolattaro, Schnitker, & Freeman, 2008). Generally, the excitatory conditioning of A develops faster than the inhibitory conditioning of B because inhibitory conditioning depends on the prior learning of a US expectation.

Negative CS–US Contingency

The standard inhibitory conditioning procedure (A+, AB⁻) is especially effective in making B a conditioned inhibitor, but there are other successful inhibitory conditioning procedures as well. In the negative CS–US contingency procedure, for example, only one explicit CS is used (e.g., a tone), together with a US (see Figure 5.6). The tone and the US occur at irregular times, with the stipulation that the US is not presented if the tone has occurred recently. This stipulation establishes a negative contingency between the tone CS and the US. It ensures that p(US/CS) will be less than p(US/noCS) and serves to make the CS a conditioned inhibitor.

Consider a child who periodically gets picked on by his classmates when the teacher is out of the room. This is similar to periodically getting an aversive stimulus or US. When the teacher returns, the child can be sure that he will not be bothered. The teacher thus serves as a CS⁻, signaling a period free from harassment. The presence of the teacher signals the absence of the US.

What provides the excitatory context for inhibitory conditioning of the tone CS in the negative contingency procedure? Because the US occurs when the CS is absent,

FIGURE 5.6

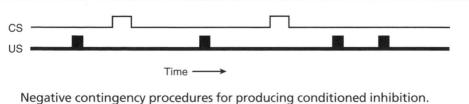

Negative contingency procedures for producing conditioned inhibition. The unconditioned stimulus (US) is presented at random times by itself, but not if the conditioned stimulus (CS) has occurred recently.

the background contextual cues of the experimental situation become associated with the US. This then enables the conditioning of inhibitory properties to the CS. The absence of the US when the CS occurs in this excitatory context makes the CS a conditioned inhibitor.

BEHAVIORAL MEASUREMENT OF CONDITIONED INHIBITION

The behavioral manifestations of excitatory conditioning are fairly obvious. Organisms come to make a new response—the conditioned response—to the CS. What happens in the case of conditioned inhibition? A conditioned inhibitory stimulus has behavioral effects that are the opposite of the behavioral effects of a conditioned excitatory cue. A conditioned inhibitor suppresses or inhibits excitatory conditioned responding. Unfortunately, special procedures are often required to see this response suppression.

Consider, for example, the eye-blink response of rabbits. Rabbits blink very infrequently, perhaps once or twice an hour. A conditioned inhibitory stimulus (CS^-) actively suppresses blinking. But because rabbits rarely blink under ordinary circumstances, the suppression of blinking during a CS^- is difficult to detect.

Summation Test of Inhibition

Inhibition of blinking would be easy to determine if the baseline rate of blinking were elevated. If rabbits blinked 60 times an hour and we presented a conditioned inhibitory stimulus (CS^-), blinking should decline substantially below the 60 per hour rate. Thus, the problem of measuring conditioned inhibition can be solved by elevating the comparison baseline rate of responding.

How can the baseline rate of responding be elevated? Perhaps the simplest way is to condition another stimulus as a conditioned excitatory cue (CS^+). Substantial responding should be evident when this new excitatory cue (CS^+) is presented by itself. Using this as a baseline, we can test the effects of a conditioned inhibitory stimulus (CS^-) by presenting the CS^- at the same time as the CS^+. Such a test strategy is called the *summation test* for conditioned inhibition.

Figure 5.7 presents hypothetical results of a summation test. Notice that considerable responding is observed when the CS^+ is presented by itself. Adding a conditioned inhibitory stimulus (CS^-) to the CS^+ results in a great deal less responding than when the CS^+ is presented alone. This is the expected outcome if the CS^- has acquired inhibitory properties. However, presentation of the CS^- might disrupt responding simply by creating a distraction. This possibility is evaluated in the summation test by determining how responding to the CS^+ is changed when a neutral stimulus with no history of either excitatory or inhibitory training is presented. Such a neutral stimulus is represented by CS^0 in Figure 5.7.

In the results depicted in Figure 5.7, CS^0 reduces responding to the CS^+ a little. This reflects the distracting effects of adding any stimulus to the CS^+. The reduction

FIGURE 5.7

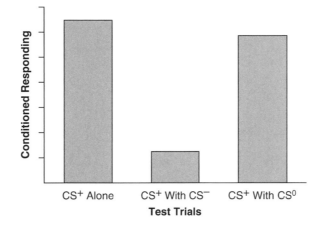

Procedure and hypothetical results for the summation test of conditioned inhibition. On some trials, a conditioned excitatory stimulus (CS⁺) is presented alone, and a high level of conditioned responding is observed. On the other trials, the CS⁺ is presented with a conditioned inhibitory stimulus (CS⁻) or a neutral stimulus (CS⁰). The fact that the CS⁻ disrupts responding to the CS⁺ much more than CS⁰ is evidence of the conditioned inhibitory properties of the CS⁻.

in responding is much greater, however, when the CS⁻ is presented with the CS⁺. This outcome shows that the CS⁻ has conditioned inhibitory properties (R. P. Cole, Barnet, & Miller, 1997).

Retardation of Acquisition Test of Inhibition

The summation test is a performance-based test of inhibition. The basic assumption is that the performance of excitatory conditioned behavior will be suppressed by a conditioned inhibitory stimulus. A second popular approach to the measurement of conditioned inhibition is an acquisition or learning test. This test is based on the assumption that conditioned inhibitory properties will interfere with the acquisition of excitatory properties to that stimulus. Hence, this is called the *retardation-of-acquisition test.*

The retardation-of-acquisition test involves comparing the rates of excitatory conditioning for two groups of participants. The same CS (e.g., a tone) is used in both groups. For the experimental group, the tone is first trained as a conditioned inhibitor. For the comparison group, a control procedure is used during this stage that leaves the tone relatively "neutral." (For example, the tone may be presented unpaired with the US.) In the second phase of the experiment, the tone is paired with the US for both groups of participants, and the development of excitatory responding to the tone is observed. If inhibitory conditioning was successful in the first stage of the experiment, excitatory conditioned responding should develop more slowly in the experimental group than in the control group during the second stage. Traditionally, the summation and the retardation-of-acquisition tests were used in combination to develop evidence of conditioned inhibition (Rescorla, 1969). In contemporary research, the use of both tests has given way to relying mostly on the summation test in studies of conditioned inhibition (e.g., Harris, Kwok, & Andrew, 2014).

Higher Order Relations in Pavlovian Conditioning: Conditioned Facilitation

In higher order stimulus relations, the focus of interest is not on the direct relationship between a CS (A) and the US but on how a second stimulus (B) provides information about the A–US relationship (Schmajuk & Holland, 1998). In a conditioned inhibition procedure, the second stimulus B indicates when the A–US relationship is not in effect. Without stimulus B, stimulus A is paired with the US. With stimulus B, stimulus A occurs without the US. Under these circumstances, stimulus B becomes a conditioned inhibitor and indicates when the participant should not respond to stimulus A. *Conditioned facilitation* involves the opposite higher order relation. In this case, stimulus B indicates when stimulus A is paired with the US.

The differences between facilitation and inhibition are illustrated in Figure 5.8. In conditioned inhibition, stimulus B occurs on trials when A is not followed by the US (AB→noUS, or AB⁻), and B is absent when A is paired with the US (A→US, or A⁺). This arrangement is reversed in a facilitation procedure. In conditioned facilitation, stimulus B occurs on trials when A is reinforced (AB→US, or AB⁺), and B is absent on trials when A is not reinforced (A→noUS, or A⁻). The result of a facilitation procedure is that the participant responds to A only when B has been presented (Holland, 1992). Stimulus B facilitates conditioned responding to A or sets the occasion for responding to A.

FIGURE 5.8

	Trials with the US	Trials without the US
Conditioned inhibition	A ⟶ US	AB ⟶ no US
Conditioned facilitation	AB ⟶ US	A ⟶ no US

Comparison of the types of trials that occur in procedures for conditioned inhibition and conditioned facilitation. A and B represent two different conditioned stimuli. US = unconditioned stimulus.

Conditional relations captured by the facilitation procedure are not limited to experimental research. Consider the road sign "Slippery When Wet." The sign indicates that ordinarily the road is safe but that it can be dangerous when it is wet. These circumstances exemplify the basic facilitation relation. In this example, the roadway stimuli are represented by "A," wetness or rain is represented by "B," and danger is the US. Danger occurs only when cues of the road are encountered in combination with rain (AB→US). No danger is present when cues of the road are encountered without rain (A→noUS).

ASSOCIATIONS LEARNED IN A CONDITIONED FACILITATION PROCEDURE

Procedures used to produce higher order associations are complex and result in more than one type of association. In a facilitation procedure, AB$^+$ trials are intermixed with A$^-$ trials, and the US is only presented on trials when stimulus B occurs. Because stimulus A is paired with the US half the time, an association develops between stimulus A and the US. Stimulus B is paired with the US each time it occurs, which allows for a direct association between stimulus B and the US. In addition to these direct associations with the US, stimulus B presumably comes to signal when stimulus A will be followed by the US. That is the higher order association. The major task in studying facilitation is to sort out what aspect of behavior reflects the direct A–US and B–US associations or reflects the higher order B(A–US) association.

Types of Conditioned Responses Elicited by Stimuli A and B

One way to sort out which type of association is responsible for the conditioned responding that occurs in a facilitation experiment is to use CSs in the role of A and B that generate different conditioned responses. This approach was used extensively in many of the early studies of facilitation in appetitive conditioning (Holland, 1992).

Rats, for example, rear in response to a light that has been paired with food, but they show a head-jerk response to a tone paired with food (Holland, 1977). Consider, then, what might occur with a facilitation procedure that consists of Tone/Light→Food and Light→noFood trials. A Light–Food association will result in rearing when the light is presented on a test trial. If the tone has come to signal the Light–Food association, the participants should show increased rearing to the light if it is announced by presentation of the tone. Notice, however, that the facilitated rearing on Tone/Light trials cannot be attributed to an association of the Tone with food because a Tone–Food association produces a head-jerk conditioned response, not a rearing response.

Another strategy for isolating the higher order B(A–US) association as the source of facilitated responding to the target A involves using background or contextual cues as the occasion setting stimulus B. Organisms typically do not respond to background or contextual cues with any overt easily observed responses. However, participants can learn to approach a target stimulus A in the context of one set of background stimuli but not another (Leising, Hall, Wolf, & Ruprecht, 2015).

A particularly interesting category of contextual or background cues is provided by drugs that change how you feel. Research has shown that subjective sensations created by various drugs can serve as occasion-setting stimuli that indicate whether a target CS will (or will not) be paired with a US (Bevins & Murray, 2011). In these studies, some experimental sessions are conducted after the rats have been injected with a drug (stimulus B) and others are conducted in the absence of the drug. During drug sessions, a light may be paired with food, providing the AB→US trials of the facilitation procedure (see Figure 5.9). During nondrug sessions, stimulus A is presented but not paired with food, providing the A→noUS trials. The typical outcome is that the drug state facilitates the food-conditioned responding to stimulus A.

Effects of Extinction of Stimulus B

An alternative strategy for distinguishing between B–US and B(A–US) relations in a facilitation procedure involves testing the effects of extinguishing stimulus B. Extinction of B involves repeatedly presenting stimulus B by itself (B–noUS). Presenting stimulus B without the US is contrary to a B–US relation and reduces responding that depends on that relation. (I have more to say about extinction in Chapter 10.) However, the repeated presentation of stimulus B by itself is not contrary to a B(A–US) relation. The opposite of B(A–US) is B(A–noUS), not B–noUS. Therefore, extinction of stimulus B should not disrupt responding mediated by a B(A–US) relation.

Numerous studies have shown that extinction of an occasion setter or facilitator (stimulus B) does not reduce the effectiveness of B in modulating responding to a target stimulus A (e.g., Holland, 1989; Leising et al., 2015; Rescorla, 1985). In fact, the lack of sensitivity of facilitation and occasion setting to extinction of the modulating stimulus is considered a signature characteristic of occasion setting.

Finally, I should point out that organisms do not invariably learn a B(A–US) relation as a result of a facilitation procedure. Sometimes procedures involving a mixture of AB–US trials and A–noUS trials result in the learning of a B–US relation only; in other cases, participants learn both a B–US relation and a higher order B(A–US) relation. A number of factors beyond the scope of the present discussion determine whether a particular procedure favors the acquisition of a B–US relation or a B(A–US) relation (Holland, 1992; Schmajuk & Holland, 1998).

FIGURE 5.9

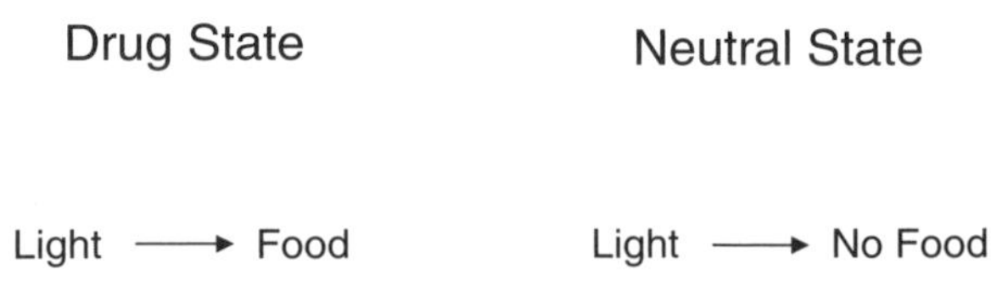

Drug State	Neutral State
Light ⟶ Food	Light ⟶ No Food

Outline of a facilitation procedure in which a drug state serves as the higher order stimulus indicating when a Light is paired with Food.

Summary

Pavlovian conditioning involves the formation of an association or connection between two events. Typically, the events are individual stimuli, the CS and the US. However, in more complex cases, one of the events may be a modulator or occasion-setting stimulus and the other is a CS–US associative unit. These cases represent higher order relations.

The development of conditioned responding is highly sensitive to the temporal relation between the CS and the US. Delayed conditioning procedures produce the most vigorous responding. Introducing a trace interval of as little as half a second between the CS and US can severely disrupt the development of conditioned behavior. Conditioned responding is also a function of the CS–US interval, but the precise quantitative relationship depends on the response system that is being conditioned.

Pavlovian conditioning is also highly sensitive to the signal relation between the CS and the US—that is, the extent to which the CS provides information about the US. This is illustrated by the blocking phenomenon and by CS–US contingency effects. Originally, variations in the contingency between CS and US were considered to influence associative processes directly. More recent evidence suggests that different degrees of context conditioning are responsible for CS–US contingency effects.

Higher order relations in Pavlovian conditioning have been investigated within the context of conditioned inhibition and conditioned facilitation. In conditioned inhibition, a modulator stimulus (stimulus B) indicates when another CS (stimulus A) *is not paired* with the US. The outcome is that B comes to inhibit conditioned responding that normally occurs to stimulus A. In conditioned facilitation, the modulator stimulus B indicates when stimulus A *is paired* with the US. The outcome is that conditioned responding occurs only when stimulus B is present. Proof that the results reflect learning a B(A–US) higher order relation often involves information concerning the topography of the conditioned response, the effects of extinguishing stimulus B, or both.

Suggested Readings

Holland, P. C. (1992). Occasion setting in Pavlovian conditioning. In G. Bower (Ed.), *The psychology of learning and motivation* (Vol. 28, pp. 69–125). Orlando, FL: Academic Press.

Lin, J.-Y., Arthurs, J., & Reilly, S. (2017). Conditioned taste aversions: From poisons to pain to drugs of abuse. *Psychonomic Bulletin & Review, 24,* 335–351. http://dx.doi.org/10.3758/s13423-016-1092-8

Molet, M., & Miller, R. R. (2014). Timing: An attribute of associative learning. *Behavioural Processes, 101,* 4–14. http://dx.doi.org/10.1016/j.beproc.2013.05.015

Raybuck, J. D., & Lattal, K. M. (2014). Bridging the interval: Theory and neurobiology of trace conditioning. *Behavioural Processes, 101,* 103–111. http://dx.doi.org/10.1016/j.beproc.2013.08.016

Urcelay, G. P., & Miller, R. R. (2014). The functions of contexts in associative learning. *Behavioural Processes, 104,* 2–12. http://dx.doi.org/10.1016/j.beproc.2014.02.008

Technical Terms

Blocking effect
Conditioned inhibition
CS–US contingency
CS–US interval
Delayed conditioning
Facilitation
Higher order stimulus relation
Interstimulus interval
Long-delay learning

Positive occasion setting
Retardation-of-acquisition test
Simultaneous conditioning
Summation test
Temporal coding
Temporal contiguity
Trace conditioning
Trace interval

Pavlovian Conditioning Mechanisms and Theories

6

Did you know that

- Pavlovian conditioning typically does not involve the learning of a new conditioned reflex or stimulus–response (S–R) connection but rather the learning of a new stimulus–stimulus (S–S) connection?
- conditioned responding can be increased or decreased by changing the value of the unconditioned stimulus (US), which is an intervention that does not involve presenting the conditioned stimulus (CS)?
- according to all contemporary models of learning, what you learn about one stimulus depends on the associative value of other concurrently present stimuli?
- a CS can lose associative strength even though it is paired with a US?
- attentional theories assume that what happens on one trial determines how much attention is devoted to the CS on the next trial?
- many major theories of learning do not consider time in their formulations?
- the absolute duration of the CS is not as important for learning as is the ratio between the CS duration and the interval between successive US presentations?
- conditioned responding depends on the associative value of the CS compared with the associative value of other cues that were present at the time the CS was conditioned?

http://dx.doi.org/10.1037/0000057-006
The Essentials of Conditioning and Learning, Fourth Edition, by M. Domjan

Originally, Pavlovian conditioning was considered to be a simple form of learning that depended only on pairings of a conditioned stimulus (CS) with an unconditioned stimulus (US) and resulted in the conditioning of a new reflex. This naive perspective has turned out to be incorrect in many ways. Long-delay taste aversion learning, selective associations, and the blocking effect all challenge the view that Pavlovian conditioning is a simple form of learning. In this chapter, I continue to document the richness and complexity of Pavlovian conditioning by focusing on the underlying mechanisms and theories that address this form of learning. I discuss two major questions: (a) What is learned in Pavlovian conditioning, and (b) how is it learned?

What Is Learned in Pavlovian Conditioning?

The signature outcome of a Pavlovian conditioning procedure is that the participant comes to perform a conditioned response (CR) when the CS is presented. What mechanism is responsible for this CR? There are two prominent alternatives. According to the first mechanism, the CS comes to elicit the CR directly. This is called *S–R learning* and is the simpler of the two mechanisms. S–R mechanisms dominated theories of learning up until the "cognitive revolution" that swept over psychology in the 1970s. That revolution encouraged more "cognitive" theories of learning and the possibility that through Pavlovian conditioning the CS comes to activate a representation of the US. That US representation or memory in turn generates the CR. This second mechanism is called *S–S learning*. Because both S–R and S–S learning mechanisms can generate the CR, how can we distinguish between them?

According to the S–R learning mechanism, classical conditioning leads to the formation of an association between the CS and the CR. As a result of this CS–CR association, presentation of the CS activates the CR directly and automatically. Such S–R learning is what is implied by the traditional notion that Pavlovian conditioning results in the learning of a new reflex response to the CS.

How S–S learning generates conditioned responding is a bit more complicated. According to the S–S learning mechanism, Pavlovian conditioning results in the learning of CS–US association. Once this association is acquired, presentation of the CS will activate a neural representation of the US (see Figure 6.1). Expressed informally, this means that upon encountering the CS, the participant will start thinking about the US. This activation of the US representation does not generate a response automatically. Rather, what the participant will do will depend on its motivation to respond to the US at that time.

A powerful technique for differentiating between S–R and S–S mechanisms was popularized by Robert Rescorla (1973) and is basically a test of performance. The test involves evaluating the vigor of conditioned responding after the individual's motivation to respond to the US has been changed. In one type of experiment, for example, motivation to respond to the US is reduced. This manipulation is called *US devaluation* (see Table 6.1).

FIGURE 6.1

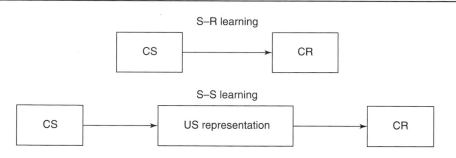

Distinction between stimulus–response (S–R) and stimulus–stimulus (S–S) learning. In S–R learning, a direct connection or association is established between the conditioned stimulus (CS) and the conditioned response (CR) such that the CR is elicited directly upon presentation of the CS. In S–S learning, the CS activates a representation of the unconditioned stimulus (US), which in turn leads to the CR.

Consider, for example, a study of sexual Pavlovian conditioning that was conducted with domesticated male quail (Holloway & Domjan, 1993). Brief exposure to a light CS was paired with access to a female bird once a day. Initially, the visual CS did not elicit any significant behavior. However, because the males were sexually motivated, they always readily approached and copulated with the female that was released at the end of each conditioning trial. With repeated conditioning trials, the males also started approaching the CS. After 10 conditioning trials, the CS elicited a strong approach or sign tracking response regardless of where the males were at the start of the trial.

According to the S–R learning mechanism, conditioned responding reflects the establishment of a direct connection between the CS and the CR. If such a direct connection has been established, then changing the animal's motivation to perform the unconditioned response should not influence its conditioned responding. Thus, an S–R interpretation predicts that once the quail has learned the sexual conditioned

TABLE 6.1

Design and Predictions of US Devaluation Study

Phase 1	Phase 2	S–R Prediction	S–S Prediction
Experimental group			
Conditioning	US devaluation	No change in CR	Decline in CR
Control group			
Conditioning	No devaluation	No change in CR	No change in CR

Note. CR = conditioned response; S–R = stimulus–response; S–S = stimulus–stimulus; US = unconditioned stimulus.

approach response, presentation of the CS will elicit the CR even if the birds are no longer sexually motivated.

Holloway and Domjan (1993) tested the S–R prediction by reducing the sex drive of one group of birds. Sexual motivation was reduced by changing the light cycle in the laboratory to mimic winter conditions, when the birds do not breed. The results of the experiment are summarized in Figure 6.2. Contrary to predictions based on the S–R mechanism, a reduction in sexual motivation reduced conditioned responding to the visual CS.

The results summarized in Figure 6.2 indicate that S–S learning had occurred in the experiment. S–S learning does not involve learning a specific CR. Rather, it involves learning an association between the CS and the US. Once the CS–US association has been established, presentation of the CS activates a representation of

FIGURE 6.2

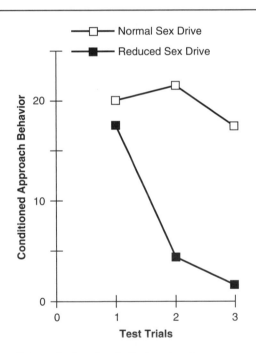

Effects of unconditioned stimulus (US) devaluation on sexual approach conditioned behavior. Three test sessions were conducted at 1-week intervals after two groups of quail had acquired a conditioned approach response. During the test phase, the sexual motivation of one group of birds was reduced. This US devaluation produced a decrease in conditioned responding. Adapted from "Sexual Approach Conditioning: Tests of Unconditioned Stimulus Devaluation Using Hormone Manipulations," by K. S. Holloway and M. Domjan, 1993, *Journal of Experimental Psychology: Animal Behavior Processes, 19,* p. 49. Copyright 1993 by the American Psychological Association.

the US. This in turn leads to conditioned responding, but only if the participants are motivated to respond to the US. In the quail experiment, the CS elicited conditioned approach behavior, but only if the birds were sexually motivated.

In the preceding experiment, motivation to respond to the US was reduced as a test for S–S learning. Another approach is to increase motivation to respond to the US. This is called *US inflation*. If conditioned responding is mediated by S–S learning, US inflation results in increased responding to the CS.

Although studies of US devaluation are more common than studies of US inflation effects, both types of results have been obtained in a variety of different forms of Pavlovian conditioning (e.g., Delamater, Campese, LoLordo, & Sclafani, 2006; Fudim, 1978; Storsve, McNally, & Richardson, 2012). These results indicate that Pavlovian conditioning typically involves S–S learning rather than the learning of a new S–R reflex.

A particularly interesting implication of these findings is that one can alter responses to a CS using procedures that involve manipulations that target the US rather than the CS itself. Most clinical interventions that seek to reduce maladaptive CRs involve changing the properties of the CS by using something like an extinction procedure (see Chapter 10, this volume). US devaluation effects suggest an alternative avenue. Focusing on changing the value of the US may be especially useful in clinical situations where the troublesome CS cannot be easily identified or manipulated.

How Are Pavlovian Associations Learned?

We next turn to considering possible mechanisms involved in the learning of Pavlovian associations. The modern era in theories of associative learning was launched by the discovery of the blocking effect, which demonstrated that CS–US contiguity is not sufficient for learning. The first and most influential modern learning theory was the Rescorla–Wagner model. Other models and theories soon followed. These alternatives sought to explore different ways of characterizing learning and to overcome some of the shortcomings of the Rescorla–Wagner model. However, the Rescorla–Wagner model remains the standard against which other theories are evaluated.

THE RESCORLA–WAGNER MODEL

Because the blocking effect was critical in shaping the development of contemporary learning theory, the basics of the blocking effect are reviewed in Figure 6.3. Participants first receive one CS (A) paired with the US. After conditioned responding to A is well established, a new stimulus (B) is added, and the A+B compound is paired with the US. Blocking is said to occur if the presence of the previously conditioned stimulus A blocks the conditioning of the new added stimulus B.

Why does the presence of the previously conditioned stimulus A block the acquisition of responding to stimulus B? Kamin (1969), who originally identified the blocking effect, explained the phenomenon by proposing that a US must be surprising to be effective in producing learning. If the US is signaled by a CS that you learned about previously, the US will not be surprising and therefore will not stimulate the "mental

FIGURE 6.3

	Phase 1	Phase 2	Test
Experimental Group	A ⟶ US	A + B ⟶ US	B
Control Group		A + B ⟶ US	B

Review of the design of a blocking experiment. In Phase 1, the experimental group gets stimulus A conditioned to asymptote. In Phase 2, both the experimental and the control groups get stimuli A and B presented simultaneously and paired with the unconditioned stimulus (US). Finally, both groups are tested for responding to stimulus B.

effort" needed for the formation of an association. Expected events are things the participant has already learned about. Hence, expected events will not activate processes leading to new learning. To be effective, the US must be unexpected or surprising.

The idea that the effectiveness of a US is determined by how surprising it is formed the basis of the Rescorla–Wagner model (Rescorla & Wagner, 1972; Wagner & Rescorla, 1972). With the use of this model, the implications of the concept of US surprisingness were extended to a wide variety of conditioning phenomena. The Rescorla–Wagner model had a huge impact on the field of conditioning and learning (Siegel & Allan, 1996) and continues to be used in a variety of areas of psychology, computer science, and neuroscience.

What does it mean to say that something is surprising? By definition, an event is surprising if it is different from what is expected. If you expect a small gift for your birthday and get a car, you will be very surprised. This is analogous to an unexpectedly large US. Likewise, if you expect a car and receive a box of candy, you will also be surprised. This is analogous to an unexpectedly small US. According to the Rescorla–Wagner model, an unexpectedly large US is the basis for excitatory conditioning or increases in associative value. In contrast, an unexpectedly small US is the basis for inhibitory conditioning or decreases in associative value. A critical component of the model is the assumption that how surprised you are by a US depends on all of the cues that are present on a conditioning trial.

Strong conditioned responding indicates a strong expectation that the US will occur, whereas weak conditioned responding indicates a low expectation of the US. Using the magnitude of the CR as a proxy for US expectancy, we can infer that the US is highly surprising at the beginning of training and not at all surprising by the end when conditioned responding has reached an asymptote or limit. Thus, distance from the asymptote of learning may be used as a measure of US surprise.

The basic ideas of the Rescorla–Wagner model are expressed mathematically by using λ to represent the asymptote of learning possible with the US that is being used and V to represent the associative value of the stimuli that precede the US. The surprisingness of the US will then be $(\lambda - V)$. According to the Rescorla–Wagner model, the amount of learning on a given trial is assumed to be proportional to $(\lambda - V)$, or US surprisingness. The value of $(\lambda - V)$ is large at the start of learning because V (the associative value of the stimuli preceding the US) is close to zero at this point. Hence, substantial increments in associative strength occur during early conditioning trials. As the associative value of the cues that precede the US increases, the difference term $(\lambda - V)$ will get smaller, and less additional learning will occur.

Learning on a given conditioning trial is the change in the associative value of a stimulus. This change can be represented as ΔV. Using these symbols, the idea that learning depends on the surprisingness of the US can be expressed as follows:

$$\Delta V = k(\lambda - V).$$

In this equation, k is a constant related to the salience of the CS and US and $(\lambda - V)$ is a measure of US surprise. $\Delta V = k(\lambda - V)$ is the fundamental equation of the Rescorla–Wagner model.

Application to the Blocking Effect

The basic ideas of the Rescorla–Wagner model clearly predict the blocking effect. In applying the model, it is important to keep in mind that expectations of the US are based on all of the cues available to the organism during the conditioning trial. As illustrated in Figure 6.3, the blocking design first involves extensive conditioning of stimulus A so that the participants acquire a perfect expectation that the US will occur based on the presentation of stimulus A. Therefore, at the end of Phase 1, V_A equals the asymptote of learning ($V_A = \lambda$). In Phase 2, stimulus B is presented together with stimulus A, and the two CSs are followed by the US. According to the Rescorla–Wagner model, no conditioning of stimulus B will occur in Phase 2 because the US is now perfectly predicted by the presence of stimulus A: $(\lambda - V_{A+B}) = 0$.

The control group receives the identical training in Phase 2, but for them the presence of stimulus A does not lead to an expectation of the US. Therefore, the US is surprising for the control group in Phase 2 and produces new learning.

Loss of Associative Value Despite Pairings With the US

The Rescorla–Wagner model is consistent with such fundamental facts of classical conditioning as acquisition and the blocking effect. However, much of the importance of the model has come from its unusual predictions. One such prediction is that under certain circumstances the conditioned properties of stimuli will decline despite continued pairings with the US. That is highly counterintuitive. Why should a CS lose associative value if it continues to be paired with the US? The Rescorla–Wagner model predicts that stimuli will lose associative value when they are paired with the US if there is an overexpectation of that US.

The design of a US overexpectation experiment is outlined in Figure 6.4. In Phase 1, stimuli A and B are paired with the same US (e.g., one pellet of food) on separate trials. This continues until each of stimuli A and B predict perfectly the one food pellet US, or $V_A = V_B = \lambda$. Phase 2 is then initiated. In Phase 2, stimuli A and B are presented simultaneously for the first time, and the A+B stimulus compound is followed by the original one food pellet US.

When stimuli A and B are presented simultaneously at the start of Phase 2, the expectations based on the individual stimuli are assumed to add together, with the result that two food pellets are predicted as the US ($V_A + V_B = 2\lambda$). This is an over-expectation, because the US remains only one food pellet. Thus, there is a discrepancy between what is expected (two pellets) and what occurs (one pellet).

At the start of Phase 2, the participants find the US surprisingly small. To bring their expectations of the US in line with what actually happens in Phase 2, the participants have to decrease their expectancy of the US based on the individual stimuli A and B. Thus, stimuli A and B are predicted to lose associative value despite continued presentations of the same US. The loss of associative value is predicted to continue until the sum of the expectancies based on A+B equals one food pellet. The predicted loss of CR to the individual stimuli A and B in the overexpectation experiment is highly counterintuitive but has been verified repeatedly (e.g., Kehoe & White, 2004; Lattal & Nakajima, 1998; Sissons & Miller, 2009).

Conditioned Inhibition

The Rescorla–Wagner model treats the development of conditioned inhibition as another illustration of the consequences of US over-expectation. Consider, for example, the standard inhibitory conditioning procedure (see Figure 5.5). This procedure

FIGURE 6.4

Phase 1	Phase 2	Test
A ⟶ US B ⟶ US	A + B ⟶ US	A, B

Design of the overexpectation experiment. In Phase 1, participants receive stimuli A and B, each paired with the unconditioned stimulus (US; one food pellet). In Phase 2, stimuli A and B are presented together, creating an expectation of more than the one pellet US. As a consequence, the associative values of stimuli A and B each decrease in Phase 2.

involves trials when the US is presented (reinforced trials) and trials when the US is omitted (nonreinforced trials). On reinforced trials, a conditioned excitatory stimulus (CS⁺) is paired with the US. On nonreinforced trials, the CS⁺ is presented together with the conditioned inhibitory stimulus (CS⁻).

To apply the Rescorla–Wagner model to the conditioned inhibition procedure, it is helpful to consider reinforced and nonreinforced trials separately. To accurately anticipate the US on reinforced trials, the CS⁺ has to gain conditioned excitatory properties. Excitatory conditioning involves the acquisition of positive associative value and ceases once the organism predicts the US perfectly on each reinforced trial. This is illustrated in the left panel of Figure 6.5.

On nonreinforced trials, both the CS⁺ and CS⁻ occur. Once the CS⁺ has acquired some degree of conditioned excitation (because of its presentation on reinforced trials), the organism will expect the US whenever the CS⁺ occurs, even on non-reinforced trials. However, the US does not happen on nonreinforced trials. This creates overexpectation of the US, similar to the example in Figure 6.4. To accurately

FIGURE 6.5

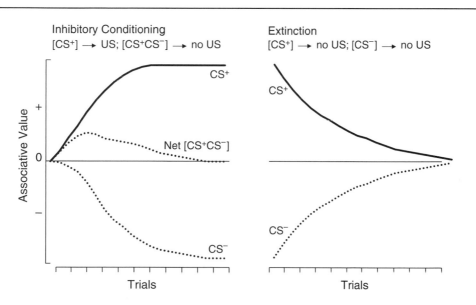

Predicted associative values of conditioned excitatory stimulus (CS⁺) and conditioned inhibitory stimulus (CS⁻) during the course of conditioned inhibition training (left panel) and extinction (right panel). During conditioned inhibition training, when the CS⁺ is presented alone, it is paired with the unconditioned stimulus (US); in contrast, when the CS⁺ is presented with the CS⁻, the US is omitted. The net associative value of CS⁺ and CS⁻ is the sum of the associative values of the individual stimuli. During extinction, the CSs are presented alone, and the US never occurs.

predict the absence of the US on nonreinforced trials, the associative value of the CS⁺ and the value of the CS⁻ have to sum to zero (the value represented by no US). Given the positive associative value of the CS⁺, the only way to achieve a net zero expectation of the US on nonreinforced trials is to make the associative value of the CS⁻ negative. Thus, the Rescorla–Wagner model explains conditioned inhibition by assuming that the CS⁻ acquires negative associative value (see the left panel of Figure 6.5).

Extinction of Conditioned Excitation and Inhibition

In an extinction procedure, the CS is presented repeatedly without the US. (I have a lot more to say about extinction in Chapter 10.) Let us consider predictions of the Rescorla–Wagner model for extinction. These predictions are illustrated in the right panel of Figure 6.5. When the CS⁺ is first presented without the US in extinction, there will be an overexpectation of the US (because the US is predicted but does not occur). With continued presentation of the CS⁺ by itself, the expectation elicited by the CS⁺ will gradually be brought in line with the absence of the US by gradual reductions in the associative value of the CS⁺. This process will continue until the associative value of the CS⁺ is reduced to zero.

The Rescorla–Wagner model predicts an analogous scenario for extinction of conditioned inhibition. At the start of extinction, the CS⁻ has negative associative value. This may be thought of as creating an underprediction of the US: The organism predicts less than the zero US that occurs on extinction trials. To bring expectations in line with the absence of the US, the negative associative value of the CS⁻ is gradually reduced until the CS⁻ ends up with zero associative strength.

Problems With the Rescorla–Wagner Model

The Rescorla–Wagner model has stimulated a great deal of research and led to the discovery of many new and important phenomena in classical conditioning (Siegel & Allan, 1996). Not unexpectedly, however, the model has also encountered some difficulties since it was proposed in 1972 (Miller, Barnet, & Grahame, 1995).

One of the difficulties with the model that became evident early on is that its analysis of the extinction of conditioned inhibition is incorrect. As I pointed out in the previous section (see Figure 6.5), the model predicts that repeated presentations of a conditioned inhibitor (CS⁻) by itself will lead to loss of conditioned inhibition. This, however, does not occur (Witcher & Ayres, 1984; Zimmer-Hart & Rescorla, 1974). In fact, some investigators have found that repeated nonreinforcement of a CS⁻ can enhance its conditioned inhibitory properties (see, e.g., DeVito & Fowler, 1987; Hallam, Grahame, Harris, & Miller, 1992). Curiously, an effective procedure for reducing the conditioned inhibitory properties of a CS⁻ does not involve presenting the CS⁻ at all. Rather, it involves extinguishing the excitatory properties of the CS⁺ with which the CS⁻ was presented during inhibitory training (Best, Dunn, Batson, Meachum, & Nash, 1985; Lysle & Fowler, 1985).

Another difficulty is that the Rescorla–Wagner model views extinction as the opposite of acquisition, or the return of the associative value of a CS to zero. However, as I discuss in Chapter 10, a growing body of evidence indicates that extinction is not simply the reversal of acquisition. Rather, extinction appears to involve the learning of a new relationship between the CS and US (namely, that the US no longer follows the CS).

ATTENTIONAL MODELS OF CONDITIONING

Given that classical conditioning has been studied for about a century, a comprehensive theory must account for many diverse findings. No theory has been entirely successful in accomplishing that goal. Nevertheless, interesting new ideas about classical conditioning continue to be proposed and examined. Some of these proposals supplement the Rescorla–Wagner model. Others are incompatible with the model and move the theoretical debate in other directions.

North American psychologists have favored learning mechanisms like the Rescorla–Wagner model that focus on changes in the surprise value or effectiveness of the US. In contrast, British psychologists have approached phenomena such as the blocking effect by postulating changes in how well the CS commands attention. The general assumption is that for conditioning to occur, participants must pay close attention to the CS. Procedures that disrupt attention to the CS are expected to disrupt learning as well (Mitchell & Le Pelley, 2010).

How noticeable a stimulus is, or how much attention it commands, is called the *salience of the stimulus*. Attentional theories differ in their assumptions about what determines the salience of a CS on a given trial. Pearce and Hall (1980), for example, assumed that how much attention a participant devotes to the CS on a given trial is determined by how surprising the US was on the preceding trial (see also Hall, Kaye, & Pearce, 1985; McLaren & Mackintosh, 2000). Individuals have a lot to learn if the US was surprising to them on the preceding trial. Therefore, under such conditions, CS salience will increase and they will pay closer attention to the CS on the next trial. In contrast, if a CS was followed by an expected US, attention to that CS will decrease.

An important feature of attentional theories is that they assume that the surprisingness of the US on a given trial alters the degree of attention commanded by the CS on future trials. For example, if Trial 10 ends in a surprising US, the salience of the CS will increase from Trial 10 to Trial 11. Thus, US surprisingness is assumed to have only a *prospective* or *proactive* influence on attention and conditioning. This is an important difference from US–reduction models such as the Rescorla–Wagner model, in which the surprisingness of the US on a given trial determines what is learned on that same trial.

The assumption that the US on a given trial can change what is learned about a CS on the next trial has received experimental support (e.g., Mackintosh, Bygrave, & Picton, 1977). However, this same assumption has made it difficult for attentional models to explain other findings. In particular, attentional models cannot explain the blocking that occurs on the first trial of Phase 2 of the blocking experiment (see, e.g., Azorlosa & Cicala, 1986; Balaz, Kasprow, & Miller, 1982; Dickinson, Nicholas, & Mackintosh, 1983). According to attentional models, blocking occurs because in Phase 2 of the blocking experiment, the lack of surprisingness of the US reduces attention to the added CS. However, such a reduction in salience can occur only after the first Phase 2 trial. Therefore, attentional models cannot explain the blocking that occurs on the first trial of Phase 2 of the blocking experiment.

TEMPORAL FACTORS AND CONDITIONED RESPONDING

Neither the Rescorla–Wagner model nor attentional models were designed to explain the effects of time in conditioning. However, time is obviously a critical factor. One important temporal variable is the CS–US interval. As I noted in Chapter 5, procedures with longer CS–US intervals produce less responding (see Figure 5.2). This relation appears to be primarily a characteristic of responses closely related to the US (e.g., focal search). If behaviors that are ordinarily farther removed from the US are measured (e.g., general search), responding is greater with procedures that involve longer CS–US intervals. Both findings illustrate that the duration of the CS is an important factor in conditioning.

Another important temporal variable is the interval between successive trials. Generally, more conditioned responding is observed with procedures in which trials are spaced farther apart. Of greater interest, however, is the fact that the intertrial interval and the CS duration act in combination to determine responding. Numerous studies have shown that the critical factor is the relative duration of these two temporal variables rather than the absolute value of either one by itself (Balsam & Gallistel, 2009).

Consider, for example, an experiment by Holland (2000). The experiment was conducted with laboratory rats, and food presented periodically in a cup was the US. Presentations of the food were signaled by an auditory CS. Initially the rats went to the food cup only when the food was delivered. However, as conditioning proceeded, they started going to the food cup as soon as they heard the auditory CS. Thus, nosing of the food cup (a form of focal search) developed as the CR. Each group was conditioned with one of two CS durations, either 10 seconds or 20 seconds, and one of six intertrial intervals (ranging from 15 seconds to 960 seconds). Each procedure could be characterized in terms of the ratio (I/T) between the intertrial interval (I) and the CS duration, which Holland called the trial duration (T).

The results of the experiment are summarized in Figure 6.6. Time spent nosing the food cup during the CS is shown as a function of the relative value of the intertrial interval (I) and the trial duration (T) for each group of subjects. Notice that conditioned responding was directly related to the I/T ratio. At each I/T ratio, the groups that received the 10-second CS responded similarly to those that received the 20-second CS.

Various interpretations have been offered for why conditioned responding is so strongly determined by the I/T ratio (Gallistel & Gibbon, 2000; Jenkins, Barnes, & Barrera, 1981). However, they all capture the notion that the I/T ratio determines how well the CS reduces ambiguity about the next occurrence of the US (Balsam & Gallistel, 2009). The CS reduces ambiguity about the US if it provides better information about the US than the background cues of the experimental situation. With a high I/T ratio, the participant spends much more time in the experimental context (I) than in the presence of the CS (T) before the US occurs. This makes the CS much

FIGURE 6.6

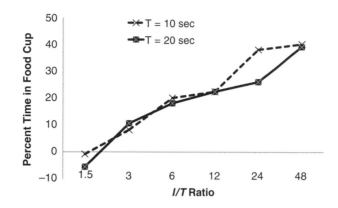

Percent time rats spent nosing the food cup during an auditory conditioned stimulus (CS) in conditioning with either a 10-second or 20-second trial duration (*T*) and various intertrial intervals (*I*) that created *I/T* ratios ranging from 1.5 to 48.0. Data are shown in relation to responding during baseline periods when the CS was absent. From "Trial and Intertrial Durations in Appetitive Conditioning in Rats," by P. C. Holland, 2000, *Animal Learning & Behavior, 28*, p. 125. Copyright 2000 by Springer. Adapted with permission.

more informative about the next occurrence of the US than background contextual cues, and therefore the CS comes to elicit a high level of conditioned responding. The informational advantage of the CS over background contextual cues is lost if durations of *I* and *T* are similar. As a consequence, less conditioned responding develops to the CS with low *I/T* ratios.

Informational models of learning that were designed to explain the effects of the *I/T* ratio are based on experiments that involve multiple conditioning trials (so that the organism can learn about the durations of *I* and *T* and the rates of US delivery during each of these intervals). However, there is substantial evidence that Pavlovian conditioning can occur in a single trial. One-trial learning occurs readily in studies of fear conditioning, taste-aversion learning, and sexual conditioning. Examples of one-trial learning are challenging for informational models of conditioning.

THE COMPARATOR HYPOTHESIS

Studies of the *I/T* ratio and informational models of learning have emphasized that conditioned responding depends not only on what happens during the CS but also on what happens in the experimental situation in general. The idea that both of these factors influence what we observed in conditioning experiments has been developed in greater detail by Ralph Miller and his collaborators in the *comparator hypothesis* (R. R. Miller & Matzel, 1988; Stout & Miller, 2007).

The comparator hypothesis is similar to informational models in assuming that conditioned responding depends on the relationship between the target CS and the US, as well as on the relationship between other cues in the situation (e.g., the background context) and the US. The associative strength of other cues present during training with the target CS is especially important. Another constraint of the comparator hypothesis is that it only allows for the formation of excitatory associations with the US. Whether conditioned responding reflects excitation or inhibition is assumed to be determined by the relative strengths of excitation conditioned to the target CS compared with the excitatory value of the contextual cues that were present with the target CS during training.

The comparator process is represented by the balance in Figure 6.7. In this figure, a comparison is made between the excitatory value of the target CS and the excitatory value of the other cues that are present during the training of that CS. If CS excitation exceeds the excitatory value of the contextual cues, the balance of the comparison will be tipped in favor of excitatory responding to the target CS. As the excitatory value of the other cues becomes stronger, the balance of the comparison will become less favorable for excitatory responding. In fact, if the excitatory value

FIGURE 6.7

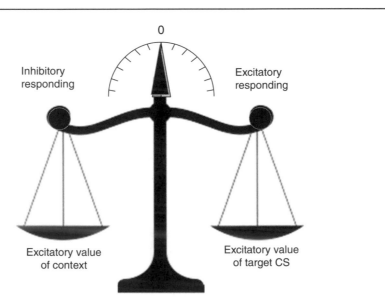

Illustration of the comparator hypothesis. Responding to the target conditioned stimulus (CS) is represented by the reading of the balance. If the excitatory value of the target CS exceeds the excitatory value of the other cues present during training of the target CS, the balance tips in favor of excitatory responding. As the associative value of the contextual cues increases, the comparison becomes less favorable for excitatory responding and may tip in favor of inhibitory responding.

of the contextual cues becomes sufficiently strong, the balance may eventually tip in favor of inhibitory responding to the target CS.

Unlike informational models, the comparator hypothesis emphasizes associations rather than time. A simplified version of the comparator hypothesis, presented in Figure 6.8, involves three different associations. The first association (Link 1 in Figure 6.8) is between the target CS (X) and the US. The second association (Link 2) is between the target CS (X) and the comparator contextual cues. Finally, there is an association between the comparator stimuli and the US (Link 3). With all of these links in place, when the CS is presented it activates the US representation directly (through Link 1) and indirectly (through Links 2 and 3). A comparison between the direct and indirect activations of the US representation determines the degree of excitatory or inhibitory responding that is observed.

It is important to note that the comparator hypothesis makes no assumptions about how associations become established. Rather, it describes how CS–US and

FIGURE 6.8

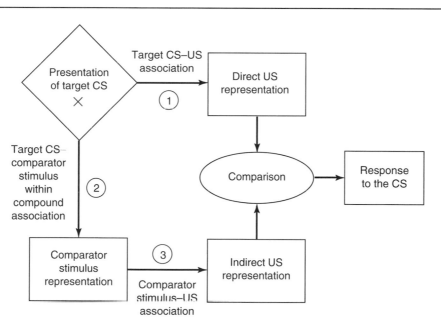

The associative structure of the comparator hypothesis. The target conditioned stimulus (CS) is represented as X. Excitatory associations result in activation of the unconditioned stimulus (US) representation, either directly by the target (Link 1) or indirectly (through Links 2 and 3). From "Comparator Mechanisms and Conditioned Inhibition: Conditioned Stimulus Preexposure Disrupts Pavlovian Conditioned Inhibition but Not Explicitly Unpaired Inhibition," by B. X. Friedman, A. P. Blaisdell, M. Escobar, and R. R. Miller, 1998, *Journal of Experimental Psychology: Animal Behavior Processes, 24*, p. 454. Copyright 1998 by the American Psychological Association.

context–US associations determine responding to the target CS. Thus, unlike US-modification and attentional models, the comparator hypothesis is a theory of *performance*, not a theory of learning.

An important corollary to the comparator hypothesis is that the comparison between CS–US and context–US associations is made at the time of testing for conditioned responding. As a consequence of this assumption, the comparator hypothesis makes the unusual prediction that extinction of context–US associations after training of a target CS will enhance responding to that target CS. This prediction has been confirmed repeatedly (e.g., Blaisdell, Gunther, & Miller, 1999). US modification and attentional theories of learning cannot explain such results.

The fact that postconditioning extinction of contextual cues enhances responding to a target CS indicates that responding to a target CS can be altered by changing the properties of comparator cues. This type of result is called a *revaluation effect*. Research on the comparator hypothesis has identified a growing number of revaluation effects. One of the more provocative revaluation effects concerns the blocking effect.

In the critical phase of the blocking experiment, a new stimulus (B) is conditioned in the presence of a previously conditioned CS (A). Because stimulus A is present when stimulus B is being conditioned, stimulus A serves as the comparator for stimulus B. According to the comparator hypothesis stimulus B will not elicit much conditioned responding because its comparator (stimulus A) has high excitatory strength, tipping balance away from stimulus B. If the lack of responding to stimulus B reflects this type of comparison, a revaluation manipulation might unmask responding to stimulus B. In particular, the comparator hypothesis predicts that participants will increase responding to stimulus B if the comparator (stimulus A) is extinguished. Interestingly, this prediction has been confirmed in several experiments (Blaisdell et al., 1999; Boddez, Baeyens, Hermans, & Beckers, 2011).

The comparator hypothesis has also been tested in studies of conditioned inhibition. The hypothesis attributes inhibitory responding to situations in which the association of the target CS with the US is weaker than the association of contextual cues with the US. The contextual cues in this case are the stimuli that provide the excitatory context for inhibitory conditioning. Interestingly, the hypothesis predicts that extinction of these conditioned excitatory stimuli after inhibitory conditioning will reduce inhibitory responding. Thus, the comparator hypothesis is unique in predicting that extinction of conditioned inhibition is best accomplished not by presenting the CS⁻ alone but by extinguishing the CS⁺ cues that provided the excitatory context for inhibitory conditioning. This unusual prediction has been confirmed in several studies (Best et al., 1985; Lysle & Fowler, 1985). (For additional revaluation effects, see McConnell, Urushihara, & Miller, 2010; Miguez, Witnauer, & Miller, 2012.)

Summary

Many instances of Pavlovian conditioning reflect the learning of an S–S association rather than an S–R association. This conclusion is supported by experiments showing that the vigor of conditioned behavior can be increased or decreased by changes in the value of the US (US inflation or devaluation) after acquisition. A variety of mechanisms have been proposed to explain Pavlovian learning. The Rescorla–Wagner model elaborated on the idea that the suprisingness of the US is the driving force that produces learning and led to the discovery of numerous novel learning phenomena. Attentional models addressed the same wide range of phenomena as the Rescorla–Wagner model, but they had some of the same difficulties as that model. Informational models focused on temporal variables in conditioning procedures, such as the *I/T* ratio. The comparator hypothesis has been extended to a wider range of phenomena, but it is a theory of performance rather than learning. It does not provide an explanation of how associations are acquired in the first place. All of these models have been important in directing our attention to previously ignored aspects of classical conditioning and each has identified important novel conditioning variables and manipulations.

Suggested Readings

Balsam, P. D., & Gallistel, C. R. (2009). Temporal maps and informativeness in associative learning. *Trends in Neuroscience, 32*, 73–78. http://dx.doi.org/10.1016/j.tins.2008.10.004

Delamater, A. R., Campese, V., LoLordo, V. M., & Sclafani, A. (2006). Unconditioned stimulus devaluation effects in nutrient-conditioned flavor preferences. *Journal of Experimental Psychology: Animal Behavior Processes, 32*, 295–306.

Hogarth, L., Dickinson, A., & Duka, T. (2010). Selective attention to conditioned stimuli in human discrimination learning: Untangling the effects of outcome prediction, valence, arousal, and uncertainty. In C. J. Mitchell & M. E. Le Pelley (Eds.), *Attention and associative learning* (pp. 71–97). Oxford, England: Oxford University Press.

McLaren, I. P. L., & Mackintosh, N. J. (2000). An elemental model of associative learning: I. Latent inhibition and perceptual learning. *Animal Learning & Behavior, 28*, 211–246. http://dx.doi.org/10.3758/BF03200258

Stout, S. C., & Miller, R. R. (2007). Sometimes-competing retrieval (SOCR): A formalization of the comparator hypothesis. *Psychological Review, 114*, 759–783. http://dx.doi.org/10.1037/0033-295X.114.3.759 [Correction published in 2008, *Psychological Review, 115*, 82.]

Technical Terms

Asymptote

Comparator hypothesis

I/T ratio

Overexpectation

S–R learning

S–S learning

Salience

US devaluation

US inflation

Instrumental or Operant Conditioning

7

Did you know that

- learning a new instrumental response often involves putting familiar response components into new combinations?
- variability in behavior is a great advantage in learning new responses?
- the deleterious effects of reinforcement delay can be overcome by presenting a marking stimulus immediately after the instrumental response?
- Thorndike's law of effect does not involve an association between the instrumental response and the reinforce?
- instrumental conditioning can result in the learning of three binary associations and one higher order association?
- Pavlovian associations acquired in instrumental conditioning procedures can disrupt performance of instrumental responses, creating biological constraints on instrumental conditioning?
- the various associations that develop in instrumental conditioning are difficult to isolate from each other, which creates major problems for studying the neurophysiology of instrumental learning?

The various procedures that I described so far (habituation, sensitization, and Pavlovian conditioning) all involve presentations of different types of stimuli according to various arrangements. The procedures produce changes in behavior—increases and decreases in responding—as a result

http://dx.doi.org/10.1037/0000057-007
The Essentials of Conditioning and Learning, Fourth Edition, by M. Domjan

of these presentation schedules. Although they differ in significant ways, an important common feature of habituation, sensitization, and Pavlovian conditioning procedures is that they are administered independently of the actions of the organism. What the participants do as a result of the procedures does not influence the stimulus presentation schedules.

In a sense, studies of habituation, sensitization, and Pavlovian conditioning represent how organisms learn about events that are beyond their control. Adjustments to uncontrollable events are important because many aspects of the environment are beyond our control. What day a class is scheduled, how long it takes to boil an egg, how far it is between city blocks, and when the local grocery store opens are all beyond our control. Although learning about uncontrollable events is important, not all learning is of this sort. Another important category of learning involves situations in which the occurrence of a significant event or unconditioned stimulus (US) depends on the individual's actions. Such cases involve *instrumental* or *operant conditioning*.

In instrumental conditioning procedures, whether or not a significant stimulus or event occurs depends on the behavior of the participant. Common examples of instrumental behavior include pulling up the covers to get warm in bed, putting ingredients together to make lemonade, changing the TV channel to find a more interesting show, and saying hello to someone to get a greeting in return. In all of these cases, a particular response is required to obtain a specific stimulus or consequent outcome. Because the response is instrumental in producing the outcome, the response is referred to as *instrumental behavior*. The consequent outcome (the warmth, the tasty lemonade, the TV show, the reciprocal greeting) is referred to as the *reinforcer*.

Operant behavior is special subset of instrumental behavior that is defined by how the behavior changes the environment. For example, turning a doorknob sufficiently to open a door is an operant response because it changes the status of the door from being closed to being open. In identifying instances of this operant response, it does not matter whether the doorknob is turned with a person's right hand, left hand, fingertips, or with a full grip of the knob. Such variations in response topography are ignored in studies of operant behavior. The focus is on the common environmental change that is produced by the operant behavior.

A common example of operant behavior in animal research involves a laboratory rat pressing a response lever in a small experimental chamber (see Figure 7.1). Whether or not a lever-press response has occurred can be determined by placing a microswitch under the lever. In a typical experiment, presses of the lever with enough force to activate the microswitch are counted as instances of the lever-press operant response. Whether the rat presses the lever with its right or left paw or its nose is ignored as long as the microswitch is activated. Another common example of operant behavior in animal research is a pigeon pecking a disk or a stimulus on a wall. Various ways of pecking are ignored provided the pecks are detected by the touchscreen on the wall.

FIGURE 7.1

A common laboratory preparation for the study of operant behavior. The drawing shows a rat in a lever-press chamber. A food cup is located below the lever.

The Traditions of Thorndike and Skinner

The intellectual traditions of classical conditioning were established by one dominant figure, Ivan Pavlov. In contrast, the intellectual traditions of instrumental or operant conditioning have their roots in the work of two American giants of 20th-century psychology, Edward L. Thorndike and B. F. Skinner (see Figures 7.2 and 7.3, respectively). The empirical methods as well as the theoretical perspectives of these two scientists were strikingly different, but the traditions that each founded have endured to this day. I first consider the distinctive experimental methods used by Thorndike and Skinner and then note some differences in their theoretical perspectives.

METHODOLOGICAL CONSIDERATIONS

Thorndike was interested in studying animal "intelligence." To do this, he designed a number of *puzzle boxes* for young cats in a project that became his PhD dissertation

FIGURE 7.2

Edward L. Thorndike. From *Wikimedia Commons.* Retrieved from https://upload.wikimedia.org/wikipedia/commons/6/66/PSM_V80_ D211_Edward_Lee_Thorndike.png. In the public domain.

(Thorndike, 1898). A different type of response was required to get out of each box. The puzzle was to figure out how to escape from the box.

Thorndike would put a kitten into a puzzle box on successive trials and measure how long the kitten took to get out of the box and obtain a piece of fish. In some puzzle boxes, the kittens had to make just one type of response to get out (e.g., turning a latch). In others, several actions were required, and these had to be performed in a particular order. Thorndike found that with repeated trials, the kittens got quicker and quicker at escaping from the box. Their escape latencies decreased.

The Discrete-Trial Method

Thorndike's experiments illustrate the *discrete-trial method* used in the study of instrumental behavior. In the discrete-trial method, the participant has the opportunity to perform the instrumental response only at certain times (during discrete trials) as determined by the experimenter. In the case of Thorndike's experiments, the kitten

FIGURE 7.3

B. F. Skinner. From *Wikimedia Commons.* Retrieved from https://commons.wikimedia.org/wiki/File:B.F._Skinner_at_Harvard_circa_1950.jpg. In the public domain.

could only perform the instrumental escape response after it was placed in a puzzle box. When it made the required response, it was released from the box. The next trial did not begin until Thorndike decided to put the kitten back in the box.

The discrete-trial method was subsequently adopted by investigators who used mazes of various sorts to study instrumental conditioning. Mazes are typically used with laboratory rats and mice. They were introduced into the investigative artillery of behavioral scientists by Willard Small, who built a maze in an effort to mimic the tunnel-like structures of the underground burrows in which rats live (Small, 1900, 1901).

A common type of maze is the *straight-alley runway* (see Figure 7.4). In a straight-alley runway, the rat is first placed in the start box. The start-box door is then lifted to allow the rat to go to the goal box at the other end of the runway. Upon reaching the goal box, the rat is given a small piece of food and then removed until it is time for the next trial. The speed of running from the start box to the goal box is measured on each trial. Learning results in increased speeds of running.

FIGURE 7.4

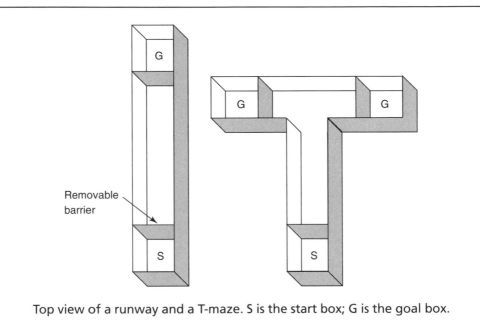

Top view of a runway and a T-maze. S is the start box; G is the goal box.

Another common apparatus is the *T-maze*. This also has a start box. After the participant is released from the start box, it is permitted to go to a choice point, where it has to select one or the other arm of the T to enter next. The T-maze is therefore particularly suited for measuring choice behavior.

The discrete-trial method requires numerous manipulations. The experimenter has to pick up the rat, place it in the start box, wait for it to reach the goal box, remove it from the goal box, and then put it in a holding area for the intertrial interval. Another distinctive characteristic of the discrete-trial method is that how long the participant has to wait between trials is determined by the experimenter.

The Free-Operant Method

The major alternative to the discrete-trial method for the study of instrumental behavior is the *free-operant method*, developed by B. F. Skinner (1938). Skinner made numerous contributions, both methodological and conceptual, to the study of behavior, and these two types of contributions were often interrelated. The free-operant method is a case in point.

Skinner's development of the free-operant method began with an interest in designing an automated maze for rats—a maze in which the rats would automatically return to the start box after each trial. Such an apparatus would have the obvious advantage that the rat would be handled only at the start and the end of a training session, freeing up the experimenter to do other things in the interim. An automated maze would also permit the rat rather than the experimenter to decide when to start its next trial. This would permit the investigation of not only how rapidly the rat completed an instrumental response but how frequently it elected to perform the response. Thus, an automated maze promised to provide new information that could not be obtained with the discrete-trial method.

Skinner tried several approaches to automating the discrete-trial maze procedure. Each approach incorporated some improvements on the previous design, but as the work progressed, the apparatus became less and less like a maze (Skinner, 1956). The end result was what has come to be known as the Skinner box, in which a rat has to press a lever to obtain a piece of food that is dropped in a food cup near the lever.

In the Skinner box, the response of interest is defined in terms of the closure of a microswitch. The computer interface ignores whether the rat presses the lever with one paw or the other or with its tail. Another important feature of the Skinner box is that the operant response can occur at any time. The interval between successive responses is determined by the participant rather than by the experimenter. Because the operant response can be made at any time, the method is called the *free-operant* method.

The primary conceptual advantage of the free-operant method is that it allows the participant to repeatedly initiate the instrumental response. Skinner focused on this aspect of behavior. How often a rat initiates the operant response can be quantified in terms of the frequency of the response in a given period of time, or the *rate of responding*. Rate of responding is the primary measure of behavior in experiments using the free-operant method.

The Initial Learning of an Instrumental or Operant Response

People often think about instrumental or operant conditioning as a technique for training new responses. Swinging a bat, throwing a football, or playing the drums all involve instrumental responses that skilled players learn through extensive practice. However, in what sense are these responses new? Does instrumental conditioning always establish entirely new responses? Alternatively, does instrumental conditioning combine familiar responses in new ways, or does it establish a familiar response in a new situation?

LEARNING WHERE AND WHAT TO RUN FOR

Consider, for example, a hungry rat learning to run from one end of a runway to the other for a piece of food. An experimentally naive rat is slow to run the length of the runway at first. This is not, however, because it enters the experiment without the motor skill of running. Rats do not have to be taught to run, just as children don't have to be taught to walk. What they have to be taught is *where* to run and what to run *for*. In the straight-alley runway, the instrumental conditioning procedure provides the stimulus control and the motivation for the running response. It does not establish running as a new response in the participant's repertoire.

CONSTRUCTING NEW RESPONSES FROM FAMILIAR COMPONENTS

The instrumental response of pressing a lever is a bit different from running. An experimentally naive rat has probably never encountered a lever before and never performed a lever-press response. Unlike running, lever pressing has to be learned in the experimental situation. But does it have to be learned from scratch? Hardly.

An untrained rat is not as naive about pressing a lever as one might think. Lever pressing consists of a number of components: balancing on the hind legs, raising one or both front paws, extending a paw forward over the lever, and then bringing the paw down with sufficient force to press the lever and activate the microswitch. Rats perform responses much like these at various times while exploring their cages, exploring each other, or handling pellets of food. What they have to learn in the operant conditioning situation is how to put the various response components together to create the new lever-press response.

Pressing a lever is a new response only in the sense that it involves a new combination of response components that already exist in the participant's repertoire. In this case, instrumental conditioning involves the construction or synthesis of a new behavioral unit from preexisting response components (Balsam, Deich, Ohyama, & Stokes, 1998).

SHAPING NEW RESPONSES

Can instrumental conditioning also be used to condition entirely new responses—responses that an individual would never perform without instrumental conditioning? Most certainly. Instrumental conditioning is used to shape remarkable feats of performance in sports, ice-skating, ballet, and musical performance—feats that almost defy nature. A police dog can be trained to climb a 12-foot vertical barrier, a sprinter can learn to run a mile in 4 minutes, and a golf pro can learn to drive a ball 200 yards in one stroke. Such responses are remarkable because they are unlike anything someone can do without special training.

In an instrumental conditioning procedure, the individual has to perform the required response before the outcome or reinforcer is delivered. Given this restriction, how can instrumental procedures be used to condition responses that never occur on their own? The learning of entirely new responses is possible because of the variability of behavior. Variability is perhaps the most obvious feature of behavior. Organisms rarely do the same thing twice in exactly the same fashion. Response variability is usually considered a curse because it reflects lack of precision and makes predicting behavior difficult. However, for learning new responses, variability is a blessing.

With instrumental conditioning, the delivery of a reinforcer (e.g., a pellet of food) does not result in repetition of the same exact response that produced the reinforcer. If a rat, for example, is reinforced with a food pellet for pressing a lever with a force of 2 grams, it will not press the lever with exactly that force thereafter. Sometimes it will respond with less pressure, other times with more.

The first panel in Figure 7.5 shows what the distribution of responses might look like in an experiment where lever pressing is reinforced only if a force greater than

FIGURE 7.5

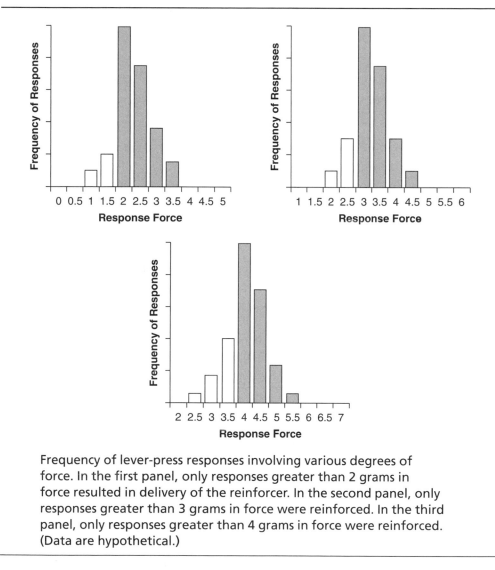

Frequency of lever-press responses involving various degrees of force. In the first panel, only responses greater than 2 grams in force resulted in delivery of the reinforcer. In the second panel, only responses greater than 3 grams in force were reinforced. In the third panel, only responses greater than 4 grams in force were reinforced. (Data are hypothetical.)

2 grams is used. Notice that many, but not all, of the responses exceed the 2-gram criterion. A few of the responses exceed a force of 3 grams, but none exceeds 4 grams.

Because the variability in behavior includes responses as forceful as 3 grams, we can change the response criterion so that the reinforcer is now only provided if the rat presses the lever with a force exceeding 3 grams. After several sessions with this new force requirement, the distribution of lever presses will look something like what is shown in the second panel of Figure 7.5.

Responding remains variable after the shift in the response requirement. Increasing the force requirement shifts the force distribution to the right so that the majority of the lever presses now exceed 3 grams. One consequence of this shift is that the rat occasionally presses the lever with a force of 4 grams or more. Notice that these responses are entirely new. They did not occur originally.

Because we now have responses exceeding 4 grams, we can increase the response requirement again. We can change the procedure so that now the food pellet is given only for responses that have a force of at least 4 grams. This will result in a further shift of the force distribution to yet higher values, as shown in the third panel of Figure 7.5. Now most of the responses exceed 4 grams, and sometimes the rat presses the lever with a force greater than 5 grams. Responses with such force are very different from what the rat started out doing.

The procedure I just described is called *shaping*. Shaping is used when the goal is to condition instrumental responses that are not in the participant's existing behavioral repertoire. New behavior is shaped by imposing a progressive series of response requirement. The progressive response requirements gradually take the participant from its starting behavioral repertoire to the desired target response (e.g., Deich, Allan, & Zeigler, 1988; Galbicka, 1988; Pear & Legris, 1987; Stokes, Mechner, & Balsam, 1999).

In setting up a shaping procedure, the desired final performance must be clearly defined. This sets the goal or end point of the shaping procedure. Next, the existing behavioral repertoire of the participant has to be documented so that the starting point is well understood. Finally, a sequence of training steps has to be designed to take the participant from its starting behavior to the final target response. The sequence of training steps involves successive approximations to the final response. Therefore, shaping is typically defined *as the reinforcement of successive approximations.*

Shaping is useful not only in training entirely new responses but also in training new combinations of existing response components. Riding a bicycle, for example, involves three major response components: steering, pedaling, and maintaining balance. Children learning to ride usually start by learning to pedal. Pedaling is a new response. It is unlike anything a child is likely to have done before getting on a bicycle. To enable the child to learn to pedal without having to balance, a child starts on a tricycle or a bicycle with training wheels. While learning to pedal, the child is not likely to pay much attention to steering and will need help to make sure she does not drive into a bush or off the sidewalk.

Once the child has learned to pedal, she is ready to combine this with steering. Only after the child has learned to combine pedaling with steering is she ready to add the balance component. Adding the balance component is the hardest part of the task. That is why parents often wait until a child is proficient in riding a bicycle with training wheels before letting her ride without them.

The Importance of Immediate Reinforcement

Instrumental conditioning is basically a response selection process. The response (or unique combination of response components) that results in the delivery of the reinforcer is selected from the diversity of actions the organism performs in the situation. It is critical to this response selection process that the reinforcer be delivered immediately after the desired or target response. If the reinforcer is delayed, other activities

FIGURE 7.6

R₁ R₂ R₃ R₄ Rₓ O   R₁ R₂ Rₓ R₃ R₄ O

Immediate reinforcement   Delayed reinforcement

Diagram of immediate and delayed reinforcement of the target response R_x. R_1, R_2, R_3, and R_4 represent different activities of the organism. O represents delivery of the reinforcer. Notice that when reinforcement is delayed after R_x, other responses occur closer to the reinforcer.

are bound to intervene before the reinforcer, and one of these other activities may be reinforced instead of the target response (see Figure 7.6).

Delivering a primary reinforcer immediately after the target response is not always practical. For example, the opportunity to go to a playground serves as an effective reinforcer for children in elementary school. However, it would be disruptive to allow a child to go outside each time he finished a math problem. A more practical approach is to give the child a star for each problem completed, and then allow these stars to be exchanged for the opportunity to go to the playground. With such a procedure, the primary reinforcer (access to the playground) is delayed after the instrumental response, but the instrumental response is immediately followed by a stimulus (the star) that is associated with the primary reinforcer.

A stimulus that is associated with a primary reinforcer is called a *conditioned* or *secondary reinforcer*. The delivery of a conditioned reinforcer immediately after the instrumental response overcomes the ineffectiveness of delayed reinforcement in instrumental conditioning (e.g., Winter & Perkins, 1982).

The ineffectiveness of delayed reinforcement can also be overcome by presenting a *marking stimulus* immediately after the target response. A marking stimulus is not a conditioned reinforcer and does not provide information about a future opportunity to obtain primary reinforcement. Rather, it is a brief visual or auditory cue that distinguishes the target response from the other activities the participant is likely to perform during a delay interval. In this way, the marking stimulus makes the instrumental response more memorable and helps overcome the deleterious effect of the reinforcer delay (Lieberman, McIntosh, & Thomas, 1979; B. A. Williams, 1999).

Associative Mechanisms in Instrumental Conditioning

Having discussed major procedural issues in instrumental conditioning, I next consider underlying associative mechanisms. Instrumental conditioning is typically distinguished from Pavlovian conditioning on the basis of procedural differences. A response is required for delivery of the reinforcer in instrumental conditioning but not in Pavlovian conditioning. The two forms of conditioning may also be distinguished on the basis of some (but not all) of the associations that are learned in instrumental and Pavlovian conditioning.

THE R–O ASSOCIATION

Methodologically, the most obvious events in instrumental conditioning are the instrumental response and the reinforcer. The response may be represented by *R* and the response outcome or reinforcer by *O*. In thinking about relationships that are learned in instrumental conditioning, an association between the instrumental response and the reinforcer may be the first one that comes to mind. This is called the *R–O association*.

Although there is strong evidence for R–O associations (Colwill & Rescorla, 1990; Hogarth & Chase, 2011; Ostlund, Winterbauer, & Balleine, 2008), an R–O association by itself is not sufficient to explain the occurrence of instrumental behavior. An R–O association means that performing R activates the memory of O. An R–O association comes into play when the response is performed, but that does not tell us why the response occurs in the first place. Thus, an R–O association is not sufficient to explain the initiation of an instrumental response.

THE S–R ASSOCIATION AND THORNDIKE'S LAW OF EFFECT

Beginning with the earliest theoretical efforts, investigators were aware that there is more to an instrumental conditioning situation than merely the response and its reinforcing outcome. Thorndike pointed out that organisms experience a unique set of stimuli when they perform an instrumental response. In Thorndike's experiments, these stimuli were provided by the puzzle box in which a participant was placed at the start of a training trial. Each puzzle box had distinctive features. Once a participant was assigned to a puzzle box, it experienced a unique set of cues whenever it performed the required escape response. Those stimuli may be represented by *S*.

Thorndike proposed that during the course of instrumental conditioning, an association comes to be established between the response R and the environmental stimuli S (see Figure 7.7). In fact, Thorndike believed that this *S–R association* was the only thing that was learned in instrumental conditioning. He summarized his thinking in the *law*

FIGURE 7.7

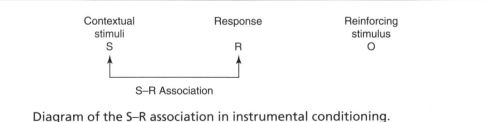

Diagram of the S–R association in instrumental conditioning.

of effect, which states that instrumental learning involves the formation of an association between the instrumental response R and the stimuli S in the presence of which the response is performed. The reinforcer delivered after the response serves to strengthen or "stamp in" the S–R association.

Thorndike's law of effect is counterintuitive and often incorrectly characterized. Note that according to the law of effect, instrumental conditioning does not involve learning to associate the response with the reinforcer. It does not involve the establishment of an R–O association or learning about the reinforcer. Rather, instrumental conditioning results only in the establishment of an S–R association. The reinforcer outcome O is significant merely as a catalyst for the learning of the S–R association but is not a part of that association.

The law of effect is an adaptation of the concept of elicited behavior to instrumental learning. Elicited behavior is a response to a particular stimulus. In an analogous fashion, the law of effect considers the instrumental response R to be a response to the stimulus context S. The law of effect thus provided a fairly straightforward causal account of instrumental behavior.

Although it was proposed more than a century ago, the law of effect remains prominent in contemporary analyses of behavior. Because S comes to produce R without any intervening processes, the S–R association of the law of effect has come to be regarded as the primary mechanism responsible for the habitual actions that people perform automatically without much thought or deliberation such as brushing teeth or sipping one's morning coffee (Duhigg, 2012; Wood & Neal, 2007).

An important area of contemporary research in which Thorndike's S–R mechanism plays a major role is the analysis of drug addiction and other forms of compulsive behavior (Hogarth, Balleine, Corbit, & Killcross, 2013; Zapata, Minney, & Shippenberg, 2010). Sitting at a bar and drinking a shot of whiskey is an instrumental response. Drugs of abuse are initially consumed because of their reinforcing effects. However, with habitual use, drug consumption becomes an automatic reaction to cues associated with the behavior. An alcoholic sitting at a bar with a shot of whisky in front of him cannot resist taking a drink. The compulsive nature of drug addiction reflects the S–R control of the behavior. Compulsive gambling and compulsive sexual behavior have similar features. Once the relevant cues for the behavior are encountered, the S–R mechanism overpowers cognitive intentions or "willpower" to abstain.

THE S–O ASSOCIATION

Although the S–R relation is compelling, it does not operate in isolation. Another important relation that has deep roots in the study of instrumental behavior is the relation between the antecedent stimuli S and the reinforcer outcome O (see Figure 7.8). Because the instrumental response R results in delivery of the reinforcer O in the presence of the particular contextual cues S, S serves as a reliable signal for O. This results in the learning of the S–O association (Hull, 1930, 1931).

The S–O association is much like a Pavlovian conditioned stimulus–unconditioned stimulus (CS–US) association and has some of the same behavioral consequences. For example, the establishment of the S–O association results in Pavlovian conditioned

FIGURE 7.8

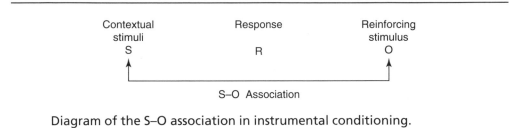

Diagram of the S–O association in instrumental conditioning.

responses being elicited by S. More important for understanding instrumental behavior, the S–O association means that Pavlovian processes contribute to the control of instrumental responding (Rescorla & Solomon, 1967). These contributions are typically studied in *Pavlovian-instrumental transfer experiments* (Holmes, Marchand, & Coutureau, 2010).

Pavlovian-instrumental transfer experiments have become common in behavioral neuroscience as a way to study the effects of incentive motivation on instrumental responding. Such experiments typically have two training phases and a transfer test phase. One training phase involves instrumental conditioning (e.g., reinforcing lever pressing with food). The second training phase involves Pavlovian conditioning (e.g., pairing a tone CS with food). As a result of the Pavlovian conditioning, the tone will come to activate the memory of food and thereby create an incentive to eat. The effects of that incentive motivation are evident during the transfer test when the presentation of the Pavlovian tone is found to increase food-reinforced lever pressing.

I previously discussed another example of Pavlovian-instrumental transfer when I described the conditioned suppression procedure as a technique for studying fear conditioning (see Chapter 4, this volume). In the conditioned suppression procedure, a Pavlovian CS paired with shock is found to suppress lever pressing for food. This is the opposite of what occurs if the Pavlovian CS is paired with food. The contrasting results illustrate that a Pavlovian CS can either facilitate or suppress instrumental responding for food depending on the extent to which the incentive properties of the Pavlovian CS are compatible with the incentive properties of the instrumental reinforcer (food).

THE S(R–O) ASSOCIATION

The three event relations we have considered thus far—R–O, S–R, and S–O—are binary or direct associations between pairs of elements of the instrumental conditioning situation. Another way in which S, R, and O may become related in instrumental conditioning is through a higher order relation that may be referred to as the *S(R–O) association* (see Figure 7.9). One of the first scientist to recognize the S(R–O) relation was B. F. Skinner (1969).

Skinner emphasized that in instrumental conditioning, the presentation of the reinforcer O is contingent on the prior occurrence of the response R, not on the prior occurrence of S. The R–O relation, however, is in effect only in the presence of S.

FIGURE 7.9

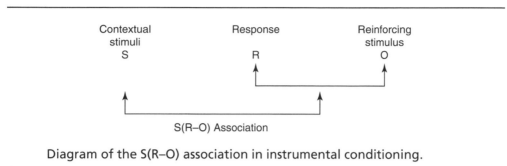

Diagram of the S(R–O) association in instrumental conditioning.

Therefore, he suggested that a higher order relation becomes established in which S signals the existence of the R–O contingency or sets the occasion for the R–O association. Skinner referred to this as a *three-term contingency*. The three-term contingency may be represented as S(R–O). The S(R–O) relation in instrumental conditioning is analogous to the higher order B(A–US) relation in Pavlovian conditioning, which I described in Chapter 5.

Experimental investigations of the associative structure of instrumental conditioning have provided evidence for all four of the associations I have described: R–O, S–R, S–O, and S(R–O). Thus, instrumental behavior is not a "simple" form of learning but involves a number of different relationships, all of which contribute to the control of instrumental responding in different ways.

Implications for Biological Constraints on Instrumental Conditioning

Understanding the associative structure of instrumental conditioning helps to solve some enduring problems in instrumental learning. In some of Thorndike's puzzle boxes, the kittens had to yawn or scratch themselves to be let out (Thorndike, 1911). Learning proceeded slowly in these boxes. Even after extensive training, the kittens did not make vigorous and bona fide yawning responses; rather, they performed rapid abortive yawns. Thorndike obtained similar results when the kittens were required to scratch themselves to be let out of the box. In this case, the kittens made rapid, half-hearted attempts to scratch themselves. These examples illustrate the general finding that self-care and grooming responses are difficult to condition with food reinforcement.

Another category of instrumental behavior that is difficult to condition with food reinforcement is the release of a coin or token. Two of Skinner's graduate students, Keller Breland and Marian Breland, became fascinated with the possibilities of animal training and set up a business that supplied trained animals for viewing in amusement parks, department store windows, and zoos. As a part of their business, the Brelands trained numerous species of animals to do various entertaining things (Breland & Breland, 1961).

For one display, they tried to get a pig to pick up a coin and drop it into a piggy bank to obtain food. Although the pig did what it was supposed to a few times, as training progressed it became reluctant to release the coin and rooted it along the ground instead. This rooting behavior came to predominate, and the project had to be abandoned. The Brelands referred to this as "misbehavior" because it was contrary to the outcome that should have occurred based on instrumental conditioning principles. Others subsequently referred to examples of such behavior as *biological constraints on learning*.

Several factors are probably responsible for the constraints on learning that have been encountered in conditioning grooming and coin-release behavior (Shettleworth, 1975). One of the most important factors seems to be the development of S–O associations in these instrumental conditioning procedures (Timberlake, Wahl, & King, 1982). In the coin-release task, the coin becomes associated with the food reinforcer and serves as stimulus S in the S–O association. In instrumental reinforcement of grooming, stimulus S is provided by the contextual cues of the conditioning situation. Because S–O associations are much like Pavlovian associations between a CS and a US, Pavlovian conditioned responses related to the reinforcer come to be elicited by S. Pavlovian responses conditioned with food consist of approaching and manipulating the conditioned stimulus. These food-anticipatory responses are incompatible with self-care and grooming. They are also incompatible with releasing and thereby withdrawing from a coin that has come to signal the availability of food.

Implications for Neural Mechanisms of Instrumental Conditioning

The complexity of the associative structure of instrumental learning presents serious challenges for scientists trying to discover the neural mechanisms and the neural circuitry underlying instrumental behavior. This is unlike the situation for Pavlovian conditioning. As we saw in Chapters 4 and 5, there are both simple and more complex forms of Pavlovian conditioning. Simple forms of Pavlovian excitatory conditioning are mediated by just an S–S association. More complex forms involve higher order relations, B(A–US). However, one can examine the neural mechanisms of S–S associations with procedures that do not involve higher order B(A–US) relations. Unfortunately, such procedural simplification is not possible in studies of instrumental conditioning.

Instrumental learning involves binary associations (S–R, S–O, and R–O), as well as the higher order S(R–O) relation. Furthermore, one cannot design an instrumental conditioning procedure that involves one of these associations to the exclusion of the others. For example, one cannot design an instrumental procedure that permits S–O associations without also allowing R–O associations, because the delivery of O contingent on R is an inherent feature of instrumental conditioning. One also cannot create an instrumental procedure that allows S–R associations without also allowing R–O and S(R–O) associations. Finally, one cannot design a procedure that only results in an R–O association because as soon as one defines a response, one has also defined a set of cues S that occur when the response is made.

The only way to isolate one of the associations to the exclusion of the others is by using complex experimental designs that keep all but one of the underlying associations constant (Colwill & Rescorla, 1990). For example, we may train two groups of participants with procedures that produce identical S–R and S–O associations, but different R–O associations. Figuring out how to successfully vary one association while keeping all of the others the same can be a major challenge. That may be one reason why we know a lot more about the neural mechanisms of Pavlovian conditioning than we know about the neural mechanisms of instrumental conditioning.

Summary

In instrumental conditioning, the delivery of a biologically significant event or reinforcer depends on the prior occurrence of a specified instrumental or operant response. The instrumental behavior may be a preexisting response that the organism has to perform in a new situation, a set of familiar response components that the organism has to put together in an unfamiliar combination, or an activity that is entirely novel to the organism. Successful learning in each case requires delivering the reinforcer immediately after the instrumental response or providing a conditioned reinforcer or marking stimulus immediately after the response.

Instrumental conditioning was first examined by Thorndike, who developed discrete-trial procedures that enabled him to measure how the latency of an instrumental response changes with successive training trials. Skinner's efforts to automate a discrete-trial procedure led him to develop the free-operant method, which allows measurement of the probability or rate of an instrumental behavior. Both discrete-trial and free-operant procedures consist of three components: contextual stimuli S, the instrumental response R, and the reinforcer outcome O. Reinforcement of R in the presence of S allows for the establishment of four types of associations: S–R, S–O, R–O, and S(R–O) associations. Because these associations cannot be isolated from one another, investigating the neurophysiology of instrumental learning is much more difficult than studying the neurophysiology of Pavlovian conditioning. Moreover, the S–O association can create serious response constraints on instrumental conditioning.

Suggested Readings

Chance, P. (1999). Thorndike's puzzle boxes and the origins of the experimental analysis of behavior. *Journal of the Experimental Analysis of Behavior, 72*, 433–440. http://dx.doi.org/10.1901/jeab.1999.72-433

Hogarth, L., Balleine, B. W., Corbit, L. H., & Killcross, S. (2013). Associative learning mechanisms underpinning the transition from recreational drug use to addiction. *Annals of the New York Academy of Sciences, 1282*, 12–24. http://dx.doi.org/10.1111/j.1749-6632.2012.06768.x

Holmes, N. M., Marchand, A. R., & Coutureau, E. (2010). Pavlovian to instrumental transfer: A neurobehavioural perspective. *Neuroscience and Biobehavioral Reviews, 34*, 1277–1295. http://dx.doi.org/10.1016/j.neubiorev.2010.03.007

Neuringer, A. (2004). Reinforced variability in animals and people: Implications for adaptive action. *American Psychologist, 59*, 891–906. http://dx.doi.org/10.1037/0003-066X.59.9.891

Wood, W., & Neal, D. T. (2007). A new look at habits and the habit-goal interface. *Psychological Review, 114*, 843–863. http://dx.doi.org/10.1037/0033-295X.114.4.843

Technical Terms

Conditioned reinforcer
Constraints on learning
Discrete-trial method
Free-operant method
Instrumental behavior
Instrumental conditioning
Law of effect
Marking stimulus
Operant behavior
Operant conditioning
Puzzle box

R–O association
Rate of responding
Reinforcer
S–O association
S–R association
S(R–O) association
Secondary reinforcer
Shaping
Straight-alley runway
T-maze

Schedules of Reinforcement 8

Did you know that

- schedules of reinforcement determine rates and patterns of responding?
- ratio schedules produce higher rates of responding than interval schedules?
- interval schedules do not provide the reinforcer automatically after the passage of a particular time interval?
- schedule effects are related to the feedback function that characterizes each schedule of reinforcement?
- some schedules of reinforcement focus on choice and provide reinforcement for two (or more) response alternatives?
- the Matching Law describes choice behavior? According to the matching law, relative rates of responding equal relative rates of reinforcement.
- self-control is investigated using concurrent-chain schedules of reinforcement?
- the value of a reward declines as a function of how long you have to wait for it?

Examples of instrumental conditioning were described in Chapter 7 with the implication that the reinforcing outcome is delivered each time the required instrumental response occurs. Situations in nature in which there is a direct causal link between an instrumental response and a reinforcer

http://dx.doi.org/10.1037/0000057-008
The Essentials of Conditioning and Learning, Fourth Edition, by M. Domjan

come close to this ideal. Nearly every time you turn on the faucet, you get running water; most of the time you send a text message to a friend, it is delivered; and most of the time you buy an attractive piece of pastry, you end up with something tasty to eat. However, even in these cases, the relation between making the response and getting the reinforcer is not perfect. The water main to your house may break, the phone may malfunction, and the pastry may be stale. In many instrumental conditioning situations, not every occurrence of the instrumental response is successful in producing the reinforcer.

Whether a particular occurrence of the instrumental response results in the reinforcer can depend on a variety of factors. Sometimes the response has to be repeated a number of times before the reinforcer is delivered. In other situations, the response is only reinforced after a certain amount of time has passed. In yet other cases, both response repetition and the passage of time are critical. The rule that specifies which occurrence of the instrumental response is reinforced is called a *schedule of reinforcement*.

Schedules of reinforcement have been of great interest because they determine many aspects of instrumental behavior (Ferster & Skinner, 1957; Jozefowiez & Staddon, 2008). The rate and pattern of responding, as well as persistence in extinction, are all determined by the schedule of reinforcement. Seemingly trivial changes in a reinforcement schedule can produce profound changes in how frequently an organism responds and when it engages in one activity rather than another. Schedules of reinforcement also determine the persistence of instrumental behavior in extinction, when reinforcement is no longer available.

The Cumulative Record

The rate and pattern of responding produced by various schedules of reinforcement are typically investigated using free-operant procedures. Computers are programmed to record occurrences of the operant response (e.g., lever pressing in rats) as well as to determine which lever press is reinforced. Training sessions last about an hour each day, and typically numerous sessions are provided. After extensive experience with a particular schedule of reinforcement, the rate and pattern of responding stabilize. The results are conveniently represented in terms of a *cumulative record*.

A cumulative record is a special kind of graph in which the horizontal axis represents the passage of time and the vertical axis represents the total or cumulative number of responses that have occurred up to a particular point in time (see Figure 8.1). If the participant does not respond for a while, its total or cumulative number of responses stays the same, and the resultant line on the cumulative record is flat, as between Points A and B in Figure 8.1. Each response is added to the previous total. Thus, each time the participant responds, the cumulative record goes up a bit. Because responses cannot be taken away, the cumulative record never goes down.

The slope of the cumulative record has special significance. Slope is calculated by dividing the vertical displacement between two points on a graph by the horizontal displacement between those two points. Vertical displacement on a cumulative

FIGURE 8.1

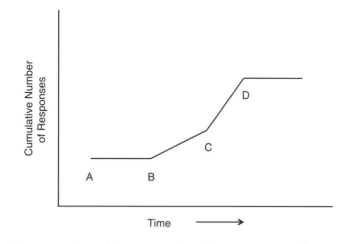

Cumulative record used to represent patterns of responding over time. There is no responding between points A and B. A low rate of responding occurs between points B and C. A higher response rate occurs from points C and D, and responding ceases after point D.

record reflects number of responses, and horizontal displacement reflects time. Thus, the slope of a cumulative record represents responses per unit of time, or the *response rate*. Low rates of responding produce a shallow slope on the cumulative record (e.g., from Point B to Point C in Figure 8.1). Higher response rates result in a steeper slope (e.g., from Point C to Point D in Figure 8.1).

Simple Schedules of Reinforcement

In simple schedules of reinforcement, which occurrence of the response is reinforced depends either on the number of repetitions of the response since the last reinforcer or on how much time has passed since the last reinforcer. If the number of repetitions of the response is the critical factor determining reinforcement, the procedure is called a *ratio schedule*. If the timing of the response since the last reinforcer is the critical factor, the procedure is called an *interval schedule*. In either case, the participant does not receive the reinforcer unless it responds.

RATIO SCHEDULES

In ratio schedules, the only thing that determines whether a response is reinforced is the number of repetitions of the response the participant has performed since the last reinforcer. How much time the participant takes to make those responses does not matter. There are two basic versions of ratio schedules, fixed and variable.

In a *fixed-ratio schedule*, the participant must repeat the response a fixed number of times for each delivery of the reinforcer. For example, each work sheet in a third-grade math class may have four problems on it, and students may receive a star for each work sheet they complete. This would be a fixed-ratio-4 schedule of reinforcement, abbreviated as FR 4.

Fixed-ratio schedules occur in situations in which there is always a fixed amount of effort required to complete a job or obtain the reinforcer. Checking attendance in a class by reading the roll requires reading the same number of names each time. Calling someone on the phone requires putting the same number of digits into the phone each time. Walking up a flight of stairs requires going up the same number of stairs each time. All of these are examples of fixed-ratio schedules.

The left side of Figure 8.2 illustrates the stable pattern of responding that results from reinforcing behavior on a fixed ratio schedule of reinforcement. The hatch marks in the records represent the delivery of the reinforcer. Two features of the FR response pattern are noteworthy. First, notice that after each hatch mark or reinforcer, the response rate is zero. The participant stops responding. This is called the *postreinforcement pause*. After the postreinforcement pause, a steady and high rate of responding occurs until the next delivery of the reinforcer. This is called the *ratio run*.

As illustrated in Figure 8.2, fixed-ratio schedules produce a break-run pattern of responding. Either the participant does not respond at all (in the postreinforcement pause), or it responds at a steady and high rate (in the ratio run). The duration of the postreinforcement pause is determined by the ratio requirement. Higher ratio

FIGURE 8.2

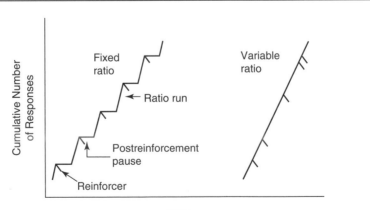

Typical results of training on a fixed-ratio and variable ratio schedule of reinforcement. The data were obtained with pigeons pecking a response key on an fixed ratio (FR) 120 and variable ratio (VR) 360 schedule of food reinforcement. The hatch marks indicate when the reinforcer was delivered. Data from Ferster and Skinner (1957).

requirements result in longer postreinforcement pauses (D. C. Williams, Saunders, & Perone, 2011).

A *variable-ratio schedule* is similar to a fixed-ratio schedule in that the only requirement for reinforcement is making a certain number of responses, irrespective of how long it takes to do that. The difference between fixed- and variable-ratio schedules is that in a variable-ratio schedule, the number of responses required varies from one reinforcer delivery to the next.

When putting in golf, for example, reinforcement is provided by the ball going into the cup. On occasion, you may get the ball into the cup on the first try. More often, you will have to hit the ball several times before you succeed. Whether the ball goes into the cup depends only on your hitting the ball with the putter. How long you take between swings is irrelevant. This, then, is a ratio schedule. But the number of putting responses required varies from one putting green to another, making it a variable-ratio schedule.

A variable-ratio schedule is abbreviated as VR. If on average you need to hit the ball three times to get it into the cup, you would be on a VR 3 schedule of reinforcement. The typical result of a variable-ratio schedule is illustrated in the right panel of Figure 8.2. Unlike fixed-ratio schedules, variable-ratio schedules produce a steady and high rate of responding, without predictable pauses (Crossman, Bonem, & Phelps, 1987).

INTERVAL SCHEDULES

Unlike ratio schedules, where the passage of time is irrelevant, in interval schedules, time is a critical factor. Specifically, whether a response is reinforced depends on when the response occurs after the start of the interval cycle. As with ratio schedules, there are two prominent types of interval schedules, fixed and variable.

In a *fixed-interval schedule*, a fixed amount of time has to pass before a response can be reinforced. Fixed-interval schedules occur in situations in which it takes a certain amount of time for the reinforcer to be prepared or set up. Consider, for example, making a gelatin dessert (e.g., Jell-O). After the ingredients are mixed, the Jell-O has to be cooled in the refrigerator for a certain amount of time before it is ready to eat. In this example, the instrumental response is taking the Jell-O out of the refrigerator to eat. If you take the Jell-O out too early, it will be watery and your response will not be reinforced. Attempts to eat the Jell-O before it solidifies will not be reinforced. Another important feature of this example (and of interval schedules generally) is that once the reinforcer is ready, it remains available until the individual responds to obtain it. When the Jell-O is done, you don't have to eat it right away. It will be there for you even if you wait to eat it the next day.

In a fixed-interval schedule of reinforcement, a fixed amount of time has to pass before the reinforcer becomes available. However, the reinforcer is not provided automatically at the end of the fixed interval. To obtain the reinforcer, the specified instrumental response has to be made. Early responses have no consequence. They do not make the reinforcer ready sooner, nor do they result in a penalty. Finally, the reinforcer can be obtained at any time after it has been set up. In a simple interval schedule, the participant does not have to respond within a set period once the reinforcer has become available.

Fixed-interval schedules are abbreviated FI, followed by a number indicating the duration of the fixed interval during which responding is not reinforced. Figure 8.3 shows data obtained from a pigeon pecking a response key on a free-operant FI 4-minute schedule of food reinforcement. On this schedule, delivery of the reinforcer at the end of one fixed interval starts the next cycle. Four minutes after the start of the cycle, the reinforcer becomes available again and is delivered if the pigeon pecks the response key.

The pattern of responding on a fixed-interval schedule is similar to what occurs on a fixed-ratio schedule. There is little or no responding at the beginning of the fixed interval. Because the interval begins just after delivery of the previous reinforcer, the lack of responding here is called a postreinforcement pause. Responding increases as the end of the interval gets closer, with the participant responding at a high rate just as the fixed interval ends. Efficient responding on a fixed interval schedule requires accuracy in time perception. For that reason, fixed interval schedules are frequently used to study the cognitive mechanisms involved in timing (Balci et al., 2009).

Variable-interval schedules are similar to fixed-interval schedules except that the amount of time it takes to set up the reinforcer varies from trial to trial. The response of checking to see whether a teacher has finished grading your paper is reinforced on a variable-interval schedule. It takes some time to grade a paper, but how long it takes varies from one occasion to the next. Checking to see whether your paper has been graded is reinforced only after some time has passed since the start of the schedule

FIGURE 8.3

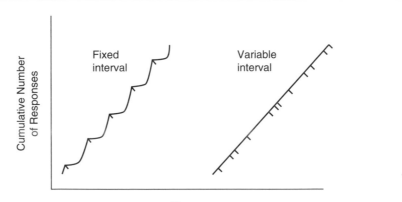

Typical results of training on a fixed-interval (FI) and variable-interval (VI) schedule of reinforcement. The data were obtained with pigeons pecking a response key on an FI 4-minute and VI 2-minute schedule of food reinforcement. The hatch marks indicate when the reinforcer was delivered. Data from Ferster and Skinner (1957).

cycle. Early responses (checking before the paper has been graded) are not reinforced. In contrast, you can get your grade any time after the paper has been graded.

Variable-interval schedules are abbreviated VI, followed by a number indicating the average duration of the intervals during which responding is not reinforced. Figure 8.3 shows data obtained from a pigeon pecking a response key on a free-operant VI 2-minute schedule of food reinforcement. On this schedule, the reinforcer became available on average 2 minutes after the start of each schedule cycle.

Responding on variable-interval schedules is similar to responding on VR schedules of reinforcement. In both cases, a steady rate of behavior occurs, with no predictable pauses or changes in rate. However, interval schedules tend to produce lower rates of responding than ratio schedules.

In simple interval schedules, once the reinforcer has become available, it remains there until the individual responds and obtains it. The cycle then starts over again. Checking on your text messages, for example, is on a variable-interval schedule. Messages arrive at unpredictable times. Checking to see whether you have any new messages does not get you a message sooner or produce more messages. In addition, once a message has been delivered, you don't have to read it right away. It will remain available even if you wait several hours to read it.

Simple interval schedules can be modified so that once the reinforcer has been set up, it remains available only for a limited period of time. This limited interval is formally called a *limited hold*. For example, it takes a certain amount of time to bake a sheet of cookies. Once the required time has passed, however, if you don't take the cookies out of the oven, they will burn. Thus, baking is on a fixed interval schedule with a limited hold. The reinforcer is "held" for a limited period of time after it becomes available, and the response must occur during this hold period to be reinforced. Adding a limited hold to an interval schedule increases the rate of responding, provided the hold is not so short that the participant frequently misses the reinforcer altogether.

Mechanisms of Schedule Performance

A key concept involved in analyses of the mechanisms of schedule effects is the *feedback function* that characterizes the schedule. Delivery of a reinforcer in an instrumental procedure can be viewed as feedback for the instrumental response. Schedules of reinforcement determine how this feedback is arranged. One way to describe the arrangement is to show how the rate of reinforcement obtained is related to the rate of responding. This relationship is the feedback function.

FEEDBACK FUNCTIONS FOR RATIO SCHEDULES

Feedback functions for ratio schedules are perhaps the easiest to understand. In a ratio schedule, how soon (and how often) the organism gets reinforced is determined only by how rapidly the required number of responses is performed. The faster the individual completes the ratio requirement, the faster it obtains the reinforcer.

Figure 8.4 shows examples of feedback functions for several ratio schedules. On an FR 1 or continuous-reinforcement schedule, the participant is reinforced for each occurrence of the instrumental response. Therefore, the rate of reinforcement is equal to the rate of responding. This results in a feedback function with a slope of 1.0.

If more than one response is required for reinforcement, the rate of reinforcement will be less than the rate of responding, and the slope of the feedback function will be less than 1.0. For example, on an FR 5 schedule of reinforcement, the participant receives one reinforcer for every fifth response. Under these circumstances, the rate of reinforcement is one fifth the rate of responding, and the slope of the feedback function is 0.2. Regardless of its slope, the feedback function for a ratio schedule is always a straight line. For this reason, an increase in the rate of responding always yields an increase in the rate of reinforcement. This is true for both fixed- and variable-ratio schedules.

FEEDBACK FUNCTIONS FOR INTERVAL SCHEDULES

Interval schedules have feedback functions that differ markedly from those of ratio schedules. Figure 8.5 shows the feedback function for a VI 3-minute schedule of reinforcement. On such a schedule, the reinforcer becomes available on average

FIGURE 8.4

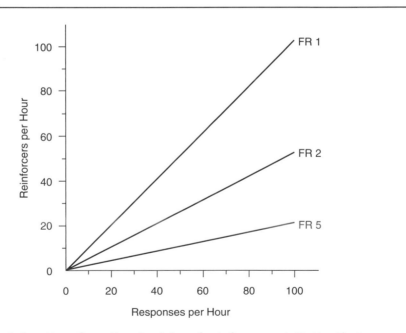

Feedback functions for ratio schedules of reinforcement. Notice that each feedback function is a straight line. Because of that, every increase in the response rate results in a corresponding increase in the rate of reinforcement. FR = fixed ratio.

FIGURE 8.5

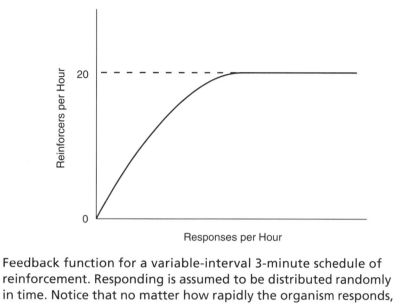

Feedback function for a variable-interval 3-minute schedule of reinforcement. Responding is assumed to be distributed randomly in time. Notice that no matter how rapidly the organism responds, its maximum reinforcement rate is 20 per hour.

3 minutes after the last time it was delivered. Therefore, no matter how often or how rapidly the organism responds, the maximum number of reinforcers it can obtain is limited to 20 per hour.

As with ratio schedules, if the participant does not make any responses on an interval schedule, it will not obtain any reinforcers. Increases in the rate of responding above zero will increase its chances of getting whatever reinforcers become available. Up to a point, therefore, increased responding is accompanied by higher rates of reinforcement. However, once the participant responds often enough to get all of the 20 reinforcers that can be obtained each hour, any further increase in response rate will have no further benefit. Thus, the feedback function for an interval schedule becomes flat once the maximum possible reinforcement rate has been achieved.

FEEDBACK FUNCTIONS AND SCHEDULE PERFORMANCE

One of the striking facts about instrumental behavior is that ratio schedules produce considerably higher rates of responding than interval schedules, even if the rate of reinforcement is comparable in the two cases (Raia, Shillingford, Miller, & Baier, 2000; Reynolds, 1975). Why ratio schedules produce higher response rates than interval schedules is related to differences in their respective feedback functions. Because the feedback function for an interval schedule reaches a maximum with a particular rate of responding, increases in the response rate beyond that point provide no additional benefit. Thus, increases in response rate are not differentially reinforced beyond a particular point on interval schedules. In contrast, no such limit exists with ratio schedules. On ratio schedules, increases in response rate always result in higher rates of reinforcement. There is no limit to the differential reinforcement of higher rates of responding. Thus, ratio schedules may produce higher rates of responding because such schedules differentially reinforce high response rates without limit.

Although feedback functions have played an important role in efforts to explain schedule performance, they have some conceptual limitations. One serious problem is that feedback functions are sometimes difficult to characterize. This is particularly true for interval-based schedules. In interval schedules, reinforcement depends not only on the rate of responding but also on how the responses are distributed in time. The feedback function for a VI 3-minute schedule presented in Figure 8.5 assumes that responses are distributed randomly in time. Other assumptions may alter the initial increasing portion of the feedback function. Despite such complications, however, investigators have found it useful to think about schedule performance as ultimately determined by how schedules of reinforcement provide feedback for instrumental behavior.

Concurrent Schedules

In each of the schedules of reinforcement considered so far, the participant could either perform the specified instrumental response or not. Only one response manipulandum was provided (a lever or a pecking key), and only responses on that manipulandum were measured and recorded. Because the procedures did not provide different response alternatives, they do not seem to involve a choice. Interestingly, however, all instrumental conditioning situations involve a choice. With simple schedules, the choice is to perform the response specified by the reinforcement schedule or to do something else that is not a part of the experiment.

Investigators have become convinced that a complete understanding of instrumental behavior requires understanding why organisms choose to engage in one response rather than another. Unfortunately, simple schedules of reinforcement are not good for analyzing the mechanisms of choice. In simple schedules, the alternative to the instrumental response, the "something else" the individual might do, is poorly specified and not measured. These shortcomings are remedied in concurrent schedules. Concurrent schedules of reinforcement provide clearly defined and measured alternative responses. Therefore, concurrent schedules are more appropriate for studying how organisms elect to engage in one activity rather than another.

As you might suspect, whether you do one thing or another depends on the benefits you derive from each activity. In the terminology of conditioning, how often you engage in activity A compared with activity B will depend on the schedule of reinforcement that is in effect for response A, compared with the schedule of reinforcement in effect for response B. On a playground, Joe could play with Peter, who likes to play vigorous physical games, or Joe could play with Matt, who prefers to play quietly in the sandbox. If Joe is not getting much enjoyment from playing with Peter, he can go play with Matt. Concurrent schedules are used to model this type of choice situation in the laboratory.

In a concurrent schedule, at least two response alternatives, A and B, are available (see Figure 8.6). Responding on alternative A is reinforced on one schedule of reinforcement (e.g., VI 5-minute), whereas responding on B is reinforced on a different schedule (e.g., VR 15). Both response alternatives (and their corresponding reinforcement schedules) are available at the same time, and the participant can switch from one activity to the other at any time. Because the two choices are available at the same time, the procedure is called a *concurrent schedule*.

Numerous factors determine how organisms distribute their behavior between two response alternatives. These include the effort required to make each response, the effort and time involved in switching from one response to the other, the attractiveness of the reinforcer provided for each response, and the schedule of reinforcement in effect for each response. Experiments have to be designed carefully so that the effects of these various factors can be studied without being confounded with other features of the choice situation.

Laboratory studies of concurrent schedules are often carried out with pigeons. One wall of the experimental chamber has two response keys positioned at about the height of the bird's head. A feeder from which the bird can obtain grain is centered below the two keys. This arrangement has the advantage that the two responses require the same effort. Although pecks on the right and left keys are reinforced on different schedules, the reinforcer in each case is the same type of food. Another advantage is that the pigeon can easily switch from one response to the other because the two response keys are located near each other.

If similar effort is required for the response alternatives, if the same reinforcer is used for both responses, and if switching from one side to the other is fairly easy, the

FIGURE 8.6

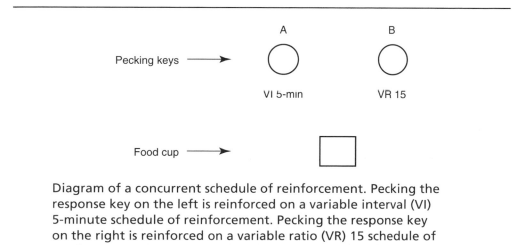

Diagram of a concurrent schedule of reinforcement. Pecking the response key on the left is reinforced on a variable interval (VI) 5-minute schedule of reinforcement. Pecking the response key on the right is reinforced on a variable ratio (VR) 15 schedule of reinforcement. The two alternatives are always available.

distribution of responses between the two alternatives will depend only on the schedule of reinforcement in effect for each response. Research has shown that choices made under these circumstances are well characterized by the *matching law*, which was originally identified by Herrnstein (1970). According to the matching law, *the relative rate of responding on a response alternative is equal to the relative rate of reinforcement obtained with that response alternative.* For example, if 70% of the responses are made on the left side of a two-key chamber, 70% of all reinforcers will be earned on the left side. (For reviews of the matching law, see Dallery & Soto, 2013; Grace & Hucks, 2013.)

In a concurrent choice situation, organisms tend to match relative rates of responding to relative rates of reinforcement. Departures from matching occur if the response alternatives require different degrees of effort, if different reinforcers are used for each response alternative, or if switching from one response to the other is made more difficult. The effects of these factors have been incorporated into what has come to be known as the *generalized matching law* (W. M. Baum, 1974).

The matching law has made a major contribution to our understanding of how behavior is controlled by schedules of reinforcement. The matching law has shown us that how individuals react when a schedule of reinforcement is set up for one response depends on the alternate activities that are available and the schedules of reinforcement that are in effect with those alternative activities. This basic conclusion has profound implications for applications of instrumental conditioning (E. A. Jacobs, Borrero, & Vollmer, 2013). Teachers usually focus on a particular response that they are trying to teach (e.g., completing math problems). However, they quickly discover that effort spent on this response depends on the availability of alternative responses and alternative sources of reinforcement. If students are allowed to play games on their cell phones, they are much less likely to work on math problems.

Concurrent-Chain Schedules and Self Control

In a concurrent schedule, the various response alternatives are available at the same time. This allows the participant to switch back and forth between alternatives at any time and with relative ease. Many situations are like that. You can easily go back and forth among entertainment programs that you watch on television. You may also have a variety of options about what to do for entertainment on the weekend. You can go to a concert, go to a ball game, or go to dinner with friends. However, in this case, once you have purchased your tickets and entered the concert venue, the other alternatives are no longer available. The basic features of such choice situations are captured in the laboratory by the design of a *concurrent-chain schedule* of reinforcement. In a concurrent-chain schedule, once you choose a particular course of action, other possible activities become unavailable.

A concurrent-chain schedule has two stages or links. Each trial begins with the choice link, during which the various choice alternatives are available. Once a selection is made during the choice link, the procedure moves to the terminal link, which only has the alternative the participant selected. The participant remains in the terminal link for the remainder of the trial. Thus, the current-chain schedule involves choice with commitment.

Concurrent-chain schedules can be used to investigate whether variability in outcomes is preferred over predictability—whether variety is in fact the spice of life. Figure 8.7 outlines a procedure to study this question in pigeons. The birds have access to two pecking keys. Pecking on one is reinforced on a VI 3-min schedule of reinforcement, whereas pecking on the other key is reinforced on an FI 3-min schedule. The FI schedule is highly predictable, whereas the VI schedule is not, but the overall rate of reinforcement is the same for the two alternatives. The choice link provides access to each alternative, but once the participant has made its selection, it is "stuck" with that alternative until the rest of the trial. Investigation of concurrent-chain procedures of this sort have indicated a preference for the variable schedule alternative (Andrzejewski et al., 2005).

Concurrent-chain schedules are also frequently used to study self-control. Self-control is involved when you have a choice between one alternative that provides a small reward quickly versus a choice that provides a larger reward but with a considerable delay. Do you opt to have a piece of cake that provides immediate gratification or forgo the dessert in favor of a healthier lifestyle whose benefits are much more delayed? Do you give in to the temptation of going out with friends in the evening or stay at home to study for an upcoming test, which will enable you to succeed in school and get a better job in a year or two? Do spend your hard-earned dollars on interesting video games that you can enjoy right away or put that money away to build your savings so you can buy a car next year? We encounter such self-control choices frequently in our daily lives.

Self-control is modeled in behavioral laboratories using a concurrent-chain schedule. During the choice link, we have the option of choosing to spend the evening with friends or stay at home to study. Once we have elected one or the other of these

FIGURE 8.7

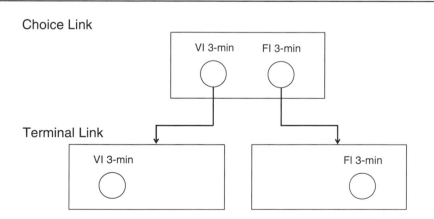

Diagram of a concurrent chain schedule of reinforcement. During the Choice Link, the participant can select either the variable interval (VI) 3-minute or the fixed interval (FI) 3-minute schedule. Choosing an alternative moves the participant into the Terminal Link in which only the chosen alternative is available.

alternatives, we move to the terminal link in which we experience either the small immediate reward or the delayed large reward. Experimental studies have confirmed what we all know: It is more tempting to go for the smaller, immediate reward than to wait for the large delayed reward. Why is that?

Central to explanations of self-control in the context of schedules of reinforcement is the concept that the longer you have to wait for a reinforcer, the less valuable it is. The discounting of reward value by waiting time is called the *delay discounting function* (Vanderveldt, Oliveira, & Green, 2016). In laboratory studies of the delay discounting function with human participants, individuals are asked to choose between hypothetical amounts of money. Would you prefer $5 now or $5 tomorrow? For most people, this is an easy decision: Obviously they would prefer to get the $5 now rather than tomorrow. This indicates that the value of $5 is reduced by having to wait a day to get the money. Because delaying a reward reduces its value, people tend to select small immediate rewards over larger delayed rewards.

Not everyone discounts the value of future rewards to the same degree (Odum & Baumann, 2010). Steeper delay discounting functions indicate greater perceived loss of reward value as a function of waiting time. Individuals with steep delay discounting functions tend to show less self-control. This relationship has been of particular interest in studies of drug abuse and drug addiction (Bickel, Koffarnus, Moody, & Wilson, 2014). The choice to consume a recreational drug is a self-control problem. Do you take the drug and enjoy its immediate effects or select another activity (studying, investing in personal relationships, developing skill in sports or music) whose benefits are more delayed? Drug addicts choose the drug, and serious addicts make this choice even if it costs them their job, marriage, and physical health.

Studies have shown that drug addicts have steeper delay discounting functions than nonaddicts, even after they have given up their drug of choice (MacKillop et al., 2011; Yi, Mitchell, & Bickel, 2010). Addicts are driven by what is reinforcing right now rather than what they can do that will improve their lives in the future. One may suggest that the inability to see the value of future rewards is a consequence of drug addiction. However, experimental research with laboratory animals has shown that the steepness of an individual's delay discounting function is predictive of the propensity to develop drug addiction (Carroll, Anker, Mach, Newman, & Perry, 2010). In a remarkable longitudinal study of children in New Zealand, the degree of self-control evident before 10 years of age was predictive of better health, higher income levels, lower rates of drug use, and lower rates of criminal behavior more than 2 decades later (Moffitt et al., 2011).

Summary

Schedules of reinforcement are of interest because, in many cases, responding does not produce a reinforcer every time. A response may be reinforced after a fixed or variable number of responses have occurred (FR and VR schedules) or after a fixed or variable amount of time has passed since the last reinforcer (FI and VI schedules). Fixed interval and ratio schedules produce rapid responding just before delivery of the reinforcer and a pause just after reinforcement. Variable interval and ratio schedules produce steady response rates. In general, ratio schedules produce higher rates of responding than interval schedules. This difference is related to the contrasting feedback functions for the two types of schedules.

Reinforcement schedules can also involve a choice between two or more activities, each associated with its own schedule of reinforcement. In a concurrent schedule, two (or more) response alternatives are available at the same, and the participant has the opportunity to switch between response alternatives at any time. Responding on concurrent schedules is characterized by the matching law. A concurrent-chain schedule also provides two response alternatives, but in this case, once one of responses is selected, the other alternative is no longer available. Concurrent-chain schedules are used to study self-control. Self-control is determined by how rapidly the value of a reinforcer is discounted by how long you have to wait for it, which is called the delay discounting function.

Suggested Readings

Cole, M. R. (1999). Molar and molecular control in variable-interval and variable-ratio schedules. *Journal of the Experimental Analysis of Behavior, 71*, 319–328. http://dx.doi.org/10.1901/jeab.1999.71-319

Dallery, J., & Soto, P. L. (2013). Quantitative description of environment–behavior relations. In G. J. Madden (Ed.), *APA handbook of behavior analysis: Vol. 1. Methods and principles* (pp. 219–250). Washington, DC: American Psychological Association.

Jozefowiez, J., & Staddon, J. E. R. (2008). Operant behavior. In J. H. Byrne (Ed.), *Learning and memory: A comprehensive reference: Vol. 1. Learning theory and behavior* (pp. 75–102). Oxford, England: Elsevier.

Vandervelt, A., Oliveira, L., & Green, L. (2016). Delay discounting: Pigeon, rat, human—Does it matter? *Journal of Experimental Psychology: Animal Learning and Cognition, 42*, 141–162. http://dx.doi.org/10.1037/xan0000097

Technical Terms

Concurrent-chain schedule

Concurrent schedule

Cumulative record

Delay discounting function

Feedback function

Fixed-interval schedule

Fixed-ratio schedule

Interval schedule

Matching law

Postreinforcement pause

Ratio run

Ratio schedule

Schedule of reinforcement

Self-control

Variable-interval schedule

Variable-ratio schedule

Theories of Reinforcement 9

Did you know that

- reinforcers need not reduce a biological drive or need?
- responses, as well as stimuli, can serve as reinforcers?
- according to contemporary perspectives, reinforcement does not "strengthen" the instrumental response?
- instrumental conditioning procedures not only increase the rate of the instrumental response; they also decrease the rate of the reinforcer response?
- instrumental conditioning procedures restrict how an organism distributes its behavior among its response alternatives?
- reinforcement effects are a by-product of the new response choices an organism makes when its activities are constrained by an instrumental conditioning procedure?
- the effect of an instrumental conditioning procedure depends on all of the activities of a participant and how these activities are organized? An important factor is the availability of substitutes for the reinforcer activity.
- behavioral economics developed from efforts to use economic concepts to better understand how instrumental conditioning procedures cause a redistribution of behavior among possible response options?

http://dx.doi.org/10.1037/0000057-009
The Essentials of Conditioning and Learning, Fourth Edition, by M. Domjan

n Chapter 8, I discussed various types of instrumental conditioning procedures and their behavioral outcomes. There is no doubt that reinforcement procedures can produce dramatic changes in behavior, and these changes are much more complex than just an increase in the probability of a response. Different schedules of reinforcement produce different patterns of response runs and pauses and also determine choices among response alternatives. The issue I turn to next is how reinforcement causes these effects. That question is addressed by a discussion of theories of reinforcement.

All good theories have to be consistent with the findings they are intended to explain. In addition, good theories should stimulate new research that serves to evaluate and increase the precision of the theory. Good theories also provide new insights and ways of thinking about familiar phenomena.

The story of the development of theories of reinforcement is a marvelous example of creativity in science. The story is peppered with examples of small refinements in thinking that brought a particular theory in line with new data. The story also includes dramatic new departures and new ways of thinking about reinforcement. And there are interesting cases in which incremental changes in thinking culminated in major new perspectives on the problem.

A theory of reinforcement must answer two questions about instrumental conditioning. First, it has to tell us what makes something a reinforcer or how can we predict whether something will be an effective reinforcer. Second, a good theory has to tell us how a reinforcer produces its effects. It has to tell us what are the mechanisms responsible for an increase in the probability of the reinforced response.

Thorndike and the Law of Effect

The first systematic theory of reinforcement was provided by Thorndike soon after his discovery of instrumental conditioning (Bower & Hilgard, 1981). According to Thorndike, a positive reinforcer is a stimulus that produces a "satisfying state of affairs." However, Thorndike did not go on to tell us why something was "satisfying." Therefore, his answer to our first question—"What makes something effective as a reinforcer?"—was not very illuminating.

One can determine whether a stimulus, such as a pat on the head for a dog, is a "satisfier" by seeing whether the dog increases a response that results in getting petted. However, such evidence does not reveal why a pat on the head is a reinforcer. By calling reinforcers "satisfiers," Thorndike provided a label for reinforcers, but he did not give us an explanation for what makes something effective as a reinforcer.

Thorndike was somewhat more forthcoming on the second question—"How does a reinforcer produce an increase in the probability of the reinforced response?" His answer was provided in the *law of effect*. As I noted in Chapter 7, according to the law of effect, a reinforcer establishes an association or connection between the instrumental response R and the stimuli S in the presence of which the response is reinforced. The reinforcer produces an S–R association (see Figure 9.1).

The law of effect explains how reinforcement increases the future probability of the instrumental response. Because of the S–R association that is established by

FIGURE 9.1

Diagram of Thorndike's law of effect. The reinforcer or response outcome O acts backward to strengthen the S–R (stimulus–response) association.

reinforcement, stimulus S comes to evoke the instrumental response R, in much the same way that an elicited response is produced by its eliciting stimulus. The basic mechanism of the law of effect was considered a reasonable explanation for increased instrumental responding and accepted by major behavioral theorists during the next 50 years. This widespread acceptance is remarkable because the mechanisms of the law were not spelled out in much detail.

Although the law of effect predicts increased instrumental responding in the training environment, it does so through a bit of magic rather than a well-established process. Thorndike did not say much about how a reinforcer can act retroactively to strengthen an association between the response and the stimuli in the presence of which the response was made. That part of the law of effect had to be taken on faith. Furthermore, despite the widespread acceptance of the law of effect during the next 50 years, no one has filled the gap left by Thorndike. The mechanism through which a reinforcer acts backward in time to strengthen an S–R association remains to be specified.

Hull and Drive Reduction Theory

The next major theorist we will consider is Clark Hull (see Amsel & Rashotte, 1984, for a review of Hullian theory). Hull accepted the S–R mechanism of the law of effect and concentrated on the question that Thorndike had pretty much ignored—namely, "What makes something effective as a reinforcer?" To answer this question, Hull made use of the concept of *homeostasis*, which had been developed to explain the operation of physiological systems.

According to the homeostatic model, organisms defend a stable state with respect to critical biologically functions. Consider, for example, food intake (see Figure 9.2). To survive, organisms must maintain a stable or optimal supply of nutrients. Food deprivation challenges to the nutritional state of the organism and creates a need for food. The psychological consequence of this is the motivational or *drive state* of hunger, which can be reduced by the ingestion of food. According to Hull, food is an effective reinforcer because it reduces the hunger drive. More generally, Hull proposed that what makes a stimulus reinforcing is its effectiveness in reducing a drive state. Hence, his theory is called the *drive reduction theory* of reinforcement.

FIGURE 9.2

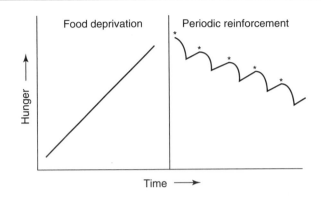

Illustration of the mechanisms of drive reduction reinforcement using hunger as an example. Deliveries of the food reinforcer are indicated by asterisks.

PRIMARY REINFORCERS

Common laboratory examples of instrumental reinforcement are consistent with Hull's drive reduction theory. Mild food deprivation is routinely used to make food an effective reinforcer for laboratory animals in experimental situations. Similarly, mild water deprivation makes water an effective reinforcer. Rats will press a response lever to obtain heat when they are in a cold environment. Conversely, they will lever-press to obtain cold air in a hot environment. Deprivation procedures and other circumstances that challenge a biological homeostatic system create drive states, and stimuli that reduce these drive states are effective reinforcers for instrumental behavior.

Hull's drive reduction theory provides a successful account of reinforcers such as food and water. Stimuli that are effective in reducing a biological need without prior training are called *primary reinforcers*. However, if Hull's theory could only characterize reinforcers that reduce primary biological drives, it would be rather limited. Many effective reinforcers do not satisfy a biological drive or need. You may find the smell of Italian food reinforcing, but the smell of food does not reduce hunger. Likewise, a $20 bill does not reduce a biological drive or need, but it is a highly effective reinforcer.

SECONDARY REINFORCERS AND ACQUIRED DRIVES

Hull's theory has been successfully extended to stimuli such as the smell of food by adding the principle of Pavlovian conditioning. As one repeatedly eats a savory food, the smell of that food becomes associated with the reduction of hunger through Pavlovian conditioning. This makes the food's aroma a *conditioned reinforcer* or *secondary reinforcer*. The concept of conditioned reinforcement increase the scope of Hull's theory to stimuli that do not reduce a drive state directly but gain their reinforcing properties through association with a primary reinforcer.

Another extension of Hull's theory beyond primary biological drives involved the concept of a conditioned drive state. Stimuli that become associated with a primary drive state are assumed to elicit a *conditioned drive* or *acquired drive*. Reduction of a conditioned or acquired drive is assumed to be reinforcing in the same manner as the reduction of a primary or biological drive state.

The concept of conditioned or acquired drive has been used extensively in the analysis of aversively motivated behavior. You can lose your balance and fall on a moving escalator. If the fall is severe enough, you may become afraid of escalators. Such conditioned fear is an example of a conditioned or acquired drive. According to Hull's drive reduction theory, a reduction in the intensity of the acquired drive will be reinforcing. Therefore, any response that enables you to escape from the conditioned fear of escalators will be reinforced. Walking away from the escalator and using an elevator will be reinforced by reduction of the conditioned fear elicited by the escalator. (I have more to say about these mechanisms when I discuss avoidance behavior in Chapter 12.)

The concept of conditioned or acquired drive is also critical in the analysis of drug addiction. Drug-associated cues elicit incentive motivation to engage in behaviors associated with the procurement and consumption of a drug such as alcohol or cocaine (Anselme & Robinson, 2016). I previously discussed such incentive motivation in Chapter 7. Incentive motivation elicited by drug-associated cues has its roots in Hull's concept of acquired drives.

SENSORY REINFORCEMENT

Although Hull's theory was successfully extended to situations that do not involve primary biological drives, the theory could not explain all instances of reinforcement. For example, investigators have found that rats kept in the dark will press a response lever to turn on a light, and rats kept in an illuminated chamber will press a response lever to produce periods of darkness. Chimpanzees will perform instrumental responses that are reinforced by nothing more than the opportunity to watch an electric toy train move around a track. These are all examples of *sensory reinforcement*. In many situations, sensory stimulation with no apparent relation to a biological need or drive state can serve as an effective reinforcer (see Berlyne, 1969). Music, beautiful paintings, and other works of art are examples of sensory reinforcers for human beings.

The growing weight of evidence for sensory reinforcement, along with the success of alternative conceptualizations of reinforcement, led to the abandonment of Hull's drive reduction theory. As we shall see, the theories that emerged were highly creative and involved radical new ways of thinking about the issues of instrumental reinforcement.

The Premack Principle

The modern era in reinforcement theory was ushered in by the work of David Premack, who approached reinforcement from an entirely different perspective. Like Hull, Premack considered basic questions such as why food is an effective reinforcer for rats pressing a response lever. However, instead of thinking of the reinforcer as a pellet of food, he thought of the reinforcer as the act of eating the food. For Premack, the question was not what makes food a reinforcing stimulus but what makes eating a reinforcing activity. Premack framed the issues of reinforcement in terms of responses, not in terms of stimuli or nutritional substances (Premack, 1965).

What makes eating different from pressing a response lever in a standard Skinner box? Many answers are possible. The rat has to learn to press the lever, but it does not have to learn to eat. Eating can occur not just in the Skinner box but anywhere the rat finds food. Eating involves a special set of muscles and activates digestive processes. Another difference between eating and pressing a lever is that a food-deprived rat in a Skinner box is much more likely to eat than to press the lever if it is given free access to both activities. Premack focused on this last difference and elevated it to a general principle.

According to Premack, the critical precondition for reinforcement is not a drive state or incentive motivation. Rather, it is the existence of two responses that differ in their likelihood when the organism is given free access to both activities. Given two such responses, Premack proposed that the opportunity to perform the higher probability response will serve as a reinforcer for the lower probability response. This general claim became to be known as *Premack's principle*. A more descriptive name for it is the *differential probability principle*.

According to the differential probability principle, the specific nature of the instrumental and reinforcer responses does not matter. Neither of them has to involve eating or drinking, and the organism need not be hungry or thirsty. The only requirement is that one response be more likely than the other. Given such a differential response probability, the more likely response will serve as a reinforcer for the less likely response.

THE PREMACK REVOLUTION

Premack's principle took the scientific community by storm. For the first time, scientists started thinking seriously about reinforcers as responses rather than as special stimuli. Premack was unconcerned with how one response might have come to be more likely than another. The only thing that mattered was that the reinforcer response be more likely than the instrumental response. Premack's principle liberated psychologists from the grip of stimulus views of reinforcement and views of reinforcement rooted in biological needs and drives. Moreover, Premack's principle provided a convenient tool for the application of instrumental conditioning procedures in a variety of educational settings, including homes, classrooms, psychiatric hospitals, mental retardation centers, and correctional institutions (Danaher, 1974).

APPLICATIONS OF THE PREMACK PRINCIPLE

In all educational settings, students are encouraged to learn and perform new responses. The goal is to get the students to do things that they did not do before and things they would not do without special encouragement or training. In other words, the goal is to increase the likelihood of low-probability responses. Instrumental conditioning procedures are ideally suited to accomplish this. But the teacher first has to find an effective reinforcer. Withholding a student's lunch so that food may be used as a reinforcer is not socially acceptable and would create a great deal of resentment. Candy and other edible treats are effective reinforcers for young children without food deprivation but are not good for them nutritionally.

Premack's principle provides a way out of this dilemma (Danaher, 1974). According to Premack, a reinforcer is any activity the participant is more likely to engage in than the instrumental response. Some students may like playing a video game; others may enjoy spending time on the playground; still others may enjoy helping the teacher. Whatever the high-probability response may be, the Premack principle suggests that one can take advantage of it by encouraging the student to engage in a less likely activity. All one needs to do is provide access to the high-probability response only if the student first performs the lower probability behavior.

Consider, for example, a child with autistic spectrum disorder who shows some form of perseverative behavior (e.g., repeatedly manipulating the same object). Studies have shown that the opportunity to perform such perseverative responses can be used as a reinforcer in efforts to teach more desirable behaviors such as simple arithmetic and language skills (Charlop, Kurtz, & Casey, 1990; Hanley, Iwata, Thompson, & Lindberg, 2000).

THEORETICAL PROBLEMS

The Premack principle has been highly influential, but it is not without complications. One major problem involves the measurement or calculation of response probabilities. We all have an intuitive sense of what it means to say that one response is more likely than another, but assigning a precise numerical value to the probability of a response can be difficult. Furthermore, the likelihood of a given response may change unexpectedly. A youngster may enjoy swimming in the morning but not later the same day.

The problems associated with using response probabilities to identify reinforcers can be avoided in applied settings with the use of a token economy (Kazdin, 1985; Matson & Boisjoli, 2009). In such a system, students are given tokens or points for performing certain target instrumental responses. The students can then exchange their points for various response opportunities (e.g., playing a video game, watching a movie, reading a comic book, or going to the playground), depending on what they want to do at the moment and how many points they have accumulated. If a wide enough range of reinforcer activities is available in exchange for tokens, one need not obtain precise measurements of the probability of each reinforcer response or worry about fluctuations in reinforcer preferences.

Token economies avoid problems associated with measuring response probabilities, but they do not solve a major conceptual problem with Premack's principle, namely, that it is merely a prescription or rule for identifying reinforcers. It does not tell us how reinforcers work. It answers the question "What makes something effective as a reinforcer?" but it does not answer the question "How does a reinforcer produce an increase in the probability of the reinforced response?"

The Response Deprivation Hypothesis

Timberlake and Allison (1974) followed in Premack's footsteps in thinking about reinforcers as responses rather than as stimuli. Their starting point, like Premack's, was to figure out what makes an instrumental response different from a reinforcer response. However, their consideration of this question led them down a different path. Timberlake and Allison suggested that the critical difference between instrumental and reinforcer responses is that the participant has free access to the instrumental response but is restricted from performing the reinforcer response.

In a typical Skinner box, for example, the rat can press the response lever at any time, but it is not at liberty to eat pellets of food at any time. Eating can occur only after the rat has pressed the lever, and even then the rat can only eat the single food pellet that is provided. Timberlake and Allison (1974) suggested that these restrictions on the reinforcer response make eating an effective reinforcer. In their view, instrumental conditioning situations deprive the participant of free access to the reinforcer response. For this reason, the Timberlake–Allison proposal, the next major development in theories of reinforcement, is called the *response deprivation hypothesis*.

RESPONSE DEPRIVATION AND THE LAW OF EFFECT

The response deprivation hypothesis captures an important idea. The idea is obvious if one considers what would happen if there were no restrictions on eating for a rat in a Skinner box. Imagine a situation in which the rat receives a week's supply of food each time it presses the response lever. According to Thorndike's law of effect, a week's worth of food should be a highly satisfying state of affairs and therefore should result in a strong S–R bond and a large increase in lever pressing. But this hardly makes sense from the rat's point of view. A more sensible prediction is that if the rat receives a week's supply of food for each lever press, it will press the response lever about once a week, when its food supple becomes depleted.

According to the response deprivation hypothesis, what makes food an effective reinforcer is not that food satisfies hunger or that eating is a high-probability response. Rather, the critical factor is that an instrumental conditioning procedure places a restriction on eating. If the response deprivation is removed, instrumental responding will not increase; the instrumental response will not be reinforced.

RESPONSE DEPRIVATION AND RESPONSE PROBABILITY

Notice that the response deprivation hypothesis does not require the computation of response probabilities. Thus, the response deprivation hypothesis avoids the first shortcoming of Premack's principle. To apply response deprivation, one merely has to determine the rate of a response during a baseline period in the absence of any restrictions and then limit access to the reinforcer response to below that baseline level (Klatt & Morris, 2001). This has made the response deprivation hypothesis a popular tool for creating effective reinforcers in applied situations.

An interesting prediction of the response deprivation hypothesis is that even a low-probability response can serve as a reinforcing event. The opportunity to perform a low-probability response can be used to reinforce a higher probability behavior if access to the low-probability response is restricted below its already low baseline rate. Such a prediction is contrary to Premack's principle but has been confirmed by experimental evidence (Allison & Timberlake, 1974; Eisenberger, Karpman, & Trattner, 1967).

RESPONSE DEPRIVATION AND THE LOCUS OF REINFORCEMENT EFFECTS

In addition to avoiding the problems involved in computing response probabilities, the response deprivation hypothesis shifted the locus of the explanation of reinforcement. In earlier theories, reinforcement was explained in terms of factors that were outside the instrumental conditioning procedure itself. With drive-reduction theory, the external factor involved procedures that established a drive state. With Premack's principle, the external factor involved the differential baseline probabilities of the reinforcer and instrumental responses. In contrast, with the response deprivation hypothesis, the locus of reinforcement rests with how the instrumental conditioning procedure constrains the organism's activities. This was a new idea. Never before had someone suggested that reinforcement effects are determined by the response restrictions that are an inherent feature of all instrumental conditioning procedures.

The response deprivation hypothesis moved our understanding of reinforcement forward in that it avoided some of the problems of Premack's principle. However, just like Premack's principle, the response deprivation hypothesis only provided an answer to the question "What makes something effective as a reinforcer?" The answer to the other major question, "How does a reinforcer produce an increase in the probability of the reinforced response?" had to await examining how instrumental conditioning changes how individuals distribute their behavior among various response options.

Response Allocation and Behavioral Economics

The response deprivation hypothesis helped to redefine the basic problem in instrumental conditioning as a problem of *response allocation*. Decreasing access to the reinforcer response creates a redistribution of behaviors such that the reinforcer response occurs less often and the instrumental response occurs more often. If instrumental conditioning involves a change in response allocation, what causes the change, and what are the rules that govern these changes? Efforts to answer such questions encouraged scientists to import concepts from the study of microeconomics into the analysis of instrumental behavior (Allison, 1989; Timberlake, 1980, 1984) and helped to establish the field of behavioral economics.

Economics basically deals with the allocation of resources among various options. One major resource is money, which is allocated among various goods and services that money can buy. In an instrumental conditioning situation, the resource is behavior, which can be allocated among various response options. A central economic concept in analyses of how people elect to spend their money is the concept of a *bliss point*. As the term implies, the bliss point refers to an individual's ideal or preferred distribution of monetary resources among the goods and services the person might wish to purchase.

A simple instrumental conditioning situation includes two obvious response options, the instrumental response and the reinforcer response. The *behavioral bliss point* may be defined as the ideal or preferred distribution of behaviors between these two response options when there are no limitations or constraints on either activity. The behavioral bliss point is the individual's preferred response choices before an instrumental conditioning procedure is imposed.

Consider, for example, a teenager named Kim. Left to her own devices, during the course of a 24-hour day, Kim might spend 4 hours talking to or texting friends, 1.5 hours eating, 2 hours driving, 10 hours sleeping, 3 hours playing video games, 3 hours listening to music, and half an hour doing schoolwork. This distribution of activities would constitute the behavioral bliss point for Kim. Notice that at the bliss point, Kim devotes only half an hour each day to doing schoolwork.

IMPOSING AN INSTRUMENTAL CONTINGENCY

Kim's parents may want to introduce an instrumental conditioning procedure to increase the amount of time Kim devotes to schoolwork. They could do this by restricting her access to music. For example, they could require that Kim spend a minute doing schoolwork for every minute that she gets to listen to music. Before the instrumental contingency, listening to music and doing homework were independent activities. How much time Kim spent on one activity had little to do with how much time she spent on the other. Once the instrumental conditioning procedure is introduced, this independence is lost.

Kim's behavioral bliss point for listening to music and studying is illustrated in the upper left quadrant of Figure 9.3. Before the instrumental contingency, Kim spends much more time on music than on studying. Requiring her to do a minute of homework for every minute of music listening ties the two activities together in a special way. Now time spent on homework must equal time spent on music. This relationship, illustrated by the 45° line in Figure 9.3, is called the *schedule line*. With the instrumental conditioning procedure in effect, Kim can no longer distribute her responses as she did at the behavioral bliss point. Notice that the schedule line does not go through the behavioral bliss point. Therefore, the instrumental contingency is a challenge to the behavioral bliss point.

How will Kim respond to the challenge to her bliss point that is created by the schedule of reinforcement that has been imposed? Behavioral economics assumes that challenges to the bliss point will trigger mechanisms of adjustment that move response allocations back toward the bliss point. Interestingly, however, every possible strategy for returning to the behavioral bliss point involves some cost or disadvantage. If Kim

FIGURE 9.3

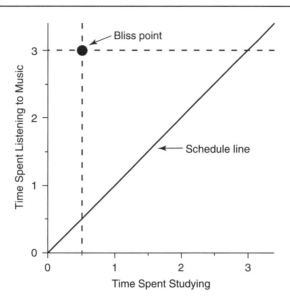

Illustration of the behavioral regulation approach to instrumental conditioning. The bliss point represents how much time a teenager spends studying and listening to music in the absence of an instrumental conditioning procedure or schedule constraint. The schedule line represents how much time the person can devote to each activity when she is required to spend 1 minute studying for each minute spent listening to music.

elects to listen to music for as long as she would like (ideally, 3 hours a day), she would have to do much more schoolwork than she likes. On the other hand, if she spent as little time doing schoolwork as she prefers (half an hour per day), she would have to settle for much less music than she likes.

Instrumental conditioning procedures constrain response options. They disrupt the free flow of behavior and interfere with how an organism selects among its available response alternatives. Furthermore, most cases are like Kim's in that the instrumental conditioning procedure does not allow the participant to return to the behavioral bliss point. The most that can be achieved is to move toward the bliss point under the constraints of the instrumental conditioning procedure.

RESPONDING TO SCHEDULE CONSTRAINTS

How an organism goes about moving back toward its behavioral bliss point after an instrumental contingency has been imposed depends on the costs and benefits of various options. Much of behavioral economics is devoted to the analysis of such cost/benefit trade-offs (Hursh, Madden, Spiga, DeLeon, & Francisco, 2013). How one navigates this problem depends on which activity one is willing to give up to defend the other. If doing schoolwork is much more unpleasant for Kim than the potential loss of music-listening time, then she will not increase her schoolwork very much but will give up time spent listening to music. In contrast, if the potential loss of music time is much more aversive for Kim than increased effort devoted to schoolwork, she will adjust to the constraint imposed by the instrumental conditioning procedure by substantially increasing the time she devotes to schoolwork.

As the preceding analysis suggests, navigating the costs and benefits of different ways of getting back to the bliss point depends on the degree of flexibility associated with one activity or the other. Economists refer to this as *elasticity of demand*. There is relatively little flexibility in how much gasoline people purchase to run their cars. Higher prices do not result in much of a drop in gas purchases, indicating that gas purchases show little elasticity of demand. In contrast, an increase in the price of candy will cause a sharp drop in purchases, showing that the purchase or consumption of candy is much more elastic. One of the hallmarks of drug addiction is lack of flexibility in consumption of the drug, illustrating low levels of elasticity of demand in that case.

If Kim insists on listening to music for 3 hours a day no matter what, she is showing little elasticity of demand for music listening and will have to substantially increase studying to defend her preferred access to music. A major factor that determines elasticity of demand is the availability of substitutes. A *substitute* is a commodity or activity that provides some of the same benefits or satisfaction as the original item. There is little elasticity of demand for gasoline because we cannot use anything else to operate our cars. In contrast, many substitutes are available for candy. If candy gets too expensive, one can switch to eating cookies or ice cream that are similarly sweet.

A particularly important factor determining how an individual responds to schedule constraints is the availability of substitutes for the reinforcer activity (Green & Freed, 1993; Murphy, Correia, & Barnett, 2007). Instrumental conditioning procedures are powerful only if no substitutes are available for the reinforcer activity. If Kim loves music and cannot derive the same satisfaction from any other type of activity, then music will be a powerful reinforcer. In this case, she will adjust to the instrumental procedure with a large increase in schoolwork. In contrast, if playing video games is a good substitute for listening to music, the instrumental contingency will have little effect on how much schoolwork Kim does. Instead, she will respond to the schedule constraint by substituting video games for listening to music, without having to increase how much time she spends on schoolwork.

Behavioral economics suggests that one must be very careful to assess the availability of substitutes in designing a practical application of instrumental conditioning principles. Unfortunately, these substitutes may not be clearly evident before an instrumental contingency is imposed. Kim's parents, for example, may not be aware that Kim considers video games a satisfactory substitute for listening to music. In fact, Kim may not be aware of this herself before the instrumental contingency links studying with listening to music. For this reason, it is important to monitor the full range of activities of the individual when an instrumental conditioning procedure is imposed to produce a desired change in behavior.

CONTRIBUTIONS OF RESPONSE ALLOCATION AND BEHAVIORAL ECONOMICS

Thinking about instrumental conditioning as a problem of response allocation guided by economic concepts has advanced our understanding by encouraging thinking about instrumental conditioning and reinforcement within the context of the participant's entire behavioral repertoire. Response allocation and behavioral economics focuses attention on the fact that instrumental conditioning procedures do not operate in a behavioral vacuum. Rather, instrumental conditioning procedures disrupt the free flow of behavior; they interfere with how individuals allocate their behavior among available response options. Behavioral economic concepts also tell us that the effects of instrumental conditioning are not limited to changes in the rate of the instrumental response. Schedule constraints can also produce changes in activities that are substitutes for the reinforce activity.

Behavioral economics encourages us to think about instrumental behavior from a broader perspective than previous conceptualizations. It encourages us to consider all of the activities of a participant—how they are organized and how that organization determines the effects of schedule constraints. This approach is a far cry from the more limited stimulus–response perspective that dominated earlier theories of reinforcement. However, it brings along with it challenges of its own. It is difficult to predict a reinforcement effect unless we know all of the features of an individual's behavioral organization that influence his or her responses to a schedule constraint.

Summary

A theory of reinforcement has to tell us (a) what makes something a reinforcer and (b) how the reinforcer produces its effects. Early theories assumed that reinforcers were special types of stimuli. According to the most influential of these theories, a stimulus will be reinforcing if it is effective in reducing a drive state. Drive reduction theory was dominant for several decades but ran into some difficulties (e.g., it could not explain sensory reinforcement) and was supplanted by response theories of reinforcement. Among the most prominent of these was Premack's principle, according to which a reinforcer is not a drive-reducing stimulus but rather the opportunity to make a response whose baseline probability is higher than the baseline probability of the instrumental response.

Premack's principle continues to form the basis of numerous applications of reinforcement in clinical and educational settings. However, shortcomings of the principle stimulated the next theoretical development, the response deprivation hypothesis. According to this hypothesis, the opportunity to perform a response will be an effective reinforcer if the instrumental conditioning procedure restricts access to that activity below its baseline rate. The response deprivation hypothesis shifted the focus of attention from reinforcers as special stimuli or responses to how an instrumental conditioning procedure constrains the organism's activities and creates a new allocation of responses among the individual's behavioral options. Analyzing the processes that are important in the reallocation of behavior was facilitated by the use of concepts from economics, and this led to the establishment of the field of behavioral economics.

Behavioral economics suggests that organisms have a preferred or optimal distribution of activities in any given situation. The introduction of an instrumental conditioning procedure disrupts this optimal response distribution, or behavioral bliss point. The disruption activates changes in response allocation in an effort to defend the bliss point. Typically, the change in the response allocation involves an increase in the instrumental response and a decrease in the rate of the reinforcer response. The extent of these changes is determined by the elasticity of each response and the availability of substitutes for the reinforcer response.

Suggested Readings

Allison, J. (1983). *Behavioral economics.* New York, NY: Praeger.

Anselme, P., & Robinson, M. J. F. (2016). "Wanting," "liking," and their relation to consciousness. *Journal of Experimental Psychology: Animal Learning and Cognition, 42,* 123–140.

Hursh, S. R., Madden, G. J., Spiga, R., DeLeon, I., & Francisco, M. T. (2013). The translational utility of behavioral economics: The experimental analysis of consumption and choice. In G. J. Madden (Ed.), *APA handbook of behavior analysis: Vol. 2. Translating principles into practice* (pp. 191–224). Washington, DC: American Psychological Association.

Matson, J. L., & Boisjoli, J. A. (2009). The token economy for children with intellectual disabilities and/or autism: A review. *Research in Developmental Disabilities, 30,* 240–248. http://dx.doi.org/10.1016/j.ridd.2008.04.001

Timberlake, W., & Farmer-Dougan, V. A. (1991). Reinforcement in applied settings: Figuring out ahead of time what will work. *Psychological Bulletin, 110,* 379–391. http://dx.doi.org/10.1037/0033-2909.110.3.379

Technical Terms

Acquired drive
Behavioral bliss point
Conditioned drive
Conditioned reinforcer
Differential probability principle
Drive reduction theory
Drive state
Law of effect

Premack's principle
Primary reinforcer
Response allocation
Response deprivation hypothesis
Schedule line
Secondary reinforcer
Sensory reinforcement

Extinction of Conditioned Behavior | 10

Did you know that

- extinction not only decreases responding, it also increases the variability of behavior?
- extinction involves learning to inhibit a previously conditioned response but leaves intact much of what was previously learned?
- extinguished behavior can reappear under a wide range of circumstances, creating challenges for behavior therapies based on extinction?
- much contemporary research is devoted to finding ways to increase the effectiveness of extinction procedures?
- the unexpected absence of reinforcement produces frustration?
- the schedule of reinforcement that was in effect during acquisition determines the persistence of behavior during extinction?
- using more reinforcement during training does not necessarily increase the persistence of behavior in extinction? Responding may decline more rapidly in extinction after more extensive training, after training with a larger reinforcer, or after training with intermittent rather than continuous reinforcement.

So far, our discussion of classical and instrumental conditioning has centered on various aspects of the acquisition and maintenance of conditioned behavior. Learning is important because it provides needed flexibility in how individuals interact with their environment. But if learned behavior

http://dx.doi.org/10.1037/0000057-010

The Essentials of Conditioning and Learning, Fourth Edition, by M. Domjan

is an adaptation to a changing environment, then the loss of conditioned behavior should be just as prevalent as its acquisition. Reinforcement schedules do not necessarily remain in effect throughout an individual's lifetime. Responses that are successful at one point in life may cease to be useful as circumstances change. Children, for example, are praised for drawing crude representations of people and objects in nursery school, but the same type of drawing is not considered appropriate if drawn by a high school student.

Acquisition of conditioned behavior involves procedures in which a reinforcing outcome or unconditioned stimulus (US) is presented. *Extinction* involves omitting the reinforcer, or US. In classical conditioning, extinction involves repeated presentations of the conditioned stimulus (CS) without the US. In instrumental conditioning, extinction involves no longer presenting the reinforcer when the individual makes the instrumental response. The typical result of an extinction procedure is that conditioned responding declines. Thus, extinction appears to be the opposite of acquisition. Indeed, that is how extinction has been characterized in traditional theories of learning, such as the Rescorla–Wagner model (see Chapter 6, this volume). However, as the evidence described in the present chapter shows, this view of extinction is seriously flawed.

It is important to distinguish extinction from forgetting. Although both involve the loss of conditioned responding, forgetting results from the passage of time. Extinction, by contrast, occurs as a consequence of repeated presentations of the CS alone or repeated instances of the instrumental response without the reinforcer. Unlike forgetting, extinction is produced by a particular procedure, not merely the passage of time.

Although research on extinction originated about a hundred years ago, extinction remains a major area of contemporary research at the level of both behavior and neural mechanisms (Delamater & Westbrook, 2014; Lattal, St. Peter, & Escobar, 2013; Todd, Vurbic, & Bouton, 2014). Contemporary research is motivated by efforts to better understand various novel extinction phenomena and by efforts to develop more effective therapeutic procedures for the treatment of maladaptive fears and phobias (Dunsmoor, Niv, Daw, & Phelps, 2015; Gillihan & Foa, 2011; Maren, 2011; Maren & Holmes, 2016).

Effects of Extinction Procedures

Imagine looking forward to getting home after a hard day's work and discovering that your key no longer opens the front door. This illustrates the basic procedure for extinction. A previously reinforced response (turning the key in the lock) is no longer effective in producing the reinforcer (opening the door). Such an unexpected absence of reinforcement produces both emotional and behavioral effects. The emotion you feel upon finding that your key no longer works is frustration and perhaps anger. Chances are you will not give up after your first attempt to open the door but will try several more times, perhaps jiggling the key in different ways. If none of these response variations works, you will eventually quit trying.

This example illustrates two basic behavioral effects of extinction. The most obvious is that responding decreases when the response no longer results in reinforcement. This is the primary behavioral effect of extinction, and the effect that has occupied most of the attention of scientists. The other important behavioral consequence of extinction is an increase in response variability (Neuringer, Kornell, & Olufs, 2001). When your key failed to open the door on the first try, you jiggled the key in various ways in an effort to make it work. This reflects the increase in response variability that is produced by extinction. In addition to these behavioral effects, extinction often also involves emotional components. Frustration and anger occur if an appetitive reinforcer is withheld, and relief occurs if an aversive US is withheld.

Extinction and Original Learning

Although extinction produces important behavioral and emotional effects, it does not reverse the effects of acquisition. Evidence that extinction does not erase what was originally learned has been obtained through studies of spontaneous recovery, renewal, reinstatement, and reinforcer devaluation effects. Understanding the mechanisms of these phenomena is of considerable interest in both basic and translational research.

SPONTANEOUS RECOVERY

The basic procedure for extinction following Pavlovian conditioning involves repeatedly presenting the CS by itself. This makes the procedure for extinction in Pavlovian conditioning similar to the standard procedure for habituation. Therefore, it is not surprising that many behavioral features of habituation are also found in extinction. One prominent feature of habituation is that it shows spontaneous recovery. If a substantial period of rest is introduced after a series of habituation trials, the habituated response is observed to return or recover.

Pavlov discovered a similar phenomenon in extinction following Pavlovian conditioning. The basic finding is illustrated in Figure 10.1. During acquisition, conditioned responding increases as a function of trials. In extinction, responding declines. A period of rest is then instituted, followed by additional extinction trials. Notice that responding is higher after the period of rest than it was at the end of the first series of extinction trials. This recovery of behavior is called *spontaneous recovery* because it does not require a special intervention other than the passage of time (Rescorla, 2004).

Spontaneous recovery typically does not restore responding to the high level that was evident during acquisition. However, the fact that responding recovers to any extent is evidence that extinction suppressed rather than eliminated the conditioned responding. This indicates that extinction does not reverse the processes of acquisition or produce unlearning. Spontaneous recovery is one of the reasons that bad habits or maladaptive fears can return after efforts to extinguish them.

FIGURE 10.1

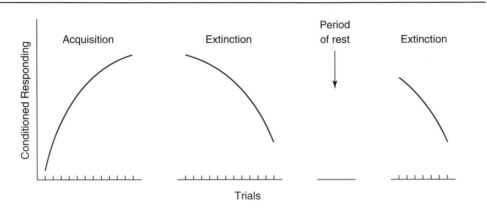

Illustration of spontaneous recovery after extinction. During the acquisition phase, conditioned responding increases. In the subsequent extinction phase, responding declines to the low level seen at the start of the acquisition phase. A period of rest is then introduced during which training trials are suspended. This results in a temporary recovery of the conditioned behavior. Data are hypothetical.

THE RENEWAL EFFECT

Another strong piece of evidence that extinction does not result in unlearning is the phenomenon of renewal identified by Mark Bouton and his colleagues (Bouton & Woods, 2008). Renewal refers to a recovery of acquisition performance when the contextual cues that were present during extinction are changed. The change may be a return to the context of original acquisition or a shift to a "neutral" context. Renewal is particularly troublesome for behavior therapy because it means that irrational fears that are extinguished in the context of a therapist's office can return when the client goes someplace else. Similarly, a bad drug habit that is extinguished in a residential treatment center can be renewed when the client returns home.

The renewal effect was discovered during the course of research on transfer of training (Bouton, 1993). The basic question in these studies was how learning that occurs in one situation transfers to other circumstances or contexts. For example, if you learn something in a noisy dormitory lounge, will that learning transfer to a quiet classroom in which you have to take a test? An equally important question concerns the transfer of extinction. If extinction is conducted in one situation so that the CS no longer elicits responding in that context, will the CS also be ineffective in eliciting the CR in other situations?

Research on the renewal effect was originally conducted with laboratory rats, but the phenomenon has since been extended to human participants (Vervliet, Baeyens, Van den Bergh, & Hermans, 2013). A schematic representation of the results of a renewal experiment is presented in Figure 10.2. In the first phase of the experiment,

FIGURE 10.2

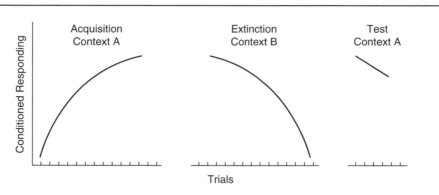

Illustration of the renewal effect. Participants originally acquire the conditioned response in Context A. They then receive extinction training in Context B, which results in a decline of the conditioned response. In the third phase, they are returned to Context A for testing. The conditioned response is "renewed" when the participants are returned to Context A. Data are hypothetical.

participants received acquisition training in a particular place, labeled Context A. Context A may be an experimental chamber or room distinguished by a particular level of illumination, odor, and flooring. As you might expect, conditioned responding increases during the acquisition phase. The participants are then moved to another experimental chamber (Context B), in which the lighting, odor, and flooring are different. Extinction is conducted in this alternate context. As is common, responding declines with repeated extinction trials. At the end of the experiment, the participants are returned to Context A to see whether the effects of extinction conducted in Context B transfer back to Context A.

If extinction involves the unlearning of a conditioned response (CR), then returning the participants to Context A after extinction in Context B should not result in recovery of the conditioned behavior. Contrary to that prediction, responding is restored when the participants are returned to Context A. As with spontaneous recovery, the restoration of performance may not be complete. But even partial return of the conditioned response indicates that extinction in Context B does not fully transfer back to the original training context. Rather, conditioned responding is "renewed" upon return to the context of original training.

The renewal effect occurs because the memory of extinction is specific to the cues that were present during the extinction phase. Therefore, a shift away from the context of extinction disrupts retrieval of the memory of extinction, with the result that extinction performance is no longer evident. But why should this restore behavior characteristic of original acquisition? To account for that, one has to make the added assumption that original acquisition performance generalizes from one context to another more easily than does extinction performance. This is indeed the case. Notice that in Figure 10.2, participants responded as vigorously at the start of the extinction phase in Context B as they had at the end of the acquisition phase in Context A. This illustrates that a shift in context does not disrupt acquisition performance. It only disrupts extinction performance.

Why is it that original acquisition is minimally disrupted (if at all) by a change in context, whereas extinction performance is highly context specific? Bouton (1993, 1994) suggested that contextual cues serve to disambiguate the significance of a CS. This function is similar to the function of semantic context in disambiguating the meaning of a word. Consider the word *cut*. *Cut* could refer to the physical procedure of creating two pieces, as in "The chef cut the carrots." Alternatively, it could refer to dropping a player from a team, as in "Johnny was cut from the team after the first game." The meaning of the word *cut* depends on the semantic context.

Conducting excitatory conditioning and then extinction with a CS makes the CS ambiguous because the CS could signify an impending US (acquisition) or the absence of the US (extinction). This ambiguity makes the CS more susceptible to contextual control. After acquisition training alone, the CS is not ambiguous because it only signifies one thing (impending US delivery). Such a CS is therefore not as susceptible to contextual control as one that has undergone both acquisition and extinction.

The renewal effect has important implications for behavior therapy, and unfortunately these implications are rather troubling. It suggests that even if a therapeutic procedure is effective in extinguishing a pathological fear or phobia in the relative safety of a therapist's office, the conditioned fear may return when the client encounters the fear CS in a different context. Equally problematic is that the effects of excitatory conditioning readily generalize from one context to another (see Figure 10.2). Thus, if you acquire a pathological fear in one situation, that fear is likely to plague you in a variety of other places. But if you overcome your fear in a particular environment or context, this benefit will not generalize as readily. The renewal effect means that problems created by conditioning are likely to be much more widespread than the solutions or remedies for those problems. (For further discussion of the implications of the renewal effect for behavior therapy, see Bouton, 2014).

REINSTATEMENT OF CONDITIONED EXCITATION

Another procedure that serves to restore responding to an extinguished CS is called *reinstatement*. The reinstatement phenomenon is illustrated in Figure 10.3. The first phase involves CS–US pairings, which result in acquisition of a Pavlovian CR. This is followed by CS-alone presentations and extinction of the CR. Once the response has declined in extinction, the participant is exposed to the US by itself. This US-alone presentation results in recovery of excitatory responding to the CS. The US-induced recovery of responding to the CS is called reinstatement.

Consider, for example, learning an aversion to french fries because you got sick on a trip after eating french fries. Your aversion is then extinguished by nibbling on french fries without getting sick on a number of occasions. In fact, you may actually regain your enjoyment of french fries because of this extinction experience. The phenomenon of reinstatement suggests that if you were to become sick again for some

FIGURE 10.3

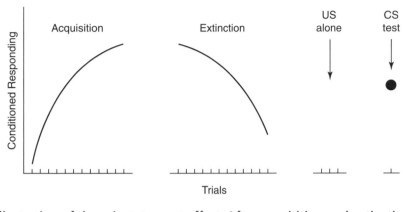

Illustration of the reinstatement effect. After acquisition and extinction training, subjects receive exposures to the unconditioned stimulus (US) alone. This is then followed by tests of responding to the conditioned stimulus (CS). The US-alone presentations produce recovery in responding to the CS. Data are hypothetical.

reason, your aversion to french fries would return even if your illness was not caused by what you ate. (For an analogous study with laboratory rats, see Schachtman, Brown, & Miller, 1985.)

As with renewal, reinstatement is a troublesome phenomenon for behavior therapy. Behavior therapy often involves trying to get clients to stop doing things that are problematic for them. Extinction is an effective technique for reducing behavior. However, because of reinstatement, responses that are successfully extinguished during the course of therapeutic intervention can recur if the individual encounters the US again. For example, reinstatement has been developed as a model for relapse after treatment for drug addiction (Bossert, Marchant, Calu, & Shaham, 2013). Drug addiction treatment typically includes an extinction component that serves to extinguish cues that elicit drug cravings. Extinguishing these cues also reduces instrumental responses involved in the procurement and consumption of the drug. However, a "free" encounter with the drug can reverse these therapeutic gains through the phenomenon of reinstatement.

Enhancing Extinction Performance

The phenomena of spontaneous recovery, renewal, and reinstatement show that conditioned responding is not eliminated by extinction procedures but can recover under various circumstances. This is because extinction does not eliminate the mechanisms that generate conditioned behavior. For example, extinction procedures do not eliminate stimulus–outcome (S–O) and response–outcome (R–O) associations (Delamater,

2012; Rescorla, 1993). Extinction operates by establishing an inhibitory process that suppresses responding without eliminating the processes that were originally responsible for the conditioned behavior (Bouton, Trask, & Carranza-Jasso, 2016). Given the significance of extinction for behavior therapy, an important area of contemporary research is to find ways to enhance the response inhibition that is created by extinction procedures.

A relatively simple strategy for enhancing extinction is to conduct more extinction trials. *Increasing the number of extinction trials* produces stronger suppression of conditioned behavior in a variety of learning situations (e.g., Leung, Bailey, Laurent, & Westbrook, 2007). However, a related variable, the interval between successive extinction trials is also important. Both basic and applied research has shown that *increasing the intertrial interval* in extinction reduces spontaneous recovery and thereby produces more enduring suppression of conditioned behavior (Tsao & Craske, 2000; Urcelay, Wheeler, & Miller, 2009).

Another procedure that helps to reduce recovery (or relapse) from extinction is to *conduct extinction in a variety of contexts*. This procedure is particularly effective in reducing the renewal effect. The renewal effect reflects the context specificity of extinction: extinguished responding reappears when participants are moved from the extinction context to someplace else. By conducting extinction in several different contexts (or locations), the context specificity of extinction can be reduced. As with the trial-spacing effect, the effectiveness of reducing renewal by conducting extinction in multiple contexts has been confirmed in research with both laboratory animals and human participants (e.g., Bandarian Balooch & Neumann, 2011; Thomas, Vurbic, & Novak, 2009).

A third strategy for enhancing extinction performance is suggested by a memory retrieval analysis of the problem of extinction. Individuals who have experienced both acquisition and extinction have competing memories guiding their behavior. The memory of acquisition encourages conditioned responding, whereas the memory of extinction discourages responding. This analysis suggests that extinction performance may be enhanced by providing reminder cues for extinction (Laborda & Miller, 2012). A tone or a light that is present only during extinction trials can come to serve as a reminder cue for extinction. Presenting such a stimulus can then be used to activate the memory of extinction.

Presenting a reminder cue for extinction has been found to reduce spontaneous recovery and the renewal effect in a variety of experimental situations (Brooks, 2000; Brooks & Bouton, 1993). Reminder cues for extinction have also been found to enhance the effectiveness of exposure therapy. For example, in a study of exposure therapy for fear of spiders, participants who were encouraged to think about the treatment context showed much less fear in novel situations than participants who did not receive this memory activation instruction (Mystkowski, Craske, Echiverri, & Labus, 2006).

The last strategy for enhancing extinction performance that I describe is based on recent research indicating that memories are not permanent but can be updated through a process called *reconsolidation*. Recent research has shown that consolidated memories are not rigid or permanent. Rather, the activation of a memory returns it to a malleable and flexible state in which it can be altered before it is returned or reconsolidated into a long-term form (Alberini & LeDoux, 2013). (I have more to say about memory updating or reconsolidation in Chapter 14.)

If reactivated memories are susceptible to change before being reconsolidation, we might be able to design extinction procedures that produce more permanent changes in how a CS is remembered. This line of thinking led to the prediction that priming extinction may enhance the long-term efficacy of extinction procedures. A priming trial consists of presenting a previously conditioned CS to activate the memory of conditioning (memory that the CS will be followed by the US). Once the acquisition memory has been activated, it becomes susceptible to change. Therefore, conducting a series of extinction trials at this point should create a new memory (that the CS is not paired with the US), and this new memory should be the one that becomes reconsolidated and permanently stored.

These considerations suggest that extinction procedures would be more effective if they were preceded by a priming trial that returns the memory of conditioning to a flexible form. This prediction has been confirmed in research with both laboratory rat and human participants in studies of the extinction of conditioned fear (Monfils, Cowansage, Klann, & LeDoux, 2009; Schiller et al., 2010). A standard extinction procedure was used in these experiments. The extinction session was preceded by a single CS-alone trial to activate the fear memory and move it to a flexible state in which it was susceptible to modification before being reconsolidated. Conducting extinction after reactivation of the fear memory with a single CS-alone trial made extinction more enduring, as evidenced by reduced levels of spontaneous recovery, renewal, and reinstatement. However, this effect occurred only if the priming CS-alone trial was presented 10 minutes or 1 hour before the extinction session. If the priming trial preceded the extinction session by 6 hours, no enhancement of extinction was observed, presumably because by the end of 6 hours, the reconsolidation window was no longer open.

Initial studies showing that priming or reactivation of a CR can enhance the effects of extinction were intriguing and stimulated numerous follow-up experiments with both laboratory animals and human participants. The original findings have been replicated, but not all efforts to enhance extinction with a reactivation treatment have been successful (Auber, Tedesco, Jones, Monfils, & Chiamulera, 2013). Nevertheless, the results hold out hope that priming and reactivation manipulations may be developed that will increase the effectiveness of exposure therapy in the treatment of maladaptive fears and phobias. Successful clinical translation of the basic research will require learning more about the boundary conditions of the extinction priming effect (Kroes, Schiller, LeDoux, & Phelps, 2016).

"Paradoxical" Reward Effects in Extinction

As I noted earlier, extinction does not degrade S–O and R–O associations but occurs because of the establishment of a new response inhibitory process. What causes that response inhibition? Why should nonreinforcement inhibit responding? In answering this question, it is important to keep in mind that extinction involves a special type of nonreinforcement—namely, nonreinforcement after a history of reinforcement. Nonreinforcement without such a prior history is not extinction but is more akin to habituation. This is an important distinction because the absence of a positive reinforcer is aversive only after a history of reinforcement.

The emotional effects of nonreinforcement depend critically on the individual's prior history. If your partner never made you coffee in the morning, you will not be disappointed if the coffee is not ready when you get up. If you never received an allowance, you will not be disappointed when you don't get one. It is only the omission of an expected reward that creates disappointment or frustration. These emotional effects are presumed to play a critical role in the behavioral decline that occurs in extinction.

As I mentioned at the outset of this chapter, extinction involves both behavioral and emotional effects. The emotional reaction, technically called *frustration*, stems from the frustration that occurs when an expected reinforcer is not forthcoming. Nonreinforcement in the face of the expectation of reward is assumed to trigger an unconditioned aversive frustrative reaction (Amsel, 1958). This aversive emotion serves to discourage responding during the course of extinction through the establishment of a process that inhibits conditioned responding (Rescorla, 2001).

If the decline in responding in extinction is due to the frustrative effects of the unexpected absence of reinforcement, then one would expect more rapid extinction after training that establishes greater expectations of reward. This is indeed the case and has led to a number of *paradoxical reward effects*. Paradoxical reward effects do not command much attention in contemporary research, but they are common in daily experience and are important to consider in applications of reinforcement principles in various settings (e.g., child-rearing).

OVERTRAINING EXTINCTION EFFECT

One of the paradoxical reward effects involves the effects of extensive reinforced training on subsequent extinction. Providing more training with reinforcement increases the expectation of reward. Because of this, when extinction is introduced, the frustrative effects of nonreinforcement will also be greater. If the decline in responding in extinction is due to the frustrative effects of nonreward, more extensive reinforcement training should produce more rapid extinction. This prediction has been confirmed (see Figure 10.4) and is called the *overtraining extinction effect* (Ishida & Papini, 1997).

The overtraining extinction effect is "paradoxical" because it involves fewer responses in extinction after more extensive reinforcement training. Thinking casually, one might suppose that more-extensive reinforcement training would create a "stronger" response, one that is more resistant to extinction. But, in fact, the opposite is the case, especially when training involves continuous reinforcement. The more accustomed you become to receiving reinforcement, the more rapidly you will give up in the face of nonreinforcement.

FIGURE 10.4

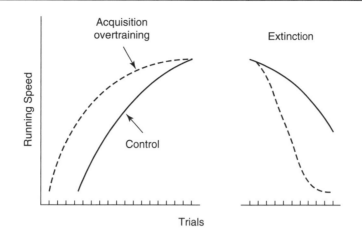

Illustration of the overtraining extinction effect. During acquisition, two groups receive continuous reinforcement for performing an instrumental response. The overtraining group is trained until it reaches asymptote, and then training continues for additional trials. In contrast, the control group is trained only until it reaches asymptote. Both groups then receive extinction trials. Responding declines more rapidly for the overtrained group than for the control group. Data are hypothetical.

MAGNITUDE OF REINFORCEMENT EXTINCTION EFFECT

Another paradoxical reward effect that reflects similar mechanisms is the *magnitude-of-reinforcement extinction effect*. This phenomenon reflects the fact that responding declines more rapidly in extinction after reinforcement with a larger reinforcer (see Figure 10.5), especially if training involves continuous reinforcement (Hulse, 1958; Wagner, 1961). The magnitude-of-reinforcement extinction effect is also readily accounted for in terms of the frustrative effects of nonreward. Nonreinforcement is apt to be more frustrative if the individual has come to expect a large reward than if the individual expects a small reward. Consider two scenarios: In one, you receive $300 per month from your parents to help with incidental expenses at college; in the other, you receive only $50 per month. In both cases, your parents stop the payments when you drop out of school for a semester. This nonreinforcement will be more aversive if you had come to expect the larger monthly allowance.

On the basis of a simple application of Thorndike's law of effect, one might predict that providing a larger reinforcer for each occurrence of an instrumental response will create a stronger S–R association and therefore produce more persistent responding in extinction. The magnitude of reinforcement extinction effect tells us that the outcome will be just the opposite. Increasing the size and frequency of the reinforcer

FIGURE 10.5

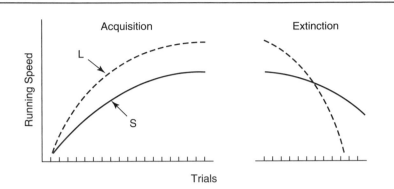

Illustration of the reward-magnitude extinction effect. During the acquisition phase, one group of participants is reinforced (on a continuous reinforcement schedule) with a small reward (S), while another group is reinforced with a large reward (L). Both groups then receive extinction trials. During the extinction phase, responding declines faster for group L than for group S. Data are hypothetical.

leads participants to give up trying more quickly when they encounter failure or non-reinforcement. As with the overtraining extinction effect, the magnitude of reinforcement extinction effect is more prominent after continuous rather than intermittent reinforcement.

PARTIAL REINFORCEMENT EXTINCTION EFFECT

A key factor that determines the vigor of both the behavioral and the emotional effects of an extinction procedure is the schedule of reinforcement that is in effect before extinction is introduced. Various subtle features of reinforcement schedules can influence the persistence of the behavior during extinction. However, the dominant schedule characteristic that determines extinction effects is whether the instrumental response is reinforced every time it occurs (*continuous reinforcement*) or only some of the times it occurs (*intermittent* or *partial reinforcement*). The general finding is that extinction is much slower and involves fewer frustration reactions if partial reinforcement rather than continuous reinforcement was in effect before introduction of the extinction procedure (see Figure 10.6). This phenomenon is called the *partial-reinforcement extinction effect* (PREE; see Horsley, Osborne, Norman, & Wells, 2012, for a recent human example). The PREE is the most extensively investigated paradoxical reward effect.

The persistence in responding that is created by intermittent reinforcement can be remarkable. Habitual gamblers are slaves to intermittent reinforcement. Occasional winnings encourage them to continue gambling during long strings of losses or non-reinforcement. Intermittent reinforcement may also have undesirable consequences

FIGURE 10.6

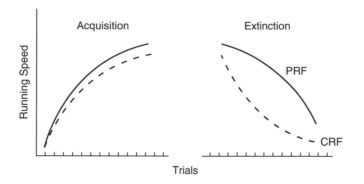

Illustration of the partial-reinforcement extinction effect. During the acquisition phase, one group of participants receives continuous reinforcement (CRF), whereas another group receives partial reinforcement (PRF). Both groups then receive extinction training. During the extinction phase, responding declines faster for the CRF group than for the PRF group. Data are hypothetical.

in parenting. Consider, for example, a child riding in a grocery cart while the parent is shopping. The child asks the parent to buy a piece of candy. The parent says no. The child asks again and again and then begins to throw a temper tantrum because the parent continues to say no. At this point, the parent is likely to give in to avoid public embarrassment. By finally buying the candy, the parent will have provided intermittent reinforcement for the repeated demands for candy. The parent will also have reinforced the tantrum behavior. The intermittent reinforcement of the requests for candy will increase the child's persistence in asking for candy during future shopping trips.

MECHANISMS OF THE PARTIAL REINFORCEMENT EXTINCTION EFFECT

Perhaps the most obvious explanation for the PREE is that the introduction of extinction is easier to detect after continuous reinforcement than after partial reinforcement. If you don't receive the reinforcer after each response during training, you may not immediately notice when reinforcers are omitted altogether during extinction. The absence of reinforcement is presumably much easier to detect after continuous reinforcement. This explanation of the PREE is called the *discrimination hypothesis*.

Although the discrimination hypothesis makes sense intuitively, the PREE is not so straightforward. In an ingenious test of the discrimination hypothesis, Jenkins (1962) and Theios (1962) first trained one group of animals with partial reinforcement and another with continuous reinforcement. Both groups then received a phase of continuous reinforcement before extinction was introduced (see Table 10.1). Because the extinction procedure was introduced immediately after continuous-reinforcement

TABLE 10.1

Design of the Jenkins/Theios Experiment to Test the Discrimination Hypothesis

Phase 1	Phase 2	Phase 3
Partial reinforcement group	Continuous reinforcement	Extinction result: slow extinction
Continuous reinforcement group	Continuous reinforcement	Extinction result: rapid extinction

training for both groups, extinction should have been equally noticeable or discriminable for both. However, participants who initially received partial-reinforcement training were slower to extinguish their behavior. These results indicate that the response persistence produced by partial reinforcement does not come from greater difficulty in detecting the start of extinction. Rather, it seems that participants learn something long lasting from partial reinforcement that is carried over through a phase of continuous reinforcement. Partial reinforcement seems to teach participants not to give up in the face of failure, and this learned persistence is retained even if they subsequently experience an unbroken string of successes.

What do participants learn during partial reinforcement that makes them more persistent in the face of a run of bad luck or failure? Numerous complicated experiments have been performed to answer this question. These studies indicate that partial reinforcement promotes persistence in two ways. One explanation, *frustration theory*, is based on what individuals learn about the emotional effects of nonreward during partial-reinforcement training. The other explanation, *sequential theory*, is based on what individuals learn about the memory of nonreward.

Frustration Theory

According to frustration theory, persistence in extinction results from learning something unusual—namely, to continue responding when you expect to be nonreinforced or frustrated (Amsel, 1992; Papini, 2003). Frustration theory assumes that intermittent reinforcement results in learning to respond in the face of expected nonreinforcement. However, this learning requires a considerable amount of experience with intermittent reinforcement.

Frustration theory characterizes the learning that occurs during the course of intermittent reinforcement in terms of stages (see Exhibit 10.1). Partial reinforcement involves both rewarded and nonrewarded trials. Rewarded trials lead individuals to expect reinforcement, whereas nonrewarded trials lead them to expect the absence of reward. Consequently, intermittent reinforcement leads individuals to expect both reward and nonreward. At first, the expectation of reward encourages participants to respond, whereas the expectation of nonreward discourages responding. Thus, early in training, individuals receiving intermittent reinforcement are conflicted about what to do. Their expectations encourage opposite response tendencies. As training continues, however, this conflict is resolved in favor of responding.

EXHIBIT 10.1

Stages of Acquisition in Frustration Theory

Partial reinforcement
Stage I. Expectancy of reward → Respond
         Expectancy of nonreward → Don't respond
Stage II. Expectancy of reward → Respond
         Expectancy of nonreward → Respond

Continuous reinforcement
Stage I. Expectancy of reward → Respond
Stage II. Expectancy of reward → Respond

The resolution of the conflict occurs because in the typical partial-reinforcement schedule, reinforcement is not predictable. Therefore, the instrumental response ends up being reinforced on some of the trials when the participant expected nonreward. As a result of such episodes, the instrumental response becomes conditioned to the expectation of nonreward. According to frustration theory, this is the key to persistent responding in extinction. With sufficient training, intermittent reinforcement results in learning to make the instrumental response in anticipation of nonreward. In a sense, intermittent reinforcement teaches us to keep going in the face of anticipated failure. Once the response has become conditioned to the expectation of nonreward, responding persists when extinction is introduced.

By contrast, there is nothing about the experience of continuous reinforcement that encourages individuals to respond when they expect nonreward. With continuous reinforcement, one only learns to expect reward and to make the instrumental response when this reward expectancy is activated. Continuous reinforcement does not teach participants to make the instrumental response when they expect nonreward, and therefore it does not produce persistence in extinction.

Sequential Theory

Sequential theory was proposed by Capaldi (1967, 1971) and is heavily based on ideas involving memory. It assumes that individuals can remember whether they were reinforced for performing the instrumental response in the recent past. They remember both recently rewarded and recently nonrewarded trials. The theory further assumes that during intermittent-reinforcement training, the memory of nonreward becomes a cue for performing the instrumental response. According to sequential theory, this produces persistence in extinction. Precisely how this happens depends a great deal on the sequence of rewarded (R) and nonrewarded (N) trials that are administered in the intermittent-reinforcement schedule. This is why the theory is labeled *sequential*.

Consider the following sequence of trials: RNN<u>R</u>RN<u>R</u>. In this sequence the participant is rewarded on the first trial, not rewarded on the next two trials, then rewarded twice, then not rewarded, and then rewarded again. The fourth and last trials are critical in this schedule and are therefore underlined. On the fourth trial, the participant is reinforced after receiving nonreward on the two preceding trials. It is assumed that the participant remembers the two nonrewarded trials when it is reinforced on the fourth trial. Because of this, the memory of two nonrewarded trials becomes a cue for responding. Responding in the face of the memory of nonreward is again reinforced on the last trial. On this trial, the participant is reinforced for responding during the memory of one nonrewarded trial. After enough experiences like these, the participant learns to respond whenever it remembers not having gotten reinforced on the preceding trials. This learning creates persistence of the instrumental response in extinction.

Some have regarded frustration theory and sequential theory as competing explanations of the PREE. Since the two mechanisms were originally proposed, however, a large and impressive body of evidence has been obtained in support of each theory. Therefore, it is inappropriate to regard one theory as correct and the other as incorrect. Rather, the two theories identify two ways in which partial reinforcement can promote persistence. Memory mechanisms may make more of a contribution when training trials are not separated by long intertrial intervals (thereby reducing the difficulty of remembering the outcome of the preceding trial). In contrast, the emotional learning described by frustration theory is less sensitive to intertrial intervals and thus provides a better explanation of the PREE when widely spaced training trials are used. However, the prudent conclusion is that both mechanisms contribute to persistence in most situations.

In exposure therapy for maladaptive fears and phobias, persistence of responding in extinction is considered a poor outcome. However, persistence in the face of nonreinforcement is an enviable trait in many other areas of life. Successful baseball players have to continue swinging at pitches even though they hit the ball less than a third of the time. Success in business, science, and politics often comes from persistence in the face of repeated failures.

Summary

Reinforcement procedures are not always permanent. The study of extinction tells us what happens when a response is no longer reinforced or a CS is no longer paired with a US. Extinction produces two prominent behavioral changes: a decrease in the CR and an increase in response variability. These changes depend on the previous circumstances of reinforcement. Overtraining and the use of a larger reinforcer produce faster decreases in responding during extinction, especially with continuous reinforcement. In contrast, partial or intermittent reinforcement slows the response decline.

The decrease in responding that occurs with extinction may look like the opposite of acquisition, but phenomena such as spontaneous recovery, renewal, and reinstatement indicate that extinction does not erase the effects of prior acquisition training. Extinction also does not erase R–O and S–O associations. Rather, extinction involves the learning of a response–inhibition process based on the frustrative and aversive effects of nonreward. Although extinction does not eliminate conditioned responding, greater suppressions of behavior occur with repetitions of the extinction procedure, spacing of extinction trials, conducting extinction in multiple contexts, providing cues that reactivate the memory of extinction, and priming extinction sessions with a CS-alone trial.

Suggested Readings

Amsel, A. (1992). *Frustration theory: An analysis of dispositional learning and memory.* Cambridge, England: Cambridge University Press.

Bouton, M. E. (2014). Why behavior change is difficult to sustain. *Preventive Medicine, 68*, 29–36. http://dx.doi.org/10.1016/j.ypmed.2014.06.010

Capaldi, E. J. (1971). Memory and learning: A sequential viewpoint. In W. K. Honig & P. H. R. James (Eds.), *Animal memory* (pp. 115–154). Orlando, FL: Academic Press.

Maren, S., & Holmes, A. (2016). Stress and fear extinction. *Neuropsychopharmacology, 41*, 58–79. http://dx.doi.org/10.1038/npp.2015.180

Todd, T. P., Vurbic, D., & Bouton, M. E. (2014). Behavioral and neurobiological mechanisms of extinction in Pavlovian and instrumental learning. *Neurobiology of Learning and Memory, 108*, 52–64. http://dx.doi.org/10.1016/j.nlm.2013.08.012

Technical Terms

Continuous reinforcement
Discrimination hypothesis
Extinction
Forgetting
Frustration
Frustration theory
Inhibitory S–R association
Intermittent reinforcement
Magnitude-of-reinforcement extinction effect

Overtraining extinction effect
Paradoxical reward effect
Partial reinforcement
Partial-reinforcement extinction effect
Priming of extinction
Reinstatement
Renewal
Sequential theory
Spontaneous recovery

Punishment 11

Did you know that

- punishment does not have to involve physical pain?
- when properly applied, punishment can produce permanent suppression of behavior in a single trial?
- the effectiveness of punishment is substantially reduced by delivering punishment intermittently or with a delay?
- mild punishment for an initial offense may immunize the individual to subsequent punishment?
- severe punishment for an initial offense may sensitize the individual to subsequent punishment?
- the effectiveness of punishment is greatly increased by positive reinforcement of alternative behavior?
- punishment facilitates responding if it signals positive reinforcement or if the punished response is a form of escape behavior?
- when one person punishes another out of anger or frustration, the parameters of effective punishment are usually violated, and no constructive changes in behavior are produced?

In discussing instrumental conditioning up to this point, I have relied primarily on examples of positive reinforcement—examples in which the instrumental response results in the delivery of an appetitive or "pleasant" event. Instrumental behavior can be also modified by aversive or "unpleasant"

http://dx.doi.org/10.1037/0000057-011
The Essentials of Conditioning and Learning, Fourth Edition, by M. Domjan

events. Perhaps the simplest aversive control procedure is *punishment*. In a punishment procedure, an aversive event is delivered contingent on the performance of an instrumental response. The expected or typical outcome is suppression of the punished behavior. However, the degree of response suppression depends on numerous factors, many of which are not intuitively obvious.

Punishment is probably the most controversial topic in conditioning and learning. It conjures up visions of cruelty and abuse, and it is the only conditioning procedure whose application is regulated by law. However, punishment need not involve unusual forms of physical cruelty or pain. A variety of aversive events have been effectively used as punishing outcomes, including verbal reprimands, monetary fines, placement in a time-out corner or time-out room, loss of earned privileges or positive reinforcers, demerits, various restitution procedures, and even water mist or a squirt of lemon juice in the mouth. Mild electric shock is used as an aversive stimulus in animal research because its intensity and duration can be precisely controlled. Shock is used rarely if ever with people, and then only under extreme circumstances.

Societal concerns and lack of research funding have discouraged research on punishment in recent years, but we learned a lot from experiments on punishment that were conducted previously. The stage for the punishment debate was set by Thorndike early in the 20th century. Thorndike (1932) claimed that punishment is ineffective in producing significant and lasting changes in behavior and therefore should not be used. On the basis of his own studies, Skinner (1953) adopted a similar point of view. He argued that we should make every effort to eliminate the use of punishment in society because punishment is cruel and ineffective. Whether punishment is cruel cannot be decided by means of empirical evidence. However, the claim that punishment is ineffective can be examined experimentally. Contrary to the early claims of Thorndike and Skinner, systematic research has indicated that punishment can be very effective in suppressing behavior, provided that punishment is properly applied.

Effective and Ineffective Punishment

Casual observation suggests that Thorndike and Skinner may have been correct in saying that punishment is ineffective. Violations of traffic laws are punished by fines and other unpleasant consequences. Nevertheless, people continue to drive through red lights and often drive faster than the posted speed limit. Grade-school children scolded by a teacher for not having their homework completed do not necessarily finish their next assignment on time. And a drug dealer apprehended for selling cocaine or heroin is likely to return to selling drugs once he is released from jail.

In contrast to the preceding examples, punishment is sometimes remarkably effective. A child who accidentally gets shocked while playing with an electric outlet is never going to poke his fingers into an outlet again. A person who falls and hurts herself rushing down a wet walkway will slow down the next time she has to negotiate the walkway in the rain. Someone who tips over a canoe by leaning too far to one side will be much more careful about staying in the middle of the canoe after that.

Why punishment is highly effective in suppressing behavior in some cases but not others has been the subject of extensive laboratory research, conducted mainly with rats and pigeons in the 1960s (Azrin & Holz, 1966; Church, 1969). In this chapter, I describe the major findings from these experiments and relate them to situations people encounter in their daily lives. Keep in mind, however, that the empirical foundations of my claims come primarily from research with laboratory animals. Let us first consider the cases in which punishment fails.

WHEN PUNISHMENT FAILS

Why do drivers often exceed the speed limit even though speeding can result in a fine? Punishment in the enforcement of traffic laws is similar to punishment in much of the criminal justice system and in many social situations. In all of these cases, punishment is administered by an individual rather than being an automatic environmental consequence of a response. Unlike a canoe, which tips over automatically when someone leans too far to one side, drivers do not automatically get a ticket when they drive too fast. A police officer has to detect the transgression, and an officer of the court has to judge the severity of the offense and decide on what penalty to apply. Requiring officers to detect the response to be punished and administer the aversive stimulus can make punishment ineffective for a variety of reasons.

One consequence of needing a police officer to detect speeders is that drivers are not caught every time they exceed the speed limit. In fact, the chances of getting caught are pretty slim. A driver may exceed the speed limit 50 times or more without getting caught for each time his speed is recorded by a patrol officer. Thus, punishment is highly intermittent. On the rare occasion when a driver who is speeding is detected, chances are that he is not detected right away but only after he has been going too fast for some time. Thus, punishment is delayed after the initiation of the behavior targeted for punishment. Further delays in punishment occur because fines do not have to be paid right away. The guilty party usually has a week or two to pay the fine. Traffic tickets can also be appealed, and an appeal may take several months.

If the appeal is unsuccessful, punishment for the first offense is likely to be fairly mild. The driver will probably just have to pay a fine. More severe penalties are imposed only if the driver is repeatedly ticketed for speeding. Thus, punishment is initially mild and increases in severity only after repeated offenses. This gradual escalation of the severity of punishment is a fundamental feature of how punishment is administered in our society. For most forms of illegal conduct, the first or second offense is not treated as harshly as the fifth or sixth transgression. We get serious about punishing someone only after repeated offenses.

Another reason punishment is not effective in discouraging speeding is that drivers can often tell when their speed is about to be measured by a patrol officer. In some cities, the location of radar checkpoints is announced on the radio each morning. The presence of an officer is also obvious from the distinctive markings of patrol cars. Some drivers have radar detectors in their cars that signal the presence of a radar patrol. Patrol cars and radar detectors provide discriminative stimuli for punishment. Thus, punishment is often signaled by a discriminative stimulus. (See Table 11.1.)

TABLE 11.1

Characteristics of Punishment

For driving too fast	For poking fingers into an electric outlet
Occurs intermittently	Occurs every time
Delayed	Immediate
Low-intensity aversive stimulus at first	High-intensity aversive stimulus every time
Signaled by a discriminative stimulus	Not signaled

WHEN PUNISHMENT SUCCEEDS

In contrast to the ineffectiveness of punishment in discouraging speeding, why does punishment work so well in discouraging a child from poking his fingers into an electric outlet? A child shocked while playing with an electric outlet is unlikely ever to do it again and may in fact develop a strong fear of outlets. What are the critical differences in the punishment contingencies involved in driving too fast and in playing with an electric outlet?

First, *punishment occurs consistently* for sticking your fingers into an electric outlet. Every time you do it, you will get shocked. If you touch an outlet and come in contact with the electrodes, you are sure to get shocked. The physical configuration of the outlet guarantees that punishment is delivered every time.

Second, *punishment is immediate.* As soon as you make contact with the electrodes, you get shocked. There is no elaborate detection or decision process involved to delay delivery of the aversive stimulus.

Third, *punishment is intense for the first transgression.* The outlet does not give you a warning the first time you touch the electrodes. The first offense is treated with the same severity as the 10th one. Each and every time you make the response, you get an intense shock.

Finally, punishment is not limited to times when a police officer or observer is watching. Thus, punishment is not signaled by a discriminative stimulus. There is no light or buzzer to tell you when the outlet will be "hot." No matter who is present in the room or what else may going on, sticking your fingers into the outlet will get you shocked. Severe and immediate punishment is always in effect for each occurrence of the target response.

Research Evidence on Punishment

All of the factors that characterize the punishment for touching the electrodes in an electric outlet have been found to be important in carefully conducted laboratory research. Moreover, research has identified several additional factors that strongly determine the effectiveness of punishment. Ironically, much of the research was done under the leadership of one of Skinner's former students, Nathan Azrin (Azrin & Holz, 1966). Complementary studies were performed in a research program conducted by Church (1969). Azrin used pigeons for much of his research, whereas Church used laboratory rats. Contrary to the early claims of Thorndike and Skinner, these experiments demonstrated that punishment can be a highly effective technique for producing rapid and long-term changes in behavior.

RESPONSE–REINFORCER CONTINGENCY

Punishment is similar to positive reinforcement in that it involves a positive contingency between the instrumental response and the reinforcer. The reinforcer is delivered only if the organism has previously performed the target response. The primary difference between punishment and positive reinforcement is that the response outcome is an aversive rather than an appetitive stimulus.

As with other instrumental conditioning procedures, a fundamental variable in punishment is the *response–reinforcer contingency*. This refers to the extent to which delivery of the aversive stimulus depends on the prior occurrence of the target response. If an aversive stimulus is administered independently of the target response, the procedure is a form of Pavlovian aversive conditioning rather than punishment. As we saw in Chapter 4 of this volume, Pavlovian aversive conditioning results in the conditioning of fear, which results in freezing and a general suppression of ongoing behavior.

Punishment procedures sometimes also produce a general suppression of ongoing behavior. However, this is not an inevitable outcome, and punishment also produces behavioral suppression specific to the target response (Camp, Raymond, & Church, 1967; Goodall, 1984). The specificity of the behavioral suppression produced by punishment depends on the contingency between the target response and the aversive reinforcer. The stronger the response–reinforcer contingency, the more specific is the response suppression produced by punishment.

RESPONSE–REINFORCER CONTIGUITY

As I previously described for positive reinforcement, the response–reinforcer contingency is just one aspect of the relation between an instrumental response and a reinforcer. Another important factor is the interval between the target response and delivery of the reinforcer. In a punishment procedure, this is the interval between the target response and the aversive consequence.

Response–reinforcer contiguity is just as important with punishment as it is with positive reinforcement. Punishment is most effective if the aversive stimulus is presented without delay after the target response (Camp, Raymond, & Church, 1967). If punishment is delayed after the target response, some suppression of behavior may occur (because of the Pavlovian conditioning of fear). However, the response suppression will not be specific to the punished response and may not be as complete.

INTENSITY OF THE AVERSIVE STIMULUS

As one might suspect, the response-suppressing effects of punishment are directly related to the intensity of the aversive stimulus. Research with rats and pigeons has shown that low intensities of punishment produce only mild suppression of behavior.

In contrast, dramatic suppressions of behavior result from the use of intense aversive stimuli (Azrin, 1960). More importantly, the effects of the intensity of punishment depend on the participant's prior experience with punishment. In general, individuals tend to respond to a new level of punishment similarly to how they responded during earlier encounters with punishment.

The historical effects of exposure to punishment can lead to somewhat unexpected results. Consider, for example, individuals who are initially exposed to a low intensity of punishment. Weak aversive stimuli produce only mild, if any, suppression of responding. Animals exposed to low-intensity punishment habituate to the aversive stimulus and learn to continue responding with little disruption in their behavior. This persistent responding in the face of mild punishment continues when higher intensities of aversive stimulation are introduced (Azrin, Holz, & Hake, 1963; N. E. Miller, 1960). As a result, the individuals continue to respond when the intensity of punishment is increased. In a sense, exposure to mild aversive stimulation serves to immunize individuals against the effects of more intense punishment (see Figure 11.1).

Interestingly, a history of exposure to intense punishment can have just the opposite effect. Initial exposure to intense punishment can increase the impact of subsequent mild punishment (see Figure 11.2). High-intensity aversive stimulation produces dramatic suppression of the punished response, and this severe suppression of responding persists when the intensity of the aversive stimulus is subsequently reduced (Church, 1969). Thus, mild punishment produces much more severe suppression of behavior in individuals who have previously received intense punishment than in individuals who

FIGURE 11.1

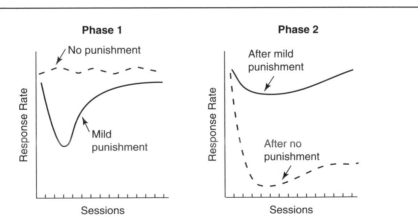

Immunizing effects of prior experience with mild punishment. During Phase 1, one group of participants is exposed to mild punishment, while another group is permitted to respond without punishment. During Phase 2, both groups receive intense punishment. Data are hypothetical.

FIGURE 11.2

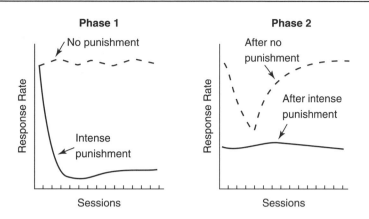

Sensitizing effects of experience with intense punishment. During Phase 1, one group of participants is exposed to intense punishment while another group is permitted to respond without punishment. During Phase 2, both groups receive mild punishment. Data are hypothetical.

were not punished previously. Exposure to intense punishment sensitizes the participant to subsequent mild aversive stimulation.

SIGNALED PUNISHMENT

Some punishment contingencies are always in effect. However, more commonly, the punishment contingency is only in effect in the presence of particular stimuli, which are usually provided by the person who administers the punishment procedure. If punishment is signaled by a distinctive stimulus, the procedure is called *discriminative punishment*. A child, for example, may be reprimanded for running through the living room when her parents are home but not when her grandparents are in charge. In this case, punishment would be signaled by cues associated with the presence of the child's parents. The parents would be discriminative stimuli for punishment.

As you might suspect, a child reprimanded by her parents but not by her grandparents will avoid running through the living room when her parents are home but will not show such restraint when the grandparents are in charge. Discriminative-punishment procedures result in discriminative suppression of behavior (Dinsmoor, 1952). Responding becomes suppressed in the presence of the discriminative stimulus but continues unabated when the discriminative stimulus is absent.

Discriminative control of a punished response can be problematic. A parent may try to get a child not to use foul language by punishing him whenever he curses. This may discourage cursing in the presence of the parent but will not stop the child from cursing around his friends or at school. The suppression of foul language will be under discriminative control, and the parent's goal will not be achieved.

In other cases, the discriminative punishment is not problematic. If a child starts talking loudly during a religious service, she is likely to be reprimanded. If the punishment procedure is effective, the child will cease talking during the service, but this will not stop her from talking enthusiastically elsewhere. Having the response suppressed only under the discriminative-stimulus control of the church service is not a problem.

PUNISHMENT AND THE MECHANISMS MAINTAINING THE PUNISHED RESPONSE

Punishment procedures are applied to responses that already occur for one reason or another. Typically, punished responses are maintained by some form of positive reinforcement. This turns out to be very important because the effects of punishment depend on the type of reinforcement and schedule of reinforcement that support the target response.

A child may talk during a church service to attract attention or to enjoy the camaraderie that comes from talking with a friend. If the child is reprimanded for talking, the aversiveness of the reprimand is pitted against the enjoyment of the attention and camaraderie. The outcome of the punishment procedure depends on how the child solves this cost–benefit problem. Research with laboratory animals has shown that, in general, punishment will be less effective if the target response is frequently reinforced. Punishment is more effective if the target response is reinforced only once in a while (Church & Raymond, 1967).

The outcome of punishment also depends on the particular schedule of positive reinforcement that maintains the target response. With variable and fixed-interval schedules, punishment reduces the overall level of responding but does not change the temporal distribution of the behavior (e.g., Azrin & Holz, 1961). In contrast, if the instrumental response is maintained on a fixed-ratio schedule of reinforcement, punishment tends to increase the postreinforcement pause (Azrin, 1959; Dardano & Sauerbrunn, 1964), with little effect on the ratio run.

PUNISHMENT AND THE REINFORCEMENT OF ALTERNATIVE BEHAVIOR

As we saw in the preceding section, the outcome of punishment procedures can be analyzed in terms of the relative costs and benefits of performing the target response. This cost–benefit analysis involves not only the punished response but also other activities the individual may perform. A powerful technique for increasing the effects of punishment is to provide positive reinforcement for some other behavior (Perry & Parke, 1975). Successful parents are well aware of this principle. Punishing children on a long car ride for quarreling among themselves is relatively ineffective if the children are not given much else to do. Punishment of quarreling is much more effective if it is accompanied by an alternative reinforced activity, such as playing a video game or watching a movie on a computer tablet in the car.

PARADOXICAL EFFECTS OF PUNISHMENT

The factors that I have described so far determine the extent to which punishment will suppress the target response. Punishment will not be very effective if the punished response is maintained by a powerful schedule of positive reinforcement, if there is no positive reinforcement for alternative behavior, or if the punishment is mild, delayed, and involves a weak response–reinforcer contingency. Weak punishment parameters make punishment ineffective. Under some circumstances, punishment may even produce the opposite of what is intended—facilitation rather than suppression of responding.

Punishment as a Signal for Positive Reinforcement

Paradoxical facilitation of responding can occur when punishment serves as a signal for positive reinforcement (Holz & Azrin, 1961). Attention, for example, is a powerful source of reinforcement for children. A child may be ignored by his parents most of the time as long as he is not doing anything dangerous or disruptive. If he starts playing with matches, he is severely reprimanded. Will punishment suppress the target response in this case? Not likely. Notice that the child receives attention from his parents only after he does something bad and is being punished. Under these circumstances, punishment can become a signal for attention or positive reinforcement, with the outcome that the child will seek out punishment as a way to obtain attention. One of the hardest things for parents to learn is to pay attention to their children when the children are not doing anything disruptive so that punishment does not become associated with getting attention.

Punishment of Escape Behavior

Paradoxical effects can also occur if punishment is applied to an escape response. An escape response serves to terminate an aversive stimulus. When a response terminates an aversive stimulus, thereby increasing the probability of the response, the stimulus is called a *negative reinforcer* and the operation is called *negative reinforcement*. (I have more to say about negative reinforcement in Chapter 12.)

Negative reinforcement is highly constrained because before an organism can terminate an aversive stimulus, the aversive stimulus must be present. Thus, an escape response is always performed in the presence of an aversive stimulus (see Figure 11.3). This makes the presence of the aversive stimulus a cue for the escape response. Punishment of an escape response facilitates rather than suppresses responding (e.g., Dean & Pittman, 1991). This paradoxical effect occurs because the aversive stimulus used to punish the response is the same stimulus that motivated the behavior in the first place. Hence, the escape response persists even though it is being punished.

FIGURE 11.3

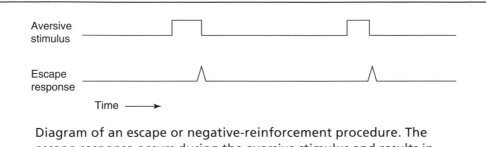

Diagram of an escape or negative-reinforcement procedure. The escape response occurs during the aversive stimulus and results in its termination.

Paradoxical effects of punishment are not common, and they should not encourage us to jump to the conclusion that punishment produces unpredictable results. Rather, if a paradoxical effect of punishment is observed, one should examine the situation carefully to determine whether punishment has come to serve as a signal for positive reinforcement. If that does not seem likely, perhaps the target response was previously reinforced as an escape response.

Can and Should We Create a Society Free of Punishment?

As I noted at the beginning of this chapter, both Thorndike and Skinner advocated that punishment should not be used, because they regarded punishment as ineffective in producing significant and lasting changes in behavior. Their recommendation was fine, but their reasoning was wrong. Laboratory experiments have shown that punishment can be highly effective in decreasing instrumental behavior. Does this mean that we should go ahead and use punishment whenever we are interested in discouraging some activity? Or should we work to build a society entirely free of punishment? Answers to these questions depend in part on what one considers to be just and ethical human conduct. Ethical questions are beyond the scope of the principles of conditioning and learning. We can consider, however, how empirical evidence about the effectiveness of punishment may inform the decisions we make about societal uses of punishment.

First, can we create a punishment-free environment? The answer to that is pretty obvious. Punishment is an inevitable consequence of various aspects of the physical and biological environment in which we live. If you mishandle a cat, the cat will scratch you. If you don't hold your glass steady as you pour from a pitcher, you will spill and make a mess. If you lift a pot out of the oven without a potholder, you will burn yourself. It would be impossible to redesign our environment to eliminate all sources of punishment.

Given that punishment cannot be eliminated entirely, what kinds of punishment should we try to get rid of, and would doing that be sensible? The kind of punishment that people in our culture find most objectionable is physical pain inflicted by one person in an effort to control the behavior of someone else. We have laws against the use of corporal punishment in schools. We also have laws against child abuse, spousal abuse, and elder abuse. Such laws are justified on moral and ethical grounds. Do such laws also make sense from the perspective of empirical principles of punishment? I think so.

Interpersonal interactions involving punishment require one individual to inflict pain on another. An important factor is the willingness of the person administering the punishment to hurt the recipient. A parent may claim to be punishing a child for having received a poor grade in school, or a husband may say that he is punishing his wife for getting home late. However, whether the punishment takes place is often related to the emotional state of the person who administers the punishment. People are more likely to punish someone if they are frustrated and angry. If someone is lashing out against another individual out of anger and frustration, principles of effective punishment are probably farthest from his or her mind.

If punishment is administered out of frustration and anger, it is not likely to be linked to an undesired response. If a poor grade on a school assignment aggravates a parent only when she is frustrated and angry, the punishment is likely to be intermittent. Frustrative punishment is also likely to occur with a long delay after the target response has taken place. A parent may become abusive when a child brings home a poor report card, even though the responses that contributed to the poor grades occurred earlier over a period of weeks.

Another disadvantage is that frustrative punishment is often under discriminative stimulus control, with the discriminative stimulus being unrelated to the punished behavior. A parent may become upset by a poor report card when his or her emotional resources are strained by difficulties at work, ill health, or drug abuse. Under these circumstances, the likelihood of punishment will be signaled by the parent's irritability, and the child will learn that she can get her report card signed without being punished if she just waits until the next day or the weekend when her mother is in a better mood.

Another shortcoming of frustrative punishment is that it is rarely accompanied by positive reinforcement of alternative behavior. When a parent punishes a child out of irritability and anger, the parent is not likely to have the presence of mind to accompany the punishment with a programmatic effort to provide positive reinforcement for more constructive activities.

Punishment as an act of aggression and frustration violates many of the parameters of effective punishment and therefore does not produce constructive changes in behavior. Because punishment out of frustration is poorly related to the targeted behavior, frustrative punishment is abusive and cannot be justified as a systematic behavior modification procedure. Societal prohibitions against the use of punishment serve to reduce instances of punishment that are motivated by frustration and anger rather than a thoughtful programmatic effort to promote better behavior. (For a more detailed discussion of problems related to the use of punishment in society, see Gershoff, 2013, 2016.)

Alternatives to Abusive Punishment

Abusive punishment cannot be justified on either ethical or empirical grounds. But undesired responses are bound to occur in homes, classrooms, and other settings. What are we to do about them? What alternatives are there to abusive punishment? Unfortunately, there are no easy answers. It has become clear that whatever procedure is adopted to suppress undesired responses, that procedure must be applied as part of a systematic program that considers not only the response to be suppressed but also the other activities other sources of reinforcement of the client. I discussed in Chapter 9 how the effects of positive reinforcement depend on a broader behavioral context. The same thing is very much the case for punishment.

TIME-OUT

A popular alternative to physical punishment in educational settings is the *time-out* procedure (Hagopian, Dozier, Rooker, & Jones, 2013). In fact, many classrooms have a time-out chair where a student has to sit if he is being punished. In a time-out procedure, the consequence of making an undesired response is not a physically aversive event but time-out from sources of positive reinforcement. A teenager who is "grounded" for a week for having taken the family car without permission is undergoing a form of the time-out procedure. Time-out is also being used when a child is told to "go to your room" as a form of punishment.

As with other instrumental conditioning procedures, the effectiveness of time-out depends on the delay between the target response and the time-out consequence. The effectiveness of the procedure also depends on how consistently it is applied. In addition, time-out involves some special considerations. To be effective, the procedure should result in a substantial reduction in the rate of positive reinforcement. A child who has many fun things to do in her room will not be discouraged by being sent to her room as a form of time-out.

Another important consideration is how much reinforcement was available before the time-out was administered compared with how much reinforcement is available in the time-out situation. Time-out is unlikely to suppress behavior if the individual is not getting much positive reinforcement anyway. A child who is not enjoying any aspect of being in a classroom will not experience much of a loss of reinforcement when he is put in time-out.

DIFFERENTIAL REINFORCEMENT OF OTHER BEHAVIOR

Another alternative to abusive punishment is *differential reinforcement of other behavior* (DRO). A DRO procedure involves a negative contingency between a target response and a reinforcer. I have previously discussed that learning produced by a negative contingency in connection with inhibitory Pavlovian conditioning. There the negative contingency was between a conditioned stimulus (CS) and an unconditioned stimulus (US). The inhibitory CS indicated that the US would not occur. In a DRO procedure, the negative contingency is between a target instrumental response and presentations of a reinforcing stimulus. Occurrence of the target response leads to the omission of the reinforcer.

In a DRO procedure, the reinforcer is scheduled to be delivered at set intervals (e.g., every 30 seconds). Occurrence of the target response causes cancellation of these scheduled reinforcers for a specified period, or resetting of the inter-reinforcer interval. This contingency results in suppression of the target response. Because the DRO procedure involves a negative response–reinforcer contingency and suppresses responding, the DRO is sometimes called *negative punishment* (Lattal, 2013).

Cancelling a teenager's weekly allowance because she stayed out too late one night is an example of a DRO schedule. The allowance is provided on a regular basis. However, the occurrence of a target undesired response results in suspension of the allowance for a specified period.

DRO is different from the time-out procedure described in the preceding section in several respects. In a DRO, reinforcers are not cancelled by having the individual go to a specific time-out chair or time-out room. Rather, previously scheduled reinforcers are omitted for a certain amount of time after the target response. Another important difference is that in the DRO procedure reinforcers are explicitly provided when the target response does not occur. Thus, activities other than the target behavior end up getting reinforced. This is why the procedure is called differential reinforcement of other behavior. It does not matter what those "other" behaviors are. Because organisms are always doing something, alternatives to the target response come to be performed more frequently in a DRO procedure (Jessel, Borrero, & Becraft, 2015).

A DRO procedure is more difficult to administer than the more common time-out procedure because it requires providing a reinforcer periodically when the target response is not made. To use a DRO procedure, a convenient reinforcer must be identified and arrangements have to be made to deliver the reinforcer periodically over extended periods of time. Thus, the DRO procedure requires interacting with the participant for long periods of time even if the response of interest does not occur.

Summary

In a punishment procedure, an aversive stimulus is presented contingent on the instrumental response. Punishment is highly effective in suppressing the target response if it is administered without delay, at a high intensity from the beginning, and each time the target response is made. The effectiveness of punishment can be further increased by providing positive reinforcement for alternative activities. Exposure to mild punishment at the beginning can result in learned resistance to the suppressive effects of more intense punishment, and signaling punishment can limit the response suppression to the presence of the signal. Punishment can result in a paradoxical increase in responding if it serves as a signal for positive reinforcement or if it is applied to escape behavior that is aversively motivated.

In daily life, the use of punishment is often related to the emotional state of the person who administers the aversive stimulus. People are likely to use punishment when they are frustrated and angry. Under these circumstances, many of the parameters of effective punishment are violated, with the result that no constructive changes in behavior are produced. Problems with the use of punishment have encouraged the use of alternatives such as time-out and differential reinforcement of other behavior. Successful application of any response-suppression procedure requires considering not only the undesired response but also the individual's other activities and other sources of reinforcement.

Suggested Readings

Azrin, N. H., & Holz, W. C. (1966). Punishment. In W. K. Honig (Ed.), *Operant behavior: Areas of research and application* (pp. 380–447). New York, NY: Appleton-Century-Crofts.

Church, R. M. (1969). Response suppression. In B. A. Campbell & R. M. Church (Eds.), *Punishment and aversive behavior* (pp. 111—156). New York, NY: Appleton-Century-Crofts.

Gershoff, E. T. (2013). Spanking and child development: We know enough now to stop hitting our children. *Child Development Perspectives, 7,* 113–137. http://dx.doi.org/10.1111/cdep.12038

Jessel, J., Borrero, J. C., & Becraft, J. L. (2015). Differential reinforcement of other behavior increases untargeted behavior. *Journal of Applied Behavior Analysis, 48,* 402–416. http://dx.doi.org/10.1002/jaba.204

Technical Terms

Differential reinforcement of
    other behavior
Discriminative punishment

Negative reinforcement
Punishment
Time-out

Avoidance Learning | 12

Did you know that

- avoidance is a form of instrumental conditioning in which the instrumental response prevents the delivery of an aversive stimulus?
- no major theory assumes that avoidance behavior is reinforced by the absence of the avoided aversive stimulus?
- although avoidance is a form of instrumental behavior, theories of avoidance learning rely heavily on concepts from Pavlovian conditioning?
- several important aspects of avoidance learning are assumed to involve learning about internal temporal cues and proprioceptive or feedback cues that accompany the avoidance response?
- avoidance behavior is strongly determined by the preexisting defensive behavior system of the organism?

Punishment is just one of the major forms of instrumental conditioning that involve aversive stimuli. Another form of aversive control is avoidance conditioning. In punishment procedures, performance of the instrumental response results in the presentation of an aversive stimulus. In avoidance conditioning, the instrumental response prevents or blocks the presentation of the aversive event.

http://dx.doi.org/10.1037/0000057-012
The Essentials of Conditioning and Learning, Fourth Edition, by M. Domjan

We do lots of things that prevent something bad from happening. Putting out one's hand when approaching a door prevents the discomfort of walking into a closed door; periodically checking the barbeque prevents burning the hot dogs you may be grilling; slowing down while driving prevents a collision with the car in front of you; putting on a coat prevents you from getting cold when you step outside. All of these are avoidance responses.

Because I have already discussed various instrumental conditioning procedures, and because people are highly familiar with avoidance learning from personal experience, one might suppose that analyses of avoidance conditioning would be fairly straightforward, if not self-evident. Unfortunately, this is not the case. In fact, avoidance learning has been one of the most difficult forms of learning to analyze and explain. Because of thorny conceptual problems in avoidance learning, much of the research has been driven by theoretical rather than practical considerations. This is in sharp contrast to research on punishment, which has been dominated by practical considerations.

Dominant Questions in the Analysis of Avoidance Learning

Avoidance procedures are clear enough: The participant performs an instrumental response that prevents the delivery of an aversive stimulus. However, it is not clear what aspect of the avoidance procedure reinforces the instrumental response. Because a successful avoidance response prevents the delivery of the aversive stimulus, successful avoidance responses are followed by nothing. Mowrer and Lamoreaux (1942) pointed out that this raises a major theoretical question: How can "nothing" reinforce behavior and produce learning?

Various hypotheses and theories have been offered to explain how "nothing" can reinforce avoidance responding. The hypotheses and theories differ in various ways. However, all of the major explanations reject the commonsense idea that avoidance responses occur because they prevent the delivery of the aversive event. As we shall see, a number of ingenious proposals have been offered in an effort to explain avoidance learning without relying on the theoretically troublesome idea that "nothing" is a reinforcer.

The second major question in analyses of avoidance behavior is: How are Pavlovian conditioning processes involved in avoidance learning? As we have seen, Pavlovian conditioning processes have also been discussed in analyses of positively reinforced instrumental behavior (see Chapter 7, this volume). However, Pavlovian conditioning concepts have not dominated thinking about positively reinforced instrumental behavior as much as they have dominated analyses of avoidance learning. Historically, avoidance learning was regarded as a special case of Pavlovian conditioning. In fact, to this day some accounts of avoidance learning regard avoidance behavior as entirely the product of Pavlovian conditioning mechanisms.

Origins of the Study of Avoidance Learning

Avoidance learning was first investigated by the Russian scientist Bechterev (1913), who set out to study the conditioning of motor rather than glandular responses. The procedure Bechterev devised was fairly simple. He asked human participants to place a finger on metal electrodes resting on a table. A mild current could be passed through the electrodes, and this triggered a finger withdrawal response. Thus, the unconditioned response was finger withdrawal. To turn the situation into one involving classical conditioning, Bechterev presented a brief warning stimulus immediately before the shock on each trial. As you might predict, the participants quickly learned to lift their fingers off the electrodes when the conditioned stimulus (CS) was presented, and this was measured as the conditioned response.

Although Bechterev considered his finger-withdrawal technique to be a convenient way to study Pavlovian conditioning, more careful consideration of his procedure shows that in fact it was an instrumental rather than a Pavlovian procedure. Recall that the electrodes rested on the surface of a table; they were not attached to the participant's finger. Therefore, if the participant lifted his finger in response to the CS, he could entirely avoid getting shocked. This differs from standard Pavlovian procedures, in which the occurrence of the conditioned response does not determine whether the unconditioned stimulus (US) is delivered. Bechterev had inadvertently given his participants control over presentation of the US. This made the finger-withdrawal technique an instrumental rather than a Pavlovian conditioning procedure.

Contemporary Avoidance Conditioning Procedures

Two types of procedures are used in contemporary research on avoidance behavior. The discriminated avoidance procedure is a discrete-trial procedure that involves an explicit warning signal. The nondiscriminated avoidance procedure is a free-operant procedure and does not involve an explicit warning stimulus.

DISCRIMINATED AVOIDANCE

Without knowing it, Bechterev invented what has come to be known as the *discriminated avoidance* procedure. In a discriminated avoidance procedure, the response–reinforcer contingency is not always in effect. Rather, responding prevents delivery of the reinforcer only during discrete periods or trials when a CS or warning stimulus is presented. As illustrated in Figure 12.1, what happens during these trials depends on the participant's behavior. If the participant responds, the CS is turned off, and the aversive US is not delivered. In contrast, if the participant fails to respond during the CS, the CS continues to be presented for its full duration and ends in the presentation of the aversive US. Thus, a discriminated avoidance procedure involves two types of

FIGURE 12.1

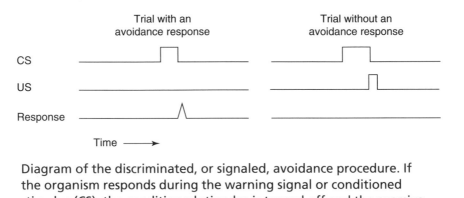

Diagram of the discriminated, or signaled, avoidance procedure. If the organism responds during the warning signal or conditioned stimulus (CS), the conditioned stimulus is turned off and the aversive unconditioned stimulus (US) is not delivered. In contrast, if the organism fails to respond during the warning signal or CS, the CS continues to be presented for its full duration and ends in the presentation of the aversive US.

trials, response trials and no-response trials, and the aversive US only occurs on trials without a response.

Since Bechterev's research, the discriminated avoidance procedure has been adapted for use with laboratory animals. In fact, most of the research on the theoretical mechanisms of avoidance learning has been done with laboratory rats. Typically the aversive US is mild electric shock delivered through a grid floor. Shock is used because its intensity and duration can be precisely controlled. In some experiments, rats are required to press a response lever during a CS or warning stimulus (a light or tone) to avoid receiving the shock. Other experiments use a *shuttle box* apparatus in which the rats have to move from one side of the apparatus to the other to avoid shock (see Figure 12.2). Each trial starts with presentation of a CS or warning stimulus (e.g., a light) while the rat is on one side of the apparatus. If the rat moves to the other side before the end of the CS, the CS is turned off and shock does not occur on that trial. If the rat does not move to the other side before the CS ends, the mild shock is applied and remains on until the rat escapes to the other side.

The shuttle box can be used to implement either a one-way or a two-way avoidance procedure. In a *one-way avoidance* procedure, the participant is always placed in the same compartment at the start of each trial (e.g., the left side). Because each trial starts on the same side (left), the avoidance response always involves going in the same direction (left to right). With this procedure, the side where the participant starts each trial is always potentially dangerous, whereas the other side is always safe. The animal never gets shocked on the other side. These features make the one-way avoidance task rather easy to learn.

In a *two-way avoidance* procedure, trials can start either on the left side or the right side, depending on which compartment the animal happens to occupy when the next

FIGURE 12.2

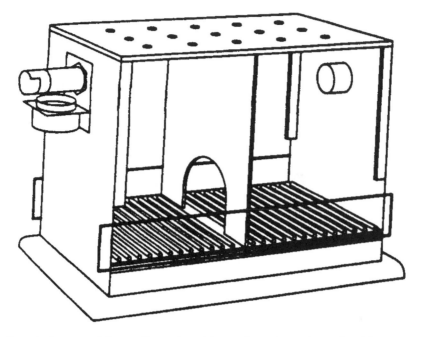

Shuttle box used in studies of avoidance learning. The animal has to cross from one compartment to the other to avoid mild shock through the grid floor.

trial is scheduled to begin. If the rat starts on the left, it must go to the right to avoid shock. If the rat starts on the right, it has to go to the left side to avoid shock. Because trials can start on either side, both sides of the shuttle box are potentially dangerous. The lack of a consistently safe side makes the two-way avoidance task more difficult to learn than the one-way procedure (Theios, Lynch, & Lowe, 1966).

NONDISCRIMINATED OR FREE-OPERANT AVOIDANCE

In discriminated avoidance procedures, responding is effective in preventing the aversive stimulus only if the response occurs during the trial period, when the warning stimulus is presented. Responses made during the intertrial interval have no effect. In fact, the participants may be removed from the apparatus during the intertrial interval. In contrast to such traditional discrete-trial procedures, Sidman (1953) devised a *nondiscriminated* or *free-operant avoidance* procedure.

Sidman's free-operant procedure was developed in the Skinnerian or operant tradition. In this tradition, trials are not restricted to periods when a discrete stimulus is present, and the participant can repeat the instrumental response at any time. On a fixed-ratio schedule in a Skinner box, for example, responses made at any time count toward completion of the ratio requirement. Sidman extended these features of operant methodology to the study of avoidance behavior.

In the free-operant avoidance procedure, an explicit warning stimulus is not used, and there are no discrete trials. The avoidance response may be performed at any time, and responding always provides some measure of benefit. Changing the oil in your car is an example. Changing the oil is an avoidance response that prevents engine problems. If you wait until the problems develop, you will encounter costly repairs. The best thing to do is to change the oil before any sign of engine difficulty. The recommended interval is every 3,000 miles. Thus, each oil change buys you 3,000 miles of trouble-free driving. You can change the oil after driving just 1,000 miles or drive another 800 miles before the oil change. Provided you change the oil before you have driven 3,000 miles, you always get 3,000 miles of trouble-free driving. Changing the oil in your car is just one example of a safety or health practice that involves doing something before signs of danger are evident. All of these are examples of free-operant avoidance contingencies.

In the laboratory, free-operant avoidance procedures use a brief shock that is programmed to occur at set intervals. For example, the shock may be scheduled to occur every 15 seconds in the absence of an avoidance response. This is the shock–shock interval, or *S–S interval*. Performance of the avoidance response creates a period of safety, during which no shocks are given. The safe period may be 30 seconds. This is the response–shock interval, or *R–S interval* (see Figure 12.3). Whether a shock occurs at the end of the R–S interval or at the end of the S–S interval, it is not preceded by an explicit warning signal.

An important aspect of free-operant avoidance procedures is that the R–S interval is reset and starts over again each time the avoidance response is made. Thus, if the R–S interval is 30 seconds, each response resets the R–S interval and starts the

FIGURE 12.3

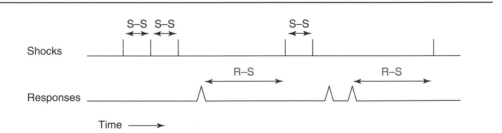

Diagram of a nondiscriminated, or free-operant, avoidance procedure. As long as the animal fails to respond, a brief shock is scheduled to occur periodically, as set by the shock–shock (S–S) interval. Each occurrence of the avoidance response creates a period without shock, as set by the response–shock (R–S) interval.

FIGURE 12.4

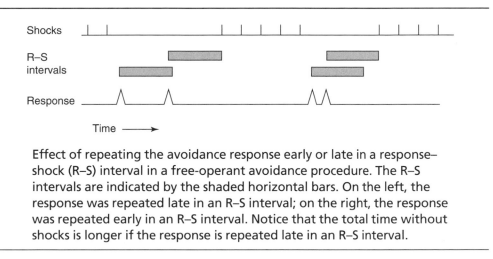

Effect of repeating the avoidance response early or late in a response–shock (R–S) interval in a free-operant avoidance procedure. The R–S intervals are indicated by the shaded horizontal bars. On the left, the response was repeated late in an R–S interval; on the right, the response was repeated early in an R–S interval. Notice that the total time without shocks is longer if the response is repeated late in an R–S interval.

30-second safe period all over again. Because of this feature, each occurrence of the avoidance response provides some benefit, just as each oil change provides some benefit. However, the degree of benefit depends on exactly when the response is made.

If the participant responds when the R–S interval is already in effect, the R–S interval will start over again, and time left on the R–S clock will be lost. The net benefit of responding will depend on whether the response occurs early or late in the R–S interval (see Figure 12.4). If the participant responds late in the R–S interval, it will lose only a small amount of time remaining on the R–S clock, and the net benefit of responding will be substantial. In contrast, if the participant responds early in the R–S interval, it will lose a lot of time remaining on the R–S clock, and the net benefit of responding will be much smaller. In either case, however, if the individual manages to respond before the end of each R–S interval, it will reset all of the R–S intervals and thereby successfully avoid all shocks.

Two-Factor Theory of Avoidance

The oldest and most influential theory of avoidance was the *two-factor theory* of avoidance learning originally proposed by O. H. Mowrer (1947; see also N. E. Miller, 1951). The two-factor theory was the dominant theoretical perspective for studies of avoidance learning for much of the 20th century, and its main components remain important in contemporary research (e.g., Maia, 2010) and clinical application (LeDoux & Gorman, 2001; van der Kolk, 2006). According to the two-factor theory, avoidance learning involves both classical and instrumental conditioning processes (those are the two factors). However, Mowrer did not describe either of these processes in ways that are intuitively obvious.

Let us first consider the classical conditioning component. Instead of thinking of classical conditioning as being directly responsible for the avoidance response (as Bechterev thought), Mowrer (1947) proposed that this process results in the conditioning of an emotional state called fear. On trials when the avoidance response does not occur, the warning stimulus or CS is paired with the aversive US, and this results in the conditioning of fear to the warning stimulus.

Conditioned fear is presumably an unpleasant or aversive state. Therefore, its reduction or elimination is assumed to be reinforcing. Fear reduction brings into play the second process in the two-factor theory. In trials when the avoidance response is made, the response turns off the warning stimulus and prevents the delivery of the US. Turning off the warning stimulus is assumed to result in the reduction of conditioned fear, and this fear reduction is assumed to provide reinforcement for the avoidance response. Thus, the second factor in the two-factor theory of avoidance is instrumental conditioning of the avoidance response through fear reduction.

Notice that according to the two-factor theory, avoidance behavior is not reinforced by "nothing" occurring after the avoidance response. Rather, the behavior is reinforced by fear reduction. Fear reduction is a form of *negative reinforcement* (removal of an aversive stimulus contingent on behavior). The instrumental response is considered to be an escape response—a response that escapes fear. Instead of focusing on the fact that avoidance behavior prevents delivery of the aversive US, the two-factor theory treats avoidance behavior as a special case of escape behavior.

The two-factor theory provides answers to many questions about avoidance learning. The answers were innovative when they were first proposed and have shaped the course of research on avoidance conditioning ever since. According to the theory, both Pavlovian and instrumental processes contribute to avoidance learning. Furthermore, the two processes are interdependent. Before fear reduction can provide instrumental reinforcement for the avoidance response, fear first has to become conditioned to the warning stimulus. Thus, classical conditioning of fear is a prerequisite for the instrumental component of the two-factor theory. The instrumental process depends on the integrity of the Pavlovian fear conditioning process.

EVIDENCE CONSISTENT WITH THE TWO-FACTOR THEORY

The interdependence of the Pavlovian and instrumental components of the two-factor theory has several major implications. First, if Pavlovian conditioned fear is the basis for avoidance behavior, then avoidance responding should decrease with extinction of the fear that has become conditioned to the warning stimulus or CS. This prediction has been confirmed by numerous studies. In these experiments, participants receive repeated exposures to the warning stimulus or CS presented by itself after acquisition of the avoidance response. The extinction procedures are typically conducted using standard Pavlovian protocols in which participants cannot control the duration of the CS-alone presentations. Subsequent tests of the avoidance responding show that avoidance behavior is significantly reduced by Pavlovian extinction of fear, with the degree of response decrement determined by the total duration of CS-alone presentations (M. Baum, 1970; Schiff, Smith, & Prochaska, 1972). These laboratory findings provide the empirical basis for exposure therapy, which is the standard treatment for maladaptive avoidance behavior such as compulsive handwashing.

A second major prediction of the two-factor theory is that fear reduction should be effective in reinforcing instrumental behavior even if the fear was not acquired in a signaled avoidance procedure. This prediction has been also confirmed in numerous studies called *escape from fear* experiments. In these studies, conditioned fear is initially established using a standard Pavlovian conditioning procedure, without an instrumental or avoidance component. For example, a tone or light may be repeatedly paired with shock under circumstances in which the participants cannot escape or avoid the shock. In the next phase of the experiment, the Pavlovian CS is presented in each trial but now the participants have the opportunity to terminate the CS by making a specified instrumental response (pressing a response lever or going from one side of a shuttle box to the other). The datum of interest is the increase in the probability of the instrumental response that occurs under these circumstances. Such an increase is routinely observed, indicating that fear reduction is an effective reinforcer for instrumental behavior (Cain & LeDoux, 2007; Esmorís-Arranz, Pardo-Vázquez, & Vázquez-García, 2003).

EVIDENCE CONTRARY TO THE TWO-FACTOR THEORY

Another major implication of the interdependence of Pavlovian and instrumental processes in the two-factor theory is that conditioned fear and avoidance responding should be highly correlated. In particular, high levels of avoidance responding should be accompanied by high levels of fear elicited by the warning stimulus in the avoidance procedure. Interestingly, this prediction has been frequently disproven. As avoidance responding increases, fear of the warning stimulus or CS that signals shock actually decreases.

The decrease in fear that accompanies mastery of an avoidance procedure has been well documented in studies with both laboratory animals (Mineka, 1979) and human participants (e.g., Lovibond, Saunders, Weidemann, & Mitchell, 2008). Studies with people provide some insight into why this occurs. Human participants report a decrease in the expectation of shock as they gain proficiency in making the avoidance response. Once you know how to prevent the shock, you have little expectation that shock will occur if you respond correctly, and therefore your level of fear declines.

Common experience also suggests that little, if any, fear exists once an avoidance response becomes well learned. Steering a car so that it does not drift off the road is basically avoidance behavior. A competent driver avoids letting the car get too close to the side of the road or too close to another lane of traffic by making appropriate steering adjustments. Even though these adjustments are avoidance responses, proficient drivers show no fear as they steer their car under normal traffic conditions.

Conditioned Temporal Cues in Avoidance Learning

Findings that are difficult to explain in terms of the two-factor theory of avoidance have encouraged modifications and additions to the theory. Efforts to integrate new findings with the theory have often involved postulating internal stimuli and ascribing important functions to these internal cues. Nondiscriminated avoidance has been a special challenge because it does not involve an explicit warning stimulus, which plays a major role in the two-factor theory. To overcome this difficulty, investigators have postulated that internal cues related to the passage of time serve the function of a warning stimulus in nondiscriminated avoidance procedures (Anger, 1963).

Recall that in a nondiscriminated avoidance procedure, shocks occur at predictable times. Free-operant avoidance procedures are constructed from two types of intervals (S–S intervals and R–S intervals), both of which are of fixed duration. In both S–S and R–S intervals, shock occurs when the intervals have been completed. Therefore, the passage of time is predictive of when the next shock will occur.

Free-operant avoidance learning can be explained in terms of the two-factor theory by assuming that individuals use the passage of time as a cue for when the next shock will occur. Animals (including people) are quite good at responding on the basis of the passage of time (Church, 2012; Crystal, 2012b). Time stimuli are referred to as *temporal cues*.

Temporal cues characteristic of the end of the S–S and R–S intervals are different from temporal cues characteristic of the beginning of these intervals. At first, participants probably do not distinguish between the beginning and end of the S–S and R–S intervals. However, they soon learn the difference because early and late temporal cues have different consequences. Temporal cues that characterize the beginning of the S–S and R–S intervals are never paired with shock. If shock occurs, it always occurs at the end of these intervals. As a consequence of this differential reinforcement, participants can learn to distinguish the early and late temporal cues.

Temporal cues characteristic of the end of an S–S or R–S interval are paired with shock and presumably acquire conditioned aversive properties. Each avoidance response starts a new R–S interval and thereby reduces the conditioned aversiveness created by temporal cues characteristic of the end of the S–S and R–S intervals (see Figure 12.5). In this way, an avoidance response can result in reduction of conditioned fear and satisfy the instrumental component of the two-factor theory.

Safety Signals and Avoidance Learning

The next explanation of avoidance learning that we consider is also based on a consideration of internal cues that participants may experience during the course of avoidance conditioning. However, instead of focusing on cues that predict danger, this account focuses on internal cues that signal the absence of shock or a period of safety. Such a *safety signal* is assumed to be a reinforcer for instrumental responding (Dinsmoor, 2001).

FIGURE 12.5

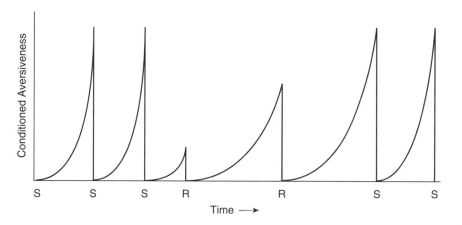

The presumed conditioned aversiveness of temporal cues during response–shock (R–S) and shock–shock (S–S) intervals in a free-operant avoidance procedure. R = occurrence of the avoidance response; S = occurrence of a brief shock. Notice the low levels of conditioned aversiveness at the beginning of each S–S and R–S interval and high levels of aversiveness at the end of these intervals. Each occurrence of the response always reduces the conditioned aversiveness of temporal cues because each response starts a new R–S interval.

In an avoidance procedure, periods of safety are best predicted by the occurrence of the avoidance response. After all, avoidance behavior cancels the delivery of an aversive stimulus. We know from biology that the movements of muscles and joints that are involved in making responses can give rise to internal *proprioceptive cues.* Such cues are also called response feedback cues, or simply *feedback cues.* The feedback cues that are produced by an avoidance response are followed by a predictable period without the aversive US, a predictable period of safety. As we saw in Chapter 5, stimuli that reliably predict the absence of a US may acquire Pavlovian conditioned inhibitory properties. Therefore, feedback cues generated by avoidance responses may also acquire Pavlovian conditioned inhibitory properties.

The safety signal explanation of avoidance learning is based on these ideas. According to the safety signal hypothesis, feedback cues from the avoidance response acquire Pavlovian conditioned inhibitory properties and thereby become signals for safety. In a situation involving potential danger, safety signals are assumed to be reinforcing. According to the safety signal account, avoidance behavior is positively reinforced by conditioned inhibitory safety signals.

Although the safety signal concept is similar to the temporal cue hypothesis in relying on stimuli internal to the organism, it has been more accessible to experimental verification. The safety signal account has been evaluated by introducing an external stimulus (e.g., a brief tone) at the time the interoceptive feedback cue is presumed to occur. That is, a brief tone is presented when the participant performs the avoidance response. If the safety signal hypothesis is correct, such an exteroceptive cue should acquire conditioned inhibitory properties. Moreover, these conditioned inhibitory properties should make the feedback stimuli effective as a positive reinforcer for instrumental behavior. Both of these predictions have been confirmed (e.g., Cándido, González, & de Brugada, 2004; Morris, 1974, 1975). (For a study of safety-signal reinforcement with human participants, see Angelakis & Austin, 2015.)

A less obvious prediction is that avoidance learning should be facilitated by increasing the salience of safety signal feedback cues. Consistent with this prediction, the introduction of an external-response feedback stimulus (which is presumably more salient than internal proprioceptive cues) substantially facilitates avoidance learning (e.g., D'Amato, Fazzaro, & Etkin, 1968).

The safety signal process is not incompatible with the two-factor theory of avoidance and need not be viewed as an alternative to that theory. Rather, positive reinforcement through a conditioned inhibitory safety signal may be considered a third factor in avoidance learning that operates in combination with classical conditioning of fear and instrumental reinforcement through fear reduction.

Extinction of Avoidance Behavior

Extinction is fairly simple following positive reinforcement: You allow the instrumental response to occur, but you no longer present the reinforcer. The common outcome is a substantial decline in responding. The situation is considerably more complicated after avoidance conditioning. One approach to the extinction of avoidance behavior is to simply turn off the shock apparatus that provided the aversive US during avoidance training. Unfortunately, just turning off the source of the shock rarely works to extinguish avoidance responding. Investigators discovered early on that avoidance responding can persist for hundreds of trials after the shock apparatus is deactivated (Solomon, Kamin, & Wynne, 1953). Why does that happen?

As I discussed earlier, there are two sources of reinforcement for the avoidance response. One is the reduction of conditioned fear that occurs when the avoidance response terminates the warning signal or CS. The second source of reinforcement comes from the conditioned inhibitory properties of response feedback cues that signal a period free from shock. Neither of these sources of reinforcement is eliminated when the shock source is deactivated after avoidance conditioning.

To eliminate fear reduction as a source of reinforcement for avoidance behavior, we have to extinguish the conditioned fear that is elicited by the warning stimulus or CS. That can be accomplished by providing repeated exposures to the CS presented alone. However, the participants cannot be permitted to terminate the CS. Highly trained individuals tend to respond quickly to turn off the warning stimulus. If they are allowed to do that, they will not receive enough exposure to the warning stimulus to extinguish much of the conditioned fear. Therefore, blocking the avoidance response is frequently a required component of fear extinction after avoidance training (M. Baum, 1970). In studies with human participants, blocking the avoidance response causes a return of fear and a return of the expectation of shock (Lovibond et al., 2008). This no doubt makes the absence of shock more salient and thereby facilitates extinction.

The second source of reinforcement for avoidance responding is provided by the safety signal properties of response feedback cues. Such safety signal properties are much more difficult to extinguish than conditioned fear. Safety signals are essentially conditioned inhibitory stimuli. Unfortunately, we know much less about the extinction of conditioned inhibition than we know about extinction of conditioned excitatory stimuli. As I pointed out in Chapter 6, repeatedly presenting a conditioned inhibitor or safety signal by itself (without a US) does not extinguish its inhibitory properties (Witcher & Ayres, 1984; Zimmer-Hart & Rescorla, 1974). Another complication is that we do not have direct access to the response feedback cues that serve as safety signals in avoidance learning. Because these cues are produced by the participant's behavior, they are not available to direct experimental control.

Another strategy for extinguishing avoidance responding is to change the procedure so that the avoidance response no longer prevents the aversive US. Unfortunately, such a procedure will maintain conditioned fear to the warning stimulus, and as we have seen, this is a strong source of motivation for avoidance responding. Difficulties in extinguishing avoidance behavior provide an ongoing challenge for behavior therapy.

Avoidance Learning and Unconditioned Defensive Behavior

As I noted in Chapter 2, learning procedures do not operate on a tabula rasa but are superimposed on an organism's preexisting behavioral tendencies, tendencies that an organism brings to the learning situation. Learned responses are the product of an interaction between the conditioning procedures used and the organism's preexisting behavioral structure. The two-factor theory and safety signal mechanisms of avoidance I described earlier are based on a simple view of what an organism brings to an aversive conditioning situation. These learning mechanisms just require that a stimulus be aversive. Given an unconditioned aversive stimulus, fear can become conditioned to a cue that predicts the aversive event, safety can become conditioned to a cue that predicts the absence of the aversive event, and fear reduction and safety can serve as reinforcers for any instrumental response.

SPECIES-SPECIFIC DEFENSE REACTIONS

As it turns out, the preexisting behavioral tendencies that organisms bring to an avoidance conditioning situation are much more complex than what I just described. Exposure to an aversive event activates a rich behavioral repertoire that has evolved to enable organisms to cope with danger quickly and effectively. Bolles (1970) pointed out that an animal being pursued by a predator must avoid the danger successfully the first time because otherwise it may not be alive for a second or third trial. Dangerous situations require effective coping without much practice, and thus Bolles suggested that organisms respond to aversive situations with a hierarchy of unconditioned defensive responses, which he called *species-specific defense reactions* (SSDRs).

SSDRs are responses such as freezing, fleeing, and fighting. Bolles suggested that which particular SSDR occurs depends on the nature of the aversive stimulus and the response opportunities provided by the environment. If a familiar and effective means of escape is available, the animal is most likely to try to flee when it encounters the aversive stimulus. Without a familiar escape route, freezing will be the predominant defensive response. In social situations, fighting may predominate.

Because SSDRs are elicited by the initial presentations of an aversive stimulus, they dominate the organism's behavior during the early stages avoidance training. This makes it difficult to use aversive conditioning procedures to condition responses that are not related to an SSDR. Running, for example, is more compatible with SSDRs than rearing. It is not surprising, then, that it is much easier to condition a rat to avoid shock by running than by rearing on its hind legs (Bolles, 1969).

THE PREDATORY IMMINENCE CONTINUUM

The concept of SSDRs encouraged investigators to consider in greater detail the structure of the defensive behavior system that is activated in aversive conditioning situations. These considerations led to the idea that unconditioned defensive behaviors depend not only whether an aversive stimulus is encountered but the likelihood or imminence of the encounter. Animals do one thing when they perceive a low likelihood of injury or attack and other things when the likelihood of injury is higher. Variations in the defensive responses that are elicited by different degrees of perceived danger constitute the *predatory imminence continuum* (Perusini & Fanselow, 2015; Rau & Fanselow, 2007).

The predatory imminence continuum has been investigated most extensively in laboratory rats (Fanselow, 1994). Rats are preyed on by hawks and snakes. Different modes of defensive behavior are activated depending on the rat's perceived likelihood of injury (see Figure 12.6). The preencounter response mode is activated if, during the course of its foraging, a rat wanders into an area where there is some chance of finding a snake, but the snake has not yet been encountered. In the preencounter mode, the rat may move to a safer area. If a safer area is not available, the rat will become more cautious in its foraging. It will venture out of its burrow less often, and it will eat larger meals when it does go out (Fanselow, Lester, & Helmstetter, 1988).

If the preencounter defensive responses are not successful and the rat encounters the snake, the predator-encounter response mode will be activated. In the predator-encounter mode, freezing is the predominant response. Finally, if this defensive behavior is also unsuccessful and the snake attacks the rat, the predator-contact response mode will be activated. In the predator-contact mode, the rat will suddenly leap into the air and strike out at the snake. This is called a *circa strike response* (see Figure 12.6).

An encounter with shock in a laboratory study activates the highest level of predatory imminence, the predator-contact response mode. The warning stimulus that occurs before the aversive US activates the predator-encounter mode. Therefore, we may

FIGURE 12.6

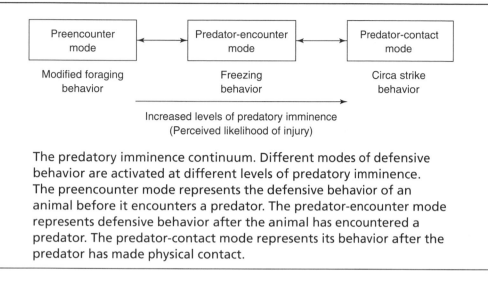

The predatory imminence continuum. Different modes of defensive behavior are activated at different levels of predatory imminence. The preencounter mode represents the defensive behavior of an animal before it encounters a predator. The predator-encounter mode represents defensive behavior after the animal has encountered a predator. The predator-contact mode represents its behavior after the predator has made physical contact.

expect responses such as freezing that are characteristic of the predator-encounter mode to develop to stimuli that become associated with an aversive US. In contrast, safety signals should elicit recuperative and relaxation responses because they signal the total absence of a potential predator. These considerations illustrate that even when organisms learn about an aversive situation, their behavior is heavily influenced by the preexisting organization of their defensive behavior system.

Summary

Studies of avoidance learning originated in studies of classical conditioning and relied on discrete-trial methods in which a warning signal ended in a brief shock unless the avoidance response was made. Subsequently, free-operant avoidance procedures that did not use explicit warning signals were developed. Regardless of which method is used, however, avoidance learning is puzzling because the consequence of an avoidance response is that nothing happens. How can "nothing" motivate learning or reinforce a response?

The first major explanation of avoidance learning, the two-factor theory, assumed that avoidance behavior is the result of a dynamic interaction between classical and instrumental conditioning. Classical conditioning occurs when the participant fails to make the avoidance response and the warning signal is followed by the aversive US. On the other hand, instrumental conditioning occurs when the avoidance response is made because this terminates the warning signal and reduces conditioned fear. Subsequent research identified a third factor, safety signal learning, that also contributes to avoidance learning. Cues that accompany the omission of the US in an avoidance procedure become safety signals or conditioned inhibitors of fear and provide positive reinforcement for the avoidance response.

Much of the experimental evidence on avoidance learning is compatible with the two-factor theory supplemented by safety signal learning, especially when temporal and proprioceptive cues are taken into account. These mechanisms are difficult to change, creating unusual problems for attempts to extinguish avoidance responding. Another source of complication in the study of avoidance learning is that organisms (human and nonhuman) have evolved a rich unconditioned defensive behavioral repertoire to deal with aversive events. The current view is that unconditioned SSDRs are organized by predatory imminence, with different defensive response modes activated by different levels of perceived danger from predatory attack. A complete account of avoidance learning has to explain how a particular avoidance conditioning procedure becomes integrated into the defensive behavior system of the organism.

Suggested Readings

Bouton, M. E., Mineka, S., & Barlow, D. H. (2001). A modern learning theory perspective on the etiology of panic disorder. *Psychological Review, 108*, 4–32. http://dx.doi.org/10.1037/0033-295X.108.1.4

Cain, C. K., & LeDoux, J. E. (2007). Escape from fear: A detailed behavioral analysis of two atypical responses reinforced by CS termination. *Journal of Experimental Psychology: Animal Behavior Processes, 33*, 451–463. http://dx.doi.org/10.1037/0097-7403.33.4.451

Dinsmoor, J. A. (2001). Stimuli inevitably generated by behavior that avoids electric shock are inherently reinforcing. *Journal of the Experimental Analysis of Behavior, 75*, 311–333. http://dx.doi.org/10.1901/jeab.2001.75-311

Krypotos, A.-M., Effting, M., Kindt, M., & Beckers, T. (2015). Avoidance learning: Review of theoretical models and recent developments. *Frontiers in Behavioral Neuroscience, 9*, Article 189. http://dx.doi.org/10.3389/fnbeh.2015.00189

Perusini, J. N., & Fanselow, M. S. (2015). Behavioral perspectives on the distinction between fear and anxiety. *Learning and Memory, 22*, 417–425. http://dx.doi.org/10.1101/lm.039180.115

Technical Terms

Aversive stimulus	R–S interval
Discriminated avoidance	S–S interval
Feedback cue	Safety signal
Free-operant avoidance	Shuttle box
Negative reinforcement	Species-specific defense response
Nondiscriminated avoidance	SSDR
One-way avoidance	Temporal cues
Predatory imminence	Two-factor theory
Proprioceptive cue	Two-way avoidance

Stimulus Control of Behavior | 13

Did you know that

- differential responding is used to identify control of behavior by a particular stimulus?
- even simple stimuli have many features or dimensions?
- control of behavior by one training stimulus often generalizes to other similar stimuli?
- stimulus generalization and stimulus discrimination are complementary concepts?
- generalization of behavior from one stimulus to another depends on the individual's training history with the stimuli?
- discrimination training produces differential responding and increases the precision of stimulus control?
- equivalence training leads to responding in the same manner to physically different stimuli?
- the learning of words and perceptual concepts involves an interplay between learning to discriminate and learning to generalize?

Throughout this book, we have seen various aspects of behavior that are controlled by antecedent stimuli or environmental events. Elicited behavior and responding that results from Pavlovian conditioning are obvious examples. Instrumental behavior can also be regarded as responding that occurs because of the presence of an antecedent stimulus. As we saw in Chapter 7, an

http://dx.doi.org/10.1037/0000057-013
The Essentials of Conditioning and Learning, Fourth Edition, by M. Domjan

antecedent stimulus may activate the instrumental response directly or may activate a representation of the response–reinforcer relation.

Proper stimulus control is a critical feature of appropriate or normal behavior. Hugging someone is an appropriate instrumental response and is reinforced by social approval if the individual is a close personal friend or family member. Hugging strangers is not appropriate and may get you slapped in the face. For a teacher to hug a student may also be inappropriate and may result in dismissal from the teaching position. These examples illustrate that whether an instrumental response is reinforced depends on the situation in which the response occurs. Taking a candy bar off the shelf and putting it in your pocket is fine in your own home but could get you accused of stealing if you do the same thing at the corner store.

Clearly, much of learned behavior occurs because of the presence of particular stimuli or environmental events. Up to this point, however, our discussion of learning has left two critical issues about the stimulus control of behavior unanswered. The first concerns the measurement of stimulus control: How can we determine whether a specific stimulus or feature of the environment is responsible for a particular response and how closely is the behavior tied to that stimulus feature? Once we know how to measure differences in stimulus control, we can tackle the second issue, which concerns the determinants of stimulus control. What factors determine which stimuli will gain control over a particular response and the degree or precision of the stimulus control that is achieved?

Measurement of Stimulus Control

Questions about stimulus control arise in part because of the complexity of environmental events. Even something as simple as a traffic light is a complex stimulus with multiple features. The red light in a traffic light has a specific color, brightness, shape, and position. How do we figure out which of these stimulus features is critical to controlling the behavior of a driver, and what makes those features critical? Once a stimulus feature has been identified, how do we figure out the degree of precision involved in the control of behavior by that stimulus feature?

The fundamental strategy for determining whether a response is controlled by a particular stimulus is to see if variations in that stimulus produce corresponding changes in the response. A response is said to be under the control of a particular stimulus if the response is altered by changes in that stimulus. A change in responding related to changes in a stimulus is called *differential responding*. We can identify which stimulus feature is responsible for the target behavior by seeing if changes in that stimulus feature cause changes in responding.

Traffic lights are often arranged in a vertical array, with the red light on top and the green light on the bottom (see Figure 13.1). Which feature is important, the color of the light or its position? Do drivers stop when they see a red light, or do they stop when the light on top is illuminated? To determine whether color rather than position is important in traffic lights, we have to test red and green lights presented in the

FIGURE 13.1

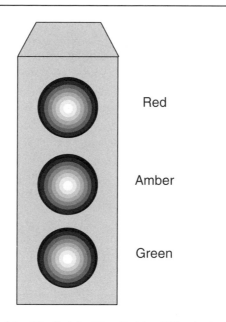

Stimulus features of traffic lights. The lights differ in both color and position.

same position. To determine whether the position rather than color is important, we have to test lights of the same color in different positions.

When we vary one feature of a stimulus while keeping all others constant, we are testing the importance of a particular *stimulus dimension* for the behavior in question. Different stimulus dimensions may be important for different drivers. Drivers who are color-blind must focus on the position of the illuminated light. Some other drivers respond primarily to the color of traffic lights. Still others probably respond to both the color and the position of the light. Thus, substantial individual differences in stimulus control may occur in the same situation.

Determining whether a particular stimulus feature is important is the first step in the analysis of stimulus control. We may be also interested in how precisely the behavior is tuned to a particular stimulus feature. Continuing with the traffic light example, let us assume that a driver stops whenever he sees a red traffic light. What shade of red does the light have to be? To answer this question, we would have to test the driver with a range of colors, including several shades of red.

The wavelength of red light is at the long end of the visual spectrum. Shorter wavelengths of light appear less red and more orange. As the wavelength becomes even shorter, the light appears more and more yellow. A detailed test of stimulus control by different colors requires systematically presenting lights of different wavelengths.

STIMULUS GENERALIZATION GRADIENTS

Several outcomes may occur if a variety of test colors ranging from deep red to deep yellow are presented. If the driver were paying very close attention to color, he would stop only if the light had a perfect red color. Lights with a tinge of orange would not cause the driver to stop. This possibility is illustrated by Curve A in Figure 13.2. At the other extreme, the driver may stop when he sees any color that has even a vague resemblance to red. This possibility is illustrated by Curve C in Figure 13.2. An intermediate outcome is shown by Curve B. In this case, the driver's behavior exhibits considerable sensitivity to differences in color, but responding is not as closely limited to a particular shade of red as in Curve A.

Each of the curves in Figure 13.2 is a *stimulus generalization gradient*. We previously encountered the concept of stimulus generalization in connection with habituation (see Figure 3.3). Generalization gradients can be obtained for any stimulus feature—stimulus position, size, brightness, shape, height, and so forth. As Figure 13.2 illustrates,

FIGURE 13.2

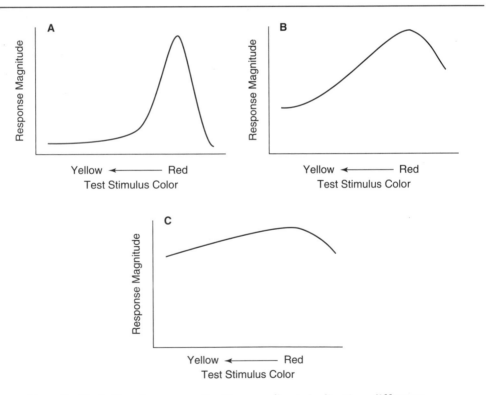

Hypothetical stimulus generalization gradients indicating different degrees of control of responding by the color of a stimulus. Curve A illustrates strongest stimulus control by color; Curve C illustrates weakest stimulus control by color.

the gradients may be very steep (Curve A) or rather shallow (Curve C). The steepness or slope of the generalization gradient indicates how closely the behavior is controlled by the stimulus feature being tested. A steep generalization gradient indicates strong control by the stimulus feature or dimension. A shallow or flat generalization gradient indicates weak stimulus control.

STIMULUS GENERALIZATION AND STIMULUS DISCRIMINATION

Stimulus generalization gradients involve two important phenomena: generalization and discrimination. In *stimulus generalization,* the responding that occurs with one stimulus is also observed when a different stimulus is presented. Points 1 and 2 in Figure 13.3 illustrate the phenomenon of stimulus generalization. Behavior that occurred at Point 1 also occurred at Point 2, or generalized to Point 2. Generalization of responding signifies similar responding to different stimuli.

Stimulus discrimination is the opposite of stimulus generalization. Here changes in a stimulus result in different levels of responding. Points 1 and 3 in Figure 13.3 illustrate the phenomenon of stimulus discrimination. More responding occurred to the stimulus at Point 1 than to the stimulus at Point 3. Thus, the participant discriminated or distinguished between Points 1 and 3. Responding at Point 1 did not generalize to Point 3.

Generalization and discrimination are complementary phenomena. A great deal of generalization among stimuli means that the participant responds the same way

FIGURE 13.3

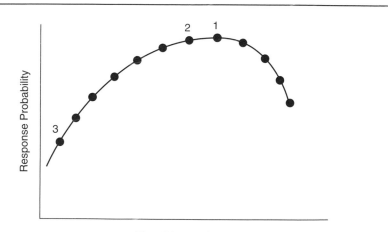

A hypothetical generalization gradient for responding to different colored stimuli. Points 1 and 2 illustrate the phenomenon of stimulus generalization. Points 1 and 3 illustrate the phenomenon of stimulus discrimination.

to these stimuli, and hence there is little discrimination. In contrast, a great deal of discrimination among stimuli means that the participant is responding differently to the stimuli, and hence there is little generalization among them.

CONTRASTING CONCEPTIONS OF STIMULUS GENERALIZATION

Why do individuals respond similarly to different stimuli? Why do they generalize from one stimulus to another? Pavlov favored a spread-of-effect interpretation. According to this idea, responses conditioned to one stimulus generalize to other cues because the effects of training spread from the original training stimulus to other similar stimuli. When a child first learns the word for cow, she is likely to use the word *cow* not only when she sees a cow but also when she sees a bull, and perhaps even a horse. According to the spread-of-effect interpretation, such generalization occurs because bulls and horses are similar to cows, and the learned response to cows spreads to other similar animals.

The spread-of-effect interpretation was challenged by Lashley and Wade (1946), who proposed that organisms respond similarly to different stimuli because they have not learned to distinguish between them. According to this hypothesis, a child will use the word *cow* when she sees cows, bulls, and horses because she has not yet learned to distinguish among these animals. The Lashley–Wade hypothesis suggests that stimulus generalization can be limited by appropriate training. I describe evidence confirming this prediction when I describe learning factors that determine the degree of stimulus control later in this chapter. Before we get to that, however, let us consider how features of a stimulus and features of the organism determine stimulus control.

Determinants of Stimulus Control: Sensory and Motivational Variables

SENSORY CAPACITY

Perhaps the most obvious factor determining whether a particular stimulus feature will influence behavior is the sensory capacity of the organism. An organism cannot respond to a stimulus if it lacks the sense organs needed to detect the stimulus. People are unable to respond to radio waves, ultraviolet light, and sounds above about 20,000 cycles per second (cps) because they lack the sense organs to detect such stimuli. Dogs are able to hear sounds of much higher frequency than human beings and are therefore capable of responding to ultrasounds that are inaudible to people.

Sensory capacity sets a limit on the kinds of stimuli that can come to control an organism's behavior. However, sensory capacity is merely a precondition for stimulus control. It does not ensure that behavior will be influenced by a particular stimulus feature. People with a normal sense of smell have the capacity to distinguish the aroma of various different red wines. However, for someone who rarely drinks wine, all red wines may smell pretty much alike.

SENSORY ORIENTATION

Another prerequisite for stimulus control is the sensory orientation of the organism. For a stimulus to gain control over some aspect of an individual's behavior, the stimulus must be accessible to the relevant sense organ. Sounds and overall levels of illumination spread throughout an environment. Therefore, such stimuli are likely to be encountered whether or not the individual is oriented toward the source of the stimulus. For this reason, tones and overhead lights are popular stimuli in learning experiments. In contrast, a localized visual cue may present a problem because it is seen only if the individual is facing toward it. If you are watching for traffic signs on the right side of a road, you may miss a sign placed on the left side.

STIMULUS INTENSITY OR SALIENCE

Other things being equal, behavior is more likely to come under the control of intense or salient stimuli than weak ones (e.g., Kamin, 1965). Stimulus intensity is important for most biological functions, and these include learning and behavior. More intense stimuli tend to elicit more vigorous behavior and more rapid learning. In addition, the presence of an intense stimulus can interfere with the control of behavior by a weaker cue. This phenomenon, first identified by Pavlov (1927), is referred to as *overshadowing*. A weak stimulus "b" may be effectively conditioned when it is presented by itself on conditioning trials. However, less learning about "b" will be evident if conditioning is conducted with a compound stimulus "Ab" that consists of "b" presented with a more intense stimulus "A." In this case, stimulus "A" may overshadow the conditioning of stimulus "b."

MOTIVATIONAL FACTORS

The extent to which behavior comes under the control of a particular stimulus is also determined by the motivational state of the organism. Motivational factors in the stimulus control of behavior have not been investigated extensively. However, the available evidence indicates that attention can be shifted away from one type of stimulus to another by a change in motivation or emotional state. In these experiments, a compound stimulus is typically used consisting of a tone and a light. With such a tone–light compound, rats and pigeons conditioned with food as the reinforcer come to respond to the light more than to the tone. In contrast, animals conditioned to avoid pain learn to respond to the tone more than to the light (Foree & LoLordo, 1973; LoLordo, 1979).

The critical factor that biases stimulus control toward the light or the tone is whether the light–tone compound acquires an appetitive or positive affective valence or a negative or aversive affective valence (Weiss & Panlilio, 2015). The motivational state elicited by the conditioned stimuli acts as a stimulus filter that biases stimulus control in favor of visual or auditory cues. When pigeons are hungry and motivated to find food, they are especially sensitive to visual cues. In contrast, when pigeons are fearful and motivated to avoid danger, they are especially sensitive to auditory cues.

For other species, these motivational influences may take different forms. A species that hunts for live prey at night, for example, may be especially attentive to auditory cues when it is seeking food.

Determinants of Stimulus Control: Learning Factors

Learning processes cannot teach you to respond to microwaves that are beyond the capacity of your sense organs. However, learning processes have a lot to do with how you come to respond to stimuli that are within the range of your senses. We turn to these learning mechanisms next. In general, behavior comes under the control of a stimulus if that stimulus becomes significant for some reason.

PAVLOVIAN AND INSTRUMENTAL CONDITIONING

As I discussed in Chapter 4, simple Pavlovian conditioning procedures make an initially ineffective and unimportant stimulus (the conditioned stimulus [CS]) significant by establishing an association between that event and unconditioned stimulus (US). Stimulus significance can also be established through instrumental conditioning. In the case of positive reinforcement, the reinforcer (O, for outcome) is presented contingent on a response (R) in the presence of an initially neutral stimulus (S). The three-term S–R–O instrumental contingency increases the significance of stimulus S by establishing an association between S and the reinforcing outcome O or by having stimulus S signal when the response will be reinforced (see Chapter 7). The situation is similar in the case of negative reinforcement (see Chapter 12). In the discriminated avoidance procedure, for example, the instrumental response results in avoidance of aversive stimulation only if the response occurs in the presence of a warning signal, which turns the warning signal into a significant event.

Although simple Pavlovian and instrumental conditioning procedures serve to bring behavior under the control of particular stimuli or events, they do not determine which feature(s) of a stimulus will become most important in controlling the conditioned behavior. Consider, for example, a compound stimulus with both auditory and visual features. Whether the visual or the auditory component will gain predominant control over the conditioned response will depend on the sensory and motivational factors that I described in the preceding section. If the participant has a keen sense of sight but poor hearing, the visual component will predominate. If both senses are adequate and the participant is motivated by fear, the auditory component may be more important. However, if the visual component is much more intense or salient than the auditory feature, the visual component may overshadow the auditory cue.

How about stimulus features that cannot be distinguished on the basis of sensory and motivational variables? How can they come to control differential responding? Consider, for example, a car that has plenty of gas and one that is about to run out of gas. There is little difference between these two types of cars in terms of the modality and intensity of the stimuli a driver encounters. The only difference is the position of the fuel gauge indicator, and that difference may be less than an inch. Nevertheless, the difference in the position of the fuel indicator between having plenty of gas and being nearly empty is highly significant to drivers. People also respond very differently to seeing the word *fire* compared with the word *hire*, even though the visual features of these two words are nearly identical. How do such highly similar stimuli come to control dramatically different responses? The answer rests with conditioning procedures that provide differential reinforcement in the presence of different stimuli.

STIMULUS DISCRIMINATION TRAINING

The most important training variable that determines the degree of stimulus control is *stimulus discrimination training*. Stimulus discrimination training provides differential reinforcement in the presence of different stimuli. Stimulus discrimination training can be conducted with either Pavlovian or instrumental methods. Simple cases of Pavlovian and instrumental conditioning involve only one CS or stimulus condition. In contrast, stimulus discrimination training requires a minimum of two stimuli. Differential reinforcement is arranged by providing the US or the reinforcer in association with one of the cues but not the other.

Any two stimuli that are initially ineffective in generating the conditioned or instrumental response may serve as stimuli in a discrimination procedure. One of the cues is called the S+, and the other is called the S−. For example, S+ and S− may be the letters *f* and *h*, a tone and a buzzer, or a light and a noise. Each trial involves presenting only one of the discriminative stimuli, and trials with the S+ and the S− are presented in a random sequence.

In a Pavlovian discrimination procedure, each presentation of S+ is paired with the US. In contrast, the US is omitted in trials when the S− occurs. Thus, S+ and S− are associated with different outcomes or differential reinforcement. S+ and S− may be two orange cats, for example, one rather friendly and the other aloof. The friendly cat (S+) is paired with tactile pleasure because she approaches and rubs up against people. The aloof cat (S−) does not approach and does not let people pet her and is therefore not paired with the positive tactile US.

Typical results of a discrimination training procedure are illustrated in Figure 13.4. Early in training, the conditioned response comes to be elicited by the S+, and this responding generalizes to the S−. At this stage of learning, the participant responds to both the S+ and the S−. With continued discrimination training (and differential reinforcement), responding to S+ continues to increase, whereas responding to S− gradually declines. The final outcome is that the participant responds much more to S+ than to S−. A strong distinction develops between S+ and S−. At this point, the two stimuli are said to be discriminated.

Let us consider again the friendly and the aloof cats. As you start to associate one of the cats with tactile pleasure, any affection that you develop for her may generalize when you encounter the other cat. However, as you have additional pleasant encounters with one cat but not with the other, your affection for the friendly cat will

FIGURE 13.4

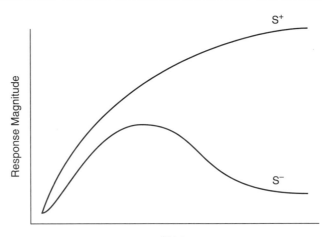

Typical results of a Pavlovian discrimination training procedure in which S⁺ is paired with an unconditioned stimulus and S⁻ is presented equally often alone. The conditioned responding that develops initially to S⁺ generalizes to S⁻. However, with continued training, a strong discrimination develops between S⁺ and S⁻.

increase, and your response to the aloof cat will decline. You will come to distinguish one cat from the other.

Discrimination training can be conducted in an analogous fashion using instrumental conditioning procedures. You again need to two stimuli, an S⁺ and an S⁻. Differential reinforcement is provided by reinforcing the instrumental response in the presence of the S⁺ but not reinforcing the response in the presence of the S⁻. Thus, the discrimination procedure consists of S⁺→R→O trials and S⁻→R→noO trials. As with Pavlovian discrimination procedures, during initial stages of training, responding on S⁺ trials may generalize to S⁻. However, eventually the participant will respond vigorously in trials with the S⁺ and little, if at all, in trials with the S⁻, as shown in Figure 13.4.

In the Skinnerian tradition of behavior analysis, the standard nomenclature for discriminative stimuli is a bit different. S⁺ is represented by the symbol S^D, and is called the "ess dee" (for *discriminative stimulus*). In contrast, the S⁻ is represented by the symbol S^Δ and is called the "ess delta" (with the delta symbol indicating lack of reinforcement).

In all stimulus discrimination procedures, different stimuli are associated with different outcomes. In the preceding examples, differential reinforcement was provided by the delivery versus omission of the US or the reinforcer. The presence versus absence of reinforcement represents a common but special case in discrimination training procedures. Any form of differential reinforcement can lead to the learning of a discrimination.

Infants, for example, quickly learn to discriminate Mom from Dad. This does not occur because Mom is a source of reinforcement but Dad is not. Both Mom and Dad provide pleasure for the infant, but they are likely to provide different types of pleasure. One parent may provide more tactile comfort and nutritional reinforcement, whereas the other may provide mostly sensory reinforcement in the form of tickling or bouncing. Each type of reinforcer is consistently associated with one of the parents, and this allows the infant to learn to discriminate between the parents.

MULTIPLE SCHEDULES OF REINFORCEMENT

Differential reinforcement may also be programmed in terms of different schedules of reinforcement in the presence of different stimuli. For example, a variable-interval schedule may be in effect in the presence of a high-pitch tone (Stimulus A), and a fixed-interval schedule may be in effect in the presence of a low-pitch tone (Stimulus B). Such a procedure is called a *multiple schedule of reinforcement*. As a result of training on a multiple variable interval–fixed interval schedule of reinforcement, participants will come to respond to Stimulus A in a manner typical of variable-interval performance and will respond to Stimulus B in a manner typical of fixed-interval performance.

A multiple schedule is in effect as you listen to different instructors in different classes. Listening behavior is reinforced by the new information you hear in each class. Some professors say lots of new things during their classes, thereby reinforcing listening behavior on a dense variable-interval schedule. Other professors predictably make just four or five important points during a lecture and spend about 10 minutes elaborating each point. This reinforces listening behavior on what is akin to a fixed-interval schedule. Each schedule of reinforcement is in effect in the presence of the distinct stimuli of each professor and class. Across both classes, therefore, listening behavior is reinforced on a multiple schedule. Because of that, your listening behavior changes when you move from one class to the other.

Determinants of the Precision of Stimulus Control

Differential reinforcement in the presence of S+ and S− produces differential responding to those stimuli. Interestingly, these effects may extend beyond the actual stimuli that are used in the discrimination procedure. The far-reaching effects of discrimination training were first identified in a landmark experiment by Jenkins and Harrison (1960). They compared the stimulus control of pecking behavior in two groups of pigeons (see Table 13.1). Group D was first conditioned to discriminate between the presence and absence of a tone. These pigeons were reinforced for pecking a response key whenever a tone with a frequency of 1,000 Hz was turned on (S+) and were not reinforced when the tone was absent (S−). The control group (Group C) received similar reinforcement for pecking the response key, but for them the tone was on

TABLE 13.1

Outline of Experiment by Jenkins and Harrison (1960)

Training	Test

Group D: discrimination training
    S⁺ (1,000-cps tone): pecks → food
    S⁻ (no tone): pecks → no food
	Tones of various frequencies

Group C: no discrimination training
    1,000-cps tone: pecks → food
    Tone always present during training
	Tones of various frequencies

continuously during the training sessions. Thus, Group C did not receive differential reinforcement associated with the tone.

After this contrasting training had taken place, the responses of both groups were measured in a test of stimulus generalization. Tones of various frequencies were presented during the test session. The results are summarized in Figure 13.5. The control group, Group C, which did not receive discrimination training, responded vigorously to the tone that had been present during training (the 1,000 Hz tone). They also

FIGURE 13.5

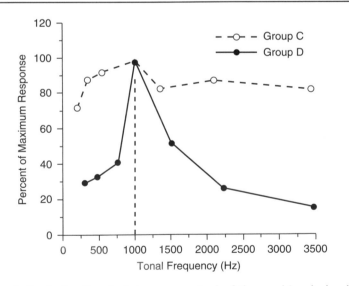

Effects of discrimination training on control of the pecking behavior of pigeons by the frequency of different tones. Before the generalization test, Group D received discrimination training in which the S⁺ was a 1,000-Hz tone, and the S⁻ was the absence of the tone. In contrast, Group C received only reinforcement for key-pecking in the presence of the 1,000-Hz tone. Data from Jenkins and Harrison (1960).

responded vigorously to most of the other tones, which they encountered for the first time during the generalization test. Thus, in the absence of discrimination training, a fairly flat generalization gradient was obtained. This indicates that the frequency of the tones did not gain much control over the behavior of these birds.

The results were dramatically different for the pigeons in Group D, which were first trained to discriminate between the presence and absence of the 1,000 Hz tone. These birds showed a steep generalization gradient. They responded a great deal to the 1,000-Hz tone (the S⁺), but their behavior quickly dropped off when tones of other frequencies were presented. This is a remarkable outcome because the other tones had not been presented during discrimination training. None of the other tones had served as the S⁻ in the discrimination procedure. Even though Group D had not encountered nonreinforcement in the presence of tones during training, tones other than the S⁺ did not support much pecking behavior.

The results presented in Figure 13.5 show that the shape of a generalization gradient can be dramatically altered by discrimination training. Discrimination training not only produces differential responding to S⁺ and S⁻ but also increases the steepness of generalization gradients. This indicates that discrimination training increases the precision of stimulus control and this increased precision extends beyond the specific stimuli that are used as S⁺ and S⁻.

INTERDIMENSIONAL VERSUS INTRADIMENSIONAL DISCRIMINATIONS

So far we have stressed the importance of differential reinforcement in discrimination training procedures. The nature of the S⁺ and S⁻ stimuli also determines the outcome of discrimination training. The similarities and differences between S⁺ and S⁻ are especially important. If S⁺ and S⁻ differ in several respects, the discrimination is called an *interdimensional discrimination*. If S⁺ and S⁻ differ in only one respect, the discrimination is called an *intradimensional discrimination*.

Interdimensional Discriminations

Perhaps the most common forms of interdimensional discrimination training are simple Pavlovian or discrete-trial instrumental conditioning procedures, although we don't usually think of these as involving discrimination training. A simple Pavlovian procedure involves just one CS and one US. Presentations of the CS end in delivery of the US. In contrast, the US is not delivered when the CS is absent. Thus, the discrimination is between times when the CS is present and times when the CS is absent (the intertrial interval). All of the features of the CS (its modality, intensity, and location) serve to distinguish the CS from its absence. Therefore, this is an interdimensional discrimination.

Discrete-trial instrumental conditioning also involves an interdimensional discrimination between cues present during a trial and cues present during the intertrial interval. The pigeons in Group D in Figure 13.5 received such a procedure. Pecking was reinforced during the 1,000-cps tone but not when the tone was absent. Periods of reinforcement differed from the intertrial interval (when the tone was absent) in both the intensity and frequency of the auditory cues the pigeons heard.

Interdimensional discriminations can be also set up between discrete stimuli serving as S⁺ and S⁻. The discrimination between a red and a green traffic light I discussed earlier in this chapter is an interdimensional discrimination because the red and green traffic lights differ in both color and position. The discrimination learned by an infant between Mom and Dad is also an interdimensional discrimination. Mom and Dad differ in many respects, including visual features, differences in how each holds the infant, differences in voice, differences in the time of day each is likely to interact with the infant, and so on.

Intradimensional Discriminations

Interdimensional discriminations are effective in establishing stimulus control. However, they do not establish a high degree of control over behavior by any particular stimulus feature. For example, because many things distinguish Mom from Dad, the infant may not respond a great deal to any one distinguishing feature. The most effective way to establish control by a specific stimulus feature is through *intradimensional* discrimination training (Jenkins & Harrison, 1960, 1962). In intradimensional discrimination training, the stimuli associated with differential reinforcement differ in only one respect.

Many forms of expert performance involve intradimensional discriminations. Reading, for example, requires discriminating between letters that differ in only one respect. The letters E and F differ only in the horizontal bottom stem, which is present in E but not in F. The physical difference is very small, but the differential consequences in terms of meaning can be substantial. The letter pairs B and P and M and N are other pairs that are similar physically but differ greatly in significance. Learning to read requires learning many intradimensional discriminations of this sort.

One of the interesting things about learning fine intradimensional discriminations is that the participant is not likely to be aware of the physical difference between the stimuli at the outset of training. Initially, the letters E and F may appear the same to a child. The child may recognize E and F as being different from O but may not be able to tell the difference between E and F. The child may come to recognize the visual difference between the two letters only after being taught to say one thing when shown E and something else when shown F. This example illustrates the general principle that *differential reinforcement serves to focus attention on physical differences that are otherwise ignored.*

Similar effects occur in the acquisition of other forms of expertise. Children learning to sing may not be able to tell at first when they are singing in tune or off-key. However, this skill develops through differential reinforcement from a teacher. Likewise, budding ballerinas learn to pay close attention to proprioceptive cues indicating the precise position of their arms and legs, and billiard players learn to make precise judgments about angles and trajectories. Intradimensional discrimination training brings behavior under the precise control of small variations in a stimulus, thereby serving to increase sensitivity to these small stimulus variations. Thus, sensitivity to variations in environmental stimuli depends not only on sensory capacity but also on one's history of discrimination training.

Stimulus Equivalence Training

As we have seen, discrimination procedures foster differential responding and increase the precision of stimulus control. There are situations, however, in which just the opposite is desired, that is, situations in which physically different stimuli must be treated the same way. Consider, for example, the same word written in different fonts and sizes. If you are concerned about the meaning of the word, you must treat the word as having the same meaning regardless of the font or size in which it is written. This raises the question: Are there learning procedures that promote responding to different stimuli in the same manner? Are there learning procedures that increase stimulus generalization?

In a discrimination procedure, stimuli are treated differently—they have different consequences. The differential treatment or significance of the stimuli leads organisms to respond to them as distinct from each other. What would happen if two stimuli were treated in the same or equivalent fashion? Would such a procedure lead organisms to respond to the stimuli as similar or equivalent? The answer seems to be yes. Just as discrimination training encourages differential responding, *stimulus equivalence* training encourages generalized responding.

There are several approaches for promoting generalization rather than discrimination among stimuli. One approach is to arrange the same consequence for responding to various physically different stimuli. This is frequently done in *perceptual concept learning*. For example, pigeons can be trained to respond in a similar fashion to different photographs, all of which include water in some form (ocean, lake, puddle, stream). The basic training strategy is to reinforce the same response (pecking a response key) in the presence of various pictures containing water, and not to reinforce that response when photographs without water appear. Herrnstein, Loveland, and Cable (1976) trained such a discrimination using 500 to 700 photographs of various scenes in New England. Once the pigeons learned the water/no-water discrimination, their behavior generalized to novel photographs that had not been presented during training. (For a more detailed discussion of perceptual concept learning, see Huber & Aust, 2012; Wasserman, 2016.)

Arranging a common outcome for different stimuli is one way to establish a stimulus equivalence class. Another common technique is to train the same response to a set of different stimuli. This is essentially what parents do when they train their children to say the same word (*fruit*) in response to a variety of types of fruit (apples, pears, bananas). The common response serves to create an equivalence class among the various specific examples that are associated with that common response (Urcuioli, 2013).

Stimulus equivalence is particularly important in analyses and training of language skills. The written word *banana*, for example, derives its meaning from the fact that it is in an equivalence class that includes the spoken word *banana* as well as a photograph or drawing of a banana and an actual banana you can eat. All of these physically different stimuli are treated as functionally equivalent and interchangeable once the meaning of the word has been learned. For example, you should be able to say the word *banana* when you see a picture of one, and you should be able to pick out the picture if asked to identify what the word *banana* signifies. (For applications of equivalence training in applied behavior analysis, see Rehfeldt, 2011.)

Summary

Individuals have to learn not only what to do but when and where to do it. When and where a response is made involves the stimulus control of behavior. Stimulus control is identified by differential responding and can be precisely measured by the steepness of generalization gradients. The extent to which a stimulus influences behavior depends on stimulus factors such as sensory capacity, sensory orientation, and stimulus intensity. Stimulus control also depends on the individual's affective or motivational state. However, most forms of stimulus control are a result of training that either facilitates discriminating among stimuli or facilitates generalizing among stimuli.

Discrimination training may involve either *inter*dimensional or *intra*dimensional stimuli. Intradimensional discrimination training produces more precise stimulus control than interdimensional training and is the basis for various forms of expert performance. However, learning fine discriminations is not always useful. Sometimes you have to learn to treat physically different objects in the same fashion. This is accomplished by stimulus equivalence learning. Stimulus equivalence is important in perceptual concept learning, language learning, and various aspects of applied behavior analysis.

Suggested Readings

Rehfeldt, R. A. (2011). Toward a technology of derived stimulus relations: An analysis of articles published in the *Journal of Applied Behavior Analysis*, 1992–2009. *Journal of Applied Behavior Analysis, 44*, 109–119. http://dx.doi.org/10.1901/jaba.2011.44-109

Urcuioli, P. J. (2013). Stimulus control and stimulus class formation. In G. J. Madden (Ed.), *APA handbook of behavior analysis: Vol. 1. Methods and principles* (pp. 361–386). Washington, DC: American Psychological Association.

Wagner, A. R. (2008). Evolution of an elemental theory of Pavlovian conditioning. *Learning & Behavior, 36*, 253–265. http://dx.doi.org/10.3758/LB.36.3.253

Wasserman, E. A. (2016). Conceptualization in pigeons: The evolution of a paradigm. *Behavioural Processes, 123*, 4–14. http://dx.doi.org/10.1016/j.beproc.2015.09.010

Technical Terms

Differential responding
Interdimensional discrimination
Intradimensional discrimination
Multiple schedule of reinforcement
Overshadowing
Perceptual concept
S$^+$

S$^-$
Stimulus dimension
Stimulus discrimination
Stimulus equivalence
Stimulus generalization
Stimulus generalization gradient

Memory Mechanisms | 14

Did you know that

- learning and memory are integrally related?
- tasks testing memory mechanisms have to be specially designed so that they cannot be solved without the use of memory?
- memories do not automatically fade through trace decay? Rather, remembering can be brought under stimulus control or instructional control.
- memory can be prospective and involve future rather than past events?
- failure to remember something is rarely due to forgetting?
- failures of memory can be caused by remembering too much?
- seemingly trivial aspects of a learning situation can help to retrieve what was learned?
- memory formation involves processes of consolidation at the level of synapses, nerve cells, and neural circuits?
- consolidated memories are not permanent but can be changed when they are retrieved or reactivated? Altered memories undergo reconsolidation.

Learning and memory are integrally related; one cannot have one without the other. In fact, research on memory mechanisms in animals makes extensive use of the basic conditioning procedures that I described in earlier chapters. This makes the discussion of memory research appropriate

http://dx.doi.org/10.1037/0000057-014
The Essentials of Conditioning and Learning, Fourth Edition, by M. Domjan

at the end of a book on basic conditioning procedures. However, a fundamental question arises: If all learning involves memory, what distinguishes studies of memory from studies of learning? The answer is that studies of memory focus on a different stage of information processing than studies of learning.

Stages of Information Processing

Memory involves the delayed effects of experience. For experience with stimuli and responses to influence behavior at a later time, three things have to happen. First, information about the stimuli and responses has to be acquired and encoded in the nervous system in some fashion. This is the *acquisition stage* of information processing. Once encoded, the information has to be stored for later use. This is the *retention stage* of information processing. Finally, when the information is needed at the end of the retention interval, it has to be recovered from storage. This is the *retrieval stage*.

Acquisition, retention, and retrieval are involved in all studies of learning as well as all studies of memory. However, which stage is the focus of interest depends on whether one is primarily concerned with learning processes or memory processes (see Table 14.1). Studies of learning focus on the acquisition stage. In studies of learning, the circumstances of acquisition are manipulated or varied while the conditions of retention and retrieval are kept constant. By contrast, in studies of memory, the conditions of acquisition are kept constant while the retention interval and the conditions of retrieval are varied. To make matters a bit more complicated, the three stages are not entirely independent. As we will see, conditions of acquisition can determine the circumstances under which a memory is retrieved (Urcelay & Miller, 2014). However, such interactions do not undermine the basic model of information processing as involving acquisition, retention, and retrieval.

The Matching-to-Sample Procedure

A variety of techniques have been used to study memory mechanisms in various species. Memory procedures often require special controls to ensure that the participant's behavior is determined by its past experience rather than by some clue that is inadver-

TABLE 14.1

Differences Between Experiments on Learning and Experiments on Memory

Stage of information processing	Learning experiments	Memory experiments
Acquisition	Varied	Constant
Retention	Constant (long)	Varied (short and long)
Retrieval	Constant	Varied

tently presented in the test situation. In addition, special procedures must be designed to isolate particular memory processes. To facilitate illustration of these complexities, I describe in detail the *matching-to-sample procedure*, which is one of the most widely used and versatile techniques for the study of memory mechanisms (Zentall & Smith, 2016).

In the matching-to-sample procedure, the participant is first exposed to a sample stimulus. The sample is then removed for a retention interval. After the retention interval, the participant receives a multiple-choice memory test. Several alternatives are presented, one of which is the same as the sample stimulus that was presented at the start of the trial. If the participant selects the previously presented sample, it is reinforced.

The matching-to-sample procedure can be used to investigate memory for a variety of stimuli and can be adapted to address various research questions. The matching procedure has been used with species as diverse as dolphins, rats, and humans (Baron & Menich, 1985; Forestell & Herman, 1988; Wallace, Steinert, Scobie, & Spear, 1980), and the procedure has been adapted for various types of sample stimuli, including visual, auditory, and spatial cues. Figure 14.1 illustrates a version of the procedure for use with pigeons. Although our discussion focuses on the matching-to-sample technique, the conceptual issues involved are relevant to all other memory tasks as well.

Pigeons are typically tested in a Skinner box with a stimulus panel on one wall that allows the presentation of stimuli and also detects pecking responses. The stimulus panel is programmed to allow the presentation of stimuli in three positions, usually arranged in a row. For example, the stimuli may be three circles of the same size

FIGURE 14.1

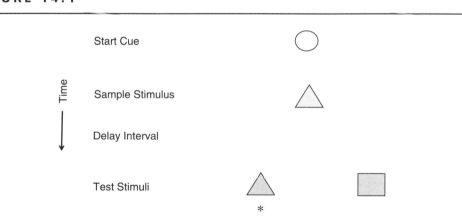

Illustration of a matching-to-sample trial. The trial begins with a white circle on a touch screen that indicates the start of the trial. The sample stimulus (a triangle) is then presented in the same location on the screen. The sample is then turned off, and a retention interval begins. At the end of the retention interval, the participant receives two test stimuli, one of which matches the sample stimulus. Responses to the test stimulus that matches the sample are reinforced, as indicated by the asterisk.

filled with various colors or patterns. Each trial begins with a start cue, which might be illumination of the center position with a white circle. One peck at the start cue results in presentation of the sample stimulus, also in the center position. In our example, the sample stimulus is a triangle. After a few seconds, the sample stimulus is turned off, and a retention interval begins. At the end of the retention interval, the pigeon receives two test stimuli, one on the left and one on the right. One of the test stimuli is the same as the previously presented sample (a triangle), whereas the other is different (a square). Pecks at the matching stimulus are reinforced. Pecks at the alternate test stimulus have no consequence.

SIMULTANEOUS VERSUS DELAYED MATCHING TO SAMPLE

As you might suspect, the difficulty of a matching-to-sample procedure depends in part on the duration of the retention interval (Grant, 1976). To facilitate learning of a matching task, it is useful to begin training without a retention interval. Such a procedure is called *simultaneous matching to sample*. In simultaneous matching, after presentation of the start cue, the sample stimulus is presented in the same position. The test stimuli are then presented on the left and right side of the sample, but the sample stimulus is not removed. Because the sample stimulus is visible at the same time as the test stimuli, the procedure is called simultaneous matching to sample.

A simultaneous matching procedure is not a good test of memory because the sample stimulus remains present during the choice component of each trial. But that feature facilitates learning the task. After the participants have learned to make the accurate choice in a simultaneous matching procedure, a retention interval can be introduced between presentation of the sample and presentation of the test stimuli, as illustrated in Figure 14.1. Because, in this case, the test stimuli are delayed after presentation of the sample, the procedure is called *delayed matching to sample*.

PROCEDURAL CONTROLS FOR MEMORY

Introducing a retention interval requires the participant to use what it remembers about the sample stimulus to respond accurately when the test choices are presented. However, having a retention interval in the procedure is not sufficient to ensure that the participant is using memory based on the sample stimulus. The sample and test stimuli must also be varied from one trial to the next.

Consider, for example, a procedure in which every trial was exactly the same as the trial illustrated in Figure 14.1. To respond accurately with repetitions of this trial, the pigeon would simply have to learn to peck the left stimulus position during the choice component of each trial. The pigeon would not have to remember anything about the shape of the triangle that was the sample on that trial.

To force participants to pay attention to and remember information about the specific stimuli that are presented in a matching procedure, the sample stimulus used and the position of the test stimuli must be varied across training trials. Figure 14.2 illustrates various types of trials in a matching procedure involving two pairs of shape

FIGURE 14.2

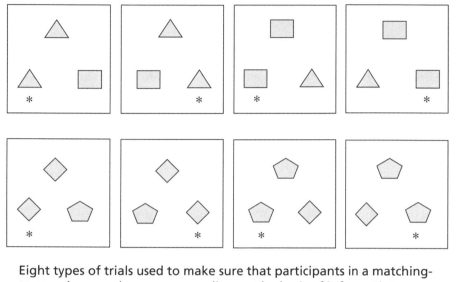

Eight types of trials used to make sure that participants in a matching-to-sample procedure are responding on the basis of information obtained from the sample stimulus. Each panel represents a different trial type, with the sample presented on top, and the two choice stimuli presented below. The correct choice is identified by an asterisk.

stimuli, triangle versus square and diamond versus pentagon. There are eight possible trial types shown in the figure. With each sample stimulus, there are two types of test trials, one with the correct stimulus on the left and one with the correct stimulus on the right. If the eight trial types are varied randomly across trials during training, the participant cannot be consistently accurate unless it uses information based on the sample to guide its selection of the correct test stimulus.

Types of Memory

Memory is not a homogeneous process. There are different kinds of memory based on the kind of information that is remembered, the types of manipulations that influence the nature of the memory, and how long the memory lasts. Common human experience involves *declarative memory*, which is memory for events, ideas, and other information that we can talk about or "declare." We are consciously aware of such memories and efforts to retrieve them. Entering the correct password on your smartphone also requires memory, but you perform that task so often that you no longer think about each individual character. That kind of automatic and unconscious recall of learned information is called *procedural memory*. Well-rehearsed Pavlovian and instrumental conditioning situations involve procedural memory. In the present section, I review research on working and reference memory and retrospective versus prospective memory and also consider whether memory involves the passive decay of learned information or more active psychological processes.

REFERENCE AND WORKING MEMORY

What kinds of memory are required to respond successfully in a matching-to-sample procedure? In our discussion of procedural controls for memory, we were concerned with making sure that responses to the test stimuli on a particular trial depended on what the participant remembered about the sample stimulus that was presented on that trial. But this information was useful only until the end of the trial. Remembering the sample on a particular trial was of no help in responding on the next trial because the next trial may have involved a different sample stimulus. Memory for information that is required to complete a task or trial is called *working memory*.

Working memory is retention of information that is needed to respond successfully on one trial or task but is not useful in responding on subsequent trials or tasks. If you are baking a cake and mixing the ingredients, you start with a certain amount of flour and then add salt, sugar, and baking powder. Because all of these ingredients are white and powdery, once each has been added to the mix it cannot be distinguished by sight. Therefore, you have to remember whether you have already added the sugar or salt. But that information is only useful until you finish preparing the cake mix; it will not help you bake the next cake. Thus, this is a form of working memory.

The control procedures that I discussed previously (variations in the sample stimulus and in the location of the correct choice stimulus) ensure that matching-to-sample procedures involve working memory. However, to respond successfully, participants must remember more than just information about the sample on a particular trial. They also have to remember general features of the matching task that remain constant from one trial to the next. For example, the pigeons have to remember to peck the start cue and to peck one of the test stimuli after the retention interval. In addition, they have to remember that correct responses are reinforced and where to obtain the reinforcer once it is delivered. These pieces of information are useful on every trial. Such memory is called *reference memory*. Reference memory involves memory for features of a task that remain constant from one trial to the next. Reference memory is of considerably longer duration than working memory.

To bake a cake, you have to remember some general information about cooking. You have to know about cake pans, ovens, various ingredients, and how to measure and mix those ingredients. These general skills are useful not just for the cake you happen to be baking but also for any future cakes you might want to make. Therefore, such information involves reference memory.

TRACE DECAY VERSUS ACTIVE MEMORY PROCESSES

Working memory and reference memory are distinguished by the type of information that is retained and by how long the information is remembered. Memory mechanisms can be distinguished as well by the kinds of procedures that influence them. A fundamental issue is whether memory is governed by a passive trace decay process that automatically leads to forgetting over time or involves more complex mechanisms that can modify the accuracy of recall.

According to the trace-decay hypothesis, presentation of a sample stimulus activates a neural trace that automatically decays after the end of the stimulus. Information about the sample is available only as long as the trace is sufficiently strong. The gradual fading or decay of the neural trace is assumed to produce progressively less accurate recall (Roberts & Grant, 1976). The concept of trace decay is one of the oldest explanations of memory loss over time. However, a growing body of evidence suggests that the simple idea of trace decay is grossly incomplete and inaccurate as an account of memory and forgetting.

According to the trace-decay hypothesis, the strength of a stimulus trace is determined primarily by its intensity and duration (Grant, 1976). However, the accuracy of memory also depends on the conditions of training. We are better at remembering things if we know that we will be tested on the information. That is, knowledge that memory will be required improves remembering. Two lines of evidence support this conclusion.

One major line of research has shown that memory processes can be brought under stimulus control. These studies were originally conducted with human participants who were presented with a series of stimulus items. Some of the items in the list were followed by a remember cue (the letter R), indicating that the participant would be tested on that item in a subsequent memory test. Other items in the list were followed by a forget cue (the letter F), which indicated that the item would not be included in the memory test. After the training, participants were tested for their memory for both the R- and the F-cued items. The results showed much better memory for the R-cued items than the F-cued items (Johnson, 1994; MacLeod, 2012; M. Williams & Woodman, 2012). This shows that memory can be brought under stimulus control and is not determined by a simple trace-decay mechanism.

Students in my classes often ask me whether what we are covering in class will be on the test. In asking that question, they are asking me to provide an R cue or an F cue. Their assumption is that an R cue will enable them to activate cognitive processes that will facilitate retention of the information.

Research on directed forgetting has been extended to nonhuman species as well, which has facilitated examination of the neural basis of the effect. In one study, for example, pigeons were trained on a matching-to-sample problem in which the sample stimulus was followed by either a high-pitched or a low-pitched tone indicating that memory for the sample stimulus would be (or would not be) tested. Probe tests at the end of the experiment indicated better performance for R-cued sample stimuli than for F-cued sample stimuli (Milmine, Watanabe, & Colombo, 2008; see also Zentall & Smith, 2016).

The directed forgetting effect shows that memory processes can be engaged (or not) on an item-by-item basis. Broader aspects of a training procedure can also activate memory processes to different degrees. We can be trained to remember something for a short period or for a longer period. This was demonstrated in an important experiment with pigeons by Sargisson and White (2001). The birds were trained on a standard delayed matching-to-sample procedure. The usual practice in such experiments is to use a relatively short delay interval between the sample stimulus and the choice alternatives during training and then test the birds with longer intervals during tests of memory. The typical outcome is that memory accuracy quickly deteriorates with longer delay intervals during the test series.

Sargisson and White (2001) departed from the standard training protocol by using delay intervals of 4 and 6 seconds during the training trials. Following training with the longer delay intervals, the deterioration in memory performance that is usually observed with longer test delays did not occur. That is, the pigeons learned to remember the sample stimulus over longer delays if they received a training procedure that required better retention. This shows that the ability to retain information for a longer period is a skill that can be trained given the right training procedure.

RETROSPECTIVE VERSUS PROSPECTIVE MEMORY

So far, we have established that the matching-to-sample task involves both working memory and reference memory, and that working memory is best characterized as an active rather than passive process. Another important issue concerns the contents of working memory, that is, what does the organism remember during the retention interval that enables it to make the correct choice at the end of a trial?

Retrospective Memory

The most obvious possibility is that information about the sample stimulus is stored during the retention interval, thus enabling the participant to select the correct test stimulus. Presumably, during the choice test at the end of the trial, the memory of the sample is compared with each of the choice alternatives to determine which alternative best resembles the sample. The participant then selects the test stimulus that best matches the sample.

Remembering attributes of the sample stimulus is a form of *retrospective memory*. Retrospective memory is memory for stimuli or events that were encountered in the past. When we think about the contents of memory, we usually think about past events. However, retrospective memory for the sample stimulus is not the only type of memory that will lead to correct performance on a matching-to-sample problem.

Prospective Memory

Recall that, in the typical matching procedure, a limited number of trial types are repeated over and over again in random order across trials. Figure 14.2, for example, illustrates a procedure in which there are four possible sample stimuli: a triangle, a square, a diamond, and a pentagon. For each sample, there is a unique correct test stimulus. Because of this, the matching procedure involves pairs of sample and test stimuli.

Let us represent a sample stimulus as S and a test stimulus as T. Different sample–test stimulus pairs may then be represented as S1–T1, S2–T2, S3–T3, and so on. Given these S–T pairings, participants could select the correct choice stimulus in a matching task by thinking of T after presentation of the sample S and storing that information during the retention interval. This involves keeping in memory information about a future choice stimulus or action and is called *prospective memory*. Prospective memory is memory for a future stimulus or response.

Distinguishing Between Retrospective and Prospective Memory

Retrospective memory involves remembering the sample stimulus S during the retention interval. Prospective memory involves remembering the test stimulus T during the retention interval. How can we distinguish between these possibilities experimentally?

In the matching-to-sample problems we have considered so far, the sample stimulus S and the correct test stimulus T are the same. If the sample is a triangle, the correct test stimulus is also a triangle. This makes it impossible to decide whether information stored during the retention interval concerns stimulus S or stimulus T. To distinguish between retrospective and prospective memory, we have to change the matching procedure somewhat, so that T is not the same physical stimulus as S. Such a procedure is called *symbolic matching to sample*.

A symbolic matching procedure is illustrated in Figure 14.3. Each row represents a different trial type in the procedure. The procedure is based on symbolic relationships between sample and test stimuli rather than the identity relationship.

FIGURE 14.3

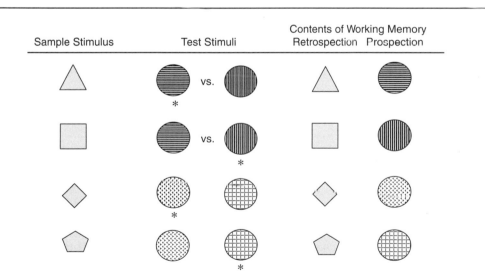

Diagram of a symbolic matching-to-sample procedure and illustration of the difference between retrospective and prospective working memory. Each row shows a different trial type. The test stimuli are shown to the right of the sample for each trial type, and the correct test stimulus is indicated by an asterisk.

In Figure 14.3, responding to the horizontal grid is reinforced after presentation of a triangle as the sample stimulus, and responding to the vertical grid is reinforced after presentation of a square as the sample. In a sense, the horizontal grid is a symbol for the triangle sample, and the vertical grid is a symbol for the square sample. Symbolic relations between other shapes and visual pattern are shown in the third and fourth rows of Figure 14.3.

As with the standard matching procedure, in a symbolic matching task the correct test stimulus appears equally often on the left and the right, and there is a delay between the sample and the test stimuli. Therefore, the task involves working memory, just as the standard matching procedure does. However, with symbolic matching, different things are remembered depending on whether the memory is retrospective or prospective. The differences are shown in the columns on the right of Figure 14.3. On trials with the triangle as the sample, retrospective memory involves retention of information about the triangle. In contrast, prospective memory involves retention of information about the horizontal-grid test stimulus, which is the correct choice after a triangle sample. On trials with the square as the sample, retrospective memory involves remembering the square, whereas prospective memory involves remembering the vertical grid.

Studies of the symbolic matching-to-sample procedure have shown that pigeons use prospective rather than retrospective memory (e.g., Roitblat, 1980; Santi & Roberts, 1985). Research using other kinds of memory tasks has also provided evidence of prospective memory (e.g., Beran, Evans, Klein, & Einstein, 2012; Crystal, 2012a; Roberts, 2012). However, not all instances of working memory involve prospection, or memory for events that are predicted to occur in the future. Whether organisms remember a past event (retrospection) or a future event (prospection) depends on which form of memory is more efficient in solving a particular task (Cook, Brown, & Riley, 1985; Zentall, Steirn, & Jackson-Smith, 1990). This shows that there is considerable flexibility in what information is encoded in memory, depending on the demands of the task.

Sources of Memory Failure

All of us encounter frustrating instances in which we cannot remember something. You may have been introduced to a new employee but when you encounter the person several days later, you struggle to remember her name. You may casually attribute such episodes to forgetting. Interestingly, however, forgetting is rarely used to explain instances of memory failure in the scientific literature. Forgetting implies that you learned and encoded the person's name when you were first introduced, but the memory trace has since faded and no longer exists. Although that may seem plausible, forgetting is difficult to prove. There are other explanations for memory failure, and these alternative accounts are easier to prove.

Memory may fail for a variety of reasons. You may not remember something because you never learned the information or never properly encoded it in the first place. Memory failure may also result from failure to effectively retrieve information that was successfully encoded or stored. You may also perform poorly in a memory task because you remember several things and are unable to choose correctly among these alternatives. In the following sections, I describe various alternative explanations of memory failure, discuss a special form of memory failure called *retrograde amnesia*, and consider the current status of the concept of memory consolidation.

INTERFERENCE EFFECTS

One of the most common sources of memory failure is interference from information that you were exposed to before or after the event that you are trying to remember. You may not recall the name of a new employee because of the other people you met for the first time before or after that particular individual. Memory failure due to interference has been extensively investigated in studies with both human participants (Postman, 1971; Underwood, 1957) and nonhuman species (e.g., Killeen, 2001; Wright, Katz, & Ma, 2012).

There are two types of interference effects depending on whether the source of the interference takes place before or after the target even that you are trying to remember (see Exhibit 14.1). If the extraneous stimuli that disrupt memory occur before the target event, the phenomenon is called *proactive interference*. In proactive interference, the interfering stimuli act forward, or proactively, to disrupt memory for the target event. Consider, for example, going to a sociology class that deals with the issue of punishment from the standpoint of the penal system and then attending a psychology class in which punishment is discussed from the perspective of conditioning procedures. You would be experiencing proactive interference if what you learned in the sociology class disrupted your memory of the psychological analysis of punishment.

Memory disruptions can also work in the opposite direction. Something you encounter later can act backward to disrupt your memory of something you learned earlier. This is called *retroactive interference*. You might be at a party, for example, where you first talk to Jane and then to Mary. When you think back on the experience the next day, you may have difficulty remembering what you discussed with Jane because of your subsequent discussions with Mary. In this case, your conversation with Mary acts backward or retroactively to disrupt your memory of talking with Jane.

Both proactive and retroactive interference have been investigated in animal studies using delayed matching-to-sample procedures. Proactive interference can occur if trials are scheduled close together in matching-to-sample training. Recall that successive trials in a matching procedure involve different sample stimuli. With short intertrial intervals, what occurs in one trial can produce proactive interference to disrupt

EXHIBIT 14.1

Distinction Between Proactive and Retroactive Interference

Proactive interference
Extraneous events → Target task → Memory test

Retroactive interference
Target task → Extraneous events → Memory test

performance in the next trial (Edhouse & White, 1988; Jitsumori, Wright, & Shyan, 1989). One account of this effect is that participants perform poorly not because they remember too little but because they remember too much. According to this interpretation, proactive interference is caused by remembering what happened on the preceding trial, which creates confusion about the correct choice on the current trial.

Retroactive interference has been investigated in matching-to-sample procedures by presenting extraneous stimuli during the delay interval between presentation of the sample stimulus and the choice alternatives. The extraneous stimulus may be provided by increasing the level of illumination in the experimental chamber, making various features of the experimental chamber more visible. Such a manipulation typically disrupts the accuracy of matching performance (Grant, 1988). In contrast to proactive interference, which results from remembering too much, retroactive interference seems to result from a failure to recall or retrieve required information. However, the precise mechanisms of retroactive interference remain under investigation (Calder & White, 2014; White & Brown, 2011).

RETRIEVAL FAILURE

Studies of proactive and retroactive interference illustrate two different causes of poor performance in a memory task. Yet another factor that contributes to memory failure is an individual's inability to effectively retrieve information that it previously learned. In principle this source of memory failure is easy to prove. If poor performance on a memory task is due to retrieval failure, then procedures that facilitate retrieval should facilitate performance. Retrieval of information is facilitated by exposure to stimuli that were previously associated with the target information. Such stimuli are called *retrieval cues*.

Remarkably insignificant features of the environment may become associated with a learning task and facilitate retrieval of information relevant to that task. In one study (Borovsky & Rovee-Collier, 1990), for example, 6-month-old infants received an instrumental conditioning procedure in their playpen at home (see Figure 14.4). Each infant was placed in a baby seat in the playpen with a mobile positioned overhead in plain view. The mobile was gently attached to one foot of the infant with a satin ribbon. By moving its foot, the infant could make the mobile move. Thus, the instrumental response was a leg movement, and the reinforcer was movement of the mobile.

Infants readily acquired the leg-movement response but showed little evidence of learning if they were tested 24 hours later. Did this deterioration of performance reflect the failure to effectively learn or encode the instrumental contingency, or a failure to retrieve what was learned the day before? If the instrumental response was not learned effectively in the first place, then there is nothing one can do to counteract the poor performance that is evident 24 hours later. In contrast, if the lack of memory was due to retrieval failure, then the presentation of retrieval or reminder cues should restore the performance.

What might be an effective retrieval cue for the infants in this situation? Borovsky and Rovee-Collier (1990) found that the pattern of the cloth liner that covered the

FIGURE 14.4

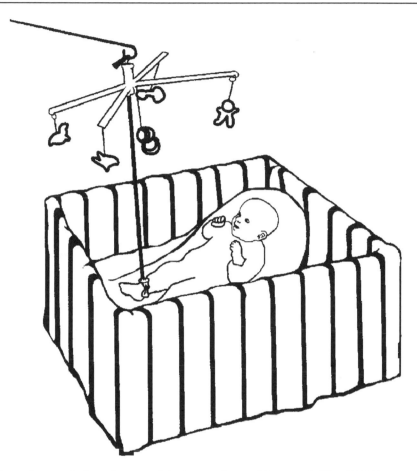

Experimental situation used by Borovsky and Rovee-Collier (1990) to study the effects of retrieval cues on the memory of human infants for an instrumental conditioning task. The instrumental response was moving a leg, and the reinforcer was consequent movement of a mobile located in the infant's view.

sides of the playpen served as an effective retrieval cue for the instrumental response. Sometimes the liner for the playpen had a striped pattern; on other occasions, the liner had a square pattern. Infants for whom the striped pattern was in the playpen during training responded better 24 hours later if they were tested with the striped liner than if they were tested with the square liner. The reverse results were obtained with infants for whom the other liner was used during original training.

The results of this experiment are remarkable because nothing was done to direct the attention of the infants to the crib liners. The square and striped patterns were both familiar to the infants, and the patterns were not predictive of reinforcement. They served as incidental background cues rather than as discriminative stimuli.

Nevertheless, the pattern present during original training became associated with the instrumental task and helped to retrieve information about the task during the memory test 24 hours later.

A variety of stimuli have been found to be effective as retrieval cues in various learning situations, including exposure to a conditioned stimulus (CS) without reinforcement exposure to the unconditioned stimulus, internal cues induced by psychoactive drugs, and exposure to the S⁻ in a discrimination procedure (Spear & Riccio, 1994). In addition, retrieval cues have been found to reverse a variety of phenomena that are characterized by low levels of conditioned responding, such as extinction, latent inhibition, overshadowing, and blocking (Urcelay & Miller, 2008).

Consolidation, Reconsolidation, and Memory Updating

For something to be remembered for a long time, a relatively permanent change has to occur in the nervous system. The translation of a learning episode into a long-term memory requires the process of memory *consolidation*. Memory consolidation involves cellular and molecular changes at the level of neural synapses (Hernandez & Abel, 2008). It also involves changes in neural circuits and neural systems (McKenzie & Eichenbaum, 2011). Both of these types of changes take time to finish, but synaptic consolidation takes place faster than consolidation in neural circuits.

Before a memory is fully consolidated, it is in a flexible or malleable state in which it can be disrupted or changed. In fact, hypotheses about memory consolidation are typically tested by introducing manipulations that disrupt the consolidation process. For example, treatment with a protein synthesis inhibitor or electroconvulsive shock after a learning episode disrupts later recall of that conditioning trial (McGaugh, 2000; McGaugh & Herz, 1972). However, the source of disruption has to occur shortly after the conditioning trial before the consolidation process has been completed. This limited period when a memory is susceptible to disruption is called the *consolidation window*.

The traditional view of memory consolidation was that once the consolidation process has been completed at the level of neural synapses and neural circuits, the memory was solidified and permanent. After a memory was consolidated, it could no longer be disrupted by the inhibition of protein synthesis or the administration of electroconvulsive shock. A previously consolidated memory could be retrieved to help deal with current situations. Retrieval or recollection moves the memory from an inactive or stored state to an active state in which the memory can guide decisions and behavior. However, the assumption was that moving the memory to an active state did nothing to change the original memory. Because the original memory remained pretty much intact, each attempt at retrieval operated on the original consolidated memory (see Figure 14.5).

The traditional view that memory consolidation creates a permanent memory has been challenged by the phenomenon of *reconsolidation*. When a memory is reactivated

FIGURE 14.5

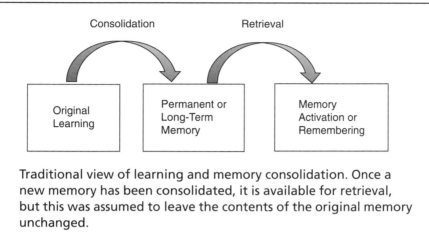

Traditional view of learning and memory consolidation. Once a new memory has been consolidated, it is available for retrieval, but this was assumed to leave the contents of the original memory unchanged.

or retrieved, the information is moved from its inactive (or stored) state to an active state. In this active state, the memory can be modified or changed, and these modifications can become incorporated into a new form of the long-term memory through the process of reconsolidation (Auber, Tedesco, Jones, Monfils, & Chiamulera, 2013). Interestingly, reconsolidation appears to involve some of the same neural mechanisms as original consolidation (McKenzie & Eichenbaum, 2011; Nader & Hardt, 2009).

The concept of reconsolidation is illustrated in Figure 14.6. Original learning and consolidation of that learning establish the first form of a long-term memory, something we may label as Form 1.0. Retrieval of that memory makes the memory subject to alteration, and these changes are then reconsolidated into a modified form of the long-term memory, which we may label as Form 1.1. This process of memory

FIGURE 14.6

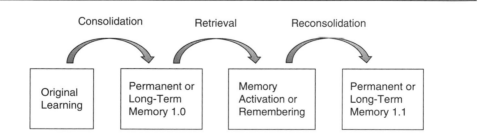

Contemporary view of learning, memory consolidation, and reconsolidation. When a memory is retrieved, it becomes labile and susceptible to reconsolidation, permitting changes in the contents of long-term memory with each episode of retrieval.

retrieval and reconsolidation is potentially repeated each time a memory is recalled, with the consequence that the long-term memory of an event becomes substantially modified as a result of repeated efforts to remember that event.

Recent research on reconsolidation has revolutionized how we think about memory mechanisms. Traditionally, we considered memory to be like a photograph that does not change each time you take out the photo and look at it. The concept of reconsolidation suggests that when you look at a photograph and then return it to storage, the photo that you store may have been modified by your current thoughts and reactions to it. In principle, each time you look at a photo and return it to long-term storage, it could be changed in some way.

I previously described how the concept of reconsolidation has been used to design a procedure that produces more effective extinction of conditioned fear (see Chapter 10, this volume). In that procedure, the memory of conditioned fear is activated by a single CS-alone trial. This memory reactivation presumably moves the conditioned fear into a malleable state such that a series of extinction trials are then more effective in changing the previous memory of the conditioned fear. However, the extinction series has to be conducted within the consolidation window (e.g., Monfils, Cowansage, Klann, & LeDoux, 2009). If the extinction trials are delayed by 6 hours after memory reactivation, they do not produced an enhanced extinction effect.

Not all reactivated memories are changed during the process of recall. If the recalled memory is not accompanied by new elements (or some form of prediction error), it is not likely to activate reconsolidation processes (Sevenster, Beckers, & Kindt, 2013). Much remains to be discovered about the circumstances that make a memory susceptible to long-term modification and the boundary conditions of such modifications. Nevertheless, the fact that long-term memories are susceptible to alteration helps us better understand how false and distorted memories develop through repeated efforts at recollection (Hardt, Einarsson, & Nader, 2010). The concept of reconsolidation is also encouraging the search for new ways to change long-term memories that are the source of recalcitrant clinical problems, such as posttraumatic stress disorder and drug addiction (Kroes, Schiller, LeDoux, & Phelps, 2016; Schwabe, Nader, & Pruessner, 2014).

Summary

Learning and memory are integrally related. Studies of learning focus on the acquisition stage of information processing, whereas studies of memory focus on the retention and retrieval stages. Working memory is used to retain information that is required just long enough to complete a trial or job. In contrast, reference memory involves aspects of the task or trial that remain constant from one occasion to the next. Early studies considered memory to be passive and retrospective. However, more recent evidence suggests that in many cases memory involves active processes and that the stored information may involve future (prospective) rather than past (retrospective) events.

Studies of what individuals forget can tell us as much about memory mechanisms as studies of successful performance. Memory failure may occur because of proactive or retroactive interference or because of retrieval failure. Proactive interference is often due to remembering both useful and irrelevant information and not being able to select between these. Retroactive interference can be due to disruptions of rehearsal processes needed for successful memory. Proper rehearsal, however, does not guarantee good memory. Information that is properly retained may not be retrieved during a memory test. Retrieval cues, some of which may be seemingly trivial features of the training situation, can facilitate memory performance in cases of retrieval failure.

Establishing a long-term memory involves processes of consolidation that operate at the level of neurons and neural circuits. However, a consolidated memory is not immune to modification. The recollection of a memory returns the memory to an active state in which it can be modified, and those modifications can be incorporated into the old memory through a process called reconsolidation. With repeated recollections, significant aspects of a memory can be altered and reconsolidated. This type of memory updating can create false memories, which may be problematic. However, research on memory updating may also enable scientists to develop more effective treatments for forms of psychopathology that are based on the maladaptive memories.

Suggested Readings

Alberini, C. M., & LeDoux, J. E. (2013). Memory reconsolidation. *Current Biology, 23,* R746–R750. http://dx.doi.org/10.1016/j.cub.2013.06.046

Schwabe, L., Nader, K., & Pruessner, J. C. (2014). Reconsolidation of human memory: Brain mechanisms and clinical relevance. *Biological Psychiatry, 76,* 274–280. http://dx.doi.org/10.1016/j.biopsych.2014.03.008

Spear, N. E., & Riccio, D. C. (1994). *Memory: Phenomena and principles.* Boston, MA: Allyn & Bacon.

Urcelay, G. P., & Miller, R. R. (2014). The functions of contexts in associative learning. *Behavioural Processes, 104,* 2–12. http://dx.doi.org/10.1016/j.beproc.2014.02.008

Zentall, T. R., & Smith, A. P. (2016). Delayed matching-to-sample: A tool to assess memory and other cognitive processes in pigeons. *Behavioural Processes, 123,* 26–42. http://dx.doi.org/10.1016/j.beproc.2015.07.002

Technical Terms

Acquisition stage
Consolidation
Delayed matching to sample
Matching-to-sample procedure
Proactive interference
Prospective memory
Reconsolidation
Reference memory

Retention interval
Retrieval cue
Retrieval stage
Retroactive interference
Retrospective memory
Simultaneous matching to sample
Working memory

Glossary

Acquired drive: A source of motivation for instrumental behavior caused by the presentation of a stimulus that was previously conditioned with a primary, or unconditioned, reinforcer.

Acquisition stage: The first stage necessary for memory performance in which information about the stimuli and responses is encoded in the nervous system in some fashion.

Afferent neuron: A neuron that transmits messages from sense organs to the central nervous system.

Appetitive behavior: The initial component of a species' typical behavior sequence. Appetitive behavior is variable, occurs in response to general spatial cues, and serves to bring the organism in contact with releasing stimuli that elicit consummatory responses.

Appetitive conditioning: A type of conditioning in which the unconditioned stimulus or reinforcer is a pleasant event or a stimulus the participant tends to approach.

Associative learning: Learning in which one event (a stimulus or a response) becomes linked to another, so that the first event activates a representation of the second.

Asymptote: The limit of learning, where no further changes occur in conditioned responding.

Autoshaping: See *sign tracking*.

Aversive conditioning: A type of conditioning in which the unconditioned stimulus or reinforcer is an unpleasant event, a stimulus that elicits aversion and withdrawal responses.

Aversive stimulus: Noxious or unpleasant stimulus that elicits aversion and/or withdrawal responses.

Behavioral bliss point: The preferred distribution of activities in the absence of constraints or limitations imposed by an instrumental conditioning procedure.

Behavior system: A sequence of response modes and corresponding behavioral and neurobiological control mechanisms that are activated in a coordinated manner to achieve a particular function such as feeding or defense against predation.

Between-subjects experiment: An experimental design in which two or more independent groups of participants are compared. The focus is on differences in the performance of the separate groups rather than the behavior of individual participants.

Blocking effect: Interference with the conditioning of a novel stimulus because of the presence of a previously conditioned stimulus during training trials for the novel stimulus.

Comparator hypothesis: The idea that conditioned responding depends on a comparison between the associative strength of the conditioned stimulus (CS) and the associative strength of other cues that were present during training of the target CS.

Concurrent-chain schedule: A schedule of reinforcement that consists of two components arranged in sequence. During the *choice link*, the participant has two alternatives available simultaneously. Selection of the one of those options provides that alternative (the *terminal link*) but makes the other one unavailable until the end of the trial.

Concurrent schedule: A reinforcement procedure in which the participant can choose to respond on one of two or more simple reinforcement schedules that are available simultaneously. Concurrent schedules allow for the measurement of choice between simple schedule alternatives.

Conditioned drive: A drive state induced by the presentation of a stimulus that was previously conditioned with a primary, or unconditioned, reinforcer. Same as *acquired drive.*

Conditioned inhibition: A type of Pavlovian conditioning in which the conditioned stimulus becomes a signal for the absence of the unconditioned stimulus.

Conditioned reinforcer: A stimulus that becomes an effective reinforcer because of its association with a primary, or unconditioned, reinforcer.

Conditioned response: A response that comes to be made to the conditioned stimulus as a result of classical conditioning.

Conditioned stimulus: A stimulus that initially does not elicit a conditioned response or activate a representation of an unconditioned stimulus but comes to do so after pairings with an unconditioned stimulus. Abbreviated CS.

Conditioned suppression: An aversive Pavlovian conditioning procedure in which conditioned responding is measured by the suppression of positively reinforced instrumental behavior.

Consolidation: The neurobiological processes whereby newly acquired information becomes encoded in a relatively permanent form in the nervous system.

Constraints on learning: Limitations on learning resulting from the evolutionary history of the organism.

Consummatory behavior: Behavior that brings an elicited behavior sequence to completion; behavior that consummates or finishes a sequence of elicited responses.

Contingency: The extent to which the occurrence of one event depends on the other, and vice versa.

Continuous reinforcement: A schedule of reinforcement in which every occurrence of the instrumental response produces the reinforcer. Abbreviated CRF.

Control condition: A condition in which participants do not receive a training procedure but are treated the same way in all other respects as participants that are trained. Performance in the control condition is compared with performance in the experimental condition in the basic learning experiment.

CS–US interval: Same as *interstimulus interval.*

CS–US relevance: Facilitated learning that occurs with certain combinations of conditioned and unconditioned stimuli (e.g., taste and illness) compared with other combinations (e.g., taste and shock).

Cumulative record: A graphical representation of the cumulative number of occurrences of a particular response as a function of the passage of time. The horizontal distance on the record represents time, the vertical distance represents the total number of responses that have occurred up to a particular point in time, and the slope represents the rate of responding.

Delay discounting function: The loss in the value of a reward as a function of how long one has to wait to obtain the reward.

Delayed conditioning: A Pavlovian conditioning procedure in which the conditioned stimulus begins before the unconditioned stimulus on each trial.

Delayed matching to sample: A procedure in which participants are reinforced for responding to a test stimulus that is the same as a sample stimulus that was presented some time earlier.

Differential probability principle: See *Premack's principle.*

Differential reinforcement of other behavior: An instrumental conditioning procedure in which a positive reinforcer is periodically delivered, but only if the participant fails to perform a particular response. Abbreviated DRO.

Differential responding: Responding in different ways or at different rates in the presence of different stimuli.

Directed forgetting: Stimulus control of memory, achieved by presenting a cue indicating when the participant will (or will not) be required to remember something.

Discrete-trial method: A method of instrumental conditioning in which the participant can perform the instrumental response only during specified periods, usually determined either by placement of the participant in an experimental chamber or by the presentation of a trial stimulus.

Discriminated avoidance: An avoidance conditioning procedure in which the occurrence of an aversive unconditioned stimulus is signaled by a warning signal or conditioned stimulus. Responding during the conditioned stimulus terminates that stimulus and prevents the delivery of the aversive unconditioned stimulus.

Discrimination hypothesis: A hypothesis that attributes the partial reinforcement extinction effect (slower extinction after partial reinforcement than after continuous reinforcement) to lack of detection or discrimination of the extinction procedure after partial reinforcement.

DISCRIMINATIVE CONTROL: A control procedure for Pavlovian conditioning in which one conditioned stimulus (the CS⁺) is paired with the unconditioned stimulus, whereas another conditioned stimulus (the CS⁻) is presented without the unconditioned stimulus. The development of responding during the CS⁺ but not during the CS⁻ is considered evidence of Pavlovian conditioning.

DISCRIMINATIVE PUNISHMENT: A type of punishment procedure in which responses are punished in the presence of a particular stimulus but not when that stimulus is absent.

DISHABITUATION: Recovery of a habituated response produced by the presentation of a strong extraneous or unrelated stimulus.

DISINHIBITION: Recovery of a partly extinguished conditioned response produced by the presentation of a novel stimulus.

DRIVE REDUCTION THEORY: A theory of reinforcement according to which reinforcers are effective because they reduce a drive state and return the participant to homeostasis.

DRIVE STATE: A motivational state that exists when a system is not at its homeostatic level. Return of the system to its homeostatic level reduces the drive state.

EFFERENT NEURON: A neuron that transmits impulses from the central nervous system to muscles.

ELICITED BEHAVIOR: A specific behavior or action pattern that occurs reliably upon presentation of a particular stimulus (its eliciting stimulus).

ETHOLOGY: A specialization in biology concerned with the analysis of species-typical behavior patterns that evolve in natural habitats.

EVOLUTION: Change in a physical or behavioral trait that occurs across successive generations because of differential reproductive success.

EXPERIMENTAL CONDITION: A condition in which participants receive a training procedure. Performance in the experimental condition is compared with performance in the control condition in the basic learning experiment.

EXPERIMENTAL OBSERVATION: Observation of behavior under conditions specifically designed by an investigator to test particular factors or variables that might influence the learning or performance of the participant.

EXTINCTION (IN CLASSICAL CONDITIONING): Reduction of a learned response that occurs because the conditioned stimulus is no longer paired with the unconditioned stimulus. Also, the procedure of repeatedly presenting a conditioned stimulus without the unconditioned stimulus.

EXTINCTION (IN INSTRUMENTAL CONDITIONING): Reduction in instrumental responding that occurs because the response is no longer followed by the reinforcer. Also, the procedure of no longer reinforcing the instrumental response.

FACILITATION: A Pavlovian conditioning procedure in which a conditioned stimulus is presented on trials when a second stimulus is paired with an unconditioned stimulus but not on trials when the second stimulus is presented alone. In such a procedure, one cue designates when another cue will be reinforced.

FATIGUE: A temporary decrease in behavior caused by repeated or excessive use of the muscles involved to perform the behavior.

Feedback cue: A stimulus that results from the performance of a response.

Feedback function: The relation between rates of responding and rates of reinforcement allowed by a particular reinforcement schedule.

Fixed-interval schedule: A reinforcement schedule in which reinforcement is delivered for the first response that occurs after a fixed amount of time following the last reinforce or the start of the trial.

Fixed-ratio schedule: A reinforcement schedule in which a fixed number of responses have to be performed for the next response to be reinforced.

Flavor neophobia: An aversion caused by the unfamiliarity of the flavor of a new food.

Focal search mode: A response mode in the feeding system that is activated once a potential source of food has been identified.

Forgetting: Loss of acquired information due to the passage of time.

Free-operant avoidance: Same as *nondiscriminated avoidance.*

Free-operant method: A method of instrumental conditioning that permits repetitions of the instrumental response at any time, in contrast to the discrete-trial method.

Frustration: An aversive emotional reaction that results from the unexpected absence of reinforcement.

Frustration theory: A theory of the partial reinforcement extinction effect according to which extinction is slower after partial reinforcement because the instrumental response becomes conditioned to the anticipation of frustrative nonreward.

General search mode: The initial response mode of the feeding system in which the organism reacts to general features of the environment with responses that enable it to come in contact with a variety of potential sources of food.

Habituation effect: A progressive decrease in the vigor of an elicited response that may occur with repeated presentations of the eliciting stimulus.

Higher order stimulus relation: A relation in which a stimulus signals a relationship between two other stimuli rather than signaling just the presence or absence of another stimulus. In a higher order Pavlovian relation, one conditioned stimulus signals whether another conditioned stimulus is paired with an unconditioned stimulus.

Homeostatic level: The optimal or defended level of a physiological system.

Hydraulic model: A model in ethology according to which certain factors lead to the buildup of a particular type of motivation or drive that increases the likelihood of corresponding modal action patterns. Performance of those modal action patterns reduces or discharges the motivational state.

Inhibitory S–R association: An S–R association in which presentation of the stimulus inhibits the associated response.

Instrumental behavior: A behavior or combination of responses that is effective in producing a particular consequence or reinforcer.

Instrumental conditioning: Conditioning that results from the relation between behavior and its consequences.

Interdimensional discrimination: A discrimination between two stimuli that differ in several respects.

INTERMITTENT REINFORCEMENT: A schedule of reinforcement in which only some of the occurrences of the instrumental response are reinforced. The instrumental response is reinforced occasionally, or intermittently. Also called *Partial reinforcement.*

INTERNEURON: A neuron in the spinal cord that transmits impulses from afferent (or sensory) to efferent (or motor) neurons.

INTERSTIMULUS INTERVAL: The interval in a Pavlovian delayed conditioning procedure between the start of the conditioned stimulus and the start of the unconditioned stimulus.

INTERVAL SCHEDULE: A reinforcement schedule in which a response is reinforced only if it occurs more than a set amount of time after the last delivery of the reinforcer.

INTRADIMENSIONAL DISCRIMINATION: A discrimination between stimuli that differ in only one stimulus characteristic, such as color, brightness, or pitch.

I/T RATIO: The ratio between the intertrial interval (I) and the duration of the conditioned stimulus or trial time (T) in Pavlovian delayed conditioning procedures.

LATENT INHIBITION: Retardation of Pavlovian conditioning that occurs because of repeated exposures or presentations of the conditioned stimulus by itself before CS–US pairings.

LAW OF EFFECT: A mechanism for instrumental behavior, proposed by Thorndike, according to which reinforcement of an instrumental response strengthens the association between the response and the stimulus in the presence of which the response occurred.

LEARNING: An enduring change in the mechanisms of behavior involving specific stimuli or responses that results from prior experience with those stimuli and responses.

LONG-DELAY LEARNING: A classical conditioning procedure in which the conditioned stimulus is presented long before the unconditioned stimulus on each conditioning trial.

LONG-TERM HABITUATION: A type of habituation that is lasts a day or more and does show spontaneous recovery.

LONG-TERM SENSITIZATION: A form of sensitization that is persistent and slow to decay.

MAGNITUDE-OF-REINFORCEMENT EXTINCTION EFFECT: Less persistence of instrumental behavior in extinction after training with a large reinforcer than after training with a small reinforcer.

MARKING STIMULUS: A brief visual or auditory cue presented after an instrumental response that makes the instrumental response more memorable and helps overcome the disruptive effect of delayed reinforcement.

MATCHING LAW: A rule for instrumental behavior, proposed by Herrnstein, according to which the relative rate of response on a particular response alternative equals the relative rate of reinforcement for that response alternative.

MATCHING-TO-SAMPLE PROCEDURE: A procedure in which participants are reinforced for selecting a stimulus that corresponds to the sample presented on that trial.

MATURATION: A change in behavior caused by physical or physiological development.

MODAL ACTION PATTERN: A response pattern that occurs in much the same fashion most of the time and in most members of a species. Modal action patterns are often used as basic units of behavior in ethological investigations of behavior.

MOTIVATION: A hypothetical state that increases the probability of a coordinated set of activities or activates a system of behaviors that functions to satisfy a goal, such as feeding, predatory defense, infant care, or copulation.

Motor neuron: Same as *efferent neuron.*

Multiple schedule of reinforcement: A procedure in which different reinforcement schedules are in effect in the presence of different stimuli presented in succession. Generally, each stimulus comes to evoke a pattern of responding that corresponds to the reinforcement schedule that is in effect in the presence of that stimulus.

Naturalistic observation: Observation of behavior as it occurs under natural conditions, in the absence of interventions or manipulations introduced by the investigator.

Negative reinforcement: An instrumental conditioning procedure in which there is a negative contingency between the instrumental response and an aversive stimulus. If the instrumental response is performed, the aversive stimulus is terminated; if the instrumental response is not performed, the aversive stimulus is not turned off.

Negative reinforcer: Same as *aversive stimulus.*

Nondiscriminated avoidance: An avoidance conditioning procedure in which the aversive stimulus is not signaled by an external warning signal. Rather, the aversive stimulus is scheduled to occur periodically, as set by the S–S interval. Each occurrence of the avoidance response prevents the delivery of the aversive stimulus for a fixed period, which is called the R–S interval.

One-way avoidance: An avoidance conditioning procedure in which the required response to avoid shock is always to cross from one compartment of a shuttle box to the other in the same direction.

Operant behavior: Behavior that is defined by the effect it produces in the environment. Examples include pressing a lever and opening a door. Any sequence of movements that depresses the lever or opens the door constitutes an instance of that particular operant behavior.

Operant conditioning: A form of instrumental conditioning in which the response required for reinforcement is an operant response, identified by its effect in manipulating the environment in some way.

Orienting response: A reaction to a novel stimulus that usually involves turning toward the source of the stimulus.

Overexpectation: Expectation of an unconditioned stimulus that is larger than what actually occurs. Overexpectation is usually produced by training each of two conditioned stimuli separately with the same unconditioned stimulus and then presenting those two conditioned stimuli at the same time.

Overshadowing: Interference with the conditioning of a stimulus due to the simultaneous presence of another stimulus that is easier to condition.

Overtraining extinction effect: Less persistence of instrumental behavior in extinction after extensive training with reinforcement (overtraining) than after only moderate levels of reinforcement training.

Paradoxical reward effect: A phenomenon in which there is more responding in extinction after training with fewer, more intermittent, or smaller reinforcers.

Partial reinforcement: A schedule of reinforcement in which only some occurrences of the instrumental response are reinforced. Also called *intermittent reinforcement.*

Partial-reinforcement extinction effect: Greater persistence of instrumental responding in extinction after partial (intermittent) reinforcement training than after continuous reinforcement training. Abbreviated PREE.

Perceptual concept: Responding the same way to a set of physically different stimuli (e.g., pictures of various types of dogs) that all belong to the same perceptual category (dog).

Performance: An organism's observable behaviors or activities at a particular time.

Persistence: The continued performance of an instrumental response after an extinction procedure has been introduced.

Positive occasion setting: Same as *facilitation*.

Postreinforcement pause: A pause in responding that typically occurs after the delivery of the reinforcer or at the start of a trial on fixed-ratio and fixed-interval schedules of reinforcement.

Practice: Repetition of a response or behavior, usually with the intent of improving performance.

Predatory imminence: The perceived likelihood of being attacked by a predator. Different species-typical defense responses are assumed to be performed in the face of different degrees of predatory imminence.

Premack's principle: Given two responses with different baseline probabilities of occurrence, the opportunity to perform the higher probability response will reinforce or increase performance of the lower probability behavior.

Primary reinforcer: A reinforcer that is effective without prior conditioning.

Proactive interference: Disruption of memory by exposure to stimuli before the event to be remembered.

Proprioceptive cue: An internal response feedback stimulus that arises from the movement of a muscle and/or joint.

Prospective memory: Memory of a plan for future action. Also called *prospection*.

Punishment: A type of instrumental conditioning procedure in which occurrence of the instrumental response results in delivery of an aversive stimulus.

Puzzle box: A type of experimental chamber used by Thorndike to study instrumental conditioning. The participant was put in the chamber and had to perform a specified behavior to be released and obtain a reinforcer.

R–O association: An association between the instrumental response (R) and the reinforcer or response outcome (O).

R–S interval: The interval between the occurrence of an avoidance response and the next scheduled presentation of the aversive stimulus in a nondiscriminated avoidance procedure.

Random control: A control procedure for Pavlovian conditioning in which the conditioned and unconditioned stimuli are presented at random times relative to each other.

Rate of responding: A measure of how often a response is repeated in a unit of time—for example, the number of responses that occur per minute.

Ratio run: The high and steady rate of responding observed after the postreinforcement pause on fixed-ratio reinforcement schedules. The ratio run ends when the necessary number of responses has been performed, resulting in delivery of the reinforcer.

Ratio schedule: A reinforcement schedule in which reinforcement depends only on the number of responses the participant performs, irrespective of when these responses occur.

Reconsolidation: The consolidation of a reactivated memory (as contrasted with consolidation of a newly acquired memory).

Reference memory: The retention of background information a participant needs to finish a task or respond successfully in a situation. (Compare with *working memory*.)

Reflex: A unit of elicited behavior involving a specific environmental event and its corresponding specific elicited response.

Reflex arc: Neural structures, consisting of the afferent (sensory) neuron, interneuron, and efferent (motor) neuron, that enable a stimulus to elicit a reflex response.

Reinforcer: A stimulus whose delivery shortly following a response increases the future probability of that response; also called *outcome*.

Reinstatement: Recovery of excitatory responding to an extinguished stimulus produced by exposures to the unconditioned stimulus.

Releasing stimulus: Same as *sign stimulus*.

Renewal: Recovery of excitatory responding to an extinguished stimulus produced by a shift away from the contextual cues that were present during extinction.

Response allocation: The distribution of instrumental responses among various options available in the situation.

Response deprivation hypothesis: An explanation of reinforcement according to which reduced access to a particular response is sufficient to make the opportunity to perform that response an effective positive reinforcer.

Retardation-of-acquisition test: A test procedure that identifies a stimulus as a conditioned inhibitor if that stimulus is slower to acquire conditioned excitatory properties than a neutral comparison stimulus.

Retention interval: The period of time between acquisition of information and a test of memory for that information.

Retrieval cue: A stimulus related to an experience that facilitates the recall of other information related to that experience.

Retrieval stage: The third stage necessary for memory performance in which information that has been retained is recovered from storage for current use.

Retroactive interference: Disruption of memory by exposure to stimuli after the event to be remembered.

Retrospective memory: Memory of a previously experienced event.

S⁺: A discriminative stimulus that signals the availability of reinforcement for an instrumental response.

S⁻: A discriminative stimulus that signals the absence of reinforcement for an instrumental response.

S–O association: An association between a stimulus (S) in the presence of which an instrumental response is reinforced and the reinforcer or response outcome (O).

S–R ASSOCIATION: An association between a stimulus and a response, enabling presentation of the stimulus to elicit the response.

S–R LEARNING: The learning of an association between a stimulus and a response, with the result that the stimulus comes to elicit the response.

S–R SYSTEM: The shortest neural pathway for elicited behavior that connects the sense organs stimulated by a stimulus and the muscles involved in making the elicited response.

S(R–O) ASSOCIATION: A higher order relation in instrumental conditioning situations, according to which a discriminative or contextual stimulus (S) activates an association between the instrumental response and the reinforcer (R–O).

S–S INTERVAL: The interval between successive presentations of the aversive stimulus in a nondiscriminated avoidance procedure when the avoidance response is not performed.

S–S LEARNING: Same as *stimulus–stimulus learning.*

SAFETY SIGNAL: A stimulus that signals the absence of an aversive event.

SALIENCE: The quality of a stimulus that makes it effective in attracting attention and controlling behavior. More intense stimuli are typically more salient.

SCHEDULE LINE: A line on a graph of rates of instrumental and reinforcer responses indicating how much access to the reinforcer activity is provided for various rates of instrumental responding on a particular schedule of reinforcement.

SCHEDULE OF REINFORCEMENT: A program or rule that determines which occurrence of an instrumental or operant response is followed by delivery of the reinforcer.

SECONDARY REINFORCER: Same as *conditioned reinforcer.*

SELECTIVE ASSOCIATIONS: Associations that are formed more readily between one combination of conditioned and unconditioned stimuli than between other combinations.

SELF-CONTROL: The choice of a delayed large reward over an immediate but smaller reward.

SENSITIZATION EFFECT: An increase in the vigor of elicited behavior that may result from repeated presentations of the eliciting stimulus or an intense unrelated event.

SENSORY NEURON: Same as *afferent neuron.*

SENSORY REINFORCEMENT: Reinforcement provided by presentation of a stimulus unrelated to a biological need or drive.

SEQUENTIAL THEORY: A theory of the partial-reinforcement extinction effect according to which extinction is retarded after partial reinforcement because the instrumental response becomes conditioned to the memory of nonreward.

SHAPING: Reinforcement of successive approximations to a target instrumental response, typically used to condition responses that are not in the participant's existing repertoire of behavior. Shaping depends on behavioral availability.

SHORT-TERM HABITUATION: A habituation effect that lasts a relatively short period of time, sometimes less than a minute.

SHORT-TERM SENSITIZATION: A form of sensitization that lasts a relatively short period of time, sometimes less than a minute.

SHUTTLE BOX: An apparatus for the study of avoidance behavior consisting of two adjacent compartments. The avoidance response involves moving from one compartment to the other (i.e., shuttling between the compartments).

SIGN STIMULUS: The specific feature of an object or animal that elicits a modal action pattern in another organism.

SIGN TRACKING: A form of appetitive classical conditioning in which a localized stimulus serves as the conditioned stimulus. During the course of conditioning, the participant comes to approach (track) and sometimes manipulate the conditioned stimulus.

SIMULTANEOUS CONDITIONING: A Pavlovian conditioning procedure in which the conditioned stimulus and the unconditioned stimulus are presented simultaneously on each conditioning trial.

SIMULTANEOUS MATCHING TO SAMPLE: A procedure in which participants are reinforced for responding to a test stimulus that is the same as a sample stimulus. The sample and the test stimuli are presented at the same time.

SINGLE-SUBJECT EXPERIMENT: A type of experiment in which learning is investigated through extensive observation of the behavior of a single individual. The individual's behavior must be sufficiently well understood to permit accurate assumptions about how the participant would have behaved if he or she had not received the training procedure.

SKINNER BOX: A small experimental chamber provided with something the participant can manipulate repeatedly, such as a response lever or a joystick. This allows the participant to perform a particular response repeatedly without being removed from the experimental situation. The chamber also has a mechanism that can deliver a reinforcer, such as a pellet of food or a sip of juice.

SPECIES-SPECIFIC DEFENSE REACTIONS: Species-typical responses individuals perform in aversive situations. The responses may involve freezing, fleeing, or fighting.

SPECIES-TYPICAL BEHAVIOR: Behavior that is characteristic of most members of a particular species.

SPONTANEOUS RECOVERY: Recovery of a response produced by a period of rest after habituation or extinction.

SSDR: Abbreviation for *species-specific defense reaction*.

STARTLE RESPONSE: A sudden jump or tensing of the muscles that may occur when an unexpected stimulus is presented.

STATE SYSTEM: Neural structures that determine the organism's general level of responsiveness or readiness to respond.

STIMULUS DIMENSION: The feature (e.g., color) that distinguishes a series of stimuli in a test of stimulus generalization.

STIMULUS DISCRIMINATION: Differential responding in the presence of two or more stimuli.

STIMULUS EQUIVALENCE: Responding to physically distinct stimuli in the same fashion because of common prior experiences with the stimuli.

STIMULUS GENERALIZATION: The occurrence of behavior learned through habituation or conditioning in the presence of stimuli that are different from the particular stimulus that was used during training.

STIMULUS GENERALIZATION GRADIENT: A gradient of responding that may be observed if participants are tested with stimuli that increasingly differ from the stimulus that was used during training.

Stimulus–stimulus learning: The learning of an association between two stimuli, such that presentation of the first stimulus activates a neural representation of the second one.

Straight-alley runway: A straight alley with a start box at one end and a goal box at the other. Animals are placed in the start box at the beginning of a trial and allowed to run to the goal box.

Summation test: A test for conditioned inhibition in which responding to an excitatory cue presented simultaneously with a conditioned inhibitor is compared with responding to the excitatory cue presented alone (or with a neutral stimulus). The conditioned inhibitor suppresses responding that is otherwise observed to the excitatory cue.

Taste aversion learning: A type of Pavlovian conditioning in which the taste of a novel food serves as the conditioned stimulus and illness serves as the unconditioned stimulus. Taste aversions can be learned even if the illness is delayed several hours after exposure to the taste.

Temporal coding: Encoding the specific temporal parameters of a conditioning procedure; learning not just that the CS is paired with the US but exactly when the US occurs relative to the CS.

Temporal contiguity: The simultaneous occurrence of two or more events.

Temporal cues: Stimuli related to the passage of time.

Time-out: A period during which the opportunity to obtain reinforcement is removed. This may involve removal of the participant from the situation in which reinforcers may be obtained.

T-maze: A maze with a start box that opens to a straight alley, at the end of which the participant can turn either right or left to reach the goal box.

Trace conditioning: A classical conditioning procedure in which the unconditioned stimulus is presented on each trial after the conditioned stimulus has been terminated for a short period.

Trace interval: The interval between the end of the conditioned stimulus and the beginning of the unconditioned stimulus in a trace conditioning procedure. The trace interval is usually much shorter than the intertrial interval.

Two-factor theory: A theory of avoidance learning involving two forms of conditioning: (a) Pavlovian conditioning of fear to a stimulus that signals aversive stimulation and (b) instrumental conditioning of the avoidance response by fear reduction.

Two-way avoidance: A shuttle avoidance procedure in which trials can start in either compartment of a shuttle box; the avoidance response consists of going back and forth from the occupied compartment to the unoccupied compartment.

Unconditioned response: A response that occurs to a stimulus without the necessity of prior training or conditioning.

Unconditioned stimulus: A stimulus that elicits vigorous responding in the absence of prior training. Abbreviated US.

Unpaired control procedure: A control procedure for classical conditioning in which both the conditioned stimulus and the unconditioned stimulus are presented periodically but never together.

US DEVALUATION: A procedure that reduces the effectiveness or value of an unconditioned stimulus in eliciting unconditioned behavior.

US INFLATION: A procedure that increases the effectiveness or value of an unconditioned stimulus in eliciting unconditioned behavior.

VARIABLE-INTERVAL SCHEDULE: A schedule of reinforcement in which the reinforcer is provided for the first response that occurs after a variable amount of time since the last reinforcer.

VARIABLE-RATIO SCHEDULE: A schedule of reinforcement in which the number of responses necessary to obtain the reinforcer varies from trial to trial. The value of the schedule refers to the average number of responses required for reinforcement.

WORKING MEMORY: The retention of information that is needed only to accomplish the task at hand, as contrasted with reference memory, which involves background information that is also needed for future similar tasks.

References

Akins, C. K. (2000). Effects of species-specific cues and the CS–US interval on the topography of the sexually conditioned response. *Learning and Motivation, 31*, 211–235. http://dx.doi.org/10.1006/lmot.2000.1050

Alberini, C. M., & LeDoux, J. E. (2013). Memory reconsolidation. *Current Biology, 23*, R746–R750. http://dx.doi.org/10.1016/j.cub.2013.06.046

Alcock, J. (2013). *Animal behavior: An evolutionary approach* (10th ed.). Sunderland, MA: Sinauer Associates.

Allan, L. G. (2005). Introduction to "Learning of contingent relationships" [Special issue]. *Learning & Behavior, 33*, 127–129. http://dx.doi.org/10.3758/BF03196057

Allison, J. (1983). *Behavioral economics.* New York, NY: Praeger.

Allison, J. (1989). The nature of reinforcement. In S. B. Klein & R. R. Mowrer (Eds.), *Contemporary learning theories: Instrumental conditioning theory and the impact of biological constraints on learning* (pp. 13–39). Hillsdale, NJ: Erlbaum.

Allison, J., & Timberlake, W. (1974). Instrumental and contingent saccharin-licking in rats: Response deprivation and reinforcement. *Learning and Motivation, 5*, 231–247. http://dx.doi.org/10.1016/0023-9690(74)90029-0

Amsel, A. (1958). The role of frustrative nonreward in noncontinuous reward situations. *Psychological Bulletin, 55*, 102–119. http://dx.doi.org/10.1037/h0043125

Amsel, A. (1992). *Frustration theory: An analysis of dispositional learning and memory.* Cambridge, England: Cambridge University Press. http://dx.doi.org/10.1017/CBO9780511665561

Amsel, A., & Rashotte, M. E. (1984). *Mechanisms of adaptive behavior: Clark L. Hull's theoretical papers, with commentary.* New York, NY: Columbia University Press.

Andrzejewski, M. E., Cardinal, C. D., Field, D. P., Flannery, B. A., Johnson, M., Bailey, K., & Hineline, P. N. (2005). Pigeons' choices between fixed-interval and random-interval schedules: Utility of variability? *Journal of the Experimental Analysis of Behavior, 83*, 129–145. http://dx.doi.org/10.1901/jeab.2005.30-04

Angelakis, I., & Austin, J. L. (2015). Maintenance of safety behaviors via response-produced stimuli. *Behavior Modification, 39*, 932–954. http://dx.doi.org/10.1177/0145445515610314

Anger, D. (1963). The role of temporal discriminations in the reinforcement of Sidman avoidance behavior. *Journal of the Experimental Analysis of Behavior, 6*, 477–506. http://dx.doi.org/10.1901/jeab.1963.6-s477

Anselme, P., & Robinson, M. J. F. (2016). "Wanting," "liking," and their relation to consciousness. *Journal of Experimental Psychology: Animal Learning and Cognition, 42*, 123–140. http://dx.doi.org/10.1037/xan0000090

Auber, A., Tedesco, V., Jones, C. E., Monfils, M. H., & Chiamulera, C. (2013). Post-retrieval extinction as reconsolidation interference: Methodological issues or boundary conditions? *Psychopharmacology, 226*, 631–647. http://dx.doi.org/10.1007/s00213-013-3004-1

Ayres, J. J. B. (2012). Conditioned suppression. In N. M. Seel (Ed.), *Encyclopedia of the sciences of learning* (pp. 749–751). New York, NY: Springer Science.

Azorlosa, J. L., & Cicala, G. A. (1986). Blocking of conditioned suppression with 1 or 10 compound trials. *Animal Learning & Behavior, 14*, 163–167. http://dx.doi.org/10.3758/BF03200051

Azrin, N. H. (1959). Punishment and recovery during fixed-ratio performance. *Journal of the Experimental Analysis of Behavior, 2*, 301–305. http://dx.doi.org/10.1901/jeab.1959.2-301

Azrin, N. H. (1960). Effects of punishment intensity during variable-interval reinforcement. *Journal of the Experimental Analysis of Behavior, 3*, 123–142. http://dx.doi.org/10.1901/jeab.1960.3-123

Azrin, N. H., & Holz, W. C. (1961). Punishment during fixed-interval reinforcement. *Journal of the Experimental Analysis of Behavior, 4*, 343–347. http://dx.doi.org/10.1901/jeab.1961.4-343

Azrin, N. H., & Holz, W. C. (1966). Punishment. In W. K. Honig (Ed.), *Operant behavior: Areas of research and application* (pp. 380–447). New York, NY: Appleton-Century-Crofts.

Azrin, N. H., Holz, W. C., & Hake, D. F. (1963). Fixed-ratio punishment. *Journal of the Experimental Analysis of Behavior, 6*, 141–148. http://dx.doi.org/10.1901/jeab.1963.6-141

Baerends, G. P. (1988). Ethology. In R. C. Atkinson, R. J. Herrnstein, G. Lindzey, & R. D. Luce (Eds.), *Stevens' handbook of experimental psychology* (Vol. 1, pp. 765–830). New York, NY: Wiley.

Balaz, M. A., Kasprow, W. J., & Miller, R. R. (1982). Blocking with a single compound trial. *Animal Learning & Behavior, 10*, 271–276.

Balci, F., Gallistel, C. R., Allen, B. D., Frank, K. M., Gibson, J. M., & Brunner, D. (2009). Acquisition of peak responding: What is learned? *Behavioural Processes, 80*, 67–75. http://dx.doi.org/10.1016/j.beproc.2008.09.010

Balsam, P. D., Deich, J. D., Ohyama, T., & Stokes, P. D. (1998). Origins of new behavior. In W. O'Donohue (Ed.), *Learning and behavior therapy* (pp. 403–420). Boston, MA: Allyn and Bacon.

Balsam, P. D., Drew, M. R., & Gallistel, C. R. (2010). Time and associate learning. *Comparative Cognition & Behavior Reviews, 5,* 1–22. http://dx.doi.org/10.3819/ccbr.2010.50001

Balsam, P. D., & Gallistel, C. R. (2009). Temporal maps and informativeness in associative learning. *Trends in Neurosciences, 32,* 73–78. http://dx.doi.org/10.1016/j.tins.2008.10.004

Balsam, P. D., & Tomie, A. (Eds.). (1985). *Context and conditioning.* Hillsdale, NJ: Erlbaum.

Bandarian Balooch, S., & Neumann, D. L. (2011). Effects of multiple contexts and context similarity on the renewal of extinguished conditioned behavior in an ABA design with humans. *Learning and Motivation, 42,* 53–63. http://dx.doi.org/10.1016/j.lmot.2010.08.008

Baron, A., & Menich, S. R. (1985). Reaction times of younger and older men: Effects of compound samples and a prechoice signal on delayed matching-to-sample performances. *Journal of the Experimental Analysis of Behavior, 44,* 1–14. http://dx.doi.org/10.1901/jeab.1985.44-1

Barrett, D. (2010). *Supernormal stimuli: How primal urges overran their evolutionary purpose.* New York, NY: Norton.

Bashinski, H. S., Werner, J. S., & Rudy, J. W. (1985). Determinants of infant visual fixation: Evidence for a two-process theory. *Journal of Experimental Child Psychology, 39,* 580–598. http://dx.doi.org/10.1016/0022-0965(85)90058-X

Baum, M. (1970). Extinction of avoidance responding through response prevention (flooding). *Psychological Bulletin, 74,* 276–284. http://dx.doi.org/10.1037/h0029789

Baum, W. M. (1974). On two types of deviation from the matching law: Bias and undermatching. *Journal of the Experimental Analysis of Behavior, 22,* 231–242. http://dx.doi.org/10.1901/jeab.1974.22-231

Bechterev, V. M. (1913). *Lapsychologie objective.* Paris, France: Alcan.

Benedict, J. O., & Ayres, J. J. B. (1972). Factors affecting conditioning in the truly random control procedure in the rat. *Journal of Comparative and Physiological Psychology, 78,* 323–330. http://dx.doi.org/10.1037/h0032296

Beran, M. J., Evans, T. A., Klein, E. D., & Einstein, G. O. (2012). Rhesus monkeys (*Macaca mulatta*) and capuchin monkeys (*Cebus apella*) remember future responses in a computerized task. *Journal of Experimental Psychology: Animal Behavior Processes, 38,* 233–243. http://dx.doi.org/10.1037/a0027796

Berlyne, D. E. (1969). The reward value of indifferent stimulation. In J. Tapp (Ed.), *Reinforcement and behavior* (pp. 178–214). New York, NY: Academic Press. http://dx.doi.org/10.1016/B978-0-12-683650-9.50012-1

Best, M. R., Dunn, D. P., Batson, J. D., Meachum, C. L., & Nash, S. M. (1985). Extinguishing conditioned inhibition in flavour-aversion learning: Effects of repeated testing and extinction of the excitatory element. *Quarterly Journal of Experimental Psychology B: Comparative and Physiological Psychology, 37,* 359–378. http://dx.doi.org/10.1080/14640748508401175

Bevins, R. A., & Murray, J. E. (2011). Internal stimuli generated by abused substances: Role of Pavlovian conditioning and its implications for drug addiction. In T. R. Schachtman & S. Reilly (Eds.), *Associative learning and conditioning theory: Human and non-human applications* (pp. 270–289). New York, NY: Oxford University Press. http://dx.doi.org/10.1093/acprof:oso/9780199735969.003.0084

Bickel, W. K., Koffarnus, M. N., Moody, L., & Wilson, A. G. (2014). The behavioral- and neuro-economic process of temporal discounting: A candidate behavioral marker of addiction. *Neuropharmacology, 76*(Part B), 518–527.

Blaisdell, A. P., Gunther, L. M., & Miller, R. R. (1999). Recovery from blocking achieved by extinguishing the blocking CS. *Animal Learning & Behavior, 27*, 63–76. http://dx.doi.org/10.3758/BF03199432

Blass, E. M., Ganchrow, J. R., & Steiner, J. E. (1984). Classical conditioning in newborn humans 2–48 hours of age. *Infant Behavior & Development, 7*, 223–235. http://dx.doi.org/10.1016/S0163-6383(84)80060-0

Boakes, R. A. (1979). Interactions between type I and type II processes involving positive rein for cement. In A. Dickinson & R. A. Boakes (Eds.), *Mechanisms of learning and motivation* (pp. 233–268). Hillsdale, NJ: Erlbaum.

Boakes, R. A., Poli, M., Lockwood, M. J., & Goodall, G. (1978). A study of misbehavior: Token reinforcement in the rat. *Journal of the Experimental Analysis of Behavior, 29*, 115–134. http://dx.doi.org/10.1901/jeab.1978.29-115

Boddez, Y., Baeyens, F., Hermans, D., & Beckers, T. (2011). The hide-and-seek of retrospective revaluation: Recovery from blocking is context dependent in human causal learning. *Journal of Experimental Psychology: Animal Behavior Processes, 37*, 230–240. http://dx.doi.org/10.1037/a0021460

Bolles, R. C. (1969). Avoidance and escape learning: Simultaneous acquisition of different responses. *Journal of Comparative and Physiological Psychology, 68*, 355–358. http://dx.doi.org/10.1037/h0027536

Bolles, R. C. (1970). Species-specific defense reactions and avoidance learning. *Psychological Review, 77*, 32–48. http://dx.doi.org/10.1037/h0028589

Borovsky, D., & Rovee-Collier, C. (1990). Contextual constraints on memory retrieval at six months. *Child Development, 61*, 1569–1583. http://dx.doi.org/10.2307/1130765

Bossert, J. M., Marchant, N. J., Calu, D. J., & Shaham, Y. (2013). The reinstatement model of drug relapse: Recent neurobiological findings, emerging research topics, and translational research. *Psychopharmacology, 229*, 453–476. http://dx.doi.org/10.1007/s00213-013-3120-y

Bouton, M. E. (1993). Context, time, and memory retrieval in the interference paradigms of Pavlovian learning. *Psychological Bulletin, 114*, 80–99. http://dx.doi.org/10.1037/0033-2909.114.1.80

Bouton, M. E. (1994). Conditioning, remembering, and forgetting. *Journal of Experimental Psychology: Animal Behavior Processes, 20*, 219–231. http://dx.doi.org/10.1037/0097-7403.20.3.219

Bouton, M. E. (2014). Why behavior change is difficult to sustain. *Preventive Medicine: An International Journal Devoted to Practice and Theory, 68*, 29–36. http://dx.doi.org/10.1016/j.ypmed.2014.06.010

Bouton, M. E., Mineka, S., & Barlow, D. H. (2001). A modern learning theory perspective on the etiology of panic disorder. *Psychological Review, 108,* 4–32. http://dx.doi.org/10.1037/0033-295X.108.1.4

Bouton, M. E., Trask, S., & Carranza-Jasso, R. (2016). Learning to inhibit the response during instrumental (operant) extinction. *Journal of Experimental Psychology: Animal Learning and Cognition, 42,* 246–258. http://dx.doi.org/10.1037/xan0000102

Bouton, M. E., & Woods, A. M. (2008). Extinction: Behavioral mechanisms and their implications. In J. H. Byrne (Ed.), *Learning theory and behavior: Vol. 1. Learning and memory: A comprehensive reference* (pp. 151–172). Oxford, England: Elsevier.

Bower, G. H., & Hilgard, E. R. (1981). *Theories of learning* (5th ed.). Englewood Cliffs, NJ: Prentice Hall.

Bradley, M. M., Moulder, B., & Lang, P. J. (2005). When good things go bad: The reflex physiology of defense. *Psychological Science, 16,* 468–473.

Breland, K., & Breland, M. (1961). The misbehavior of organisms. *American Psychologist, 16,* 681–684. http://dx.doi.org/10.1037/h0040090

Brooks, D. C. (2000). Recent and remote extinction cues reduce spontaneous recovery. *The Quarterly Journal of Experimental Psychology, 53,* 25–58. http://dx.doi.org/10.1080/027249900392986

Brooks, D. C., & Bouton, M. E. (1993). A retrieval cue for extinction attenuates spontaneous recovery. *Journal of Experimental Psychology: Animal Behavior Processes, 19,* 77–89. http://dx.doi.org/10.1037/0097-7403.19.1.77

Burns, M., & Domjan, M. (2001). Topography of spatially directed conditioned responding: Effects of context and trial duration. *Journal of Experimental Psychology: Animal Behavior Processes, 27,* 269–278. http://dx.doi.org/10.1037/0097-7403.27.3.269

Cain, C. K., & LeDoux, J. E. (2007). Escape from fear: A detailed behavioral analysis of two atypical responses reinforced by CS termination. *Journal of Experimental Psychology: Animal Behavior Processes, 33,* 451–463. http://dx.doi.org/10.1037/0097-7403.33.4.451

Calder, A., & White, K. (2014). In search of consolidation of short-term memory in nonhuman animals. *Learning & Behavior, 42,* 83–92. http://dx.doi.org/10.3758/s13420-013-0127-5

Camp, D. S., Raymond, G. A., & Church, R. M. (1967). Temporal relationship between response and punishment. *Journal of Experimental Psychology, 74,* 114–123. http://dx.doi.org/10.1037/h0024518

Campolattaro, M. M., Schnitker, K. M., & Freeman, J. H. (2008). Changes in inhibition during differential eyeblink conditioning with increased training. *Learning & Behavior, 36,* 159–165. http://dx.doi.org/10.3758/LB.36.2.159

Cándido, A., González, F., & de Brugada, I. (2004). Safety signals from avoidance learning but not from yoked classical conditioning training pass both summation and retardation tests for inhibition. *Behavioural Processes, 66,* 153–160. http://dx.doi.org/10.1016/j.beproc.2004.01.011

Capaldi, E. J. (1967). A sequential hypothesis of instrumental learning. In K. W. Spence & J. T. Spence (Eds.), *The psychology of learning and motivation* (Vol. 1, pp. 67–156). Orlando, FL: Academic Press.

Capaldi, E. J. (1971). Memory and learning: A sequential viewpoint. In W. K. Honig & P. H. R. James (Eds.), *Animal Memory* (pp. 115–154). Orlando, FL: Academic Press.

Carroll, M. E., Anker, J. J., Mach, J. L., Newman, J. L., & Perry, J. L. (2010). Delay discounting as a predictor of drug abuse. In G. J. Madden & W. K. Bickel (Eds.), *Impulsivity: The behavioral and neurological science of discounting* (pp. 243–271). Washington, DC: American Psychological Association. http://dx.doi.org/10.1037/12069-009

Chance, P. (1999). Thorndike's puzzle boxes and the origins of the experimental analysis of behavior. *Journal of the Experimental Analysis of Behavior, 72,* 433–440. http://dx.doi.org/10.1901/jeab.1999.72-433

Charlop, M. H., Kurtz, P. F., & Casey, F. G. (1990). Using aberrant behaviors as reinforcers for autistic children. *Journal of Applied Behavior Analysis, 23,* 163–181. http://dx.doi.org/10.1901/jaba.1990.23-163

Church, R. M. (1964). Systematic effect of the random error in the yoked control design. *Psychological Bulletin, 62,* 122–131. http://dx.doi.org/10.1037/h0042733

Church, R. M. (1969). Response suppression. In B. A. Campbell & R. M. Church (Eds.), *Punishment and aversive behavior* (pp. 111–156). New York, NY: Appleton-Century-Crofts.

Church, R. M. (2012). Behavioristic, cognitive, biological, and quantitative explanations of timing. In T. R. Zentall & E. A. Wasserman (Eds.), *The Oxford handbook of comparative cognition* (pp. 409–433). New York, NY: Oxford University Press. http://dx.doi.org/10.1093/oxfordhb/9780195392661.013.0022

Church, R. M., & Raymond, G. A. (1967). Influence of the schedule of positive reinforcement on punished behavior. *Journal of Comparative and Physiological Psychology, 63,* 329–332. http://dx.doi.org/10.1037/h0024382

Cole, M. R. (1999). Molar and molecular control in variable-interval and variable-ratio schedules. *Journal of the Experimental Analysis of Behavior, 71,* 319–328.

Cole, R. P., Barnet, R. C., & Miller, R. R. (1997). An evaluation of conditioned inhibition as defined by Rescorla's two-test strategy. *Learning and Motivation, 28,* 323–341. http://dx.doi.org/10.1006/lmot.1997.0971

Colombo, J., & Mitchell, D. W. (2009). Infant visual habituation. *Neurobiology of Learning and Memory, 92,* 225–234. http://dx.doi.org/10.1016/j.nlm.2008.06.002

Colwill, R. M., & Rescorla, R. A. (1990). Evidence for the hierarchical structure of instrumental learning. *Animal Learning & Behavior, 18,* 71–82. http://dx.doi.org/10.3758/BF03205241

Cook, R. G., Brown, M. F., & Riley, D. A. (1985). Flexible memory processing by rats: Use of prospective and retrospective information in the radial maze. *Journal of Experimental Psychology: Animal Behavior Processes, 11,* 453–469. http://dx.doi.org/10.1037/0097-7403.11.3.453

Craske, M. G., Hermans, D., & Vansteenwegen, D. (Eds.). (2006). *Fear and learning: From basic procedures to clinical implications.* Washington, DC: American Psychological Association. http://dx.doi.org/10.1037/11474-000

Crossman, E. K., Bonem, E. J., & Phelps, B. J. (1987). A comparison of response patterns on fixed-, variable-, and random-ratio schedules. *Journal of the Experimental Analysis of Behavior, 48,* 395–406. http://dx.doi.org/10.1901/jeab.1987.48-395

Crystal, J. D. (2012a). Prospective cognition in rats. *Learning and Motivation, 43,* 181–191. http://dx.doi.org/10.1016/j.lmot.2012.05.006

Crystal, J. D. (2012b). Sensitivity to time: Implications for the representation of time. In T. R. Zentall & E. A. Wasserman (Eds.), *The Oxford handbook of comparative cognition* (pp. 434–450). New York, NY: Oxford University Press.

Dallery, J., & Soto, P. L. (2013). Quantitative description of environment-behavior relations. In G. J. Madden (Ed.), *APA handbook of behavior analysis: Vol. 1. Methods and principles* (pp. 219–250). Washington, DC: American Psychological Association. http://dx.doi.org/10.1037/13937-010

D'Amato, M. R., Fazzaro, J., & Etkin, M. (1968). Anticipatory responding and avoidance discrimination as factors in avoidance conditioning. *Journal of Experimental Psychology, 77,* 41–47. http://dx.doi.org/10.1037/h0025763

Danaher, B. G. (1974). Theoretical foundations and clinical applications of the Premack principle: Review and critique. *Behavior Therapy, 5,* 307–324. http://dx.doi.org/10.1016/S0005-7894(74)80001-8

Dardano, J. F., & Sauerbrunn, D. (1964). An aversive stimulus as a correlated block counter in FR performance. *Journal of the Experimental Analysis of Behavior, 7,* 37–43. http://dx.doi.org/10.1901/jeab.1964.7-37

Darwin, C. (1897). *The descent of man and selection in relation to sex.* New York, NY: Appleton-Century-Crofts.

Davis, M. (1970). Effects of interstimulus interval length and variability on startle-response habituation in the rat. *Journal of Comparative and Physiological Psychology, 72,* 177–192. http://dx.doi.org/10.1037/h0029472

Davis, M. (1974). Sensitization of the rat startle response by noise. *Journal of Comparative and Physiological Psychology, 87,* 571–581. http://dx.doi.org/10.1037/h0036985

Davis, M., Antoniadis, E. A., Amaral, D. G., & Winslow, J. T. (2008). Acoustic startle reflex in rhesus monkeys: A review. *Reviews in the Neurosciences, 19,* 171–185. http://dx.doi.org/10.1515/REVNEURO.2008.19.2-3.171

Dean, S. J., & Pittman, C. M. (1991). Self-punitive behavior: A revised analysis. In M. R. Denny (Ed.), *Fear, avoidance, and phobias* (pp. 259–284). Hillsdale, NJ: Erlbaum.

Deich, J. D., Allan, R. W., & Zeigler, H. P. (1988). Conjunctive differentiation of gape during food reinforced key pecking in the pigeon. *Animal Learning & Behavior, 16,* 268–276. http://dx.doi.org/10.3758/BF03209076

Delamater, A. R. (2012). Issues in the extinction of specific stimulus-outcome associations in Pavlovian conditioning. *Behavioural Processes, 90,* 9–19. http://dx.doi.org/10.1016/j.beproc.2012.03.006

Delamater, A. R., Campese, V., LoLordo, V. M., & Sclafani, A. (2006). Unconditioned stimulus devaluation effects in nutrient-conditioned flavor preferences. *Journal of Experimental Psychology: Animal Behavior Processes, 32,* 295–306. http://dx.doi.org/10.1037/0097-7403.32.3.295

Delamater, A. R., & Lattal, K. M. (2014). The study of associative learning: Mapping from psychological to neural levels of analysis. *Neurobiology of Learning and Memory, 108,* 1–4. http://dx.doi.org/10.1016/j.nlm.2013.12.006

Delamater, A. R., & Westbrook, R. F. (2014). Psychological and neural mechanisms of experimental extinction: A selective review. *Neurobiology of Learning and Memory, 108,* 38–51. http://dx.doi.org/10.1016/j.nlm.2013.09.016

Delaunay-El Allam, M., Soussignan, R., Patris, B., Marlier, L., & Schaal, B. (2010). Long-lasting memory for an odor acquired at the mother's breast. *Developmental Science, 13,* 849–863. http://dx.doi.org/10.1111/j.1467-7687.2009.00941.x

DeVito, P. L., & Fowler, H. (1987). Enhancement of conditioned inhibition via an extinction treatment. *Animal Learning & Behavior, 15,* 448–454. http://dx.doi.org/10.3758/BF03205055

Dickinson, A., Nicholas, D. J., & Mackintosh, N. J. (1983). A re-examination of one-trial blocking in conditioned suppression. *The Quarterly Journal of Experimental Psychology, 35,* 67–79. http://dx.doi.org/10.1080/14640748308400914

Dinsmoor, J. A. (1952). A discrimination based on punishment. *The Quarterly Journal of Experimental Psychology, 4,* 27–45. http://dx.doi.org/10.1080/17470215208416601

Dinsmoor, J. A. (2001). Stimuli inevitably generated by behavior that avoids electric shock are inherently reinforcing. *Journal of the Experimental Analysis of Behavior, 75,* 311–333. http://dx.doi.org/10.1901/jeab.2001.75-311

Domjan, M. (1976). Determinants of the enhancement of flavored-water intake by prior exposure. *Journal of Experimental Psychology: Animal Behavior Processes, 2,* 17–27. http://dx.doi.org/10.1037/0097-7403.2.1.17

Domjan, M. (1977). Attenuation and enhancement of neophobia for edible substances. In L. M. Barker, M. R. Best, & M. Domjan (Eds.), *Learning mechanisms in food selection* (pp. 151–179). Waco, TX: Baylor University Press.

Domjan, M. (2005). Pavlovian conditioning: A functional perspective. *Annual Review of Psychology, 56,* 179–206. http://dx.doi.org/10.1146/annurev.psych.55.090902.141409

Domjan, M. (2015). The Garcia–Koelling selective association effect: A historical and personal perspective. *International Journal of Comparative Psychology, 28.* Retrieved from http://escholarship.org/uc/item/5sx993rm

Domjan, M. (2016). Elicited versus emitted behavior: Time to abandon the distinction. *Journal of the Experimental Analysis of Behavior, 105,* 231–245. http://dx.doi.org/10.1002/jeab.197

Domjan, M., & Akins, C. K. (2011). Applications of Pavlovian conditioning to sexual behavior and reproduction. In T. R. Schachtman & S. Reilly (Eds.), *Associative learning and conditioning theory: Human and nonhuman applications* (pp. 507–531). New York, NY: Oxford University Press. http://dx.doi.org/10.1093/acprof:oso/9780199735969.003.0159

Domjan, M., & Gillan, D. (1976). Role of novelty in the aversion for increasingly concentrated saccharin solutions. *Physiology & Behavior, 16,* 537–542. http://dx.doi.org/10.1016/0031-9384(76)90211-0

Domjan, M., & Krause, M. (in press). Generality of the laws of learning: From biological constraints to ecological perspectives. In J. H. Byrne (Ed.), *Learning and behavior theory: Vol. 1. Learning and memory: A comprehensive reference* (2nd ed.). Oxford, England: Elsevier.

Domjan, M., Mahometa, M. J., & Matthews, R. N. (2012). Learning in intimate connections: Conditioned fertility and its role in sexual competition. *Socioaffective Neuroscience & Psychology, 2,* 17333. http://dx.doi.org/10.3402/snp.v2i0.17333

Domjan, M., & Nash, S. (1988). Stimulus control of social behaviour in male Japanese quail, *Coturnixcoturnixjaponica. Animal Behaviour, 36,* 1006–1015. http://dx.doi.org/10.1016/S0003-3472(88)80060-5

Duhigg, C. (2012). *The power of habit.* New York, NY: Random House.

Dunsmoor, J. E., Niv, Y., Daw, N., & Phelps, E. A. (2015). Rethinking extinction. *Neuron, 88,* 47–63. http://dx.doi.org/10.1016/j.neuron.2015.09.028

Edhouse, W. V., & White, K. G. (1988). Sources of proactive interference in animal memory. *Journal of Experimental Psychology: Animal Behavior Processes, 14,* 56–70. http://dx.doi.org/10.1037/0097-7403.14.1.56

Eisenberger, R., Karpman, M., & Trattner, J. (1967). What is the necessary and sufficient condition for reinforcement in the contingency situation? *Journal of Experimental Psychology, 74,* 342–350. http://dx.doi.org/10.1037/h0024719

Epstein, L. H., Temple, J. L., Roemmich, J. N., & Bouton, M. E. (2009). Habituation as a determinant of human food intake. *Psychological Review, 116,* 384–407. http://dx.doi.org/10.1037/a0015074

Esmorís-Arranz, F. J., Pardo-Vázquez, J. L., & Vázquez-García, G. A. (2003). Differential effects of forward or simultaneous conditioned stimulus-unconditioned stimulus intervals on the defensive behavior system of the Norway rat (*Rattus norvegicus*). *Journal of Experimental Psychology: Animal Behavior Processes, 29,* 334–340. http://dx.doi.org/10.1037/0097-7403.29.4.334

Fanselow, M. S. (1994). Neural organization of the defensive behavior system responsible for fear. *Psychonomic Bulletin & Review, 1,* 429–438. http://dx.doi.org/10.3758/BF03210947

Fanselow, M. S., Lester, L. S., & Helmstetter, F. J. (1988). Changes in feeding and foraging patterns as an antipredator defensive strategy: A laboratory simulation using aversive stimulation in a closed economy. *Journal of the Experimental Analysis of Behavior, 50,* 361–374. http://dx.doi.org/10.1901/jeab.1988.50-361

Ferster, C. B., & Skinner, B. F. (1957). *Schedules of reinforcement.* New York, NY: Appleton-Century-Crofts. http://dx.doi.org/10.1037/10627-000

Flagel, S. B., Akil, H., & Robinson, T. E. (2009). Individual differences in the attribution of incentive salience to reward-related cues: Implications for addiction. *Neuropharmacology, 56*(Suppl. 1), 139–148. http://dx.doi.org/10.1016/j.neuropharm.2008.06.027

Flagel, S. B., Clark, J. J., Robinson, T. E., Mayo, L., Czuj, A., Willuhn, I., . . . Akil, H. (2011). A selective role for dopamine in stimulus–reward learning. *Nature, 469,* 53–57. http://dx.doi.org/10.1038/nature09588

Foree, D. D., & LoLordo, V. M. (1973). Attention in the pigeon: Differential effects of food-getting versus shock-avoidance procedures. *Journal of Comparative and Physiological Psychology, 85,* 551–558. http://dx.doi.org/10.1037/h0035300

Forestell, P. H., & Herman, L. M. (1988). Delayed matching of visual materials by a bottlenosed dolphin aided by auditory symbols. *Animal Learning & Behavior, 16,* 137–146. http://dx.doi.org/10.3758/BF03209056

Friedman, B. X., Blaisdell, A. P., Escobar, M., & Miller, R. R. (1998). Comparator mechanisms and conditioned inhibition: Conditioned stimulus preexposure disrupts Pavlovian conditioned inhibition but not explicitly unpaired inhibition. *Journal of Experimental Psychology: Animal Behavior Processes, 24*, 453–466. http://dx.doi.org/10.1037/0097-7403.24.4.453

Fudim, O. K. (1978). Sensory preconditioning of flavors with a formalin-produced sodium need. *Journal of Experimental Psychology: Animal Behavior Processes, 4*, 276–285. http://dx.doi.org/10.1037/0097-7403.4.3.276

Galbicka, G. (1988). Differentiating the behavior of organisms. *Journal of the Experimental Analysis of Behavior, 50*, 343–354. http://dx.doi.org/10.1901/jeab.1988.50-343

Gallistel, C. R., & Gibbon, J. (2000). Time, rate, and conditioning. *Psychological Review, 107*, 289–344. http://dx.doi.org/10.1037/0033-295X.107.2.289

Garcia, J., Ervin, F. R., & Koelling, R. A. (1966). Learning with prolonged delay of reinforcement. *Psychonomic Science, 5*, 121–122. http://dx.doi.org/10.3758/BF03328311

Garcia, J., & Koelling, R. A. (1966). Relation of cue to consequence in avoidance learning. *Psychonomic Science, 4*, 123–124. http://dx.doi.org/10.3758/BF03342209

Gershoff, E. T. (2013). Spanking and child development: We know enough now to stop hitting our children. *Child Development Perspectives, 7*, 133–137. http://dx.doi.org/10.1111/cdep.12038

Gershoff, E. T. (2016). Should parents' physical punishment of children be considered a source of toxic stress that affects brain development? *Family Relations, 65*, 151–162. http://dx.doi.org/10.1111/fare.12177

Gillihan, S. J., & Foa, E. B. (2011). Fear extinction and emotional processing theory: A critical review. In T. R. Schachtman & S. Reilly (Eds.), *Associative learning and conditioning theory: Human and non-human applications* (pp. 27–43). New York, NY: Oxford University Press. http://dx.doi.org/10.1093/acprof:oso/9780199735969.003.0017

Goodall, G. (1984). Learning due to the response-shock contingency in signalled punishment. *Quarterly Journal of Experimental Psychology B: Comparative and Physiological Psychology, 36*, 259–279. http://dx.doi.org/10.1080/14640748408402206

Gormezano, I., Kehoe, E. J., & Marshall, B. S. (1983). Twenty years of classical conditioning research with the rabbit. In J. M. Sprague & A. N. Epstein (Eds.), *Progress in psychobiology and physiological psychology* (Vol. 10, pp. 197–275). Orlando, FL: Academic Press.

Grace, R. C., & Hucks, A. D. (2013). The allocation of operant behavior. In G. J. Madden (Ed.), *APA handbook of behavior analysis: Vol. 1. Methods and principles* (pp. 307–338). Washington, DC: American Psychological Association. http://dx.doi.org/10.1037/13937-014

Grant, D. S. (1976). Effect of sample presentation time on long-delay matching in the pigeon. *Learning and Motivation, 7*, 580–590. http://dx.doi.org/10.1016/0023-9690(76)90008-4

Grant, D. S. (1988). Sources of visual interference in delayed matching-to-sample with pigeons. *Journal of Experimental Psychology: Animal Behavior Processes, 14*, 368–375. http://dx.doi.org/10.1037/0097-7403.14.4.368

Green, L., & Freed, D. E. (1993). The substitutability of reinforcers. *Journal of the Experimental Analysis of Behavior, 60*, 141–158. http://dx.doi.org/10.1901/jeab.1993.60-141

Groves, P. M., Lee, D., & Thompson, R. F. (1969). Effects of stimulus frequency and intensity on habituation and sensitization in acute spinal cat. *Physiology & Behavior*, *4*, 383–388. http://dx.doi.org/10.1016/0031-9384(69)90194-2

Groves, P. M., & Thompson, R. F. (1970). Habituation: A dual-process theory. *Psychological Review*, *77*, 419–450. http://dx.doi.org/10.1037/h0029810

Hagopian, L. P., Dozier, C. L., Rooker, G. W., & Jones, B. A. (2013). Assessment and treatment of severe problem behavior. In G. J. Madden (Ed.), *APA handbook of behavior analysis: Vol. 2. Translating principles into practice* (pp. 353–386). Washington, DC: American Psychological Association. http://dx.doi.org/10.1037/13938-014

Halberstadt, A. L., & Geyer, M. A. (2009). Habituation and sensitization of acoustic startle: Opposite influences of dopamine D1 and D2–family receptors. *Neurobiology of Learning and Memory*, *92*, 243–248. http://dx.doi.org/10.1016/j.nlm.2008.05.015

Hall, G., Kaye, H., & Pearce, J. M. (1985). Attention and conditioned inhibition. In R. R. Miller & N. E. Spear (Eds.), *Information processing in animals: Conditioned inhibition* (pp. 185–207). Hillsdale, NJ: Erlbaum.

Hallam, S. C., Grahame, N. J., Harris, K., & Miller, R. R. (1992). Associative structure underlying enhanced negative summation following operational extinction of a Pavlovian inhibitor. *Learning and Motivation*, *23*, 43–62. http://dx.doi.org/10.1016/0023-9690(92)90022-E

Hanley, G. P., Iwata, B. A., Thompson, R. H., & Lindberg, J. S. (2000). A component analysis of "stereotypy as reinforcement" for alternative behavior. *Journal of Applied Behavior Analysis*, *33*, 285–297. http://dx.doi.org/10.1901/jaba.2000.33-285

Hardt, O., Einarsson, E. Ö., & Nader, K. (2010). A bridge over troubled water: Reconsolidation as a link between cognitive and neuroscientific memory research traditions. *Annual Review of Psychology*, *61*, 141–167. http://dx.doi.org/10.1146/annurev.psych.093008.100455

Harris, J. A., Kwok, D. W. S., & Andrew, B. J. (2014). Conditioned inhibition and reinforcement rate. *Journal of Experimental Psychology: Animal Learning and Cognition*, *40*, 335–354. http://dx.doi.org/10.1037/xan0000023

Hearst, E., & Jenkins, H. M. (1974). *Sign tracking: The stimulus–reinforcer relation and directed action*. Austin, TX: Psychonomic Society.

Hernandez, P. J., & Abel, T. (2008). The role of protein synthesis in memory consolidation: Progress amid decades of debate. *Neurobiology of Learning & Memory*, *89*, 293–311. http://dx.doi.org/10.1016/j.nlm.2007.09.010

Herrnstein, R. J. (1970). On the law of effect. *Journal of the Experimental Analysis of Behavior*, *13*, 243–266. http://dx.doi.org/10.1901/jeab.1970.13-243

Herrnstein, R. J., Loveland, D. H., & Cable, C. (1976). Natural concepts in pigeons. *Journal of Experimental Psychology: Animal Behavior Processes*, *2*, 285–302. http://dx.doi.org/10.1037/0097-7403.2.4.285

Hock, A., White, H., Jubran, R., & Bhatt, R. S. (2016). The whole picture: Holistic body posture recognition in infancy. *Psychonomic Bulletin & Review*, *23*, 426–431. http://dx.doi.org/10.3758/s13423-015-0902-8

Hogarth, L., Balleine, B. W., Corbit, L. H., & Killcross, S. (2013). Associative learning mechanisms underpinning the transition from recreational drug use to addiction. *Annals of the New York Academy of Sciences*, *1282*, 12–24.

Hogarth, L., & Chase, H. W. (2011). Parallel goal-directed and habitual control of human drug-seeking: Implications for dependence vulnerability. *Journal of Experimental Psychology: Animal Behavior Processes, 37*, 261–276. http://dx.doi.org/10.1037/a0022913

Hogarth, L., Dickinson, A., & Duka, T. (2010). Selective attention to conditioned stimuli in human discrimination learning: Untangling the effects of outcome prediction, valence, arousal, and uncertainty. In C. J. Mitchell & M. E. Le Pelley (Eds.), *Attention and associative learning* (pp. 71–97). Oxford, England: Oxford University Press.

Holland, P. C. (1977). Conditioned stimulus as a determinant of the form of the Pavlovian conditioned response. *Journal of Experimental Psychology: Animal Behavior Processes, 3*, 77–104. http://dx.doi.org/10.1037/0097-7403.3.1.77

Holland, P. C. (1989). Feature extinction enhances transfer of occasion setting. *Animal Learning & Behavior, 17*, 269–279. http://dx.doi.org/10.3758/BF03209799

Holland, P. C. (1992). Occasion setting in Pavlovian conditioning. In D. L. Medin (Ed.), *Psychology of learning and motivation* (Vol. 28, pp. 69–125). San Diego, CA: Academic Press.

Holland, P. C. (2000). Trial and intertrial durations in appetitive conditioning in rats. *Animal Learning & Behavior, 28*, 121–135. http://dx.doi.org/10.3758/BF03200248

Hollis, K. L. (1999). The role of learning in the aggressive and reproductive behavior of blue gouramis, *Trichogaster trichopterus. Environmental Biology of Fishes, 54*, 355–369. http://dx.doi.org/10.1023/A:1007529628117

Holloway, K. S., & Domjan, M. (1993). Sexual approach conditioning: Tests of unconditioned stimulus devaluation using hormone manipulations. *Journal of Experimental Psychology: Animal Behavior Processes, 19*, 47–55. http://dx.doi.org/10.1037/0097-7403.19.1.47

Holmes, N. M., Marchand, A. R., & Coutureau, E. (2010). Pavlovian to instrumental transfer: A neurobehavioural perspective. *Neuroscience and Biobehavioral Reviews, 34*, 1277–1295. http://dx.doi.org/10.1016/j.neubiorev.2010.03.007

Holz, W. C., & Azrin, N. H. (1961). Discriminative properties of punishment. *Journal of the Experimental Analysis of Behavior, 4*, 225–232. http://dx.doi.org/10.1901/jeab.1961.4-225

Horsley, R. R., Osborne, M., Norman, C., & Wells, T. (2012). High-frequency gamblers show increased resistance to extinction following partial reinforcement. *Behavioural Brain Research, 229*, 438–442. http://dx.doi.org/10.1016/j.bbr.2012.01.024

Huber, L., & Aust, U. (2012). A modified feature theory as an account of pigeon visual categorization. In T. R. Zentall & E. A. Wasserman (Eds.), *The Oxford handbook of comparative cognition* (pp. 497–512). New York, NY: Oxford University Press. http://dx.doi.org/10.1093/oxfordhb/9780195392661.013.0026

Hull, C. L. (1930). Knowledge and purpose as habit mechanisms. *Psychological Review, 37*, 511–525. http://dx.doi.org/10.1037/h0072212

Hull, C. L. (1931). Goal attraction and directing ideas conceived as habit phenomena. *Psychological Review, 38*, 487–506. http://dx.doi.org/10.1037/h0071442

Hulse, S. H., Jr. (1958). Amount and percentage of reinforcement and duration of goal confinement in conditioning and extinction. *Journal of Experimental Psychology, 56*, 48–57. http://dx.doi.org/10.1037/h0046279

Hursh, S. R., Madden, G. J., Spiga, R., DeLeon, I., & Francisco, M. T. (2013). The translational utility of behavioral economics: The experimental analysis of consumption and choice. In G. J. Madden (Ed.), *APA handbook of behavior analysis: Vol. 2. Translating principles into practice* (pp. 191–224). Washington, DC: American Psychological Association.

Ishida, M., & Papini, M. R. (1997). Massed-trial overtraining effects on extinction and reversal performance in turtles *(Geoclemys reevesii). The Quarterly Journal of Experimental Psychology B: Comparative and Physiological Psychology, 50*, 1–16. http://dx.doi.org/10.1080/027249997393619

Jacobs, E. A., Borrero, J. C., & Vollmer, T. R. (2013). Translational applications of quantitative choice models. In G. J. Madden (Ed.), *APA handbook of behavior analysis: Vol. 2. Translating principles into practice* (pp. 165–190). Washington, DC: American Psychological Association. http://dx.doi.org/10.1037/13938-007

Jacobs, N. S., Cushman, J. D., & Fanselow, M. S. (2010). The accurate measurement of fear memory in Pavlovian conditioning: Resolving the baseline issue. *Journal of Neuroscience Methods, 190*, 235–239. http://dx.doi.org/10.1016/j.jneumeth.2010.04.029

Jenkins, H. M. (1962). Resistance to extinction when partial reinforcement is followed by regular reinforcement. *Journal of Experimental Psychology, 64*, 441–450. http://dx.doi.org/10.1037/h0048700

Jenkins, H. M., Barnes, R. A., & Barrera, F. J. (1981). Why autoshaping depends on trial spacing. In C. M. Locurto, H. S. Terrace, & J. Gibbon (Eds.), *Autoshaping and conditioning theory* (pp. 255–284). New York, NY: Academic Press.

Jenkins, H. M., & Harrison, R. H. (1960). Effect of discrimination training on auditory generalization. *Journal of Experimental Psychology, 59*, 246–253. http://dx.doi.org/10.1037/h0041661

Jenkins, H. M., & Harrison, R. H. (1962). Generalization gradients of inhibition following auditory discrimination learning. *Journal of the Experimental Analysis of Behavior, 5*, 435–441. http://dx.doi.org/10.1901/jeab.1962.5-435

Jessel, J., Borrero, J. C., & Becraft, J. L. (2015). Differential reinforcement of other behavior increases untargeted behavior. *Journal of Applied Behavior Analysis, 48*, 402–416. http://dx.doi.org/10.1002/jaba.204

Jitsumori, M., Wright, A. A., & Shyan, M. R. (1989). Buildup and release from proactive interference in a rhesus monkey. *Journal of Experimental Psychology: Animal Behavior Processes, 15*, 329–337. http://dx.doi.org/10.1037/0097-7403.15.4.329

Johnson, H. M. (1994). Processes of successful intentional forgetting. *Psychological Bulletin, 116*, 274–292. http://dx.doi.org/10.1037/0033-2909.116.2.274

Jozefowiez, J., & Staddon, J. E. R. (2008). Operant behavior. In J. H. Byrne (Ed.), *Learning theory and behavior: Vol. 1. Learning and memory: A comprehensive reference* (pp. 75–102). Oxford, England: Elsevier. http://dx.doi.org/10.1016/B978-012370509-9.00087-5

Kalmbach, B. E., Ohyama, T., Kreider, J. C., Riusech, F., & Mauk, M. D. (2009). Interactions between prefrontal cortex and cerebellum revealed by trace eyelid conditioning. *Learning & Memory, 16*, 86–95. http://dx.doi.org/10.1101/lm.1178309

Kamin, L. J. (1965). Temporal and intensity characteristics of the conditioned stimulus. In W. F. Prokasy (Ed.), *Classical conditioning* (pp. 118–147). New York, NY: Appleton-Century-Crofts.

Kamin, L. J. (1969). Predictability, surprise, attention, and conditioning. In B. A. Campbell & R. M. Church (Eds.), *Punishment and aversive behavior* (pp. 279–296). New York, NY: Appleton-Century-Crofts.

Kaplan, P. S., Werner, J. S., & Rudy, J. W. (1990). Habituation, sensitization, and infant visual attention. In C. Rovee-Collier & L. P. Lipsitt (Eds.), *Advances in infancy research* (Vol. 6, pp. 61–109). Norwood, NJ: Ablex.

Kavšek, M. (2013). The comparator model of infant visual habituation and dishabituation: Recent insights. *Developmental Psychobiology, 55*, 793–808. http://dx.doi.org/10.1002/dev.21081

Kazdin, A. E. (1985). The token economy. In R. M. Turner & L. M. Ascher (Eds.), *Evaluating behavior therapy outcome* (pp. 225–253). New York, NY: Springer.

Kehoe, E. J., & White, N. E. (2004). Overexpectation: Response loss during sustained stimulus compounding in the rabbit nictitating membrane preparation. *Learning & Memory, 11*, 476–483. http://dx.doi.org/10.1101/lm.77604

Killeen, P. R. (2001). Writing and overwriting short-term memory. *Psychonomic Bulletin & Review, 8*, 18–43. http://dx.doi.org/10.3758/BF03196137

Kimble, G. A. (1961). *Hilgard and Marquis' conditioning and learning* (2nd ed.). New York, NY: Appleton-Century-Crofts.

Kirkpatrick, K., & Church, R. M. (2004). Temporal learning in random control procedures. *Journal of Experimental Psychology: Animal Behavior Processes, 30*, 213–228. http://dx.doi.org/10.1037/0097-7403.30.3.213

Klatt, K. P., & Morris, E. K. (2001). The Premack principle, response deprivation, and establishing operations. *The Behavior Analyst, 24*, 173–180.

Krause, M. A., & Domjan, M. (2017). Ethological and evolutionary perspectives on Pavlovian conditioning. In J. Call (Ed.), *APA handbook of comparative psychology: Vol. 2. Perception, learning, and cognition* (pp. 247–266). Washington, DC: American Psychological Association.

Kroes, M. C. W., Schiller, D., LeDoux, J. E., & Phelps, E. A. (2016). Translational approaches targeting reconsolidation. *Current Topics in Behavioral Neurosciences, 28*, 197–230. http://dx.doi.org/10.1007/7854_2015_5008

Krypotos, A.-M., Effting, M., Kindt, M., & Beckers, T. (2015). Avoidance learning: Review of theoretical models and recent developments. *Frontiers in Behavioral Neuroscience, 9. Article, 189*, 1–16.

Laborda, M. A., & Miller, R. R. (2012). Reactivated memories compete for expression after Pavlovian extinction. *Behavioural Processes, 90*, 20–27. http://dx.doi.org/10.1016/j.beproc.2012.01.012

Lashley, K. S., & Wade, M. (1946). The Pavlovian theory of generalization. *Psychological Review, 53*, 72–87. http://dx.doi.org/10.1037/h0059999

Lattal, K. A. (2013). The five pillars of the experimental analysis of behavior. In G. J. Madden (Ed.), *APA handbook of behavior analysis: Vol. 1. Methods and principles* (pp. 33–63). Washington, DC: American Psychological Association. http://dx.doi.org/10.1037/13937-002

Lattal, K. A., St. Peter, C., & Escobar, R. (2013). Operant extinction: Elimination and generation of behavior. In G. J. Madden (Ed.), *APA handbook of behavior analysis: Vol. 2. Translating principles into practice* (pp. 77–107). Washington, DC: American Psychological Association.

Lattal, K. M., & Nakajima, S. (1998). Over expectation in appetitive Pavlovian and instrumental conditioning. *Animal Learning & Behavior, 26,* 351–360. http://dx.doi.org/10.3758/BF03199227

LeDoux, J. E., & Gorman, J. M. (2001). A call to action: Overcoming anxiety through active coping. *The American Journal of Psychiatry, 158,* 1953–1955. http://dx.doi.org/10.1176/appi.ajp.158.12.1953

Leising, K. J., Hall, J. S., Wolf, J. E., & Ruprecht, C. M. (2015). Occasion setting during a spatial-search task with pigeons. *Journal of Experimental Psychology: Animal Learning and Cognition, 41,* 163–178. http://dx.doi.org/10.1037/xan0000048

Leung, H. T., Bailey, G. K., Laurent, V., & Westbrook, R. F. (2007). Rapid reacquisition of fear to a completely extinguished context is replaced by transient impairment with additional extinction training. *Journal of Experimental Psychology: Animal Behavior Processes, 33,* 299–313. http://dx.doi.org/10.1037/0097-7403.33.3.299

Lieberman, D. A., McIntosh, D. C., & Thomas, G. V. (1979). Learning when reward is delayed: A marking hypothesis. *Journal of Experimental Psychology: Animal Behavior Processes, 5,* 224–242. http://dx.doi.org/10.1037/0097-7403.5.3.224

Lin, J.-Y., Arthurs, J., & Reilly, S. (2017). Conditioned taste aversions: From poisons to pain to drugs of abuse. *Psychonomic Bulletin & Review, 24,* 335–351.

LoBue, V., & DeLoache, J. S. (2010). Superior detection of threat-relevant stimuli in infancy. *Developmental Science, 13,* 221–228. http://dx.doi.org/10.1111/j.1467-7687.2009.00872.x

Logue, A. W., Ophir, I., & Strauss, K. E. (1981). The acquisition of taste aversions in humans. *Behaviour Research and Therapy, 19,* 319–333. http://dx.doi.org/10.1016/0005-7967(81)90053-X

LoLordo, V. M. (1979). Selective associations. In A. Dickinson & R. A. Boakes (Eds.), *Mechanisms of learning and motivation* (pp. 367–398). Hillsdale, NJ: Erlbaum.

Lorenz, K. Z. (1981). *The foundations of ethology.* New York, NY: Springer. http://dx.doi.org/10.1007/978-3-7091-3671-3

Lovibond, P. F., Saunders, J. C., Weidemann, G., & Mitchell, C. J. (2008). Evidence for expectancy as a mediator of avoidance and anxiety in a laboratory model of human avoidance learning. *The Quarterly Journal of Experimental Psychology, 61,* 1199–1216. http://dx.doi.org/10.1080/17470210701503229

Lubow, R. E. (2011). Aberrant attentional processes in schizophrenia as reflected in latent inhibition data. In T. R. Schachtman & S. Reilly (Eds.), *Associative learning and conditioning theory: Human and non-human applications* (pp. 152–167). New York, NY: Oxford University Press. http://dx.doi.org/10.1093/acprof:oso/9780199735969.003.0048

Lubow, R. E., & Weiner, I. (Eds.). (2010). *Latent inhibition: Cognition, Neuroscience and applications to schizophrenia.* Cambridge, England: Cambridge University Press. http://dx.doi.org/10.1017/CBO9780511730184

Lysle, D. T., & Fowler, H. (1985). Inhibition as a "slave" process: Deactivation of conditioned inhibition through extinction of conditioned excitation. *Journal of*

Experimental Psychology: Animal Behavior Processes, 11, 71–94. http://dx.doi.org/10.1037/0097-7403.11.1.71

MacKillop, J., Amlung, M. T., Few, L. R., Ray, L. A., Sweet, L. H., & Munafò, M. R. (2011). Delayed reward discounting and addictive behavior: A meta-analysis. *Psychopharmacology, 216*, 305–321. http://dx.doi.org/10.1007/s00213-011-2229-0

Mackintosh, N. J. (1974). *The psychology of animal learning.* Oxford, England: Academic Press.

Mackintosh, N. J., Bygrave, D. J., & Picton, B. M. B. (1977). Locus of the effect of a surprising reinforcer in the attenuation of blocking. *The Quarterly Journal of Experimental Psychology, 29*, 327–336. http://dx.doi.org/10.1080/14640747708400608

MacLeod, C. M. (2012). Directed forgetting. In N. M. Seel (Ed.), *Encyclopedia of the sciences of learning* (pp. 993–995). New York, NY: Springer.

Maia, T. V. (2010). Two-factor theory, the actor-critic model, and conditioned avoidance. *Learning & Behavior, 38*, 50–67. http://dx.doi.org/10.3758/LB.38.1.50

Maren, S. (2011). Seeking a spotless mind: Extinction, deconsolidation, and erasure of fear memory. *Neuron, 70*, 830–845. http://dx.doi.org/10.1016/j.neuron.2011.04.023

Maren, S., & Holmes, A. (2016). Stress and fear extinction. *Neuropsychopharmacology, 41*, 58–79. http://dx.doi.org/10.1038/npp.2015.180

Matson, J. L., & Boisjoli, J. A. (2009). The token economy for children with intellectual disability and/or autism: A review. *Research in Developmental Disabilities, 30*, 240–248. http://dx.doi.org/10.1016/j.ridd.2008.04.001

McConnell, B. L., Urushihara, K., & Miller, R. R. (2010). Contrasting predictions of extended comparator hypothesis and acquisition-focused models of learning concerning retrospective revaluation. *Journal of Experimental Psychology: Animal Behavior Processes, 36*, 137–147. http://dx.doi.org/10.1037/a0015774

McGaugh, J. L. (2000). Memory—a century of consolidation. *Science, 287*, 248–251. http://dx.doi.org/10.1126/science.287.5451.248

McGaugh, J. L., & Herz, M. J. (1972). *Memory consolidation.* San Francisco, CA: Albion.

McKenzie, S., & Eichenbaum, H. (2011). Consolidation and reconsolidation: Two lives of memories? *Neuron, 71*, 224–233. http://dx.doi.org/10.1016/j.neuron.2011.06.037

McLaren, I. P. L., & Mackintosh, N. J. (2000). An elemental model of associative learning: I. Latent inhibition and perceptual learning. *Animal Learning & Behavior, 28*, 211–246. http://dx.doi.org/10.3758/BF03200258

Meyer, P. J., Cogan, E. S., & Robinson, T. E. (2014). The form of a conditioned stimulus can influence the degree to which it acquires incentive motivational properties. *PLoS One, 9*(6), e98163. http://dx.doi.org/10.1371/journal.pone.0098163

Miguez, G., Witnauer, J. E., & Miller, R. R. (2012). The role of contextual associations in producing the partial reinforcement acquisition deficit. *Journal of Experimental Psychology: Animal Behavior Processes, 38*, 40–51. http://dx.doi.org/10.1037/a0024410

Miller, D. B. (1985). Methodological issues in the ecological study of learning. In T. D. Johnston & A. T. Pietrewicz (Eds.), *Issues in the ecological study of learning* (pp. 73–95). Hillsdale, NJ: Erlbaum.

Miller, N. E. (1951). Learnable drives and rewards. In S. S. Stevens (Ed.), *Handbook of experimental psychology* (pp. 435–472). New York, NY: Wiley.

Miller, N. E. (1960). Learning resistance to pain and fear: Effects of overlearning, exposure, and rewarded exposure in context. *Journal of Experimental Psychology, 60,* 137–145. http://dx.doi.org/10.1037/h0043321

Miller, R. R., Barnet, R. C., & Grahame, N. J. (1995). Assessment of the Rescorla–Wagner model. *Psychological Bulletin, 117,* 363–386. http://dx.doi.org/10.1037/0033-2909.117.3.363

Miller, R. R., & Matzel, L. D. (1988). The comparator hypothesis: A response rule for the expression of associations. In G. H. Bower (Ed.), *The psychology of learning and motivation* (pp. 51–92). Orlando, FL: Academic Press.

Milmine, M., Watanabe, A., & Colombo, M. (2008). Neural correlates of directed forgetting in the avian prefrontal cortex. *Behavioral Neuroscience, 122,* 199–209. http://dx.doi.org/10.1037/0735-7044.122.1.199

Mineka, S. (1979). The role of fear in theories of avoidance learning, flooding, and extinction. *Psychological Bulletin, 86,* 985–1010. http://dx.doi.org/10.1037/0033-2909.86.5.985

Mineka, S., & Öhman, A. (2002). Phobias and preparedness: The selective, automatic, and encapsulated nature of fear. *Biological Psychiatry, 52,* 927–937. http://dx.doi.org/10.1016/S0006-3223(02)01669-4

Mitchell, C. J., & Le Pelley, M. E. (Eds.). (2010). *Attention and associative learning.* Oxford, England: Oxford University Press.

Moffitt, T. E., Arseneault, L., Belsky, D., Dickson, N., Hancox, R. J., Harrington, H., . . . Caspi, A. (2011). A gradient of childhood self-control predicts health, wealth, and public safety. *Proceedings of the National Academy of Sciences of the United States of America, 108,* 2693–2698. http://dx.doi.org/10.1073/pnas.1010076108

Molet, M., & Miller, R. R. (2014). Timing: An attribute of associative learning. *Behavioural Processes, 101,* 4–14. http://dx.doi.org/10.1016/j.beproc.2013.05.015

Monfils, M. H., Cowansage, K. K., Klann, E., & LeDoux, J. E. (2009). Extinction-reconsolidation boundaries: Key to persistent attenuation of fear memories. *Science, 324,* 951–955. http://dx.doi.org/10.1126/science.1167975

Morris, R. G. M. (1974). Pavlovian conditioned inhibition of fear during shuttlebox avoidance behavior. *Learning and Motivation, 5,* 424–447. http://dx.doi.org/10.1016/0023-9690(74)90002-2

Morris, R. G. M. (1975). Preconditioning of reinforcing properties to an exteroceptive feedback stimulus. *Learning and Motivation, 6,* 289–298. http://dx.doi.org/10.1016/0023-9690(75)90029-6

Mowrer, O. H. (1947). On the dual nature of learning: A reinterpretation of "conditioning" and "problem-solving." *Harvard Educational Review, 17,* 102–150.

Mowrer, O. H., & Lamoreaux, R. R. (1942). Avoidance conditioning and signal duration: A study of secondary motivation and reward [Monograph]. *Psychological Monographs, 54*(247).

Murphy, J. G., Correia, C. J., & Barnett, N. P. (2007). Behavioral economic approaches to reduce college student drinking. *Addictive Behaviors, 32,* 2573–2585. http://dx.doi.org/10.1016/j.addbeh.2007.05.015

Mystkowski, J. L., Craske, M. G., Echiverri, A. M., & Labus, J. S. (2006). Mental reinstatement of context and return of fear in spider-fearful participants. *Behavior Therapy, 37,* 49–60. http://dx.doi.org/10.1016/j.beth.2005.04.001

Nader, K., & Hardt, O. (2009). A single standard for memory: The case for reconsolidation. *Nature Reviews Neuroscience, 10,* 224–234. http://dx.doi.org/10.1038/nrn2590

Neuringer, A. (2004). Reinforced variability in animals and people: Implications for adaptive action. *American Psychologist, 59,* 891–906. http://dx.doi.org/10.1037/0003-066X.59.9.891

Neuringer, A., Kornell, N., & Olufs, M. (2001). Stability and variability in extinction. *Journal of Experimental Psychology: Animal Behavior Processes, 27,* 79–94. http://dx.doi.org/10.1037/0097-7403.27.1.79

Newsweek Staff. (2001, February 12). How it all starts inside your brain. *Newsweek,* p. 40. Retrieved from http://www.newsweek.com/how-it-all-starts-inside-your-brain-155189

Odum, A. L., & Baumann, A. A. L. (2010). Delay discounting: State and trait variable. In G. J. Madden & W. K. Bickel (Eds.), *Impulsivity: The behavioral and neurological science of discounting* (pp. 39–65). Washington, DC: American Psychological Association. http://dx.doi.org/10.1037/12069-002

Oehlberg, K., & Mineka, S. (2011). Fear conditioning and attention to threat: An integrative approach to understanding the etiology of anxiety disorders. In T. R. Schachtman & S. Reilly (Eds.), *Associative learning and conditioning theory: Human and non-human applications* (pp. 44–78). Oxford, England, and New York, NY: Oxford University Press. http://dx.doi.org/10.1093/acprof:oso/9780199735969.003.0020

Ostlund, S. B., Winterbauer, N. E., & Balleine, B. W. (2008). Theory of reward systems. In J. H. Byrne (Ed.), *Learning theory and behavior: Vol. 1. Learning and memory: A comprehensive reference* (pp. 701–720). Oxford, England: Elsevier. http://dx.doi.org/10.1016/B978-012370509-9.00089-9

Papini, M. R. (2003). Comparative psychology of surprising nonreward. *Brain, Behavior and Evolution, 62,* 83–95. http://dx.doi.org/10.1159/000072439

Papini, M. R., & Bitterman, M. E. (1990). The role of contingency in classical conditioning. *Psychological Review, 97,* 396–403. http://dx.doi.org/10.1037/0033-295X.97.3.396

Pavlov, I. (1927). *Conditioned reflexes* (G. V. Anrep, Trans.). London, England: Oxford University Press.

Pear, J. J., & Legris, J. A. (1987). Shaping by automated tracking of an arbitrary operant response. *Journal of the Experimental Analysis of Behavior, 47,* 241–247. http://dx.doi.org/10.1901/jeab.1987.47-241

Pearce, J. M., & Hall, G. (1980). A model for Pavlovian learning: Variations in the effectiveness of conditioned but not of unconditioned stimuli. *Psychological Review, 87,* 532–552. http://dx.doi.org/10.1037/0033-295X.87.6.532

Pelchat, M. L., & Rozin, P. (1982). The special role of nausea in the acquisition of food dislikes by humans. *Appetite, 3,* 341–351. http://dx.doi.org/10.1016/S0195-6663(82)80052-4

Perry, D. G., & Parke, R. D. (1975). Punishment and alternative response training as determinants of response inhibition in children. *Genetic Psychology Monographs, 91,* 257–279.

Perusini, J. N., & Fanselow, M. S. (2015). Neurobehavioral perspectives on the distinction between fear and anxiety. *Learning & Memory, 22,* 417–425. http://dx.doi.org/10.1101/lm.039180.115

Postman, L. (1971). Transfer, interference, and forgetting. In J. W. Kling & L. A. Riggs (Eds.), *Woodworth and Schlosberg's experimental psychology* (3rd ed., pp. 1019–1132). New York, NY: Holt, Rinehart and Winston.

Premack, D. (1965). Reinforcement theory. In D. Levine (Ed.), *Nebraska symposium on motivation* (Vol. 13, pp. 123–180). Lincoln: University of Nebraska Press.

Rachlin, H. (1976). *Behavior and learning* (pp. 102–154). San Francisco, CA: W. H. Freeman.

Raia, C. P., Shillingford, S. W., Miller, H. L., Jr., & Baier, P. S. (2000). Interaction of procedural factors in human performance on yoked schedules. *Journal of the Experimental Analysis of Behavior, 74*, 265–281. http://dx.doi.org/10.1901/jeab.2000.74-265

Rankin, C. H., Abrams, T., Barry, R. J., Bhatnagar, S., Clayton, D. F., Colombo, J., . . . Thompson, R. F. (2009). Habituation revisited: An updated and revised description of the behavioral characteristics of habituation. *Neurobiology of Learning and Memory, 92*, 135–138. http://dx.doi.org/10.1016/j.nlm.2008.09.012

Rau, V., & Fanselow, M. S. (2007). Neurobiological and neuroethological perspectives on fear and anxiety. In L. J. Kirmayer, R. Lemelson, & M. Barad (Eds.), *Understanding trauma: Integrating biological, clinical, and cultural perspectives* (pp. 27–40). Cambridge, England: Cambridge University Press. http://dx.doi.org/10.1017/CBO9780511500008.005

Raybuck, J. D., & Lattal, K. M. (2014). Bridging the interval: Theory and neurobiology of trace conditioning. *Behavioural Processes, 101*, 103–111. http://dx.doi.org/10.1016/j.beproc.2013.08.016

Rehfeldt, R. A. (2011). Toward a technology of derived stimulus relations: An analysis of articles published in the journal of applied behavior analysis, 1992–2009. *Journal of Applied Behavior Analysis, 44*, 109–119. http://dx.doi.org/10.1901/jaba.2011.44-109

Reilly, S., & Schachtman, T. R. (Eds.). (2009). *Conditioned taste aversion: Behavioral and neural processes.* New York, NY: Oxford University Press.

Rescorla, R. A. (1967). Pavlovian conditioning and its proper control procedures. *Psychological Review, 74*, 71–80. http://dx.doi.org/10.1037/h0024109

Rescorla, R. A. (1969). Pavlovian conditioned inhibition. *Psychological Bulletin, 72*, 77–94. http://dx.doi.org/10.1037/h0027760

Rescorla, R. A. (1973). Effect of US habituation following conditioning. *Journal of Comparative and Physiological Psychology, 82*, 137–143. http://dx.doi.org/10.1037/h0033815

Rescorla, R. A. (1985). Conditioned inhibition and facilitation. In R. R. Miller & N. E. Spear (Eds.), *Information processing in animals: Conditioned inhibition* (pp. 299–326). Hillsdale, NJ: Erlbaum.

Rescorla, R. A. (1993). Preservation of response-outcome associations through extinction. *Animal Learning & Behavior, 21*, 238–245. http://dx.doi.org/10.3758/BF03197988

Rescorla, R. A. (2001). Experimental extinction. In R. R. Mowrer & S. B. Klein (Eds.), *Contemporary learning theories* (pp. 119–154). Mahwah, NJ: Erlbaum.

Rescorla, R. A. (2004). Spontaneous recovery. *Learning & Memory, 11*, 501–509. http://dx.doi.org/10.1101/lm.77504

Rescorla, R. A., & Solomon, R. L. (1967). Two-process learning theory: Relationships between Pavlovian conditioning and instrumental learning. *Psychological Review, 74*, 151–182. http://dx.doi.org/10.1037/h0024475

Rescorla, R. A., & Wagner, A. R. (1972). A theory of Pavlovian conditioning: Variations in the effectiveness of reinforcement and nonreinforcement. In A. H. Black & W. F. Prokasy (Eds.), *Classical conditioning II: Current research and theory* (pp. 64–99). New York, NY: Appleton-Century-Crofts.

Reynolds, G. S. (1975). *A primer of operant conditioning.* Glenview, IL: Scott Foresman.

Roberts, W. A. (2012). Evidence for future cognition in animals. *Learning and Motivation, 43,* 169–180. http://dx.doi.org/10.1016/j.lmot.2012.05.005

Roberts, W. A., & Grant, D. S. (1976). Studies of short-term memory in the pigeon using the delayed matching to sample procedure. In D. L. Medin, W. A. Roberts, & R. T. Davis (Eds.), *Processes of animal memory* (pp. 79–112). Hillsdale, NJ: Erlbaum.

Roitblat, H. L. (1980). Codes and coding processes in pigeon short-term memory. *Animal Learning & Behavior, 8,* 341–351. http://dx.doi.org/10.3758/BF03199615

Romanes, G. J. (1882). *Animal intelligence.* New York, NY: Appleton.

Santi, A., & Roberts, W. A. (1985). Prospective representation: The effects of varied mapping of sample stimuli to comparison stimuli and differential trial outcomes on pigeons' working memory. *Animal Learning & Behavior, 13,* 103–108. http://dx.doi.org/10.3758/BF03199261

Sargisson, R. J., & White, K. G. (2001). Generalization of delayed matching to sample following training at different delays. *Journal of the Experimental Analysis of Behavior, 75,* 1–14. http://dx.doi.org/10.1901/jeab.2001.75-1

Schachtman, T. R., Brown, A. M., & Miller, R. R. (1985). Reinstatement-induced recovery of a taste–LiCl association following extinction. *Animal Learning & Behavior, 13,* 223–227. http://dx.doi.org/10.3758/BF03200013

Schein, M. W., & Hale, E. B. (1965). Stimuli eliciting sexual behavior. In F. A. Beach (Ed.), *Sex and behavior* (pp. 440–482). New York, NY: Wiley.

Schiff, R., Smith, N., & Prochaska, J. (1972). Extinction of avoidance in rats as a function of duration and number of blocked trials. *Journal of Comparative and Physiological Psychology, 81,* 356–359. http://dx.doi.org/10.1037/h0033540

Schiller, D., Monfils, M. H., Raio, C. M., Johnson, D. C., LeDoux, J. E., & Phelps, E. A. (2010). Preventing the return of fear in humans using reconsolidation update mechanisms. *Nature, 463,* 49–53. http://dx.doi.org/10.1038/nature08637

Schmajuk, N. A. (2010). *Mechanisms in classical conditioning: A computational approach.* Cambridge, England: Cambridge University Press. http://dx.doi.org/10.1017/CBO9780511711831

Schmajuk, N. A., & Holland, P. C. (Eds.). (1998). *Occasion setting: Associative learning and cognition in animals.* Washington, DC: American Psychological Association. http://dx.doi.org/10.1037/10298-000

Schneiderman, N., & Gormezano, I. (1964). Conditioning of the nictitating membrane of the rabbit as a function of the CS–US interval. *Journal of Comparative and Physiological Psychology, 57,* 188–195. http://dx.doi.org/10.1037/h0043419

Schwabe, L., Nader, K., & Pruessner, J. C. (2014). Reconsolidation of human memory: Brain mechanisms and clinical relevance. *Biological Psychiatry, 76,* 274–280. http://dx.doi.org/10.1016/j.biopsych.2014.03.008

Sevenster, D., Beckers, T., & Kindt, M. (2013). Prediction error governs pharmacologically induced amnesia for learned fear. *Science, 339*, 830–833. http://dx.doi.org/10.1126/science.1231357

Shapiro, K. L., Jacobs, W. J., & LoLordo, V. M. (1980). Stimulus–reinforcer interactions in Pavlovian conditioning of pigeons: Implications for selective associations. *Animal Learning & Behavior, 8*, 586–594. http://dx.doi.org/10.3758/BF03197773

Shettleworth, S. J. (1975). Reinforcement and the organization of behavior in golden hamsters: Hunger, environment, and food reinforcement. *Journal of Experimental Psychology: Animal Behavior Processes, 1*, 56–87. http://dx.doi.org/10.1037/0097-7403.1.1.56

Sidman, M. (1953). Avoidance conditioning with brief shock and no exteroceptive warning signal. *Science, 118*, 157–158. http://dx.doi.org/10.1126/science.118.3058.157

Sidman, M. (1960). *Tactics of scientific research*. New York, NY: Basic Books.

Siegel, S. (2008). Learning and the wisdom of the body. *Learning & Behavior, 36*, 242–252. http://dx.doi.org/10.3758/LB.36.3.242

Siegel, S. (2016). The heroin overdose mystery. *Current Directions in Psychological Science, 25*, 375–379.

Siegel, S., & Allan, L. G. (1996). The widespread influence of the Rescorla–Wagner model. *Psychonomic Bulletin & Review, 3*, 314–321. http://dx.doi.org/10.3758/BF03210755

Simons, R. C. (1996). *Boo! Culture, experience, and the startle reflex*. New York, NY: Oxford University Press.

Sissons, H. T., & Miller, R. R. (2009). Overexpectation and trial massing. *Journal of Experimental Psychology: Animal Behavior Processes, 35*, 186–196. http://dx.doi.org/10.1037/a0013426

Skinner, B. F. (1938). *The behavior of organisms: An experimental analysis*. New York, NY: Appleton-Century-Crofts.

Skinner, B. F. (1953). *Science and human behavior*. New York, NY: Macmillan.

Skinner, B. F. (1956). A case study in scientific method. *American Psychologist, 11*, 221–233. http://dx.doi.org/10.1037/h0047662

Skinner, B. F. (1969). *Contingencies of reinforcement: A theoretical analysis*. New York, NY: Appleton-Century-Crofts.

Small, W. S. (1900). An experimental study of the mental processes of the rat: I. *The American Journal of Psychology, 11*, 133–164. http://dx.doi.org/10.2307/1412267

Small, W. S. (1901). An experimental study of the mental processes of the rat: II. *The American Journal of Psychology, 12*, 206–239. http://dx.doi.org/10.2307/1412534

Smith, J. C., & Roll, D. L. (1967). Trace conditioning with X-rays as an aversive stimulus. *Psychonomic Science, 9*, 11–12.

Smith, M. C., Coleman, S. R., & Gormezano, I. (1969). Classical conditioning of the rabbit's nictitating membrane response at backward, simultaneous, and forward CS–US intervals. *Journal of Comparative and Physiological Psychology, 69*, 226–231. http://dx.doi.org/10.1037/h0028212

Solomon, R. L., Kamin, L. J., & Wynne, L. C. (1953). Traumatic avoidance learning: The outcomes of several extinction procedures with dogs. *Journal of Abnormal Psychology, 48*, 291–302. http://dx.doi.org/10.1037/h0058943

Spear, N. E., & Riccio, D. C. (1994). *Memory: Phenomena and principles*. Boston, MA: Allyn & Bacon.

Stephens, D. W., Brown, J. S., & Ydenberg, R. C. (Eds.). (2007). *Foraging: Behavior and ecology*. Chicago, IL: University of Chicago Press. http://dx.doi.org/10.7208/chicago/9780226772653.001.0001

Stokes, P. D., Mechner, F., & Balsam, P. D. (1999). Effects of different acquisition procedures on response variability. *Animal Learning & Behavior, 27*, 28–41. http://dx.doi.org/10.3758/BF03199429

Storsve, A. B., McNally, G. P., & Richardson, R. (2012). Renewal and reinstatement of the conditioned but not the unconditioned response following habituation of the unconditioned stimulus. *Behavioural Processes, 90*, 58–65. http://dx.doi.org/10.1016/j.beproc.2012.03.007

Stout, S. C., & Miller, R. R. (2007). Sometimes-competing retrieval (SOCR): A formalization of the comparator hypothesis. *Psychological Review, 114*, 759–783 [Correction published in 2008. *Psychological Review, 115*, 82]. http://dx.doi.org/10.1037/0033-295X.114.3.759.

Theios, J. (1962). The partial reinforcement effect sustained through blocks of continuous reinforcement. *Journal of Experimental Psychology, 64*, 1–6. http://dx.doi.org/10.1037/h0046302

Theios, J., Lynch, A. D., & Lowe, W. F., Jr. (1966). Differential effects of shock intensity on one-way and shuttle avoidance conditioning. *Journal of Experimental Psychology, 72*, 294–299. http://dx.doi.org/10.1037/h0023496

Thomas, B. L., Vurbic, D., & Novak, C. (2009). Extensive extinction in multiple contexts eliminates the renewal of conditioned fear in rats. *Learning and Motivation, 40*, 147–159. http://dx.doi.org/10.1016/j.lmot.2008.10.002

Thompson, R. F. (2009). Habituation: A history. *Neurobiology of Learning and Memory, 92*, 127–134. http://dx.doi.org/10.1016/j.nlm.2008.07.011

Thompson, R. F., & Spencer, W. A. (1966). Habituation: A model phenomenon for the study of neuronal substrates of behavior. *Psychological Review, 73*, 16–43. http://dx.doi.org/10.1037/h0022681

Thorndike, E. L. (1898). Animal intelligence: An experimental study of the association process in animals [Monograph]. *Psychological Review Monographs, 2*(8).

Thorndike, E. L. (1911). *Animal intelligence: Experimental studies*. New York, NY: Macmillan. http://dx.doi.org/10.5962/bhl.title.55072

Thorndike, E. L. (1932). *The fundamentals of learning*. New York, NY: Teachers College Press. http://dx.doi.org/10.1037/10976-000

Timberlake, W. (1980). A molar equilibrium theory of learned performance. In G. H. Bower (Ed.), *The psychology of learning and motivation* (Vol. 14, pp. 1–58). Orlando, FL: Academic Press. http://dx.doi.org/10.1016/S0079-7421(08)60158-9

Timberlake, W. (1984). Behavior regulation and learned performance: Some misapprehensions and disagreements. *Journal of the Experimental Analysis of Behavior, 41*, 355–375. http://dx.doi.org/10.1901/jeab.1984.41-355

Timberlake, W. (2001). Motivational modes in behavior systems. In R. R. Mowrer & S. B. Klein (Eds.), *Handbook of contemporary learning theories* (pp. 155–209). Mahwah, NJ: Erlbaum.

Timberlake, W., & Allison, J. (1974). Response deprivation: An empirical approach to instrumental performance. *Psychological Review, 81*, 146–164. http://dx.doi.org/10.1037/h0036101

Timberlake, W., Wahl, G., & King, D. (1982). Stimulus and response contingencies in the misbehavior of rats. *Journal of Experimental Psychology: Animal Behavior Processes, 8*, 62–85. http://dx.doi.org/10.1037/0097-7403.8.1.62

Tinbergen, N. (1951). *The study of instinct*. Oxford, England: Clarendon Press.

Tinbergen, N. (1952). The behavior of the stickleback. *Scientific American, 187*, 22–26. http://dx.doi.org/10.1038/scientificamerican1252-22

Tinbergen, N., & Perdeck, A. C. (1950). On the stimulus situation releasing the begging response in the newly hatched herring gull chick (*Larus argentatus argentatus* Pont.). *Behaviour, 3*, 1–39. http://dx.doi.org/10.1163/156853951X00197

Todd, T. P., Vurbic, D., & Bouton, M. E. (2014). Behavioral and neurobiological mechanisms of extinction in Pavlovian and instrumental learning. *Neurobiology of Learning and Memory, 108*, 52–64. http://dx.doi.org/10.1016/j.nlm.2013.08.012

Tomie, A., Brooks, W., & Zito, B. (1989). Sign-tracking: The search for reward. In S. B. Klein & R. R. Mowrer (Eds.), *Contemporary learning theories: Pavlovian conditioning and the status of learning theory* (pp. 191–223). Hillsdale, NJ: Erlbaum.

Tomie, A., Murphy, A. L., Fath, S., & Jackson, R. L. (1980). Retardation of autoshaping following pretraining with unpredictable food: Effects of changing the context between pretraining and testing. *Learning and Motivation, 11*, 117–134. http://dx.doi.org/10.1016/0023-9690(80)90024-7

Tsao, J. C. I., & Craske, M. G. (2000). Timing of treatment and return of fear: Effects of massed, uniform- and expanding-spaced exposure schedules. *Behavior Therapy, 31*, 479–497. http://dx.doi.org/10.1016/S0005-7894(00)80026-X

Underwood, B. J. (1957). Interference and forgetting. *Psychological Review, 64*, 49–60. http://dx.doi.org/10.1037/h0044616

Urcelay, G. P., & Miller, R. R. (2008). Retrieval from memory. In J. H. Byrne (Ed.), *Learning theory and behavior: Vol. 1. Learning and memory: A comprehensive reference* (pp. 53–74). Oxford, England: Elsevier. http://dx.doi.org/10.1016/B978-012370509-9.00075-9

Urcelay, G. P., & Miller, R. R. (2014). The functions of contexts in associative learning. *Behavioural Processes, 104*, 2–12. http://dx.doi.org/10.1016/j.beproc.2014.02.008

Urcelay, G. P., Wheeler, D. S., & Miller, R. R. (2009). Spacing extinction trials alleviates renewal and spontaneous recovery. *Learning & Behavior, 37*, 60–73. http://dx.doi.org/10.3758/LB.37.1.60

Urcuioli, P. J. (2013). Stimulus control and stimulus class formation. In G. J. Madden (Ed.), *APA handbook of behavior analysis: Vol. 1. Methods and principles* (pp. 361–386). Washington, DC: American Psychological Association. http://dx.doi.org/10.1037/13937-016

van der Kolk, B. A. (2006). Clinical implications of neuroscience research in PTSD. *Annals of the New York Academy of Sciences, 1071*, 277–293. http://dx.doi.org/10.1196/annals.1364.022

Vanderveldt, A., Oliveira, L., & Green, L. (2016). Delay discounting: Pigeon, rat, human—does it matter? *Journal of Experimental Psychology: Animal Learning and Cognition, 42*, 141–162. http://dx.doi.org/10.1037/xan0000097

Vervliet, B., Baeyens, F., Van den Bergh, O., & Hermans, D. (2013). Extinction, generalization, and return of fear: A critical review of renewal research in humans. *Biological Psychology, 92*, 51–58. http://dx.doi.org/10.1016/j.biopsycho.2012.01.006

Waddell, J., Morris, R. W., & Bouton, M. E. (2006). Effects of bed nucleus of the stria terminalis lesions on conditioned anxiety: Aversive conditioning with long-duration conditional stimuli and reinstatement of extinguished fear. *Behavioral Neuroscience, 120*, 324–336. http://dx.doi.org/10.1037/0735-7044.120.2.324

Wagner, A. R. (1961). Effects of amount and percentage of reinforcement and number of acquisition trials on conditioning and extinction. *Journal of Experimental Psychology, 62*, 234–242. http://dx.doi.org/10.1037/h0042251

Wagner, A. R. (2008). Evolution of an elemental theory of Pavlovian conditioning. *Learning & Behavior, 36*, 253–265. http://dx.doi.org/10.3758/LB.36.3.253

Wagner, A. R., & Rescorla, R. A. (1972). Inhibition in Pavlovian conditioning: Application of a theory. In R. A. Boakes & M. S. Halliday (Eds.), *Inhibition and learning* (pp. 301–335). London, England: Academic Press.

Wallace, J., Steinert, P. A., Scobie, S. R., & Spear, N. E. (1980). Stimulus modality and short-term memory in rats. *Animal Learning & Behavior, 8*, 10–16. http://dx.doi.org/10.3758/BF03209724

Wasserman, E. A. (2016). Conceptualization in pigeons: The evolution of a paradigm. *Behavioural Processes, 123*, 4–14. http://dx.doi.org/10.1016/j.beproc.2015.09.010

Wasserman, E. A., Franklin, S. R., & Hearst, E. (1974). Pavlovian appetitive contingencies and approach versus withdrawal to conditioned stimuli in pigeons. *Journal of Comparative and Physiological Psychology, 86*, 616–627. http://dx.doi.org/10.1037/h0036171

Weiss, S. J., & Panlilio, L. V. (2015). Hedonics and the "selective associations": Biological constraints on learning. *International Journal of Comparative Psychology, 28*. Retrieved from http://escholarship.org/uc/item/1102v2b8

White, K. G., & Brown, G. S. (2011). Reversing the course of forgetting. *Journal of the Experimental Analysis of Behavior, 96*, 177–189. http://dx.doi.org/10.1901/jeab.2011.96-177

Williams, B. A. (1999). Associative competition in operant conditioning: Blocking the response-reinforcer association. *Psychonomic Bulletin & Review, 6*, 618–623. http://dx.doi.org/10.3758/BF03212970

Williams, D. C., Saunders, K. J., & Perone, M. (2011). Extended pausing by humans on multiple fixed-ratio schedules with varied reinforcer magnitude and response requirements. *Journal of the Experimental Analysis of Behavior, 95*, 203–220. http://dx.doi.org/10.1901/jeab.2011.95-203

Williams, M., & Woodman, G. F. (2012). Directed forgetting and directed remembering in visual working memory. *Journal of Experimental Psychology: Learning, Memory, and Cognition, 38*, 1206–1220. http://dx.doi.org/10.1037/a0027389

Winter, J., & Perkins, C. C. (1982). Immediate reinforcement in delayed reward learning in pigeons. *Journal of the Experimental Analysis of Behavior, 38*, 169–179. http://dx.doi.org/10.1901/jeab.1982.38-169

Witcher, E. S., & Ayres, J. J. B. (1984). A test of two methods for extinguishing Pavlovian conditioned inhibition. *Animal Learning & Behavior, 12,* 149–156. http://dx.doi.org/10.3758/BF03213134

Wood, W., & Neal, D. T. (2007). A new look at habits and the habit-goal interface. *Psychological Review, 114,* 843–863. http://dx.doi.org/10.1037/0033-295X.114.4.843

Wright, A. A., Katz, J. S., & Ma, W. J. (2012). How to be proactive about interference: Lessons from animal memory. *Psychological Science, 23,* 453–458. http://dx.doi.org/10.1177/0956797611430096

Yi, R., Mitchell, S. H., & Bickel, W. K. (2010). Delay discounting and substance abuse-dependence. In G. J. Madden & W. K. Bickel (Eds.), *Impulsivity: The behavioral and neurological science of discounting* (pp. 191–211). Washington, DC: American Psychological Association. http://dx.doi.org/10.1037/12069-007

Zapata, A., Minney, V. L., & Shippenberg, T. S. (2010). Shift from goal-directed to habitual cocaine seeking after prolonged experience in rats. *The Journal of Neuroscience, 30,* 15457–15463. http://dx.doi.org/10.1523/JNEUROSCI.4072-10.2010

Zentall, T. R., & Smith, A. P. (2016). Delayed matching-to-sample: A tool to assess memory and other cognitive processes in pigeons. *Behavioural Processes, 123,* 26–42. http://dx.doi.org/10.1016/j.beproc.2015.07.002

Zentall, T. R., Steirn, J. N., & Jackson-Smith, P. (1990). Memory strategies in pigeons' performance of a radial-arm-maze analog task. *Journal of Experimental Psychology: Animal Behavior Processes, 16,* 358–371. http://dx.doi.org/10.1037/0097-7403.16.4.358

Zimmer-Hart, C. L., & Rescorla, R. A. (1974). Extinction of Pavlovian conditioned inhibition. *Journal of Comparative and Physiological Psychology, 86,* 837–845. http://dx.doi.org/10.1037/h0036412

Zito, B., & Tomie, A. (2014). *The tail of the raccoon: Secrets of addiction.* Princeton, NJ: ZT Enterprises.

Index

A

Abusive punishment, 171–173
Acquired drives, 133, 227
Acquisition stage (information processing), 210, 227
Action pattern, 19. *See also* modal action pattern
Active memory processes, 214–216
Afferent neuron, 38, 227
Aggression, punishment as act of, 171
Allison, J., 136
Alternative behavior, reinforcement of, 168–169
Animals
 learning by, 15–16
 reflexes of, 17
 used in research, 13. *See also specific types of conditioning*
Appetitive behavior, 23–24, 227
Appetitive conditioning, 45–47, 89, 227
Appropriate behavior, stimulus control and, 192
Arousal, sensitization and, 39
Associative learning, 227. *See also* Pavlovian conditioning
 attentional models of, 87–88
 comparator hypothesis of, 89–92
 in conditioned facilitation procedure, 73–74
 in discriminative control procedures, 55
 in instrumental conditioning procedures, 105–109
 in random control procedures, 53–54

Rescorla–Wagner model, 81–87
 temporal factors in, 88–89
Attentional models, 87–88
Autoshaping, 46
Aversion learning, selective association effect in, 51–52
Aversive conditioning, 46–48, 227. *See also* Avoidance learning; Fear conditioning; Punishment
 and defensive behavior system, 49
 eye-blink conditioning, 46, 47
 fear conditioning, 47–48
 and response–reinforcer contingency, 165
Aversive stimulus, 228
 escape response and, 169
 in punishment, 162, 165–167
 unconditioned, 187–189
Avoidance learning, 175–190
 conditioned temporal cues in, 184
 contemporary procedures in research on, 177–181
 early studies of, 177
 extinction of, 186–187
 major questions in analysis of, 176
 nondiscriminated avoidance procedure, 177–179
 safety signals and, 184–187
 two-factor theory of, 181–184
 and unconditioned defensive behavior, 187–189
Azrin, Nathan, 164–165

B

Bashinski, H. S., 29–30
Bechterev, V. M., 177
Behavioral bliss point, 138, 140, 142, 228
Behavioral economics, 137–142
Behaviorally silent learning, 6–7
Behavior therapy
    reinstatement and, 149
    renewal and, 148
    and extinction procedures, 149–150, 187
Behavior change, 4–6. *See also individual topics*
    context for, 16
    forms of, 4–6
Behavior systems, 24–25, 48–49, 51, 188–189, 228
Between-subjects experimental design, 12
Bhatt, R. S., 32, 33
Biological constraints on learning
    and general-process approach, 13
    in avoidance learning, 187–189
    in instrumental conditioning, 109–110
    in Pavlovian conditioning, 51–52
    in discrimination learning, 197–198
Bliss point. *See* Behavioral bliss point
Blocking effect, 64–65, 81, 83, 87–88, 92,
        222, 228
Bolles, R. C., 187–188
Borovsky, D., 220–222
Bouton, M. E., 146, 148
Breland, Keller, 109–110
Breland, Marian, 109–110

C

Cable, C., 205
Capaldi, E. J., 157
Causes of behavior, 9–10
Church, R. M., 164–165
Circa strike response, 188, 189
Classical conditioning. *See* Pavlovian conditioning
Cognitive revolution, 78
Comparator hypothesis, 89–92, 93, 228
Complex forms of elicited behavior, 18–22
    modal action patterns, 19–20
    sign stimuli, 20–22
Compulsive behavior, 107, 183
Concurrent-chain schedules, 124–126, 127, 228
Concurrent schedules, 122–124, 127, 228
Conditioned drives, 133, 228
Conditioned facilitation, 72–74, 75
Conditioned inhibition, 67–72, 75, 228
    behavioral measurement of, 70–72
    extinction of, 86
    and feedback cues from avoidance response,
        185–187
    negative CS–US contingency in, 69–70
    in Rescorla–Wagner model, 84–86
    standard procedure, 68–69
Conditioned reinforcer, 105, 111, 132, 228

Conditioned response (CR), 44, 228. *See also*
        Extinction; *specific types of conditioning*
    in conditioned facilitation procedure, 73–74
    conditioned modifications of unconditioned
        response, 49–50
    nature of, 48–49
Conditioned stimulus (CS), 44, 228. *See also specific*
        types of conditioning
    contingency between US and, 65–67
    and extinction, 144
    factors in effectiveness of, 50–52
    in higher-order relations, 67–74
    and nature of US, 51–52
    novelty of, 51
    signal relation between US and, 64–67
    temporal relation between US and, 60–64
Conditioned suppression, 47–48, 51–52, 228.
        See also Punishment
    CS–US interval in, 62
    and Pavlovian-instrumental transfer, 108
Consolidation, 150, 222–223, 225, 228
Consolidation window, 151, 222, 224
Constraints on learning. *See* Biological constraints
        on learning
Consummatory behavior, 24, 25, 26, 48, 229
Contiguity
    response–reinforcer, 165
    temporal, 60–61
Contingency(-ies), 229
    CS–US, 65–67, 69–70
    instrumental, 138–139
    response–reinforcer, 165
    in signaled punishment, 167–168
    three-term, 109
Continuous reinforcement, 154, 157, 229
Control condition, 10, 11, 229
Control group, 10–12
Control problem
    in the fundamental learning experiment,
        10–12
    in Pavlovian conditioning, 53–55
CR. *See* Conditioned response
CS. *See* Conditioned stimulus
CS-alone control, 53
CS–US contingency, 65–67, 69–70
CS–US interval, 62–63, 88, 229
CS–US relevance, 51–52, 229. *See also* Selective
        association
Cumulative record, 114–115, 229

D

Darwin, C., 3
Declarative memory, 213
Defensive behavior, 19, 24, 49, 187, 190
    predatory imminence continuum, 188–189
    species-specific defense reactions, 187–188
    avoidance learning and, 187–189

Delay discounting function, 126, 127, 229
Delayed conditioning, 60, 61, 62, 75, 229
Delayed matching to sample, 212, 216, 219, 229
Dependent variable (DV), 10
Descartes, René, 17–18, 28, 38
Differential probability principle, 134. *See also*
    Premack principle
Differential reinforcement, 122, 184, 199–204
Differential reinforcement of other behavior (DRO),
    172–173, 174, 229
Differential responding, 57, 192, 198, 201, 203,
    205, 237, 229
Directed forgetting, 215–216, 229
Discrete-trial method, 98–100, 111, 177, 203–204,
    229
Discriminated avoidance, 177–179, 198, 229
Discrimination hypothesis (for extinction),
    155–156, 229
Discrimination
    interdimensional, 203–204
    intradimensional, 204–205
    stimulus, 195–196
    stimulus discrimination training, 199–201
Discriminative control, 54–55, 230
Discriminative or signaled punishment, 167–168,
    230
Discriminative stimulus, 163, 164, 167, 168, 171,
    173, 200, 235
Dishabituation, 35–36, 40, 53, 230
Domjan, M., 20–21, 79–81
Drive reduction theory, 131–133, 230
Drive state, 23–24, 131–134, 137, 230
DRO (differential reinforcement of other behavior),
    172–173, 174
Drug tolerance, 50, 56
Dual-process theory of habituation and sensitization,
    37–40
DV (dependent variable), 10

E
Efferent neuron, 38, 230
Elasticity of demand, 140
Elicited behavior
    complex forms of, 18–22
    defined, 17, 230
    and ethology, 18
    and law of effect, 107
    organization of, 23–25
    and repeated presentation of stimulus, 29–37
    and sensitization, 39
    S–R system and, 37–40
Equivalence training, 205–206
Ervin, F. R., 62, 63
Escape behavior, punishment of, 169–170
Escape from fear experiments, 183
Ethology, 18, 19, 23, 24, 230
Evolution, change due to, 5, 6, 18, 230

Evolutionary predisposition, 52. *See also* Biological
    constraints on learning
Experimental condition, 10, 11, 230
Experimental designs
    between-subjects, 12
    single-subject, 12
Experimental group, 10–12
Experimental observations, 8, 9, 230
Expert performance, 204–205
Exposure therapy
    empirical basis for, 183
    persistence in responding in, 158
    reminder cues for extinction in, 150, 151
Extinction, 143–159
    and avoidance learning, 182, 186–187
    in conditioned facilitation procedure, 74
    defined, 230
    enhancing, 149–151
    and memory, 150–151
    and original learning, 145–149
    paradoxical reward effects in, 151–158
    and reinstatement of conditioned excitation,
        148–149, 151, 158, 235
    and renewal effect, 146–148, 149, 150, 151, 158
    in Rescorla–Wagner model, 86–87
    and spontaneous recovery, 145–146, 149, 150,
        151, 158, 237
Eye-blink conditioning, 46–48, 61, 62, 70

F
Facilitation
    conditioned, in Pavlovian conditioning, 72–74
    defined, 230
    inhibition vs., 72
Fatigue, 4, 32, 230
Fear conditioning, 47–48, 49, 50, 61, 65, 89,
    CS–US interval in, 62
    in escape from fear experiments, 183
    and Pavlovian conditioning, 56
    and renewal effect, 148
    selective association effect in, 51–52
Fear reduction
    as source of reinforcement for avoidance
        behavior, 186–187
    in two-factor theory of avoidance, 182–183
Feedback cues, 185–187, 231
Feedback functions, 119, 127, 231
    for interval schedules, 120–121
    for ratio schedules, 119–120
    and schedule performance, 121–122
Fixed action patterns, 19. *See also* Modal action
    patterns
Fixed-interval schedules, 117–118, 119, 168,
    201, 231
Fixed-ratio schedules, 116–117, 118, 168, 179, 231
Flavor neophobia, 34, 37, 231
Focal search mode, 24–25, 48–49, 88, 231

Forgetting, 144, 218, 231
  directed, 215–216
  extinction vs., 144
  and memory failure, 218
Free-operant avoidance, 179–181, 184, 185, 189, 231. *See also* Nondiscriminated avoidance
Free-operant method, 100–101, 114, 118, 231
Frustration, 144, 145, 152, 154, 171, 231
Frustration theory, 156–157, 158, 231
Frustrative punishment, 171
Fundamental learning experiment, 9–13
  control problem in, 10–12
  general-process approach to, 12–13
  use of nonhuman participants in research, 13

G
Garcia, J., 62, 63
Garcia–Koelling selective association effect, 52
Generalization
  of learning, 5
  stimulus, 194–196
  theories of, 196
  after equivalence training, 205–206
Generalized matching law, 124
General-process approach, 12–13
General search mode, 24–25, 48–49, 88, 231
Goal tracking, 46, 48, 61
Groves, P. M., 37

H
Habituation, 27–41
  defined, 30, 231
  difference from sensitization and, 37
  difference from instrumental conditioning, 96
  and dishabituation, 35–36
  dual-process theory of, 37–40
  effects of repeated stimulus presentations on, 29–37
  and extinction, 145
  and latent inhibition, 51
  in reflex systems, 28
  short- and long-term, 34–35, 40
  and stimulus change, 31–32
  stimulus specificity of, 31–32
Habituation effects/phenomena
  characteristics of, 31–36
  habituation process vs., 37
  observable, 38, 39
  relation to Pavlovian conditioning, 53
Habituation process, 37–40
Hall, G., 87
Harrison, R. H., 201–203
Herrnstein, R. J., 124, 205
Heterogeneous behavioral structure, 16–17
Higher-order stimulus relations, 231
  conditioned facilitation, 72–74
  conditioned inhibition, 67–72
Hock, A., 32, 33

Holloway, K. S., 79–81
Homeostasis, 50, 131, 231
Homogeneous substrate of behavior, 17
Hull, Clark, 131–133
Human causal judgment, 55
Hydraulic model of behavior, 23, 231

I
Immediate reinforcement, 104–105
Incentive motivation, 46, 50
  and acquired drives, 133
  Pavlovian-instrumental transfer experiments on, 108
Independent variable (IV), 10
Informational models, 89–90
Information processing, stages of, 210
Inhibition
  conditioned. *See* Conditioned inhibition
  facilitation vs., 72
  latent inhibition effect, 51
  response, 151–152
Inhibitory S–R association, 151–152, 158, 231
Initial learning of responses, in instrumental conditioning, 101–104
Instrumental behavior, 96, 231. *See also* Instrumental conditioning
  and choice of response, 122
  fear reduction as reinforcer for, 183
  stimulus discrimination in, 199
Instrumental (or operant) conditioning, 95–111, 231. *See also specific topics, e.g.:* Schedules of reinforcement
  associative mechanisms in, 105–109
  biological constraints on, 109–110
  discrete-trial method, 98–100
  free-operant method, 100–101
  immediate reinforcement, 104–105
  initial learning of responses, 101–104
  interdimensional discriminations in, 203–204
  neural mechanisms of, 110–111
  new responses from familiar components, 102
  response allocation and behavioral economics, 137–141
  R–O association in, 106
  S(R–O) association in, 108–109
  schedules of reinforcement in. *See* Schedules of reinforcement
  shaping new responses, 16, 102–104, 236
  Skinner tradition in, 99–101
  S–O association in, 107–108
  S–R association in, 106–107
  and stimulus control, 198–199
  Thorndike's law of effect, 106–107
  Thorndike tradition in, 97–99
  in two-factor theory of avoidance, 182, 183
Intensity of punishment, 165–167, 169
Interdimensional discriminations, 203–204, 231
Interference effects, memory failure and, 219–220

Intermittent reinforcement, 154, 156, 232. *See also* Schedules of reinforcement
Interneuron, 38, 232
Interstimulus interval, 62–63, 232. *See also* CS–US interval
Interval
    CS–US, 62–63, 88
    between extinction trials, 150, 158
    between response and delivery of positive reinforcer, 104-105
    between response and delivery of punishment, 165
    R–S, 180–181
    S–S, 180
    between successive trials, 88
Interval schedules, 117–122, 232
    feedback functions for, 120–121
    fixed-interval, 117–118
    response rates for, 121–122
    variable-interval, 118–119
Intradimensional discriminations, 204–205, 232
I/T ratio, 88–89, 232
IV (independent variable), 10

J
Jacobs, W. J., 51–52
Jenkins, H. M., 155–156, 201–204
Jubran, R., 32, 33

K
Kamin, L. J., 61, 62, 63, 64, 81
Kaplan, P. S., 35
Koelling, R. A., 52

L
Lamoreaux, R. R., 176
Lashley, K. S., 196
Lashley–Wade hypothesis, 196
Latent inhibition effect, 51, 222, 232
Law of effect (Thorndike), 106–107, 130–131, 136, 153, 232
Learning, 3–4
    in acquisition stage of information processing, 210
    behaviorally silent, 6–7
    defined, 8, 232
    fundamental learning experiment, 9–13
    levels of analysis of, 7–8
    and memory, 209–210
    other forms of behavior change vs., 4–6
    performance and, 7
Learning factors, in stimulus control, 198–201
Levels of analysis, 7–8
Limited hold, 119
Locus of reinforcement in response deprivation, 137
LoLordo, V. M., 51–52
Long-delay learning, 62, 63, 78, 232

Long-term habituation, 34–35, 40, 232
Long-term sensitization, 37, 40, 232
Loveland, D. H., 205
Lukas, Scott, 56

M
Magnitude-of-reinforcement extinction effect, 153–154, 232
MAP (modal action pattern), 19–22, 232
Marking stimulus, 105, 232
Matching law, 124, 232
Matching-to-sample procedure, 210–213, 232
    procedural controls for memory, 212–213
    simultaneous vs. delayed, 212
    symbolic, 217–218
Maturation, 5–6, 232
Matzel, L. D., 89
Mazes, 99–101
Measurement of stimulus control, 192–196
Memory, 209–225
    active memory processes, 214–216
    consolidation, 150, 222–224, 225, 228
    declarative, 213
    and enhancement of extinction performance, 150–151
    failure of, 218–222
    and interference effects, 219–220
    and learning, 209–210
    matching-to-sample procedure, 210–213
    procedural, 213
    prospective, 216–218, 234
    reconsolidation, 222–224, 235
    for enhancing extinction performance, 150–151
    reference, 214, 216, 235
    retrieval failure, 220–222
    retrospective, 216–218, 235
    and sequential theory, 157–158
    stages of information processing, 210
    and trace decay, 214–216
    types of, 213–218
    updating, 222–224. *See also* Reconsolidation
    working, 214, 216, 217, 218, 239
Miller, R. R., 89, 91
Modal action pattern (MAP), 19–22, 232
Molecular level of analysis, 7
Motivation, 232. *See also* Incentive motivation
    and short-term behavior change, 4
    in stimulus control, 197–198
Motivational state, 197
Motor neuron, 18, 38
Mowrer, O. H., 176, 181–182
Multiple schedules of reinforcement, 201, 233

N
Nash, S., 20–21
Naturalistic observations, 8–9, 233
Negative punishment, 173

Negative reinforcement, 169,170, 233
    fear reduction as, 182
    in punishment, 169
    stimulus control and, 198
Negative reinforcers, 169. *See also* Aversive stimulus
Neural mechanisms, of instrumental conditioning, 110–111
Neural processes, in state system, 38
Neural systems level of analysis, 8
Nondiscriminated avoidance, 177, 179–181, 184, 233
Nonhuman research participants, 13
"Nothing," as reinforcer, 176. *See also* Avoidance learning

O
Observations
    experimental, 8, 9
    naturalistic, 8–9
One-way avoidance, 178, 233
Operant behavior, 96–97, 233
Operant conditioning, 96. *See also* Instrumental (or operant) conditioning
Organization of elicited behavior, 23–25
    appetitive behavior, 23–24
    behavior systems, 24–25
    consummatory behavior, 24
    motivational factors, 23
Orienting response, 28, 233
Overexpectation 84–86, 233
Overshadowing, 197, 233
Overtraining extinction effect, 152–153, 233

P
Pain, as punishment, 171
Paradoxical effects of punishment, 169–170, 233
Paradoxical reward effects, 151–158
    magnitude-of-reinforcement extinction effect, 153–154
    overtraining extinction effect, 152–153
    partial-reinforcement extinction effect, 154–158
Partial reinforcement, 154, 156–157, 234. *See also* Intermittent reinforcement
Partial-reinforcement extinction effect (PREE), 154–158, 234
    and frustration theory, 156–157
    mechanisms of, 155–158
    and sequential theory, 157–158
Pavlov, Ivan, 7, 44, 145, 196, 197
Pavlovian (classical) conditioning, 43–57
    appetitive conditioning, 45–47
    attentional models of, 87–88
    aversive conditioning, 46–48
    and avoidance learning, 176, 177
    comparator hypothesis, 89–92
    conditioned facilitation in, 72–74
    conditioned inhibition in, 67–72

conditioned modifications of unconditioned response, 49–50
control problem in, 53–55
dogs salivating to a bell experiment, 44
extinction following, 145–146
fear conditioning, 47–48
interdimensional discriminations in, 203
mechanisms of learning in, 77–93
nature of conditioned response, 48–49
outcomes of, 78–81
presentation schedule in, 95–96
prevalence of, 55–56
Rescorla–Wagner model, 81–87
signal relation in, 64–67
and stimulus control, 198–199
stimulus discrimination in, 199, 200
stimulus factors in, 50–52
stimulus relations in, 59–75
temporal factors and conditioned responding, 88–89
temporal relation in, 60–64
theories related to, 77–93
in two-factor theory of avoidance, 182, 183
Pavlovian-instrumental transfer experiments, 108
Pearce, J. M., 87
Perceptual concept learning, 205, 234
Performance, 7, 234
Physical pain, as punishment, 171
Positive occasion setting, 67. *See also* Facilitation
Positive reinforcement, 95–101, 115–119,
    extinction following, 144–145, 151–156
    in avoidance learning, 185–186, 187
    in punishment, 168–169
    punishment as signal for, 169
    punishment vs., 162, 165
    stimulus control and, 198
    theories of, 129–141
    through conditioned inhibitory safety signal, 185–186, 187
Postreinforcement pause, 116, 234
Practice, 5, 234
Predatory imminence continuum, 188–189, 234
PREE. *See* Partial-reinforcement extinction effect
Premack, David, 133–134, 138
Premack principle, 133–135, 234
Primary reinforcers, 105, 132, 234
Priming of extinction, 151
Proactive interference, 219–220, 234
Procedural controls, for memory, 212–213
Procedural memory, 213
Proprioceptive cues, 185, 186, 204, 234
Prospective memory, 216–218, 234
Punishment, 161–174, 234
    abusive, 171–173
    effective and ineffective, 162–164
    of escape behavior, 169–170
    intensity of aversive stimulus, 165–167

mechanisms maintaining punished response, 168
  paradoxical effects of, 169–170
  and reinforcement of alternative behavior, 168–169
  research evidence on, 164–170
  response–reinforcer contiguity, 165
  response–reinforcer contingency, 165
  signaled, 167–168
  as signal for positive reinforcement, 169
  societal uses of, 170–171
Puzzle boxes, 97, 98, 99, 106, 109, 234

R
Rachlin, H., 16
Random control, 53–54, 234
Rate of responding, 101, 234
Ratio run, 116, 168, 235
Ratio schedules, 115–117, 235
  feedback functions for, 119–120
  fixed-ratio, 116–117, 168, 179, 231
  response rates for, 121–122
  variable-ratio, 117, 239
Reconsolidation, 235
  definition of, 235
  for enhancing extinction performance, 150–151
  memory, 222–224
Reference memory, 214, 216, 235
Reflex arc, 17, 18, 38, 235
Reflexes, 17–18, 28, 38, 235
Reinforcers, 96, 102–104, 235. *See also* Schedules of reinforcement; Theories of reinforcement
  delivery of, 105–106
  "nothing" as, 176. *See also* Avoidance learning
  primary, 105, 132, 234
  as responses, 133–135
  as satisfiers, 130
  secondary/conditioned, 105, 132–133, 228
  unconditioned, *same as* primary reinforcer
Reinstatement, 148–149, 151, 235
Releasing stimulus, 23
Relevance, CS–US, 51–52. *See also* Selective association
Renewal effect, 146–148, 150, 151, 235
Rescorla, R. A., 53, 78, 81–87, 88, 93, 144
Rescorla–Wagner model, 81–87, 88, 93, 144
Response allocation, 137–141, 235
Response deprivation hypothesis, 136–137, 235
Response feedback cues, 185–187. *See also* Proprioceptive cues
Response inhibition, 151–152, 158, 231
Response rate
  defined, 234
  in cumulative record, 115
  matching law, 124
  for ratio vs. interval schedules, 121–122
Response–reinforcer contiguity, 104–105, 165

Response–reinforcer contingency, 165. *See also* Schedules of reinforcement
Response–shock (R–S) interval, 180–181, 184, 185, 234
Retardation-of-acquisition test, 71–72, 235
Retention interval, 210–212, 214, 216, 217, 235
Retention stage (information processing), 210
Retrieval cues, 150, 220–222, 235
Retrieval failure (memory), 220–222
Retrieval stage (information processing), 210, 235
Retroactive interference, 219, 220, 235
Retrograde amnesia, 219
Retrospective memory, 216–218, 235
Revaluation effect, 92. *See also* US devaluation, and US inflation
R–O association, 106, 107, 108, 109, 198, 234
  and extinction, 149
  and neural mechanisms of conditioning, 110–111
Rovee-Collier, C., 220–222
R–S interval, 180–181, 184, 185, 234
Rudy, J. W., 29–30, 35

S
S⁻, 199–204, 235
S⁺, 199–204, 235
Safety signals, avoidance learning and, 184–187, 189, 236
Salience of the stimulus, 87–88, 186, 197, 236
Sargisson, R. J., 215–216
S(R–O) association, 108–109, 110, 236
Satisfiers, 130
Schedule line, 138–139, 236
Schedules of reinforcement, 113–127
  defined, 236
  concurrent-chain schedules, 124–126
  concurrent schedules, 122–124
  and cumulative records, 114–115
  feedback functions and schedule performance, 121–122
  feedback functions for interval schedules, 120–121
  feedback functions for ratio schedules, 119–120
  interval schedules, 117–119
  mechanisms of schedule performance, 119–122
  in punishment, 168
  ratio schedules, 115–117
  simple, 115–119
  and stimulus control, 199–201
  in studies of self-control, 125–126
Secondary reinforcer, 105, 132–133. *See also* Conditioned reinforcer
Selective association, 51–52, 197–198, 236
Self-control studies, concurrent-chain schedules in, 125–126

Sensitization, 27–41
    difference between habituation and, 37
    dual-process theory of, 37–40
    effects of repeated presentation on, 29–37
    in reflex systems, 28
    short- and long-term, 37, 40
Sensitization effects/phenomena
    characteristics of, 36–37
    defined, 30, 236
    in Pavlovian conditioning, 53, 54
    sensitization process vs., 37
Sensitization process, 37–40
Sensory adaptation, 35
Sensory capacity, stimulus control and, 196
Sensory neuron, 38, 236
Sensory orientation, stimulus control and, 197
Sensory reinforcement, 133, 236
Sequential theory, 157–158, 236
Sexual conditioning, 46, 49, 50, 56, 79–81, 89
Shaping, 16, 102–104, 236
Shapiro, K. L., 51–52
Shock–shock (S–S) interval, 180, 184, 185, 236
Short-term habituation, 34, 35, 40, 236
Short-term sensitization, 37, 40, 236
Shuttle box, 178–179, 183, 236
Sidman, M., 179–180
Signaled punishment, 167–168
Signal relations
    in conditioning inhibition, 67–72
    in Pavlovian conditioning, 64–67
Sign stimulus, 20–23, 237
Sign tracking, 45–46, 48, 50, 61, 79, 237
Simple schedules of reinforcement, 115–119
Simultaneous conditioning, 60–61, 237
Simultaneous matching to sample, 212, 237
Single-stimulus learning, 44. *See also* Habituation.
Single-subject experimental designs, 12, 237
Skinner, B. F., 97, 99–101
    on classical conditioning, 44
    and free-operant method, 100–101
    on punishment, 162, 170
    and S(R–O) association, 108–109
    and shaping, 16
    and single-subject experiments, 12
    and three-term contingency, 109
Skinner box, 45, 101, 179–180, 211, 212, 237
Small, William, 99
S–O association, 107–108, 235
    and constraints on learning, 110
    and extinction, 149
    and neural mechanisms of conditioning,
        110, 111
    and Pavlovian-instrumental transfer
        experiments, 108
Social behavior, 18–19
Society free of punishment, 170–171
Species-specific defense reactions (SSDRs),
    187–188, 237

Species-typical behavior, 19, 20, 24, 237
Spencer, W. A., 36
Spinal reflexes, 38
Spontaneous recovery
    in extinction, 145–146, 150, 151, 237
    in habituation, 32–35
Spread-of-effect interpretation
    (stimulus generalization), 196
S–R association
    in Pavlovian conditioning, 78–81
    in instrumental conditioning, 106–107
    and neural mechanisms of conditioning,
        110, 111
S–R system, in dual process theory, 37–40, 236
SSDRs (species-specific defense reactions), 187–188
S–S interval, 180, 184, 185, 236
S–S learning, 7, 78–81, 238
Startle response, 31, 37, 237
State system, 40, 237
    in dual process theory, 37–40
    sensitization in, 39
Stimulus(—i)
    aversive, 162, 165–167, 169, 187–189, 228
    conditioned, 44. *See also* Conditioned
        stimulus [CS]
    discriminative, 163, 164, 167, 171, 200
    marking, 105
    releasing, 23
    as retrieval cues, 220–222
    salience of, 87–88, 186, 197, 236
    sign, 20–23, 237
    unconditioned, 44. *See also* Unconditioned
        stimulus [US]
    warning, 177–180, 182–184, 186, 188, 189
Stimulus control of behavior, 191–206
    conceptions of stimulus generalization, 196
    determinants of, 196–205
    and interdimensional discriminations, 203–204
    and intradimensional discriminations, 204–205
    learning factors in, 198–201
    measurement of, 192–196
    and motivational factors, 197–198
    and multiple schedules of reinforcement, 201
    and Pavlovian and instrumental conditioning,
        198–199
    precision of, 201–205
    and sensory capacity, 196
    and sensory orientation, 197
    stimulus discrimination, 195–196, 237
    and stimulus discrimination training, 199–201
    stimulus equivalence training, 205–206, 237
    stimulus generalization, 195–196, 237
    stimulus generalization gradients, 194–195, 237
    and stimulus intensity or salience, 197
Stimulus control of memory, 215. *See also* Directed
    forgetting
Stimulus dimensions, 193
Stimulus discrimination, 195–196

Stimulus discrimination training, 199–201
Stimulus equivalence training, 205–206
Stimulus factors, in Pavlovian conditioning, 50–52
Stimulus frequency, habituation and, 35
Stimulus generalization
    conceptions of, 196
    gradients of, 194–195
    and stimulus discrimination, 195–196
Stimulus generalization gradients, 194–195
Stimulus intensity
    and habituation, 35
    stimulus control, 197
Stimulus relations (Pavlovian conditioning), 59–75
    conditioned facilitation, 72–74
    conditioned inhibition, 67–72
    signal relation, 64–67
    temporal relation, 60–64
Stimulus salience, 87–88, 186, 197, 236
Stimulus specificity of habituation, 31–32
Stimulus–stimulus (S-S) learning, 7, 78–81, 238
Stout, S. C., 89
Straight-alley runway, 99–101, 238
Structure of unconditioned behavior, 15–26.
        See also Behavior systems
    complex forms of elicited behavior, 18–22
    organization of elicited behavior, 23–25
    reflexes, 17–18
    substrates of behavior, 16–17
Substitutes (in behavioral economics), 140, 141, 142
Substrates of behavior, 16–17
Suckling conditioning, 56
Summation test, for conditioned inhibition,
        70–72, 238
Supernormal stimuli, 22
Surprising stimuli, 82–83, 87
Symbolic matching to sample, 217–218

T

Taste-aversion learning, 51–52, 62–62, 64, 89, 238
    blocking effect in, 64
    CS–US interval in, 62, 63
Temporal coding, 63, 238
Temporal contiguity, 60–61, 65, 104–105, 238
Temporal cues, 63, 184, 238
Temporal factors, in conditioned responding,
        88–89, 184
Temporal relation, between CS and US, 60–64
Theios, J., 155–156
Theories of reinforcement, 129–142
    Hull and drive reduction theory, 131–133
    Premack principle, 133–135
    response allocation and behavioral economics,
        137–141
    response deprivation hypothesis, 136–137
    Thorndike and law of effect, 130–131
Thompson, R. F., 36, 37
Thorndike, Edward L., 97–99, 106, 109, 130–131,
        162, 170

Thorndike's law of effect, 106–107, 130–131, 136,
        153, 232
Three-term contingency, 108–109. *See also* S(R–O)
        association
Timberlake, W., 24, 136
Time-out, 172, 238
T-maze, 100, 238
Token economies, 135
Trace conditioning, 60–62, 238
Trace decay (memory), 214–216
Trace interval, 61, 238
Two-factor theory of avoidance learning,
        181–184, 238
Two-way avoidance, 178, 179, 238

U
Unconditioned behavior
    defensive, avoidance learning and, 187–189
    reflexes, 17–18
    structure of. *See* Structure of unconditioned
        behavior
Unconditioned response (UR), 44, 49–50, 238.
        See also specific types of conditioning
Unconditioned stimulus (US), 44, 238. *See also*
        specific types of conditioning
    contingency between CS and, 65–67
    and effectiveness of CS, 51–52
    and extinction, 144
    in higher-order relations, 67–74
    signal relation between CS and, 64–67
    temporal relation between CS and, 60–64
    unexpected/surprising, 82–83, 87
Unpaired control procedure, 55, 238
UR (unconditioned response), 44, 49–50
US. *See* Unconditioned stimulus
US-alone control, 53
US devaluation, 78–79, 81, 239
US inflation, 81, 239

V
Variability in behavior
    during acquisition, 102–104
    during extinction, 145
Variable-interval schedule (VI), 118–119,
        168, 239
Variable-ratio schedule (VR), 117, 239

W
Wade, M., 196
Wagner, A. R., 81–88, 92. *See also* Rescorla–Wagner
        model
Warning stimulus, in avoidance learning, 177–180,
        182–184, 186, 188, 189
Werner, J. S., 29–30, 35
White, H., 32, 33
White, K. G., 215–216
Woods, A. M., 146
Working memory, 214, 216, 217, 218, 239

About the Author

Michael Domjan, PhD, is a professor of psychology at the University of Texas at Austin, where he has taught learning to undergraduate and graduate students for four decades. He also served as department chair from 1999 to 2005 and was the founding director of the Imaging Research Center from 2005 to 2008. Dr. Domjan is noted for his functional approach to classical conditioning, which he has pursued in studies of sexual conditioning and taste aversion learning. His research was selected for a MERIT Award by the National Institute of Mental Health. Dr. Domjan is a past president of the Pavlovian Society and also served as president of the Society for Behavioral Neuroscience and Comparative Psychology of the American Psychological Association (APA). In 2014, he received the D. O. Hebb Distinguished Scientific Contributions Award from APA Division 6 (Society for Behavioral Neuroscience and Comparative Psychology). Dr. Domjan also enjoys playing the viola and is the director of the Tertis/Pavlov Project, which consists of a series of minilectures (available on YouTube) that describe how learning is involved in musical experience and performance.